A.I. SILVER is associate professor in the Department of History at the University of Toronto.

At Confederation, most French Canadians felt their homeland was Quebec; they supported the new arrangement because it separated Quebec from Ontario, creating an autonomous French-Canadian province loosely associated with the others. Unaware of other French-Canadian groups in British North America, Quebeckers were not concerned with minority rights, but only with the French character and autonomy of their own province.

However, political and economic circumstances necessitated the granting of wide linguistic and educational rights to Quebec's Anglo-Protestant minority. Growing bitterness over the prominence of this minority in what was expected to be a French province was amplified by the discovery that French-Catholic minorities were losing their rights in other parts of Canada. Resentment at the fact that Quebec had to grant minority rights, while other provinces did not, intensified French-Quebec nationalism.

At the same time, French Quebeckers felt sympathy for their co-religionists and co-nationals in other provinces and tried to defend them against assimilating pressures. Fighting for the rights of Acadians, Franco-Ontarians, or western Métis eventually led Quebeckers to a new concern for the French fact in other provinces.

Professor Silver concludes that by 1900 they had become thoroughly committed to French-Canadian rights not just in Quebec but throughout Canada, and had become convinced that the very existence of Confederation was based on such rights.

A.I. SILVER

THE FRENCH-CANADIAN IDEA OF CONFEDERATION 1864-1900

UNIVERSITY OF TORONTO PRESS

Toronto Buffalo London

© University of Toronto Press 1982
Toronto Buffalo London
PRINTED IN CANADA

ISBN 0-8020-5557-5 cloth
ISBN 0-8020-6441-8 paper

Canadian Cataloguing in Publication Data
Silver, Arthur I., 1940–
The French-Canadian idea of Confederation, 1864–1900
ISBN 0–8020–5557–5 (bound). – ISBN 0–8020–6441–8 (pbk.)
1. Canadians, French-speaking – Attitudes – History –
19th century.* 2. Canada – English-French relations –
History – 19th century. 3. Canada – History – 1867–
1914. I. Title.
FC144.S58   971'.004114   c81-094801-x
F1027.S58

Cover illustration:
Le Monument Mercier, Quebec City
Paul Chevré, sculptor

This book has been published with the help of
a grant from the Social Science Federation of
Canada, using funds provided by the Social
Sciences and Humanities Research Council of
Canada, and from the Publications Fund of
University of Toronto Press.

CONTENTS

PREFACE

During the past two decades separatism and bilingualism have been hotly debated issues in Canada, and more than once advocates of one policy or another have appealed to history for support. It's always tempting to argue that because a certain conception prevailed at the founding of Confederation, that same conception must dictate our policies today – that we must be constant to an original 'spirit of Confederation' or to the intentions of its 'fathers'. But it's a temptation that ought to be resisted.

One of the main findings of this study is that when Confederation was devised in the 1860s, French Canadians were not concerned to establish their nationality and their culture throughout the new dominion, but only in Quebec. There can be no justification, however, for concluding from this that the establishment of French rights outside Quebec is inappropriate today. Living people change, and acquire new needs; hence the need for constitutions to be amendable. Indeed, it will be seen in the following pages that the post-Confederation decades brought the discovery of new needs not foreseen in 1867, and especially the discovery that manifest good will toward French Canadians in the other provinces was necessary if Quebec were to live together peacefully with the rest of Canada. The way in which French Canadians were treated in other provinces turned out to be important, not because French Canadians expected to be as much at home in Toronto or Calgary as in Trois-Rivières or St-Hyacinthe, but because it was an indication of English Canada's attitude toward Quebec's majority nationality – an indication, therefore, of English Canada's willingness to treat Quebec itself with respect and consideration.

This is a study of French-Canadian attitudes, and in it English Canadians are seen through the eyes of nineteenth-century French Canadians. The view is

often unflattering, and the inhabitants of Ontario and the West frequently
appear as intolerant bigots and fanatics. We should not be quick to condemn
them, however, nor should we take this representation of them at face value.
It may well be that a study of English-Canadian opinion similar to this one
would show French Canada in a pretty bad light too. In any case, until such a
study is made, we oughtn't to judge severely. Even if people like McDougall
and McCarthy, as they represented themselves on paper, seem unpleasant and
unsympathetic to us today, it's worth remembering that they represented a
point of view that was held in good faith in their own time, and which seemed
reasonable and legitimate then to a large part of the Canadian population.

In this book the evidence to support my assertions consists mainly of
quotations from what French Canadians wrote down in various places.
Naturally, they usually wrote in French, and if my evidence were to be
presented with the greatest possible degree of accuracy, I should have quoted
it in the original French. However, this is the twentieth century, not the
eighteenth, and it must be admitted that for most readers, the constant
interruption of an English text by frequent French quotations, long and short,
would be, if not an impediment to understanding, at least a confounded
nuisance.

So, holding my breath, as it were, I've translated. A risky business, and one
that exposes me to trouble, no doubt. I've tried to alleviate the obvious
problems in some measure by giving the original French passage in a footnote
where it seemed that my translation was open to question or where the French
was ambiguous or susceptible of different interpretations. One word that is
constantly ambiguous is *Canadien*, which, in the nineteenth century, meant
French-Canadian more often than not. Where this meaning was only
probable but not certain, I've used square brackets: [French] Canadian.

The habit of reading and copying what French Canadians wrote in the
nineteenth century has probably affected my own writing. In any case, I've
repeatedly used the word 'race' here in the way in which they used it,
speaking, for example, of 'the French-Canadian race'. They meant by it
nationality, ethnic group, a group of people sharing common experience and
cultural characteristics, and, in their own case at least, descended from a
distinct group of ancestors. Of course, English dictionaries also define the
word in this way, but it has to be admitted that since the Second World War
such usage has become distasteful to many people. I'd be sorry to have
offended anyone, and hope that readers will see in my use of this word not a
sign of unhealthy proclivities but only an indication of how close I have got to
the society I've been studying, how totally I immersed myself in the period

about which I was writing. Isn't that a recommendation rather than cause for reproach?

A last word before I begin, and that is to say thank you to Ramsay Cook for his guidance, advice, and friendship, not only during the preparation of this book, but so constantly over the years. I am sincerely grateful.

THE
FRENCH-CANADIAN
IDEA OF
CONFEDERATION

INTRODUCTION

I N 1864, when the fathers of Confederation sat down to their conference table, there were about a million people of French origin in British North America, and more than 85 per cent of them lived in what would become the province of Quebec. In all other places they lived in small and scattered groups surrounded by great majorities of strangers; in Lower Canada they were a compact and organized society comprising more than three-quarters of the population. Everywhere else they were weak and without influence; in Lower Canada their language was heard daily in public life, and their values and traditions shaped the laws and institutions of the province. Thus, Quebec was the most particular homeland of the French Canadians, though it was not the sole theatre of their activities or interests.

This had always been so. Even before the Conquest, in an age when French North America stretched from the Atlantic to the Rockies, from Hudson Bay to the Gulf of Mexico, Quebec's position was always special. It was, indeed, the very centre and the heart of that empire; it alone was called Canada. On its east, Acadia guarded, perhaps, the entrance to the St Lawrence, but the tiny settlements there were of little account. They were administered separately from Canada, and that so weakly and sporadically that they were destroyed or conquered by British forces at least seven times before French diplomacy finally failed, in 1713, to return the stolen horse to the unlocked barn once more.

To the west of Canada lay the vast sweep of a wild interior: Indian country, a fur traders' and a military frontier. Exploited by Canada, traversed by Canadians, it was certainly no part of Canada itself. Those who left for the West – and by the eighteenth century they represented a small, specialized, and distinct part of the Canadian population[1] – separated themselves from the St Lawrence valley not only by distance, but also by type of environment and way of life. The world to which they went was wild and wooded, and there Indian society maintained itself. The world they left behind was settled and cultivated, covered with farms, scattered with towns and villages, organized into parishes and seigneuries. In Quebec an orderly and Christian civilization was established; at Toronto fur traders might still do the *Gan8ary*, running naked between the lodges with a keg of brandy under each arm.[2]

No wonder the moral distinction was soon made between the good people who stayed in the colony to plough their land and lead upright lives, and the bad ones who ran off to the depravities of the *pays d'en haut*.[3] No wonder, either, that men who spent years in the tramping life of the interior were never able afterwards to adapt themselves to the civilization of the St Lawrence valley.[4] And how much more was this the case when the fur trade had penetrated so far westward that return trips had become difficult for those who worked at the frontier. *Voyageurs* remained away from Quebec for longer and longer periods of time, until there were hundreds of Canadians in the West who never returned at all.[5]

Thus, differences of identity, of self-awareness, between the Canadians and the other French of North America appeared during the French régime itself. Acadia and Louisiana were separated from Canada by geography, economics and administration; the interior, though connected to Canada by commerce and by strategy, differed from it in the way of life and in the attitudes of its

---

1 Louise Dechêne, *Habitants et marchands de Montréal au XVIIe siècle* (Montreal: Plon 1974), pp. 176–83; also pp. 217–26.

2 *Histoire de l'eau de vie en Canada* (n.p., c.1705), p. 19.

3 Marcel Giraud, *Le Métis canadien* (Paris: Institut d'Ethnologie 1945), p. 298. The evolution of the meaning of the word *habitant* in Canada during the seventeenth and eighteenth centuries is instructive. Its original signification, of course, was 'inhabitant', but it came gradually to mean a 'permanent settler in the colony' and, finally, a 'farmer' or 'peasant'. This seems to reflect the growing distinction between the *real* 'inhabitants' of Canada, who remained in the St Lawrence valley and cultivated the land, and the others, who travelled in the interior. See Konrad Fillion, 'Essai sur l'évolution du mot *habitant* (xviie–xviiie siècles)', in the *Revue d'histoire de l'Amérique Française*, xxiv, 3 (Dec., 1970). This semantic evolution parallels a shift in the distribution of population away from the town where the interior trade was organized and into the Quebec countryside. See Louise Dechêne, 'La Croissance de Montréal au xviiie siècle', in the *RHAF*, xxvii, 2 (Sept., 1973).

4 W.J. Eccles, *The Canadian Frontier, 1534–1760* (Albuquerque: University of New Mexico Press 1974), p. 128. Also, Georges Dugas, *Un Voyageur des pays d'en haut* (Montreal: Beauchemin 1890), pp. 123–4.

5 Dechêne, *Habitants et marchands*, pp. 180, 226: 'Chaque voyage est un pas de plus vers cette émigration définitive.'

tiny, scattered, and largely wandering population. Above all, the vast majority of French North Americans lived in the St Lawrence valley. Throughout the French régime censuses of New France, or Canada, began with the Quebec district and never went farther west than Les Cèdres.[6]

Conquest accentuated the differences between the Canadians and the other French North Americans. But it was still the intensity of their settlement that distinguished the former from all the rest. The Acadians' sparse numbers (1,773 in Nova Scotia at the time of France's final surrender of the peninsula) had encouraged British immigration by the end of the 1740s and made possible the dramatic expulsions of the 1750s. But Quebec's 65,000 population at the Conquest ensured her a different destiny. The Quebec Act was a recognition of this numerical strength; it acknowledged that the St Lawrence valley was and would continue to be inhabited by a preponderantly French and Catholic population. True, the act included Ontario and the Ohio country in its provisions (strategic as well as commercial considerations might make this desirable); but British censuses of Quebec from 1774 to 1791 still stopped at Les Cèdres.

The success of the American Revolution only emphasized the fact that the area west of the Ottawa River was not a truly French-Canadian country. South of the Great Lakes the triumph of Anglo-American democracy precluded any possibility of a permanently constituted French fact. And while this enabled the British to persuade some of Michigan's French to cross the Detroit River, by holding up the fact that the Quebec Act still applied in Ontario,[7] the Loyalist immigration which was a by-product of the revolution ensured that Ontario, in the long run, would be English.

The Loyalists, by the magnitude of their settlement, staked out the same claim to Ontario as had saved the French fact in Quebec. Both claims were registered in the 1791 Constitutional Act, which finally re-confined the French establishment to the old Canada of the French régime. The first session of the Upper Canadian legislature might resolve that its acts be published in French as well as in English, at a time when strategy advised the attraction of French from Detroit to Sandwich and the securing of their

---

6 *Censuses of Canada*, 1665–1871 (vol. 4 of the 1871 census; Ottawa: Taylor 1876), pp. 60–1. Unless otherwise indicated, all pre-Confederation population figures in this chapter are based on the figures given in this volume. Les Cèdres is about twelve miles west of Montreal island, or half way to the present-day Ontario border.

7 Télésphore Saint-Pierre, *Histoire des Canadiens du Michigan et du Comté d'Essex, Ontario* (Montreal: La Gazette 1895), pp. 182–4. Saint-Pierre reported, though, that by the turn of the century the Detroit parish still numbered 1,800, while Sandwich parish counted no more than 1,000 souls (p. 192).

loyalty,[8] but clearly, the predominant character of the province was going to be English.

Thus was confirmed the distinction between the French Canadians of Lower Canada and the French minorities in the rest of North America. Henceforth, the development of French-Catholic communities outside Quebec would depend on relations with Anglo-Protestant majorities; only in Lower Canada could French Canadians hope to exert the influence of a majority in their own land.[9]

The Acadians were the oldest minority group. Estimates of their pre-expulsion numbers vary widely, as do accounts of the numbers expelled.[10] In any case, the 1767 census of Nova Scotia, taken after the deportations had ended, showed 921 Acadians among a total population of 11,779, with 147

8 Leopold Lamontagne, 'Ontario: The Two Races', in Mason Wade and J.-C. Falardeau, eds., *Canadian Dualism / La Dualité canadienne* (Toronto: University of Toronto Press 1960), p. 353. The policy was not ill advised, especially since the association of British authority with the maintenance of the fur trade had already attracted the sympathies of the French traders. Thus, according to Saint-Pierre, 400 Franco-Ontarians participated in Brock's 1812 campaign against Detroit (p. 204), while the French of the Michigan interior took Michilimackinac for the British that same year (p. 201).

9 See Jacques-Yvan Morin, 'Les Origines historiques du statut particulier', in the *RHAF*, xx, 1 (June, 1966). Though Morin is interested only in the *legal* status of Quebec within the context of the British Empire and British-dominated Canada, his quotation from William Pitt referring to the 1791 constitutional act (p. 8) shows clearly that legal status depended on effective occupation of territory. As for the influence of population on the authors of the Quebec Act, one need only recall, for example, the oft-quoted argument of Governor Carleton, that 'barring Catastrophe shocking to think of, this Country must, to the end of Time, be peopled by the Canadian Race. ... '

10 Emery LeBlanc, for example, in *Les Acadiens* (Montreal: Editions de l'Homme 1963), p. 19, calculates that more than 9,500 were sent to various parts of the British Empire, not counting those who escaped to the woods or made their way to Quebec. But Rameau de Saint-Père, in *La France aux colonies* (Paris: A. Jouby 1859), p. 42, claimed there were only 9,215 Acadians altogether in Nova Scotia on the eve of the expulsion. Naomi Griffiths, in *The Acadians: Creation of a People* (Toronto: McGraw-Hill Ryerson 1973), p. 60, reckons the Acadians numbered about 10,000 in 1755, and that about 8,000 were expelled. A most detailed attempt to trace the movements of the Acadian population was made by the compilers of the 1871 census, who based their work not only on eighteenth-century censuses, but on a wide variety of documents in French and British archives. In their introduction to the volume, *Censuses of Canada, 1665–1871*, they reckoned that 18,500 Acadians lived in the Maritimes in 1755, of whom 8,200 were on the Nova Scotia peninsula, 3,000 on Cape Breton, an equal number on Prince Edward Island, and the remainder in what would become New Brunswick. The expulsion of that year hit 6,000 from the peninsula, while a thousand more appear to have fled to Prince Edward Island and New Brunswick. By 1758, after the fall of Louisbourg, another 2,000 or even 3,000 more appear to have been expelled from Cape Breton and the Shediac district of New Brunswick.

more in the part of the province which was to become New Brunswick, and 197 on Prince Edward Island. These figures, however, certainly underrate the real numbers of Acadians still in the maritime colonies, for many were hiding in the woods, or removed to isolated regions where the British authorities would not be apt to find them.[11]

Subsequent growth of Acadian population is not easy to follow, especially since pre-Confederation censuses did not distinguish Acadians either by language or by national origin. The Catholic Bishop of Quebec, who toured the Maritimes in 1803, is reported to have found more than 8,000 Acadians there.[12] The French commentator Edmé Rameau de Saint-Père calculated there were 80,000 in 1859,[13] and the first dominion census, in 1871, announced there were 92,740 Acadians in Nova Scotia, New Brunswick, and Prince Edward Island.[14]

Increase in numbers was one thing, social development was another. Fearful both of the authorities and of the Loyalists, who poured into the Maritimes after 1783, forcing a last displacement of Acadians from the St John River in 1784, the French avoided the well-organized older regions of settlement, huddling in the wild northern and gulf coast areas. Not eager to show themselves too openly, and having, in any case, returned from exile or from hiding in small, unconnected groups, they remained isolated from each other as well as from English-speaking society.[15] They struggled for a century without the important unifying forces that promoted French-Canadian development in Quebec: Church, schools, press, and political spokesmen.

The first necessity, an Acadian clergy, was hard to acquire. The Seven

---

11 Robert Rumilly speaks of this hiding-out in the woods in his *Histoire des Acadiens* (2 vols.; Montreal: Fides 1955), II, ch. 43. The authors of *Censuses of Canada, 1665 to 1871* reckon that the real numbers of Acadians still in the Maritimes were far higher than what the 1767 census showed. They give a total of 10,150 for the year 1765: 2,500 in Nova Scotia (of whom 800 were on Cape Breton), 1,400 on Prince Edward Island, and the rest in New Brunswick. These figures, again, are much higher than those of Antoine Bernard, who, in his *Histoire de la survivance acadienne* (Montreal: Les Clercs de Saint-Viateur 1935), pp. 30–1, estimates there were only 2,800 Acadians in the Maritimes by 1763, of whom 1,000 were in New Brunswick, 1,000 on the Nova Scotia peninsula, and 400 each on Cape Breton and Prince Edward Island.

12 LeBlanc, p. 22. Antoine Bernard, in his account of Mgr Denaut's 1803 tour of the Maritimes, reports (p. 79) that the bishop confirmed 8,800 souls in the faith, but makes no distinction between Acadians and other Catholics. It may be that LeBlanc has assumed all these Catholics were Acadians.

13 Rameau, p. 92.

14 *Census of Canada, 1870–71* (Ottawa: I.B. Taylor 1873), vol. 1; and *Censuses of Canada, 1665–1871*, p. xxvi.

15 Rumilly, II, ch. 43. On the return from exile and early isolation, see also Griffiths, pp. 73–6, and Rameau, chs. 5–6.

Years' War had left not a single French-Catholic priest in the Maritimes, and, although the Bishops of Quebec, with some help from the seminary for foreign missions in Paris, managed to send a few missionaries into the lower provinces between 1767 and 1818, they were hardly enough to establish an adequately served parish system. In any case, the Maritimes were separated from the diocese of Quebec in 1818, and from that moment, their Church was controlled by Scotch and Irish clergy. By 1844, four dioceses had been created in the Maritimes, none of which had a French-speaking bishop. After that year, there was not a single French priest in Nova Scotia,[16] though a few Quebec missionaries laboured on in New Brunswick. Even there, however, by 1860, of thirty priests at work, only seven were French-speaking, and only one an Acadian.[17] Maritime bishops often held to the theory that, in the interest of Church unity and of good relations with the Protestant majority, English should be the sole language of Catholicism in their dioceses; they tended, therefore, to name English-speaking priests even to parishes with overwhelmingly Acadian populations, and were accused of discouraging French-language life in other ways too.[18]

Under these circumstances, Acadian education developed with difficulty. A century after the expulsion Rameau could still report that while many had learned to read and write, this was the limit of their knowledge.[19] Circumstances had opposed greater progress. A Nova Scotia law of 1766 had forbidden the operation of Catholic schools, so that lessons had to be either private or secret, given in barns, the backs of houses, and so on.[20] By the second decade of the nineteenth century, most teaching was done by itinerant instructors, who travelled through the bush giving a lesson here and a class there, for a fee – though two priests finally did open schools in 1817.[21] As late as the 1860s, the condition of Acadian education was still so bad that a French sailor who jumped ship off the coast of New Brunswick found himself the

---

16 Rumilly, II, 705, 711.
17 Bernard, p. 136.
18 Rumilly, II, 794–5, 789–91, 798–9, 862–5, etc. Also, see Martin Spigelman, 'Race et religion: Les Acadiens et la hiérarchie catholique irlandaise du Nouveau-Brunswick', in the *RHAF*, XXIX, 1 (June, 1975), pp. 69–85, especially pp. 73–4 and 79–81.
19 Rameau, p. 113. In 1885, H.R. Casgrain wrote that since the expulsions the Acadians had been virtually without any means of instruction. See his *Un Pèlerinage au pays d'Evangeline* (Quebec: Demers 1888), p. 23.
20 LeBlanc, pp. 46–7; Rumilly, II, 688.
21 Rumilly, II, 688. Although most of Nova Scotia restrictions on Catholic education were removed in 1786, poverty and lack of priests still retarded the establishment of Acadian schools. See G.A. Rawlyk and Ruth Hafter, *Acadian Education in Nova Scotia* (Study No. 11 of the Royal Commission on Bilingualism and Biculturalism; Ottawa, 1970), p. 6.

best-educated man in the village of Bouctouche, where he landed, and successfully opened and ran a school.[22]

By this time the State had begun to lend a hand. An 1841 Nova Scotia law authorized government grants to Catholic schools, where French (or German or Gaelic, for that matter) might be the language of instruction. These were not long enjoyed, however, since the province set up a non-denominational public school system in 1864, making it compulsory and universal the following year. French was eliminated, except as a subject of instruction in upper grades, and certification rules made it impossible to import teachers from the religious orders of Lower Canada.[23] Meanwhile, however, Prince Edward Island had begun granting subsidies to Catholic schools in 1852 (though French-speaking teachers apparently received 18 per cent less than English),[24] and New Brunswick began making similar grants in 1858.[25] The first Acadian secondary school opened at Memramcook, New Brunswick, in 1854, closed after a few years of financial struggle, and finally re-opened in 1864, though it was largely English in the origin of its pupils and in its language of instruction.[26]

Educational difficulties prevented the growth of other elements of national life. No French newspaper was published in the Maritimes till 1867; its first issue appeared a week after Confederation was inaugurated.[27] It had not been till 1846 that a first Acadian had been elected to the New Brunswick legislature. In 1864 he was still the only Acadian MPP, and, though another was elected in 1865, the Acadians were without representation in the Maritime governments and delegations that participated in the making of Confederation.[28] Nor was their economic situation such as to give them influence. Still mainly poor fishermen, they were little engaged in agriculture and not at all in business.[29]

In these circumstances, we need hardly be surprised to find no significant expression of Acadian opinion about the making of Confederation. Largely ignorant of its coming.[30] having had no part in its preparation, Acadians had

---

22 Rumilly, II, 688. Bernard, p. 148. This sailor became the first French-speaking MP from the Maritimes. He was Auguste Renaud.
23 LeBlanc, p. 47; Rumilly, II, 727–8; Rawlyk and Hafter, pp. 13–14.
24 LeBlanc, p. 47.
25 Rumilly, II, 749. The 1858 act did not actually recognize Catholic schools as such, but it left local school boards so much autonomy that in Catholic areas they were able to make their public schools Catholic in practice.
26 Ibid., p. 718. Also, Spigelman, pp. 76–7.
27 It was *Le Moniteur Acadien*, published at Shediac, N.B.
28 LeBlanc, p. 82.
29 Rameau, p. 110; Rumilly, II, 735; Bernard, pp. 99–100.
30 Rumilly, II, 735.

no reason to greet it with enthusiasm.[31] They could only follow their clergy's advice to accept it passively as a *fait accompli*.[32] 'Today,' commented the *Moniteur Acadien* in its first issue, 'there is only one thing for us to do: resign ourselves to our fate and try to make the best of it.'[33]

On the other side of Quebec, the Franco-Ontarians were far more closely connected in every way with the French Canadians of Lower Canada than were the Acadians. Their old Windsor-area community had declined in relative importance since the beginning of the century, but, at the time of Confederation, their build-up of strength in eastern Ontario was still beginning. The 1861 census, on which the fathers of Confederation had to base their considerations, showed that Canadians of French origin comprised only 2.4 per cent of Upper Canada's population, though they were close to half in the eastern counties of Russell, Prescott and Nipissing, and a quarter of Ottawa city. In all of Upper Canada, 13 per cent of Catholics were of French origin.

Small though it was, this group was able to lead a French-Canadian life, largely because of the decentralized nature of pre-Confederation society. Especially in the frontier period, there was relatively little pressure for cultural uniformity. At a time, for instance, when schools were hard pressed to find teachers who could disseminate the elements of reading, writing and arithmetic, there was little point in insisting on this or that language, or on conformity to this or that curriculum. Thus, in 1851, Upper Canada's Council of Public Instruction refused to challenge a local school board's hiring of a unilingual French teacher, not only on the grounds that the majority of pupils in the area were French-Canadian, but also because it was too hard to find people qualified to teach in English. The Council ordered that teachers should be able to qualify for certification in French, if they chose, rather than English. This was a strictly practical decision, not a matter of natural, historical, or constitutional rights, and the facilities given to French were also allowed to German, just as the 1841 Nova Scotia law had applied to German and Gaelic as well as to French.[34]

While the language of Upper Canadian education was, thus, not a political

---

31 *La Revue Canadienne* (Montreal), III, 5 (May 1866), p. 316, observed that even the prospect of being united with the French Canadians did not seem to make Confederation attractive to the Acadians. Indeed, Griffiths notes (p. 80) that at Confederation the Acadians 'knew nothing of "Bas Canada, sinon qu'il y avait, à Québec et à Montréal, des Français qui s'appelaient des Canadiens."'
32 Rumilly, II, 738.
33 *Le Moniteur Acadien*, 8 July 1867.
34 C.B. Sissons, *Bi-lingual Schools in Canada* (Toronto: Dent 1917), pp. 17–22, 30.

question before Confederation, religion was one. And here the Upper Canadian Catholics were aided by the Union in 1840. though they and their allies were a minority in Upper Canada, the support of their Lower Canadian co-religionists enabled them to obtain separate school privileges. In 1855, and again in 1863, bills defining and expanding the rights of the Catholic school system in Ontario were passed against the opposition of the Upper Canadian majority, thanks to the votes of Lower Canadians in the united legislature of the two Canadas.

The important support which Franco-Ontarians received from Quebec was demographic as well as political. Beginning around 1850, emigration from Lower Canada doubled the French-Canadian population of the southwestern counties of Essex and Kent in twenty years.[35] More strikingly, it was Lower Canadian emigrants who accounted for the growing importance of French Canadians in the Upper Canadian counties that touched the Ottawa River.[36] The contact of these counties with Lower Canada meant that settlers in them formed part of a large French-Canadian bloc of population centred in Quebec, and could more easily maintain their cultural identity. Thus, the diocese of Ottawa was part of the ecclesiastical province of Quebec, and its French-Canadian bishops were ready to appoint French-speaking priests as the Maritime hierarchy were not. Again, the proximity of the east bank population made it easier to launch a French-language newspaper on the west side. Attempts were made at Ottawa in 1858 and 1861; a more successful venture began in 1865, as Ottawa was about to become the Canadian capital, and Le Canada was published there till two years after Confederation.[37]

Nevertheless, the Franco-Ontarians were not a political force of their own in the 1860s. There was no French Upper Canadian father of Confederation, no Franco-Ontarian voice in the councils that planned the new régime, that wrote the new constitution. For these people there was much to be lost in the break-up of the old union of the Canadas, and they were much dependent on the French-Canadian leaders of Lower Canada to obtain what securities could be had for them in the new dominion.

---

35 Saint-Pierre, p. 220.

36 Census of Canada, 1870–71, vol. 1, showed that the Quebec-born were 52 per cent of the French-origin population in Prescott county, 59 per cent in Russell, 85 per cent in Ottawa, 82 per cent in Nipissing county, and 71 per cent in Renfrew North. This is based on the assumption that in these areas, whose French-origin population was growing spectacularly, and where there was an emigration of English Canadians, virtually all the Quebec-born settlers were French Canadians.

37 André Beaulieu and Jean Hamelin La Presse québécoise des origines à nos jours (vol. 2; Quebec: Presses de l'Université Laval 1975), p. 151. The last issue of Le Canada was followed within days by the first of a new French newspaper, and so it continued.

Like the Acadians, the French Métis of the northwestern plains were French-Catholic cousins of the Quebeckers, but were not, properly speaking, French Canadians themselves. Descendants of old-time *voyageurs* and Indian women, they had come, by the beginning of the nineteenth century, to form, together with the English-speaking descendants of Hudson's Bay men, distinct half-breed communities, apart from both Indians and whites. In these communities the French and Catholic element slightly predominated. Censuses of Assiniboia (the Hudson's Bay Company's administrative district corresponding roughly to the Manitoba of 1870) did not note either language or national origin; but the census of 1843 showed that 54 per cent of Assiniboia's families (including the tiny minority of whites) were Catholic. The first Manitoba census, taken in 1870–1, counted 5,757 French Métis and 4,083 English Métis.[38]

The numerical importance of the French Catholics was reflected in the Company's administration of the North-West. From the time of its establishment, the Bishop of St Boniface was always a member of the Council of Assiniboia, and from 1853 on, at least one French Métis was also appointed. Four years before, the council had officially sanctioned the use of French in court cases involving francophone inhabitants, and in 1850 several French magistrates had been appointed. Two years later, the council began making an annual grant to the Catholic, Anglican, and Presbyterian Churches for the support of their schools, establishing some precedent for separate Catholic and Protestant schools systems in the North-West. The French and Catholic fact had, thus, considerable institutional basis in Rupert's Land, and it is not for nothing that Assiniboia has been referred to as 'a little Quebec.'[39]

But the differences between Assiniboia and Quebec were at least as great as their similarities. Commerical relations between the two areas had ended with the demise of the Montreal fur trade in 1822, and if there had been a religious connection since 1818, when the first Catholic missionaries were sent from Quebec to Red River, the very establishment of that connection had been a manifestation of the difference between the two places. It was Lord Selkirk who had appealed to Quebec's Bishop Joseph-Octave Plessis to send those missionaries, when Métis, fearing that his agricultural settlement would destroy the buffalo hunt on which their livelihood depended, were led into

---

38 And 1,565 whites. These are probably the most frequently quoted and easily accessible census figures in Canadian history. See, eg., G.F.G. Stanley, *The Birth of Western Canada* (London: Longmans Green 1936), p. 13; W.L. Morton, *Manitoba: A History* (Toronto: University of Toronto Press 1957), p. 145; A.G. Morice, *Histoire abrégée de l'Ouest canadien* (St Boniface 1914), p. 89, Auguste-Henri de Trémaudan, *Histoire de la nation métisse dans l'Ouest canadien* (Montreal 1936).
39 A.S. Morton, *A History of the Canadian West to 1870–71* (London: Nelson n.d.) p. 802.

violence. Selkirk wanted the missionaries to tame these savage Métis, to settle them down into an agricultural life like that of the French Canadians.

But agriculture was not easy to establish on the prairies. A group of French Canadians, who followed the first missionaries with the task of providing an example and a nucleus around which Métis farmers could settle, gave up within a few years and fled to the United States or back to Canada. Bishop Provencher was later to write that for six or seven years after his arrival in the North-West, though he dined at the governor's table, he never saw any bread.[40] Though churches were built and plots of land marked off along the Red River, stability was hard to achieve. Even in the late 1860s, the twice-yearly buffalo hunts still uprooted the entire community from its Red River homes and transported it across the plains for six weeks at a time. On the eve of the Canadian takeover, J.J. Hargrave was writing that one of the chief problems for the colony's future would 'lie in persuading the hunting portion of the partially-civilized community to devote themselves to sedentary or agricultural labour. This is the French half-breed race. ... '[41]

Like any great social change, in fact, the settling of the Métis was a gradual one, affecting some more quickly and more thoroughly than others.[42] The greatest degree of adaptation was found in the Assiniboia area, while those who resisted change drifted into the farther North-West. A.S. Morton sums up the situation thus: 'The more sedentary portion made good farmers, but every grade of settler was found among them, down to those whose homes differed little from their former camps among the Indians, and whose livelihood continued to be hunting and fishing as of old.'[43]

Not surprisingly, the Métis were unenthusiastic about joining the Canadian confederation. Fearing a sudden flooding of the plains by Canadian agricultural settlement, in the face of which their hunting life could no longer survive, they would have preferred maintenance of Hudson's Bay Company rule, if possible.[44] But if the status quo could not be maintained, they were at least determined to have a say in the conditions on which they would join the dominion. The Acadians and the Franco-Ontarians had not shared in the making of the Confederation in the 1860s; but the Assiniboians

40 J.-N. Provencher, *Mémoire ou notice sur l'établissement de la mission de la Rivière-Rouge* (Rome 1836), p. 2.
41 J.J. Hargrave, *Red River* (Montreal: Lovell 1871), p. 466.
42 Marcel Giraud, pp. 631–2.
43 A.S. Morton, p. 804.
44 This is expressed clearly in Louis Riel's explanation to the Council of Assiniboia of why his people had resisted the Canadian takeover. The English half-breeds, less dependent on the hunt than their French cousins, and for some time increasingly accustomed to associate with immigrants from Ontario, were less eager to block the Canadian takeover. Indeed, Frits Pannekoek argues that religious hostility toward the Catholic Métis had led them,

made an uprising in 1869–70 in order to share in the making of Confederation as it affected them. And in that uprising, it was repeatedly the French Métis who took the initiatives – the section of the community still most attached to the hunt and least comfortable with agriculture.

The only French-Catholic group that played any direct part in making the original confederation, between 1864 and 1867, was French Lower Canada. Despite various challenges, this group maintained the essential numerical strength which had made it unique already in the eighteenth century. British immigration had, for a time, after 1815, seemed to threaten the integrity of French Lower Canada. By 1822, officials estimates suggested that almost 15 per cent of Lower Canadians were living in the new townships or Protestant seigneuries. But the flood of immigration had scarcely begun. The census of 1844 showed that only 75 per cent of Lower Canadians were French-Canadian. By this time, too, a new problem had appeared to accentuate the effect of British immigration: the exodus of French Canadians from Quebec to the United States. A committee of the Canadian legislature reckoned in 1849 that 20,000 French Canadians had emigrated to the States merely in the five preceding years.[45] The movement accelerated in the following decades, as French Canadians felt increasingly the lack of good agricultural land and the absence of jobs in Quebec. By 1890, the United States census showed that there were 302,496 people born in Canada of French origin then living in the U.S.,[46] and it has been estimated that, all in all, as many as 500,000 French Canadians left Canada to live in the republic between 1851 and 1901.[47] Nevertheless, despite this exodus, and despite the lesser movement to Upper Canada, the French Canadians began slowly to regain their strength in Quebec after the middle of the nineteenth century. The 1861 census showed that they now constituted over 76 per cent of the provincial population. In 1871 the figure would be 78 per cent, and by 1901, over 80 per cent.

These facts encouraged people to continue looking on Lower Canada as a particularly French-Canadian country. It was in Lower Canada that French-Canadian nationalism emerged, in the politics and literature of Lower Canada

well before 1869, to identify themselves actively with the Ontarians and to seek Canadian annexation as a desirable thing. See Pannekoek's article, 'The Rev. Griffiths Owen Corbett and the Red River Civil War of 1869–70', in the *Canadian Historical Review*, LVII, 2 (June, 1976), pp. 133–49.

45 Fernand Ouellet, *Histoire économique et sociale du Québec, 1760–1850* (2 vols.; Montreal: Fides 1971), II, 473.

46 United States Department of Commerce and Labor, Bureau of the Census, *A Century of Population Growth* (Washington 1909), p. 226.

47 Jean Hamelin and Yves Roby, *Histoire économique du Québec, 1851–1896* (Montreal: Fides 1971), p. 66.

that that nationalism expressed itself. It was not without reason that Lord Durham looked on the 1791 separation of Lower Canada from Upper as the green flag to French-Canadian national aspirations. Already in 1822, the petitions which French Canadians drew up to oppose a proposed reunion of the Canadas expressed their belief that this province had been set aside for all time as a homeland for their nationality, a territory to be characterized by their laws, their institutions, and their language.[48]

These beliefs were not extinguished by the union of 1840, for although the legislatures of the Canadas were merged, it soon became clear that the separate laws and institutions, and hence, inevitably, the separate administration and language of Lower Canada, would continue to flourish.[49] Indeed, during the very period of the union, the identity of French Canada with Lower Canada became formalized in literature, and there emerged a well-defined theory of a French-Canadian nationality domiciled in a Lower Canadian homeland.[50]

The work of Louis-François Laflèche, at the end of the Union period, was a particularly elaborate expression of this theory. Having demonstrated that the French Canadians constituted a nation, and that every nation, in order to live out its national life in accord with the will of Providence, had to have a homeland of its own, Laflèche concluded that 'we have a homeland; that homeland is the land bequeathed to us by our fathers, the fine, rich valley of the St Lawrence. Providence itself gave it to our forefathers. ... ' Significantly, in defining what constituted a nation, Laflèche stressed common laws, customs, and social organization, as well as language and religion: a national homeland had to be a place where more than linguistic and religious privileges were guaranteed.[51]

Thus, on the eve of Confederation, Lower Canada stood out, as always in

---

48 Public Archives of Canada: Mouvement Anti-Unioniste, Bas-Canada, 1822–1825: Papers (MG 24, B22): Copies of petitions, especially pp. 4, 9, 19, 21–2, 93. These ideas were also repeated in the Reform polemics of the 1820s and 1830s. See, eg., D.-B. Viger, *Analyse d'un entretien sur la conservation des établissemens du Bas-Canada* ... (Montreal: James Lane 1826), p. 31; or Papineau's speech in *Chambre d'assemblée, vendredi, 21 février, 1834* (n.p., n.d.), pp. 32–3.

49 Indeed, the Union of the Canadas soon became a sort of semi-federalism. See, eg., William Ormsby, *The Emergence of the Federal Concept in Canada, 1839–1845* (Toronto: University of Toronto Press 1969).

50 Expressions or reflections of this theory can be seen in the most varied sorts of works – eg., *Douze missionnaires des townships de l'est, Le Canadien émigrant* (Québec: Côté et Cie 1851), p. 17; Stanislas Drapeau, *La Colonisation du Canada envisagée au point de vue national* (Quebec: Lamoureux 1858), p. 4; L.J.C. Fiset, *Jude et Grazia* (Quebec: Brousseau et Frères 1861), pp. 17, 24; *La St-Jean-Baptiste à Québec en 1865* (Quebec: Duquet et Cie 1865), p. 36; *Coup d'oeil sur la colonisation* (Montreal: Plinguet et Laplante 1865), p. iv, etc., etc. All these equated French Canada with Lower Canada.

51 Louis-François Laflèche, *Quelques considérations sur les rapports de la société civile avec la religion et la famille* (Trois-Rivières 1866), pp. 70, 23–5.

the past, as the most particular homeland of the French Canadians: the one place where their laws and institutions predominated, and where their elected representatives were in a position to participate fully in the making of the new régime.

In the light of what we have seen so far, we shall not be surprised to discover that the province of Quebec was the only part of the new confederation in which French-Canadian and Catholic institutions were fully and effectively established. Since Section 94 of the British North America Act provided for uniformity of civil laws in provinces other than Quebec, and since French Canadians would be able to control future legislation only in Quebec, where alone they would be a majority, there was no question of having French-Canadian laws outside that province. Section 133 established the official status of the French language, but only in Quebec and in the *federal* Parliament and courts.[52] Finally, section 93 limited, to some degree, the provinces' powers to deprive Catholics of separate school systems once they officially possessed them – though, as the future would show, the degree of limitation was slight indeed, and official possession most difficult to demonstrate.

If these provisions did not do much to guarantee the flourishing of French-Catholic institutions outside Quebec, neither did they deprive them of any rights they had possessed before Confederation. What the new constitution did do for the minorities was to put them into the same political unit with the Quebeckers. Though the break-up of the Canadian Union deprived Franco-Ontarians of the kind of direct French-Quebec support that the united legislature had allowed, the jurisdiction of the federal Parliament was, nevertheless, sufficient to ensure that questions of the cultural rights of the minorities would come before it, and would, thus, be discussed by the French-Quebec MPs who sat in it. Moreover, the association of the British North American provinces in a single confederation might have encouraged, in some measure, either the movement of French Canadians to areas outside Quebec, where they could reinforce the minorities, or at least the idea that such a movement could be desirable.

During the first decades of Confederation the French-origin population grew at about the same rate as the Canadian population in general. It fell off only

---

52 The Red River uprising of 1869–70 brought an extension of French language rights, when the Manitoba Act of 1870 applied to that province the same provisions which Section 133 had applied to Quebec. French only enjoyed its official status in Manitoba, however, until 1890. Another section of the Manitoba Act was intended to give stronger protection to Catholic separate schools than was provided by the 1867 act, but in the end it proved as frail a reed as Section 93 itself.

slightly, from 31.1 per cent of the total in 1871 to 31.0 per cent in 1901. But the distribution of French population throughout the dominion changed significantly in this period. While its relative importance grew in the Maritimes, Quebec, Ontario, and even British Columbia, it declined drastically on the prairies.

We have already seen that in Quebec the French-origin population grew more quickly than the non-French population, constituting 78.0 per cent of the total in 1871 and 80.2 per cent in 1901. At the same time, there was a movement of French Quebeckers into parts of the province which had previously been mainly English. Thus the French-origin population grew from 56.1 per cent of Quebec City's total in 1861 to 82.8 per cent in 1901; at Sherbrooke the increase was from 24.1 per cent in 1861 to 62.7 per cent in 1901.[53] French-origin population thus gradually strengthened its place in the one province in which it had been a controlling majority to begin with.

The Acadian population also gained significantly in relative numbers during this period, especially in New Brunswick, where it increased from 16 per cent of the total population in 1871 to 24 per cent at the turn of the century. Acadians were a less significant part of the populations of Nova Scotia and Prince Edward Island, but there, too, their share of the total increased, from 8.5 per cent to 9.8 per cent in Nova Scotia, and, in Prince Edward Island, from 9.8 per cent in 1881 to 13 per cent in 1901.

This increase in Acadian strength corresponded, first of all, to a high rate of natural increase. In all three provinces, Acadian families were consistently larger than those of other Maritimers. Indeed, if one compares census figures on family size in those Maritime counties with the largest proportion of French-origin population with the figures for the Quebec counties that were most thoroughly French, one finds that the Acadians beat even the French Quebeckers in point of large families.

A second factor which contributed to the relative strengthening of the Acadians was the movement of non-French population away from the maritime provinces. New Brunswick and Prince Edward Island both experienced absolute decreases in their non-Acadian population during the 1880s and 1890s, as did Nova Scotia in the latter decade. This emigration was particularly noticeable in those counties where Acadians were most densely concentrated. For the Acadians were not spread evenly through these provinces, but were gathered together in specific regions – the southwestern

---

53 These and the following population figures come from vol. 1 of each of the appropriate federal censuses. In Montreal, the French-origin population grew from 48 per cent of the total in 1861 to 56 per cent in 1881. By 1901, in Montreal City itself, it was still 56 per cent, though in the greater Montreal urban area it was much stronger. Even in Montreal City, though, it had grown from 43,509 in 1861 to 114,245 in 1901.

tip of Nova Scotia, Cape Breton, and the northern and gulf coast areas of New Brunswick. In the last regions especially, the Acadians constituted more than half the population in three out of six counties as early as 1871, and by 1901 formed more than a third of the population in all but Northumberland County. This concentration gave the Acadians a better chance to maintain their separate language and identity than would have been expected from the general proportion in which they stood to the Maritime population as a whole. It was not surprising, therefore, that non-French population often tended to move away from Acadian districts.

One factor that contributed very little to the growth of French-origin population in the Maritimes was reinforcement by emigrants from Quebec. After Confederation as before, the Acadian and French-Canadian peoples remained distinct and separate from each other. In Nova Scotia and Prince Edward Island, immigration of Quebeckers was negligible, and even in northern New Brunswick, the Quebec-born element was usually equivalent to no more than one to three per cent of the French-origin population. It was only in the two counties directly bordering on Quebec that the figure ever ran above ten per cent, and even there it was never anywhere near the proportions to be found in eastern Ontario.

As before Confederation, emigrants from Quebec continued to pour into the eastern counties of Ontario. In 1871, the Quebec-born were equivalent to more than half of the French-origin population in the four eastern counties of Glengarry, Prescott, Russell and Nipissing. In the last, the figure ran as high as 79 per cent in 1871 and 82 per cent in 1891. Thanks largely to this kind of movement, the proportion of Ontario's population that was of French origin increased from 4.7 per cent in 1871 to 7.3 per cent in 1901. In the latter year there were 158,671 Franco-Ontarians; they had become far more numerous than any other provincial minority outside Quebec. Like the Acadians, they showed a striking rate of natural increase; families in the most densely French county, Prescott, were consistently larger than those of other Ontarians, and larger than those of French Quebeckers as well. Again, as in New Brunswick, the relative strength of the French in Ontario was boosted by the exodus of English-origin population from the areas where the Franco-Ontarians were most numerous. These areas were mainly the ones contiguous to the province of Quebec, so that the local strength of the French Ontarians was much greater than their province-wide force. Between 1871 and 1901 the number of counties whose populations were more than one-third French increased from two to six – all but Essex being in the eastern fringe. Two of the southeastern counties had French majorities.

Far different from the experience of the Acadians and of the Franco-Ontarians was that of the francophones in the North-West, for their population declined most dramatically in relative strength after Confederation.[54] Between 1870 and the end of the century, the prairie population grew at a much faster rate than that of Canada as a whole,[55] so that by 1901 the prairies had been completely transformed and the balance of Canadian population greatly changed. The important factor, of course, was new settlement. But the lack of French-Canadian settlers left the region open to a mainly English flow of pioneers, more of whom came from Ontario than from any other place.[56] Within a decade, the French element was swamped in Manitoba and sinking in the territories. By 1891 it had dropped to a fairly permanent level: about seven per cent of Manitoba's population and four to five per cent in the rest of the prairie region. Moreover, the French or francophone population in the West had few centres of concentration. Only in the Manitoba district of Provencher did it remain above ten per cent of the population, running at about a third during most of our period.

Not only was French settlement on the Canadian plains meagre, but Métis families fled the census districts as white men came in, thus reducing the strength of the French-speaking community. Despite an increase in the size of the province, Manitoba's French-Métis population fell from 5,757 in 1871 to 4,369 in 1885. The desperate desire to keep up the hunting way of life had drawn Métis away from the province and into the more distant North-West. They were replaced in Manitoba by French-Canadian settlers from Quebec and the United States, and by a high rate of natural increase among the French-Manitobans – a characteristic which the different French-Canadian and Acadian minorities all seem to have shared. It is interesting to note that despite the efforts of a repatriation movement that attempted particularly to go after those French Canadians who had gone to the United States, in order to bring them back as settlers in the Canadian West, the 1885 census of

---

54 This was also different from the experience of the French British Columbians, whose numbers increased five-fold between 1881 and 1901. Despite this growth, however, the French element in B.C. remained insignificant, constituting only 1.9 per cent of the province's population in 1881 and still only 2.6 per cent in 1901.

55 In those three decades the Canadian population grew by 52.6 per cent, from 3,485,761 to 5,318,606. In the same period the population of the Canadian prairies grew by over 1200 per cent, from about 30,000 to well over 410,000. In the single decade of the 1880s, Manitoba's population jumped by 145 per cent, and the rest of the prairies' by 158 per cent. In 1871, less than one per cent of Canadians lived on the prairies; by 1901, almost eight per cent lived there.

56 The 1881 census showed that of 41,512 Manitobans who had not been born on the Canadian prairies, almost half – 19,125 – came from Ontario. A further 8,161 had been born in the United Kingdom, but only 4,085 in Quebec (including, of course, English Quebeckers). The Ontario-born were, in fact, more than twice as numerous as any other group in Manitoba, save only those born in the province itself.

Manitoba indicated that more Quebeckers had been attracted there, in fact, than Franco-Americans. The Quebec-born population of Provencher, in that year, was equivalent to 62 per cent of the non-Métis French-origin community, but the American born to only 11 per cent.[57]

It was not primarily a movement of population that brought French Quebeckers into contact with the minorities after Confederation; rather, it was the social and political conflicts in which the minorities became engaged, and whose repercussions were felt at Ottawa. The first decades of Confederation saw, in fact, a dramatic succession of conflicts in which French and Catholic minorities found themselves fighting for their interests, their rights, or even, at times, their physical safety. And French Quebeckers could not avoid becoming involved in these affairs, for again and again, the minorities appealed for help in their battles, not only to the federal Parliament, in which French Quebeckers participated, but even directly to the Quebec press and population.

The entry of the North-West into the dominion involved the first such conflict, and it dragged on long after the passing of the Manitoba Act. The question of an amnesty for participants in the Red River uprising remained unresolved until 1875, while extremists – usually from Ontario – encouraged the use of violence, especially against the French-Catholic Métis.[58] The arrest of Ambroise Lépine in 1873, and his trial the following year, for the murder of Thomas Scott, as well as Riel's expulsion from the Commons in 1874, were aspects of a continuing crisis at whose centre was the French-Catholic element. In Manitoba, press campaigns were soon launched against the separate school system and the official use of French.[59] The latter was nearly abolished in 1879 during a provincial cabinet crisis with racial overtones.

Meanwhile, the very advance of white settlement was a threat to the Métis, pushing them out of Manitoba in the 1870s and leading them to rise up, with their Indian allies, in the North-West rebellion of 1885. That rebellion, as well as the controversy surrounding the fate of its leader, Riel, provoked further expressions of anti-French feeling in Ontario and the West.

---

57 Even considering that many who moved to Manitoba from the u.s. had probably been born in Quebec, the disproportion seems striking.

58 Eg., see George Taylor Denison, *The Struggle for Imperial Unity* (London: Macmillan 1909), pp. 42–3; A.G. Archibald's testimony in Canada, Parliament, *Rapport du Comité spécial sur les causes des troubles du territorie du Nord-Ouest en 1869–70* (Ottawa: Taylor 1874), p. 140; A.-A. Taché, *L'Amnistie* (Montreal: Le Nouveau Monde 1874), p. 59.

59 R.O. MacFarlane, 'Manitoba Politics and Parties after Confederation', in the Candian Historical Association, *Report*, 1940, p. 48. By 1877, Archbishop Taché had been obliged to take to print in defence of the separate schools. See A.-A. Taché, *Denominational or Free Christian Schools in Manitoba* (Winnipeg: Standard Printing 1877).

Two years later, one of a series of territorial ordinances weakened the position which federal legislation of 1875 had given Catholic schools in the territories, and this would be repeated, with increasing provocation of passions at Ottawa (where territorial ordinances were reviewed) until the establishment of the provinces of Alberta and Saskatchewan in 1905.[60]

Meanwhile, in 1890, D'Alton McCarthy's initiative in the House of Commons opened the way to the undoing of the 1877 establishment of the French language in the North-West Territories.[61] The same year saw the disestablishment of French in Manitoba and the beginning of the Manitoba schools controversy. The latter would rage with increasing ferocity, engaging the passions of French Quebeckers to an ever-greater extent, as federal politics became increasingly involved, until it was temporarily resolved by an 1896 compromise. This left the province with the common school system it had given itself in 1890, but allowed certain privileges, in practice, to the French language and Catholic religion, in school districts with sufficiently large French or Catholic enrolments. In a sense, the controversy had been far from a strictly French-Canadian question, since, by the end of the 1890s, less than half of Manitoba's Catholics were of French origin.[62] Nevertheless, the issue had become a French-Canadian national question because of the political atmosphere in 1889–90, in which the Manitoba school law had been passed at the same time as attacks were launched against the French language, and because of the unprecedented involvement of Quebec politics and opinion in the matter.

The school question, as a matter of fact, had already been raised in the first years after Confederation, when the New Brunswick government had passed a common school act, ending the 1858 practice of allowing local school boards to raise tax support for denominational schools. This law, a blow to Catholicism, did not, however, affect the position of the French language in New Brunswick schools.[63] Moreover, when it was passed in 1871, less

---

60 The use of French was similarly limited in territorial schools. The 1892 ordinance restricted it to one primary year in classes where children did not understand English. In 1930, Saskatchewan would further restrict even this much use of French. See G.F.G. Stanley's essay in Wade and Falardeau, p. 330.

61 McCarthy's bill was amended to permit a partial disestablishment of French, and the territorial council took advantage of the permission in 1892.

62 *Fourth Census of Canada*, 1901, vol. 1, showed 35,672 Catholics in Manitoba, but a French-origin population of only 16,021.

63 French-Canadian historiography has consistently, but wrongly, assumed that the French language was aimed at by this legislation. But see, eg., Maud Hody, 'The Anglicising Common Schools Act of 1871: A Study in Folklore', in the Société Historique Acadienne *19ᵉ Cahier* (Apr.–June, 1968), pp. 347–9. Also Report of the Royal Commission on Bilingualism and Biculturalism, book II: 'Education' (Ottawa: Queen's Printer 1968), p. 44.

than half of the province's Catholics were of French origin.[64] Because of this, and because the Acadians were the weakest, worst organized, and least conspicuous part of the Maritime Catholic community, the battle against the common schools was mainly waged by English-speaking Catholics.

Nevertheless, in a series of motions of 1872, 1873, and 1875, the MP John Costigan put the New Brunswick schools question before the federal House of Commons, and, thus, before the French Quebeckers, who, as Catholics, might be expected particularly to concern themselves with it. Costigan's resolutions failed to bring about either disallowance of the school law or a constitutional amendment giving greater protection to Catholic schools. Equally unsuccessful was a Catholic appeal to the courts; the Privy Council upheld the validity of the school law in the summer of 1874.

Nevertheless, Costigan had attracted Quebec's attention, and the aftermath of the Privy Council's decision was such as to excite that attention even more. Even before that decision was announced, resistance against the school legislation had led to violence, arrests, and seizures of property to pay taxes. The climax came in January 1875 in the mainly Acadian village of Caraquet. When the province tried to coerce the local school board, violence erupted. Two men were killed and several townsmen arrested.

The seriousness of the situation finally forced both sides to give in. Negotiations between prominent Catholics and the provincial government led to a compromise agreement that summer.[65]

Although the New Brunswick Catholics had appealed to Ottawa for help in their dispute, and although the Caraquet affair had brought the Acadians in particular to the attention of French Quebeckers, the Acadians, nevertheless, remained distinct and separate from the French Canadians. In 1881 the Acadians held their first national congress, bringing together 5,000 delegates from the three maritime provinces. Half a century after the founding of French Canada's Saint-Jean-Baptiste Society, these Acadians set out to

---

64 The 1871 census showed that 47 per cent of New Brunswick's Catholics were of French origin. By 1881, the proportion had become 52 per cent.

65 This account is based mainly on Rumilly's *Histoire des Acadiens*, II, 760ff. The 1875 compromise provided that nuns and priests could obtain certification without attending the provincial teachers' college, and that they would be allowed to wear clerical costume in the classroom; formal religious instruction could be given in the classroom after normal school hours; textbooks containing material offensive to Catholic consciences could be amended or replaced for schools in Catholic areas; and Catholic children could be allowed to attend school outside their own district if the local board of a Catholic area accepted them. Rumilly mistakenly asserts that permission to use the French language was also part of the 1875 compromise, but French, in fact, had never stopped being used. As for the men arrested at Caraquet, they were eventually released, but only after one had been convicted of murder and then had the conviction quashed.

found a national society of their own, and in so doing, they consciously and determinedly rejected the French-Canadian identity. The congress spent much of its time trying to choose an Acadian national holiday. Two dates were proposed: June 24, Saint-Jean-Baptiste day; and August 15, the feast of the Assumption. The former would identify the Acadians with the French Canadians; the latter would distinguish them. Although speakers who favoured the identification were not lacking, it was August 15 that was chosen, after a debate which made clear the desire of the Acadians to remain a people distinct from the French Canadians.[66]

Confederation, then, did not end the ambivalence in the relations between French Quebeckers and the Métis, on the one hand, French Quebeckers and the Acadians, on the other. The one minority which did remain clearly and fully French-Canadian was the Franco-Ontarians. They, too, however, saw some diminution of their cultural privileges in the first decades after Confederation. The unilingual French schools tolerated since the early nineteenth century were rendered bilingual in 1885, and in the following years the religious and racial tensions associated with the Riel affair and the nationalist stances of the Mercier government brought increasingly loud calls for the abolition of the Ontario separate school system. Though these led to no action, pressure on the French language did continue to mount until 1912, when the Department of Education's Regulation 17 made Ontario schools unilingually English.[67]

All these changes in the position of the Acadians, Métis, and Franco-Ontarians were followed much more closely by French Quebeckers after 1867 than they had been before. Confederation, by enabling the minorities to bring their cases to Ottawa, made them, in some sense, the affairs of the French Quebeckers. But there was one more minority, not even resident in Canada, to whom the Quebeckers were also related, and whose tribulations they could also follow with regularity and interest: the Franco-Americans.

Although, as we have seen, there was some movement to Upper Canada after 1783, the old French community continued strong in Michigan after the American Revolution. As late as 1820, when the census showed Michigan had a population of 8,896, most were still French. Settlement, however, soon changed the proportions, and by 1840, five years after Michigan had attained statehood, even the most sanguine estimate could not number its French at more than 15,000 out of a total population of 220,000. In that year, the

---

66 LeBlanc, pp. 30–3. See also Griffiths, p. 80.
67 See Robert Choquette, *Language and Religion: A History of English-French Conflict in Ontario* (Ottawa: University of Ottawa Press 1975).

governor's speech to the legislature was, for the first time, no longer translated into French.[68]

But just as French Canadians moved into Upper Canada after 1850, so they moved, in much greater numbers, to the United States. Indeed, the movement had begun even before mid-century, as we have already seen.[69] This emigration reinforced the French communities in the American West. The Canadian-born population of Michigan grew from 14,000 in 1850 to 88,275 in 1870, and it has been reckoned that over half were French Canadians.[70] Moreover, in the early 1850s, the Abbé Chiniquy led about six or seven thousand French Canadians to Illinois, where they joined an existing French community of about 8,000 and founded a French newspaper, the *Tribune de Chicago*. At the end of the decade, Rameau de Saint-Père wrote that Wisconsin, Minnesota, and Montana were also receiving significant French-Canadian immigration from Quebec.[71]

The great bulk of French-Canadian emigration to the United States, however, was directed to New England. From the time of the Civil War, rapid industrial development created a great demand for labour, and thousands of French Quebeckers moved each year to fill the jobs in New England factory towns. Their numbers were so great that they were able to form entire French-Canadian communities, with parishes of their own, schools, and a French-language press. In the midst of the American melting pot, they kept alive their patriotism and their desire to maintain their national institutions. From 1852 on, Saint-Jean-Baptiste Societies, Lafayette Societies, and Unions Françaises sprang up throughout New England – indeed, across the United States. While British North Americans were planning Confederation, in 1865, these societies were holding the first national convention of French Canadians of the United States.[72]

---

68 Saint-Pierre, pp. 206, 217–18.

69 Above, p. 14.

70 Saint-Pierre, p. 221. He calculated that the French-origin population constituted about six per cent of Michigan's total in 1870. It is interesting to note that the 1871 census set the French-origin group at only 4.7 per cent of Ontario's population.

71 Rameau, pp. 173–4.

72 This convention saw expressions of hostility toward the project of Confederation in British North America, and calls for annexation of Canada to the u.s. Such a move, by uniting Lower Canadians with their compatriots in New England, would reinforce the position of the latter by forming a large, solid, French-Canadian bloc in the northeastern United States – a bloc strong enough numerically to resist assimilation, dominate the area, and exert considerable influence even at Washington. See E. Hamon, *Les Canadiens-Français de la Nouvelle-Angleterre* (Quebec: Hardy 1891), pp. 129–30. This 1869 Detroit convention of Franco-Americans passed a series of annexation resolutions, but the idea lost support soon after, and was hurt beyond revival when one of its leading advocates, Médéric Lanctôt, publicly abandoned Catholicism. (Saint-Pierre, pp. 233–46.)

One thing that helped keep alive French Canadianism in New England was the proximity of Quebec. Distances were short enough that visits could be made, ties to old friends and old places maintained. Quebeckers, too, could easily keep up with the activities of their compatriots across the border. Saint-Jean-Baptiste congresses frequently brought representatives of the two communities together, and Franco-American newspapers, whose columns were frequently reprinted in those of Quebec, also maintained the connection.

Thus, Quebeckers could follow the vicissitudes of Franco-American destinies as closely and with as much interest as those of any other minority. This was significant, because Franco-Americans experienced the same difficulties as the others. They too had their school questions, their difficulties with the English-speaking catholic clergy, their struggle to maintain their language.[73]

What the following chapters discuss is not the position of the minorities, but the attitudes of French Quebeckers toward that position. To what extent did the experience of Confederation overcome the old separateness between Lower Canada and the other French-Catholic communities? Did it lead at all to a new sense of solidarity in a wider homeland than the old Lower Canada? What, in fact, were the attitudes of French Quebeckers toward Confederation and the place of their nationality in it? Was their concern for French rights in the other provinces different from their interest in the rights of Franco-Americans?

The answers to these questions will be sought mainly in the press, but also in the pamphlets, private letters, and general literature of Quebec in the first decades of Confederation. We shall look largely at reactions to those critical affairs – school questions, western uprisings, and so on – in which minority rights were so affected. But between crises as well, we shall look for expressions of feeling about the position of the minorities and about Quebec's uniqueness as a French-Canadian country. And underlying all will be the question: what place did French-Canadians see for their nationality in a bilingual Canada, in a separate Quebec?

Merely to ask this sort of question is to look for trouble. After all, are we not asking about 'public opinion'? And what was public opinion in nineteenth-century Quebec? Was the ordinary Quebecker even aware of the issues which

---

73 Robert Rumilly, *Histoire des Franco-Américains* (Montreal 1958), pp. 45, 113, 122–4, 129–30, 138, 146–7, etc.; Hamon, pp. 57–61, 75–86; G.F. Thériault, 'The Franco-Americans of New England', in Wade and Falardeau, pp. 405–7.

we are discussing? How much did he know or care about what parliamentarians debated: about Confederation, the New Brunswick schools, or the language question in the North-West?

In 1865, just after the Canadian legislature had debated the Quebec resolution, *La Revue Canadienne* had to admit that the mass of ordinary people seemed 'indifferent to the project, or didn't understand anything about it. Some said, "Oh well, I suppose it'll be a good thing!" and the others, "I don't know – *M. le curé* hasn't breathed a word about it."'[74] Two years later, when the Confederation project had got as far as the British Parliament, many Lower Canadians still, it seemed, did not know about it:

There are still a lot of people, especially in the countryside, who may be completely unaware of the fact that while they go quietly about their petty domestic affairs, a new constitution is being prepared for us in the imperial parliament.[75]

Those who opposed Confederation laid much stress on the absence of any sign of mass awareness or support of it. If public opinion was characterized by a profound apathy,[76] if ignorance was widespread, it was because the government carefully avoided publicizing the project, knowing full well that if French Canadians knew what was being planned, they would exert themselves to oppose it.[77] Indeed, the opposition was convinced that there was a public opinion, that it opposed Confederation, and that if only it were consulted, it would express itself clearly enough. It was a chief complaint of the Rouge MPPs that 'the people of this province have never had the chance to express their opinion about the confederation plan. ... '[78] Let Macdonald only hold general elections, let him ask the electorate, in the way prescribed by the constitution, whether they shared his views, and he would see Lower Canadians express their opinions in the same way New Brunswickers had done when they voted Tilley out of office in 1865.[79]

Would general elections in Canada have produced such results? And would election results, in any case, have proved a reliable guide to public opinion on the question of Confederation? The contrast between the Confederationists' success in Quebec in the general elections of 1867 and their catastrophic defeat

---

74 *La Revue Canadienne*, II, (1865), p. 240.
75 *Le Pionnier de Sherbrooke*, 9 March 1867.
76 *Le Défricheur* (L'Avenir), 7 Feb. 1866.
77 *L'Union Nationale* (Montreal), 8 November 1864.
78 *Représentation de la Minorité parlementaire du Bas-Canada à Lord Carnarvon, Secrétaire des Colonies ...* (Montreal: Le Pays 1866), p. 3.
79 Ibid., pp. 6, 9–10. Also, *La Confédération couronnement de dix années de mauvaise administration* (Montreal: Le Pays 1867), pp. 10–13; *Le Pays* (Montreal), 27 March 1867; *L'Ordre* (Montreal), 1 July 1867.

in Nova Scotia, the ratification of the confederation project by a majority of French-Canadian MPs in March 1865, and the success of Confederationists in Lower Canadian by-elections held between the summer of 1864 and the passing of the BNA Act – all this suggests that the Lower Canadian opposition had, in fact, much less support than it claimed to hold.[80] So, perhaps, does the electoral fate of the twenty-one French-Canadian MPPs who voted against Confederation in the legislature. Of those twenty-one men, seven lost their seats in the 1867 federal elections. Three more, who were not candidates themselves, saw their ridings won by Confederationists. Three were re-elected but rallied to Confederation. Only five were re-elected as anti-Confederates, with the last three seats won by new opponents of the scheme.[81]

One of the anti-Confederates who lost his seat in 1867 was J.-F. Perrault of Richelieu riding. A Rouge, Perrault had early announced his opposition to the Quebec Resolutions, and had immediately received this warning from the *Gazette de Sorel:*

If you want to go on being the MP for Richelieu (and we'd be happy to go on giving you our support) you'll have to respect our wishes and be guided by the views and the desires of your electors ... otherwise, you'll never be re-elected in Richelieu, even though, as far as the interests of the riding itself are concerned, everyone admits that you are a zealous and useful MP.[82]

Was Perrault's defeat, then, a judgement by his electors against his anti-Confederate stand? Can one interpret the 1867 elections in general in this way? It would surely be rash to do so, for close analysis of the campaign suggests that Confederation may often not have been an issue at all.[83] And

---

80 The suggestion is accepted, at any rate, by J.-C. Bonenfant, eg., in 'L'Esprit de 1867', in the *RHAF*, XVII, 1 (June 1963), p. 34; also in his *La Naissance de la Confédération* (Montreal: Leméac 1969), p. 10.

81 Based on information in Jean-Paul Bernard, *Les Rouges: libéralisme, nationalisme et anti-cléricalisme au milieu du XIXe siècle* (Montreal: Les Presses de l'Université du Québec 1971), pp. 295–311; in Henry J. Morgan, *The Candian Parliamentary Companion* (Montreal: The Gazette 1871); and in Marcel Hamelin, *Les Premières années du parlementarisme québécois* (Quebec: Les Presses de l'Université Laval 1974), pp. 17–25. The anti-Confederationists were even worse beaten in the 1867 Quebec provincial elections. Only five of the twenty-one ridings whose French-Canadian MPPs had voted against the Quebec Resolutions returned anti-Confederates, and one of the five men elected was so moderate in his opposition that he soon crossed the floor, and ran as a Bleu in the following election.

82 *La Gazette de Sorel,* 21 Jan. 1865. Perrault was a candidate in the federal election only, in 1867, but his riding also elected a Bleu provincially.

83 See Marcel Hamelin, *Les Premières années,* p. 24: 'L'étude de la campagne au niveau local ne nous permet pas de considérer les élections de 1867 comme un plébiscite sur la Confédération.' Hamelin argues that in most ridings it was strictly local questions and not

even if the voters were expressing an acceptance of Confederation, would that mean that they had wanted it in the first place? The bishops had told them, after all, that whatever they had thought of the plan before it was adopted, they ought now to accept the *fait accompli* wrought by legitimate authority and to vote for men willing to accept it and make it work.[84]

No, election results are no sure guide to public opinion. If those of 1867 cannot be relied on to tell us what Quebeckers thought of Confederation, can we expect any more from later ones? How can we tell what French Quebeckers felt about the Riel affair from seeing that the Conservatives held Quebec in 1887, though they had lost power provincially as a result of elections held only a few months before? And how much ink has flowed in contradictory attempts to deduce what they thought of the Manitoba schools question from the way they voted in 1896? Elections to federal and provincial parliaments were simply not public opinion polls – and alas, no such polls were held in the decades with which we are concerned. The claims of the Rouges that a general election on the issue would show opinion to oppose Confederation were as vain as the claims of the Sorel newspaper that voters would punish those MPPs who did not support it. It was easy for partisan editors to claim that public opinion was what they wanted it to be, but neither their own claims nor the elections to which they often appealed can be of great help to us.[85]

In inquiring into attitudes and opinions, then, we are obliged to be content, most of the time, with those that were put into writing or circulated in print. Occasionally we may find that more concrete public behaviour – mass rallies and demonstrations, migrations of thousands of people to one place in preference to another – correspond, somehow, to what was expressed or

---

the great theme of Confederation that determined how people voted. Jean-Paul Bernard, in *Les Rouges*, contends that Confederation was, in fact, an important issue in the campaign, but so much mixed up with other issues, particularly the conflict between the clergy and liberalism, that its significance cannot be isolated. 'Ainsi,' he write (p. 296), 'les élections ont-elles permis de mesurer le sentiment populaire face à la Confédération et les forces relatives du clergé et des Rouges, sans qu'il soit possible de distinguer une chose de l'autre.'

84 The Bishops of Tloa, Trois-Rivières, St-Hyacinthe, and Rimouski, in *Nouvelle constitution du Canada* (Ottawa: Le Canada 1867), pp. 54, 61–2, 66, 78ff.

85 While Rouges claimed that opinion was against Confederation, Bleu supporters wrote with apparently equal conviction that the Lower Canadian population was mightily pleased with the scheme, or even that the very idea of Confederation arose from a groundswell of public opinion. See, eg., *La Gazette de Sorel*, 1 Sept. 1866, and 29 June 1867; J.-C. Taché, *Des Provinces de l'Amérique du Nord et d'une union fédérale* (Quebec: Brousseau 1858), pp. iii, 7; *Le Courrier du Canada* (Quebec), 4 July 1867; *Le Journal de Québec*, 2 July 1867.

reported of mass opinion in the press or letters of the time; but in the main, we must depend on opinions that were set down on paper.

But who wrote things in Quebec in the last decades of the nineteenth century? Who read what was written? And how far did Quebeckers in general share the opinions – come to share the opinions – that were put down on paper? As late as 1901, the census reported that only 78 per cent of Quebec's school-age and older population knew how to read and write, while 18 per cent had admitted that they could do neither the one nor the other. Even this represented a considerable accomplishment, for ten years earlier the census had shown that as much as 31 per cent of Quebec's school-age and older population could neither read nor write. And at the time of Confederation, hardly more than half of French-Quebec adults were literate.[86] Apparently, the portion of French Quebeckers who read newspapers was even smaller, for the combined circulation of all French-language newspapers reported in G.P. Rowell's *American Newspaper Directory* for 1873 was equivalent to only about 33 per cent of the number of French-origin families in Quebec (given by the 1871 census). The press, at least around the time of Confederation, would seem, then, to have been read only by a certain class of people – undoubtedly the familiar élite of professionals, clerics, merchants and shop-keepers, and some well-to-do farmers.

Nevertheless, there are reasons for taking it seriously as a guide to opinion. In the first place, both literacy and newspaper circulation increased dramatically in the decades which concern us. By 1889, the total of French-language newspaper circulations reported to the *American Newspaper Directory* had become large enough to cover about 80 per cent of French-Quebec families (1891 census). Clearly, newspapers were growing enormously in this period. Before 1880, only one (*La Minerve* of Montreal) had had a press run of over 10,000. But by 1884, *Le Nouveau Monde* had set a new record with a distribution of 26,400. By the end of the decade, *Le Canadien, La Patrie, La Presse*, and probably *L'Electeur* (though this last did not report its circulation in 1889) had also passed the 10,000 mark. And the age of big circulations was only beginning; the 1890s saw the take-off of the mass-circulation daily in Quebec as in the rest of Canada.

Moreover, the influence of the press probably did not stop with its actual circulation, for facts and opinions picked up by one reader might be spread to many other people by word of mouth. What an editor wrote one day in his paper, he (or a political colleague) might say the next (or perhaps had said the

---

86 For elaboration on the last figure and on much of what follows in this section, see Paul Rutherford, *The Making of the Canadian Media* (Toronto: McGraw-Hill Ryerson 1978), especially pp. 29–37, 48–53.

day before) at a public meeting – at a political picnic or one of those boisterous and often violent political confrontations which, as Paul Rutherford points out, were a kind of nineteenth-century equivalent of our professional hockey games. What's more, in a society in which deference to the *notables* was both a duty in the official ideology and a practice in much of the social life (note the reference to *M. le curé* in the quotation from *La Revue Canadienne*, above, p. 26), it is not unlikely that what the élite read in the papers was listened to with interest later on by many non-readers.

Certainly, those who wished the support of public opinion seemed to think it important to have newspapers on their side. One has only to glance at the Beaulieu-Hamelin accounts of how papers came to be founded to see how often this politician or that bishop took the initiative in order to create a 'healthy' influence on public opinion.[87] Thus, an individual paper was usually the organ of a particular political, religious, or other interest; together, the papers represented the official point of view, that is, the views of the professional-political élite that dominated French-Canadian life in the province. They put forward the ideas which that élite wanted to set before the electorate. What newspapers expressed became the body of 'acceptable' ideas, to which politicians or other leaders could refer for justification or legitimation of policies or positions, and in terms of which issues were discussed – at least in so far as they *were* discussed.

In saying this, I am implying that even papers that represented positions as far apart as rouge and ultramontane nevertheless shared certain common points of view. And indeed, the questions which we have asked of public opinion are particularly the sort to bring out common points of view. For in asking about awareness of the minorities the sense of belonging to a homeland, feelings of solidarity with French-Catholic groups outside of

---

87 André Beaulieu and Jean Hamelin, *La Presse québécoise des origines à nos jours*, vol. 1 (Quebec: Les Presses de l'Université Laval 1973), pp. 113–14 on the founding of the *Mélanges Religieux*, p. 204 on the *Courrier du Canada*, vol. 2 (PUL, 1975), p. 65 on the *Journal des Trois-Rivières*, p. 106 on *Le Nouveau Monde*, pp. 188–9 on *Le National*, p. 288 on *La Patrie*, etc., etc. During the whole of the period we shall be looking at – even in the 1890s when the mass-circulation paper financed by advertising was beginning to appear – the French-Quebec press remained highly partisan and closely connected with political or other interests which could become its patrons. Not only did newspapers often depend on government printing contracts or other forms of political patronage for their survival, but journalists often looked for appointment to public positions at the end of periods of faithful journalistic service. Frequently, journalists were also party organizers (Arthur Dansereau, for example) or even politicians. Hector Langevin, Joseph Cauchon, Wilfrid Laurier, Honoré Mercier, Joseph-Israel Tarte were only a few of an enormous number of men who either passed from journalism to politics, or practised both professions at the same time.

Quebec, we are not as apt to be answered by party policies or platforms as by more generally held attitudes. We shall, naturally, wish to be aware of these areas of agreement, and when we find them – when we find, moreover, attitudes expressed not only in the newspapers but in the pamphlet literature, letters, novels, even poetry – we shall probably be justified in feeling that we have got pretty close to 'French-Canadian opinion.'

Nevertheless, differences – important differences – will occur, and it is important, therefore, to notice certain changes which appeared in the French-Quebec press during the third of a century which interests us. At the beginning of the period, the French-language press in Quebec was dominated by organs of the Conservative Party or by organs of Church authorities that were careful to support the Conservatives politically. At the time when Confederation was being discussed, the pro-Confederation press easily dominated that of the opposition.[88] During the 1870s, the Liberals had continuing difficulty in keeping alive newspapers to compete with the disseminators of Conservative opinion. In the following decade, however, the balance of press power began to change. Thoroughgoing ultramontane-nationalist papers like *L'Etendard* and *La Vérité* achieved prominence. Though they did not support the Liberals, their rebellion against the Bleus helped weaken traditional points of view in Quebec. At the same time, important Liberal papers began to emerge, notably *La Patrie* (1879) and *L'Electeur* (1880). Thus, by the time of the Riel affair, there was a strong opposition press ready to express outrage at the federal government's conduct. In the 1890s, some of the Liberal papers were among those whose circulations soared the highest, while the same decade saw the demise of some of the great names of the old Conservative press. *Le Canadien, Le Journal des Trois-Rivières*, and *La Minerve* disappeared from the scene in 1889, 1893, and 1899, to be followed by *Le Monde* and *Le Courrier du Canada* in 1900 and

---

88 At Trois-Rivières, Sorel, and (after the middle of 1866) Sherbrooke, pro-Confederation papers were the only ones published. At St-Hyacinthe each side was represented, but the weak anti-Confederate organ collapsed in 1868, while the *Courrier* is still published today. At Quebec City, the combined 1873 circulations of the pro-Confederation *Journal de Québec* and *Courrier du Canada* (1873 was the first year for which Rowell's directory is available) exceeded by four-to-three that of *Le Canadien*, which in any case, did not oppose the principle of Confederation, but only details of the Quebec Resolutions. In the Eastern Townships, *Le Défricheur* opposed Confederation, but it collapsed in 1866 (at the age of four years) just after two new pro-Confederation papers had appeared in the area. At Montreal there were three anti-Confederate papers, *L'Ordre, L'Union Nationale*, and *Le Pays*, but not one of them was still publishing when Rowell's first directory appeared in 1873. In that year, in any case, the Bleu *La Minerve* had a circulation greater than all the rest of the Montreal press combined. Finally, Quebec's only review journal, *La Revue Canadienne*, also supported Confederation.

1901. Even before the Liberal victory in the 1896 elections, the party's newspaper wing had scored impressive triumphs over the Conservatives.

So the scene has been set. The disposition of the French in Canada has been described, the question we wish to answer has been posed, and the sources we shall consult have been discussed. Let us now begin our enquiry.

II

CONFEDERATION
AND QUEBEC

W HEN French Lower Canadians were called on to judge the proposed confederation of British North American provinces, the first thing they wanted to know was what effect it would have on their own nationality. Before deciding whether or not they approved, they wanted to hear 'what guarantees will be offered for the future of the French-Canadian nationality, to which we are attached above all else.'[1] From Richelieu's Rouge MPP to Quebec's Catholic-Conservative *Courrier du Canada*, everyone promised to judge the work of the Great Coalition according to the same criterion.[2] Even Montreal's *La Minerve*, known to be George-Etienne Cartier's own organ, promised to make its judgement from a national point of view:

If the plan seems to us to safeguard Lower Canada's special interests, its religion and its nationality, we'll give it our support; if not, we'll fight it with all our strength.[3]

But this quotation reminds us that concern for the French-Canadian nationality had geographical implications, that Canadians in the 1860s generally considered French Canada and Lower Canada to be equivalent. When French Canadians spoke of their *patrie*, their homeland, they were invariably referring to Quebec. Even the word *Canada*, as they used it, usually referred to the lower province, or, even more specifically, to the valley of the St Lawrence, that ancient home of French civilization in America,

---

1 *La Gazette de Sorel*, 23 June 1864.
2 Perrault quoted in the *Gazette de Sorel*, 3 Sept. 1864; *Le Courrier du Canada*, 24 June 1864.
3 *La Minerve*, 9 Sept. 1864. After the Quebec Resolutions were known, journalists, politicians, and clergy still claimed to judge them by the same criterion. See, eg., *Le Journal de Québec*, 24 Dec. 1864. Joseph Cauchon, *L'Union des provinces de l'Amérique britannique du Nord* (Quebec: Côté 1865), pp. 19, 41; *Nouvelle constitution du Canada*, p. 59.

whose special status went back to the seventeenth century. Thus, when
Cartier sang 'O Canada! mon pays! mes amours!' he was referring to the
'majestic course of the Saint-Laurent';[4] and Cartier's protégé, Benjamin
Sulte, versifying like his patron, also found French Canada's 'Patrie ... on the
banks of the Saint-Laurent.'[5]

Throughout the discussion of Confederation, between 1864 and 1867,
there ran the assumption that French Canada was a geographical as well as an
ethnic entity, forming, as the *Revue Canadienne* pointed out optimistically,
'the most considerable, the most homogeneous, and the most regularly
constituted population group' in the whole Confederation.[6] *La Minerve*,
which, as has been seen, characterized Lower Canada by a religion and a
nationality, referred also to a 'Franco-Canadian nationality, which really
exists today on the banks of the St Lawrence, and which has affirmed itself
more than once.'[7] Nor was the equation of Lower Canada with French
Canada only a pro-Confederationist notion. The editors of the *Union
Nationale* also maintained that the way to defend the French-Canadian
nationality was to defend the rights of Lower Canada.[8]

It followed from this equation that provincial autonomy was to be sought
in the proposed constitution as a key safeguard of the interests of French
Canada. 'We must never forget,' asserted the *Gazette de Sorel*, 'that French
Canadians need more reassurance than the other provinces for their civil and
religions immunities. ...' But since French Canada was a province, its
immunities were to be protected by provincial autonomy; hence, 'this point is
important above all for Lower Canada. ...'[9]

On this key issue, French Canadians felt themselves to have different
interests from those of other British North Americans. Thus, Cartier's organ:

---

4 Most relevantly quoted in Auguste Achintre and J.B. Labelle, *Cantate: La Confédération* (n.p., n.d.), p. 4. Cartier, indeed, saw French Canada as geographically defined. J.-C.
Bonenfant claims that while he fought for the French Canadians, 'seuls à ses yeux
comptent ceux qui habitent le Bas-Canada.' See Bonenfant's article. 'Le Canada et les
hommes politiques de 1867', in the *RHAF*, XXI, 3a (1967), pp. 579-80. At the 1855 funeral
of Ludger Duvernay, the founder of the Saint-Jean-Baptiste Society, Cartier had warned that
every nationality, including French Canada, must possess an 'élément territorial' in
order to survive. See Joseph Tassé, ed., *Discours de Sir Georges Cartier* (Montreal: Senécal et
Fils 1893), p. 95. Cartier also used the very expression 'French Canada' in a geographical
sense, meaning Lower Canada. See, eg., Tassé, p. 83.
5 *La Revue Canadienne*, I (1864), p. 696.
6 Ibid., IV (1867), p. 477.
7 *La Minerve*, 25 Sept. 1865.
8 *L'Union Nationale*, 3 Sept. 1864. All of these quotations, of course, are merely variations of
Louis-François Laflèche's statement (in *Quelques considérations*, p. 43), 'Les Canadiens-
français sont réellement une nation; la vallée du St-Laurent est leur patrie.'
9 *La Gazette de Sorel*, 14 Jan. 1865. Also, *La Minerve*, 10 and 14 Sept. 1864.

The English ... have nothing to fear from the central government, and their first concern is to ensure its proper functioning. This is what they base their hopes upon, and the need for strong local governments only takes second place in their minds.

The French press, on the contrary, feels that guarantees for the particular autonomy of our nationality must come before all else in the federal constitution. It sees the whole system as based on these very guarantees. [10]

Le Courrier de St-Hyacinthe agreed that 'we do not have the same ideas as our compatriots of British origin concerning the powers which are to be given to the central government. ... We cannot consent to the loss of our national autonomy. ...' [11] The Rouges also saw opposition between French and English-Canadian interests. It was because of this opposition, they commented pessimistically, that George Brown had been able to reveal details of the Quebec Resolutions in Toronto, to the evident satisfaction of Upper Canadians, while in Lower Canada the ministers refused to make any information public. [12]

New Brunswick's governor, A.H. Gordon, in whose house Cartier had been a guest after the Charlottetown Conference, also saw an opposition between English and French-Canadian aspirations. He reported to the Colonial Secretary that while the former seemed to expect a very centralized union, ' "federal union" in the mouth of a Lower Canadian means the independence of his Province from all English or Protestant influences. ... ' [13] This was, indeed, what it seemed to mean to the French-Canadian press. Thus:

We want a confederation in which the federal principle will be applied in its fullest sense – one which will give the central power control only over general questions in no way affecting the interests of each separate section, while leaving to the local legislatures everything which concerns our particular interests. [14]

A confederation would be a fine thing, but only 'if it limited as much as possible the rights of the federal government, to general matters, and left complete independence to the local governments.' [15] As early as 1858, French-Canadian advocates of a British North American confederation had argued that 'it would certainly be necessary to give the separate [provincial]

---

10 *La Minerve*, 14 Sept. 1864.
11 *Le Courrier de St-Hyacinthe*, 23 Sept. 1864. Also, *Le Journal de Québec*, 4 July 1867.
12 *Le Pays*, 8 Nov. 1864.
13 In G.P. Browne, ed., *Documents on the Confederation of British North America* (Toronto: McClelland and Stewart 1969), pp. 42–3. Also, pp. 47, 49, 168 for Gordon's other assertions on the matter.
14 *Le Courrier de St-Hyacinthe*, 2 Sept. 1864.
15 *La Gazette de Sorel*, 30 July 1864.

legislatures the greatest possible share of power', and even that the federal government should only have its powers 'by virtue of a perpetual but limited concession from the different provinces.'[16]

While most papers did not go so far as to support the provincial sovereignty which that last implied,[17] they did opt for co-ordinate sovereignty:

The federal power will be sovereign, no doubt, but it will have power only over certain general questions clearly defined by the constitution.

This is the only plan of confederation which Lower Canada can accept. ... The two levels of government must both be sovereign, each within its jurisdiction as clearly defined by the constitution.[18]

What, after all, could be simpler than that each power, federal or provincial, should have complete control of its own field?

Isn't that perfectly possible without having the local legislatures derive their powers from the central legislature or vice versa? Isn't it possible for each of these bodies to have perfect independence within the scope of its own jurisdiction, neither one being able to invade the jurisdiction of the other?[19]

To be sure, the fathers of Confederation were aware that French Canadians would reject complete centralization. John A. Macdonald told the Assembly that though he would have preferred a legislative union, he realized it would be unacceptable to French Canadians. Nevertheless, he felt the Quebec Resolutions did not provide for a real federalism, but would 'give to the General Government the strength of a legislative and administrative union.' They represented 'the happy medium' between a legislative and a federal union, which, while providing guarantees for those who feared the former, would also give 'us the strength of a Legislative union.'[20] In short, he appeared to understand the Quebec scheme to provide for the closest thing possible to a legislative union, saving certain guarantees for the French Canadians' 'language, nationality and religion'.

---

16 J.-C. Taché, *Des Provinces*, pp. 147, 148.
17 Some did support provincial sovereignty, however – at least at times. See, eg., *La Gazette de Sorel*, 27 Aug. 1864.
18 *Le Courrier de St-Hyacinthe*, 2 Sept. 1864. Also, 28 Oct. 1864.
19 *Le Journal de Québec*, 1 Sept. 1864. Also, 6 Sept. 1864; *Le Courrier du Canada*, 30 Sept. 1864, and 10 Oct. 1864.
20 In P.B. Waite, ed., *The Confederation Debates in the Province of Canada, 1865* (Toronto: McClelland and Stewart 1963), pp. 40, 41, 43. Macdonald's belief that he had obtained something more centralized than a federation is dramatically expressed in his well-known letter of 19 Dec. 1864 to M.C. Cameron (PAC, Macdonald papers), in which he predicts that within a lifetime, 'both local Parliaments and Governemtns [will be] absorbed in the General power.'

This interpretation was hotly rejected by French Canadians of both parties, including those who spoke for Macdonald's partner, Cartier:

Whatever guarantees may be offered here, Lower Canada will never consent to allowing its particular interests to be regulated by the inhabitants of the other provinces. ... We want a solid constitution ... but we demand above all perfect freedom and authority for the provinces to run their own internal affairs.[21]

Let there be no mistake about it: anything close to a legislative union 'cannot and will not be accepted by the French-Canadian population.' A centralized union would be fatal to the French-Canadian nationality.[22] The *Courrier de St-Hyacinthe*, in fact, summed up the whole French-Canadian position when it said:

But whatever guarantees they decide to offer us, we cannot accept any union other than a federal union based on the well-understood principles of confederations.[23]

In taking this view, French Canadians were led to reject another position adopted by John A. Macdonald: that the United States example proved the necessity of a strong central government. He argued that the Civil War had occurred there because the individual states had too much power under the American constitution – power which had given the federation too much centrifugal thrust. To avoid this, British North America must have a dominant central authority.[24]

In French Canada, even *La Minerve* considered Macdonald's reasoning to be nonsensical. 'We believe that this is a specious argument. The United States have a strongly centralized government, which is even capable of acting despotically, as we can see every day.' If you gave a central government too much power over too many localities, it would inevitably antagonize some of them.

This is precisely what happened in the United States, where the war was caused not by the excessive power of the local governments, but by the central government, whose tyrannical actions came into direct opposition to the particular interests of a considerable part of the confederation.[25]

---

21 *La Minerve*, 15 Oct. 1864. See also *Le Courrier de St-Hyacinthe*, 2 Sept. 1864.

22 *Le Courrier du Canada*, 16 Sept. 1864.

23 *Le Courrier de St-Hyacinthe*, 18 Oct. 1864. See also *Le Pays*, 13 Oct. 1864; *L'Ordre*, 14 Oct. 1864; *Contre-poison: la Confédération c'est le salut du Bas-Canada* (Montreal: Senécal 1867), p. 9.

24 The argument is stated clearly and briefly in the letter to M.C. Cameron mentioned above, p. 36n. See also Donald Creighton, *John A. Macdonald* (2 vols.; Toronto: Macmillan 1966), I, 369, 375–6, 378–80; P.B. Waite, 'The Quebec Resolutions and the *Courrier du Canada*, 1864–1865', in the *CHR*, XL, 4 (Dec., 1959), p. 294; etc., etc.

25 *La Minerve*, 15 Oct. 1864.

Le Journal de Québec agreed whole-heartedly. The causes of the American Civil War were to be sought, not in the powers of the states, but in 'the awful tyranny which the central government of the Unites States imposes on the state authorities, by taking them over and stealing their most inalienable powers. ...'[26]

There was agreement between Bleus and Rouges that the autonomy of a French-Canadian Lower Canada was the chief thing to be sought in any new constitution. Accordingly, the Confederation discussion revolved around whether or not the Quebec plan achieved that aim. As far as the opposition was concerned, it did not. The Rouges maintained that this was an 'anglicizing bill',[27] the latest in a line of attempts to bring about the 'annihilation of the French race in Canada', and thus realize Lord Durham's wicked plans.[28] And it would achieve this goal because it was not really a confederation at all, but a legislative union in disguise, a mere extension of the Union of 1840.[29] 'It is in vain,' cried C.-S. Cherrier at a Rouge-sponsored rally, 'that they try to disguise it under the name of confederation. ... This *quasi* legislative union is just a step toward a complete and absolute legislative union.'[30]

The evidence of Confederation's wickedness could be seen by its opponents on every hand. Did it not involve representation by population – the dreaded 'Rep by Pop' which French Canadians had resisted so vigorously till now?[31] And were not English Canadians proclaiming that centralization was to be the chief characteristic of the new regime? The Canadian legislature had even ordered the translation and publication of Alpheus Todd's essay on the provincial governments – an essay which included the remark that these would be 'subject to the legal power of the federal parliament.'[32] Indeed,

---

26 *Le Journal de Québec*, 27 Aug. 1864. See also Joseph Cauchon, *L'Union des provinces*, p. 39. *Le Courrier du Canada*, far from seeing the u.s. constitution as embodying the error of excessive decentralization, found it an apt model for the Quebec Conference to follow. See J.-C. Bonenfant, 'L'Idée que les Canadiens-français de 1864 pouvaient avoir du fédéralisme', in *Culture*, xxv (1964), p. 316. Some Rouges, notably Médéric Lanctôt in *L'Union Nationale*, went so far as to maintain that it would be more desirable for Lower Canada to join the u.s. than the British North American Union, precisely because it would have more autonomy as an American state.

27 *Le Pays*, 27 Mar. 1867.

28 Ibid., 2 Apr. 1867. Also, 23 July 1864; and *La Confédération couronnement*, p. 5.

29 *La Confédération couronnement*, pp. 5, 8; *Le Pays*, 12 Nov. 1864, 9 Feb. 1865, 2 Apr. 1867.

30 C.-S. Cherrier, et al, *Discours sur la Confédération* (Montreal: Lanctot, Bouthillier et Thompson 1865), p. 13.

31 *Le Pays*, 23 and 28 June, 14 July, 8 Nov. 1864; *L'Ordre*, 27 June 1864; *L'Union Nationale*, 8 Nov. 1864; *Confédération couronnement*, p. 13.

32 Alpheus Todd, *Quelques considérations sur la formation des Gouvernements locaux du Haut et du Bas-Canada* ... (Ottawa: Hunter, Rose et Lemieux 1866), p. 5.

argued the Rouges, it was hardly worth while for Quebec to have such an elaborate, two-chamber parliament as was proposed, since, as Todd made clear, the federal legislature 'will be able to quash and annul all its decisions.'[33]

The Quebec Reolutions themselves indicated that Todd was right, that the provincial powers would be scarcely more than a mirage:

Mind you, according to everything we hear from Quebec, the prevailing idea in the conference is to give the central government the widest powers and to leave the local governments only a sort of municipal jurisdiction. ... [34]

Le Pays had been afraid of this from the time the Great Coalition had annouced its programme. 'Without finances, without power to undertake major public works, the local legislature will hardly be anything other than a big municipal council where only petty matters will be discussed.'[35] When the Quebec Conference had ended, opposition papers still had the same impression: 'In short, the general parliament will have supreme control over the local legislatures.'[36] Even provincial control of education was an illusion, since the governor-general at Ottawa could veto any provincial legislation in the field.[37]

Finally, English-Canadian talk of creating a new nationality only strengthened Rouge fears that Confederation meant centralization and assimilation. When the legislature refused to pass A.-A. Dorion's resolution of January, 1865, that Canadians neither desired nor sought to create a new nationality, his brother's newspaper became convinced that it was all over for Lower Canada and its French-Canadian nationality.[38]

In answering all these opposition arguments, the Bleus certainly did not attempt to defend the notion of a strong or dominant central government. But, they maintained, that was not at all what British North America was going to get. Lower Canada, liberated from the forced Union of 1840, would become a distinct and autonomous province in a loose and decentralized Confederation – that was the real truth of the matter.

The defenders of Confederation refuted the opposition's arguments one after another. Did the Rouges speak of Rep by Pop? Why, any schoolboy

---

33 *Le Pays*, 28 July 1866. Also, 27 Sept. 1864, and 19 July 1866.
34 *Le Pays*, 25 Oct. 1864.
35 Ibid., 23 July 1864. Also, *L'Ordre*, 22 July 1864.
36 *L'Union Nationale*, 11 Nov. 1864. Also, 3 Sept. 1864; *Le Pays*, 14 and 23 July 1864.
37 *L'Ordre*, 14 Nov. 1864.
38 *Le Défricheur*, 25 Jan. 1865. All these fears which inspired the opposition also provoked doubts in the minds of some people who were otherwise supporters of the government. 'Nous avons toujours dit,' remarked *Le Canadien*, on 3 Aug. 1866, 'que dans le plan de confédération actuel, on n'avait pas laissé assez de pouvoir aux gouvernements locaux et trop au gouvernement général.' See also, eg., 3 Feb. 1865.

ought to see the difference between Rep by Pop, which the Bleus had opposed as long as the legislative union remained, and a 'confederation which would give us, first of all, local legislatures for the protection of our sectional interests, and then a federal legislature in which the most populous province would hve a majority *only in the lower house.*'[39] As long as there was only a single legislature for the two Canadas, Rep by Pop would have put 'our civil law and religious institutions at the mercy of the fanatics.' But Confederation would eliminate that danger by creating a separate province of Quebec with its own distinct government:

We have a system of govenment which puts under the exclusive control of Lower Canada those questions which we did not want the fanatical partisans of Mr Brown to deal with. ...

Since we have this guarantee, what difference does it make to us whether or not Upper Canada has more representatives than we in the Commons? Since the Commons will be concerned only with general questions of interest to all provinces and not at all with the particular affairs of Lower Canada, it's all the same to us, as a nationality, whether or not Upper Canada has more representation.[40]

This was central to the Bleu picture of Confederation: all questions affecting the French-Canadian nationality as such would be dealt with at Quebec City, and Ottawa would be 'powerless, if it should want to invade the territory reserved for the administration of the local governments.'[41] As for the questions to be dealt with at Ottawa, they might divide men as Liberals and Conservatives, but not as French and English Canadians. 'In the [federal] Parliament,' said Hector Langevin, 'there will be no questions of race, nationality, religion or locality, as this Legislature will only be charged with the settlement of the great general questions which will interest alike the whole Confederacy and not one locality only.'[42] Cartier made the same point when he said that 'in the questions which will be submitted to the Federal parliament, there will be no more danger to the rights and privileges of the French Canadians than to those of the Scotch, English or Irish.'[43] Or, as his organ, *La Minerve*, put it, Ottawa would have jurisdiction only over those matters 'in which the interests of everyone, French Canadians, English, or Scotch, are identical.'[44] For the rest – for everything which concerned the

39 *Le Journal de Québec*, 5 July 1864.
40 *Réponses aux censeurs de la Confédération* (St-Hyacinthe: Le Courrier 1867), pp. 47–9.
41 *La Minerve*, 20 Sept. 1864. Also, *Le Courrier du Canada*, 11 July 1864.
42 *Parliamentary Debates on the Subject of the Confederation of the British North American Provinces* (Ottawa 1865), p. 368.
43 Ibid., pp. 54–5.
44 *La Minerve*, 15 Oct. 1864.

French Canadians *as* French Canadians – for the protection and promotion of their national interests and institutions, they would have their own province with their own parliament and their own government.

And what a parliament! and what a government! Why, the very fact that Quebec was to have a bicameral legislature was proof of the importance they were to have. 'In giving ourselves a complete government,' argued the Bleus, 'we affirm the fact of our existence as a separate nationality, as a complete society, endowed with a perfect system of organization.'[45] Indeed, the very fact that Ontario's legislature was to have only one house while Quebec's had two served to underline the distinctiveness, the separateness, and the autonomy of the French-Canadian province:

It is very much in our interest for our local legislature to have enough importance and dignity to gain respect for its decisions. ... For us, French Canadians, who are only entering Confederation on the condition of having our own legislature as a guarantee of our autonomy, it is vital for that legislature not to be just a simple council whose deliberations won't carry any weight. ...

The deeper we can make the demarcation line between ourselves and the other provinces, the more guarantee we'll have for the conservation of our special character as a people.[46]

Here was the very heart and essence of the pro-Confederation argument in French Lower Canada: the Union of the Canadas was to be broken up, and the French Canadians were to take possession of a province of their own – a province with an enormous degree of autonomy. In fact, *separation* (from Upper Canada) and *independence* (of Quebec within its jurisdictions) were the main themes of Bleu propaganda. 'As a distinct and separate nationality,' said *La Minerve*, 'we form a state within the state. We enjoy the full exercise of our rights and the formal recognition of our national independence.'[47]

The provinces, in this view, were to be the political manifestations of distinct nationalities. This was the line taken in 1858 by J.-C. Taché, when he wrote that in the provincial institutions, 'the national and religious elements will be able to develop their societies freely, and the separate populations realize ... their aspirations and their dispositions.' And it was widely understood that Taché had played a vital role in influencing the course of the Quebec Conference.[48] Cartier himself had told that conference that a federal

45 Ibid., 17 July 1866.
46 *Le Journal des Trois-Rivières*, 24 July 1866. Also, *Le Courrier de St-Hyacinthe*, 10 July 1866.
47 *La Minerve*, 1 July 1867. Also, 2 July 1867: '[Comme] nation dans la nation, nous devons veiller à notre autonomie propre. ... '
48 Taché, *Des Provinces*, p. 151: 'Les éléments nationaux et religieux pourront à l'aise opérer

rather than a unitary system was necessary, 'because these provinces are peopled by different nations and by peoples of different religions.'[49] It was in this light that *La Minerve* saw the Quebec programme as establishing 'distinctly that all questions having to do with our religion or our nationality will be under the jurisdiction of our local legislature.'[50] All the pro-Confederation propagandists were agreed that 'the future of our race, the preservation of everything which makes up our national character, will depend directly on the local legislature.'[51] It was the Lower Canadian ministers who had insisted, at the Quebec Conference, that education, civil and religious institutions should be under provincial jurisdiction, in order that Quebec should have the power to take charge of the French-Canadian national future.[52] Indeed, that power extended well beyond civil and religious institutions. It included 'the owernership and control of all their lands, mines, and minerals; the control of all their municipal affairs'[53] – everything 'which is dearest and most precious to us'[54] – all power, in fact, necessary to promote the national life of French Canada.

All these powers were to be entrusted to the government of a province in which French Canadians would form 'almost the whole' of the population, and in which everyone would have to speak French to take part in public life.[55] Yes, Confederation, by breaking up the union of the two Canadas, would make the French Canadians a majority in their own land,[56] so that 'our beautiful French language will be the only one spoken in the Parliament of the Province of Quebec. ...'[57]

---

leurs mouvements de civilisation, et les populations séparées donner cours ... à leurs aspirations et à leurs tendances.' During the Confederation Debates, Joseph Blanchet claimed that the Quebec Resolutions were, essentially, the very scheme which Taché had presented in his 1858 pamphlet (p. 457 of the Ottawa edition of the debates). Joseph Tassé asserted in 1885 that Taché had acted as special adviser to the Canadian ministers at the Quebec Conference. (See J.-C. Bonenfant, 'L'Idée que les Canadiens-français de 1864', p. 314.) And Taché's son told an interviewer in 1935 that his father (whose uncle, Sir E.-P. Taché, had repeatedly recommended the nephew's scheme to the conference) had several times been called into the sessions, 'vraisemblablement pour donner des explications sur son projet.' See Louis Taché, 'Sir Etienne-Pascal Taché et la Confédération canadienne', in the *Revue de l'Université d'Ottawa*, v (1935), p. 24.

49 In Browne, *Documents*, p. 128.
50 *La Minerve*, 30 Dec. 1864. See also *Le Journal de Québec*, 24 Dec. 1864.
51 *Le Courrier de St-Hyacinthe*, 28 Oct. 1864. Also, 23 Sept. and 22 Nov. 1864.
52 *Le Courrier du Canada*, 7 Nov. 1864. See also 11 Nov. 1864.
53 *Le Courrier du Canada*, 13 Mar. 1867. Also, 28 June 1867.
54 *La Minerve*, 1 July 1867. Also, 2 July 1867; and the speech of Sir Narcisse Belleau in the *Confederation Debates* (Waite edition), p. 29.
55 *Le Courrier de St-Hyacinthe*, 10 July 1866.
56 Cauchon, *L'Union*, p. 45.
57 *Contre-poison*, p. 20. See also *Réponses aux censeurs*, p. 48.

What was more, the control which French Canadians would exercise over their wide fields of jurisdiction would be an absolute control, and 'all right of interference in these matters is formally denied to the federal government.'[58] The Bleus, in fact, claimed to have succeeded in obtaining a system of co-ordinate sovereignty. 'Each of these governments,' they explained, 'will be given absolute powers for the questions within its jurisdiction, and each will be equally sovereign in its own sphere of action.'[59] Some over-enthusiastic advocates of the new régime even claimed that the provinces alone would be sovereign, 'the powers of the federal govenment being considered only as a concession of specifically designated rights.'[60] But even the moderate majority was firm in maintaining that the provinces would be in no way inferior or subordinate to the federal govenment, that they would be at least its equal, and that each government would be sovereign and untouchable in its own sphere of action:

In the plan of the Quebec conference there is no delegation of power either from above or from below, because the provinces, not being independent states, receive their powers, as does the federal authority, from the imperial parliament.[61]

Politicians and journalists expressed this same view, in the legislature as well as in print. Thus, Joseph Blanchet told the Assembly: 'I consider that under the present plan of confederation the local legislatures are sovereign with regard to the powers accorded to them, that is to say in local affairs.'[62]

It may be that French-Canadian Confederationists went farther than they ought to have done in interpreting the Quebec Resolutions the way they did. Part of the reason for this may have been ignorance. A Bleu back-bencher like C.B. de Niverville of Trois-Rivières could admit in the legislative debates that he had not read the resolutions, and what's more, that his ignorance of the English language had prevented him from following much of the debate. In this very situation he saw – or thought he saw – an argument for Confederation. For as he understood it, the new arrangement would remove

---

58 *Contre-poison*, p. 20. Also, *Le Journal de Québec*, 15 Nov. 1864, and 24 Dec. 1864; Cauchon, *L'Union*, pp. 45–6; *L'Union des Cantons de l'Est* (Arthabaskaville), 4 July 1867; Governor Gordon in Brown, *Documents*, p. 75; Bishop Larocque in *Nouvelle constitution*, p. 75.

59 *Le Courrier de St-Hyacinthe*, 28 Oct. 1864.

60 E.-P. Taché, quoted in Bonenfant, 'L'Idée que les Canadiens', p. 315.

61 Joseph Cauchon, *Discours ... sur la question de la Confédération* (n.p., n.d.), p. 8: 'les provinces, n'étant pas des états indépendants, reçoivent, avec l'autorité supérieure, leurs organisations politiques du Parlement de l'Empire. Il n'y a que des attributs distincts pour l'une et pour les autres.' See also Cauchon's *L'Union*, pp. 40, 52; *Le Courrier du Canada*, 7 Nov. 1864, and in Waite's 'The Quebec Resolutions and', pp. 299–300.

62 Joseph Blanchet in *Débats parlementaires sur la question de la Confédération des provinces de l'Amérique Britannique du Nord* (Ottawa: Hunter, Rose et Lemieux 1865), p. 551.

French-Canadian affairs from an arena where men such as he were at a disadvantage, and place them before a group of French-speaking legislators:

Indeed, what sort of liberty do we have, we who do not understand the English language? We have the liberty to keep quiet, to listen, and to try to understand! (Hear! hear! and prolonged laughter.) Under Confederation, the Upper Canadians will speak their language and the Lower Canadians will speak theirs, just as today; only, when a man finds that his compatriots form the great majority in the assembly in which he sits, he'll have more hope of hearing his language spoken, and as they do today, members will speak the language of the majority.[63]

Such an argument seems virtually to have ignored the very existence of the federal parliament, or at least of the authority it would have over French Canadians.

The case of de Niverville may have been extreme, but it was certainly not the only case of Bleus interpreting the Confederation plan in such a way as to maximize the powers of the provinces and minimize those of Ottawa far beyond anything we have been accustomed to. The federal power to raise taxes 'by any mode or system of taxation' was interpreted so as to exlude the right of direct taxation.[64] The federal veto power was represented not as a right to interfere with provincial legislation, but only as as an obligation upon Ottawa to act as 'guardian of the constitution' by keeping clear the distinction between federal and provincial jurisdictions.[65]

But more important than any of these *specific* arguments was the wide-ranging exuberance of pro-Confederation propaganda. Here was a source of rhetoric that seemed to be promising that Confederation would give French Canadians virtual independence. Quebec was 'completely separated from Upper Canada and has a complete governmental organization to administer *all its local affairs* on its own.'[66] In the legislative council, E.-P. Taché interrupted his English-language speech on Confederation to tell his French-Canadian followers in French: 'If a Federal Union were obtained, it would be tantamount to a separation of the provinces, and Lower Canada would thereby preserve its autonomy together with all the institutions it held so dear.'[67] This could not be too often repeated: 'The first, and one of the principal clauses of the constitution is the one that brings about the repeal of

---

63 Ibid., p. 949.
64 *L'Union des Cantons de l'Est*, 12 Sept. 1867. This argument about direct taxation will not be as unfamiliar to historians as to other payers of federal income tax.
65 *La Minerve*, 3 Dec. 1864. Also, 11 Nov. 1864; *Le Courrier de St-Hyacinthe*, 22 Nov. 1864; *Le Courrier du Canada*, 7 Nov. 1864.
66 *Contre-poison*, p. 13.
67 *Confederation Debates* (Waite edition), p. 22.

the Union, so long requested by the Rouges, and separates Lower Canada from Upper Canada.'[68] What patriotic French Canadian could fail to be moved by what the fathers of Confederation had achieved?

We've been separated from Upper Canada, we're called the Province of Quebec, we have a French-Canadian governor ... we're going to have our own government and our own legislature, where everything will be done by and for French Canadians, and in French. You'd have to be a renegade ... not to be moved to tears, not to feel your heart pound with an indescribable joy and a deserved pride at the thought of these glorious results of the patriotism and unquenchable energy of our statesmen, of our political leaders, who ... have turned us over into our own hands, who have restored to us our compete autonomy and entrusted the sacred heritage of our national traditions to a government chosen from among us and composed of our own people.[69]

This sort of exaggerated rhetoric invited an obvious reponse from the opposition. If you really are serious about separation from Upper Canada, they asked, if you really do want to obtain autonomy for French Lower Canada, then why not go the whole way? Why not break up the old union altogether, instead of joining this confederation? 'Everyone is agreed that only the repeal of the union would give us the independence of action needed for the future of Lower Canadians.'[70] If necessary, some sort of commercial association would be sufficient to satisfy Upper Canada in return for political separation.[71]

The Confederationists answered this, not by saying that Quebec's independence was an undesirable goal, not by saying that French Canadians wanted to join together with English Canadians to form a Canadian nation, but by claiming that complete indpendence was simply not practicable:

The idea of making Lower Canada an independent State ... has appealed to all of us as schoolboys; but we don't believe that any serious adult has taken it up so far. ... We simply cannot do everything on our own. ...[72]

---

68 *Contre-poison*, p. 11. Episcopal statements recommended Confederation on the same basis. Bishop Baillargeon of Tloa, who administered the diocese of Quebec, noted in his pastoral letter that, although there would be a central government, Confederation would, nevertheless, comprise four distinct provinces. 'C'est ainsi que le Bas-Canada, désormais séparé du Haut, formera sous le nouveau régime une province séparée qui sera nommé "la Province de Québec" ' (in *Nouvelle constitution*, p. 53).

69 *Contre-poison*, p. 3.

70 *L'Union Nationale*, 3 Sept. 1864. Also, *Confédération couronnement*, p. 5.

71 *L'Union Nationale*, 7 Nov. 1864. Even the pro-Conservative *Gazette de Sorel* admitted, on 23 June 1864, that it had always preferred a straightforward breakup of the union as the best solution for French Canada. Also, 30 July 1864.

72 *La Minerve*, 5 Jan. 1865.

This was, perhaps, a temporary condition, and it was to be hoped that one day Quebec *would* be in a position to make good her independence. Yes, French Canada 'can and must one day aspire to be come a nation';[73] for the moment, however, 'we are too young for absolute independence.'[74] Of course, whoever says 'we are too young' implies that one day we shall be old enough – and Confederation, in the mean while, would preserve and prepare French Quebec for that day of destiny.[75]

One obvious reason why complete independence was not a realistic goal for the present was that Lower Canada was still part of the British Empire, and imperial approval, without which no constitutional change was possible, could not be obtained in the face of intense English-Canadian opposition.[76] But beyond that, it should be clear that an independent Quebec would inevitably be gobbled up by the United States. 'We would be on our own, and our obvious weakness would put us at the mercy of a stronger neighbour.'[77] French Canadians must understand, therefore, that, 'unless we hurry up and head with all sails set toward Confederation, the current will carry us rapidly toward annexation.'[78]

The weakness of an independent Quebec would be both military and economic. The first of these weaknesses could hardly be more apparent to Quebeckers than it was in the mid-1860s, for just as the Anglo-American frictions created by the Civil War were impressing upon them the dangers arising from American hostility, the desire of British politicians to disengage themselves from colonial defence reponsibilities was causing Canadians to think as never before of their own defences. Intercolonial co-operation seemed a natural response to the situation:

No-one could deny that the annexation of the British colonies, either by their consent or by force, is intended and desired by the northern states; it is a no less evident truth that, as things stand today, we could resist their armies with help from Europe; but that on their own, without a political union, without a strong common organization,

---

73 *Le Journal de Québec*, 17 Dec. 1864.
74 *Le Pionnier de Sherbrooke*, 9 Mar. 1867.
75 See Cauchon, *L'Union*, p. 29.
76 *La Minerve*, 28 Sept. 1864.
77 *Le Courrier de St-Hyacinthe*, 25 Nov. 1864. Also, *Le Courrier du Canada*, 10 Oct. 1864.
78 Cauchon, *L'Union*, p. 25. Cartier put the same alternative to the legislative assembly, when he said: 'The matter resolved itself into this, either we must obtain British American Confederation or be absorbed in an American Confederation.' (*Confederation Debates*, Waite edition, p. 50.) See also *La Minerve*, 13 Jan. 1865; and *Nouvelle constitution*, pp. 60, 66–7, 78ff.; *La Revue Canadienne*, II (1865), p. 116, on Confederation as an alternative to 'le gouffre et le néant de la république voisine'.

the colonies could, in the foreseeable future, sustain such a combat – that is something which no-one would dare to maintain. ...[79]

It was in these circumstances that the Confederation project presented itself. Only weeks after the end of the Quebec Conference, the St Alban's raid brought the fear of imminent war with the United States. Yet at the same time, recent British military reports on colonial defence made Quebeckers wonder how much help they could expect if war broke out. 'We must not place unlimited hopes on the support of the mother-country in case of war with our neighbours. Circumstances more powerful than the will of men could render such confidence illusory.'[80] Yet the prospect for the separate British North American colonies without British support was bleak: 'separate from each other, we'd be sure to be invaded and crushed one after the other.'[81] Not only would Confederation give Quebec the advantage of a joint defence organization with the other colonies, but also, by this very fact, it would make Britain willing to give more help in case of war than she would have been willing to give to the isolated and inefficient defence effort of a separate Quebec.[82]

Quebec's economic weakness could be seen already in the flood of emigration directed toward the United States. Clearly, French Lower Canada's economy was not able, on its own, to support all its population. To keep her people at home, the province must co-operate with others to create opportunities. As French Canadians went to seek manufacturing jobs in New England, manufacturing must be established in Lower Canada;[83] by 1867, Quebec papers were appealing to outside capital to set up mills in the province.[84] Long before, Hector Langevin, in a prize-winning essay, had looked to the development of the St Lawrence transportation system to check emigration by providing jobs in commercial enterprises.[85] But the St

---

79 *La Revue Canadienne*, II (1865), p. 159.
80 *La Minerve*, 7 Dec. 1864. The danger of war with the u.s. was announced not only by *La Minerve* in December 1864, but also by *Le Courrier du Canada*, 26 Nov. 1866, and *La Gazette de Sorel*, 19 Nov. 1864, while the need to prepare for British disengagement was urged by the *Journal de Québec*, 17 Dec. 1864, and *Le Courrier du Canada*, 5 Oct. 1864.
81 Cauchon, *L'Union*, p. 32. See also Jules Fournier, *Le Canada: Son présent et son avenir* (Montreal: *La Minerve* 1865), p. 4.
82 *Contre-poison*, p. 8.
83 *L'Union Nationale*, 19 July 1866.
84 *L'Union des Cantons de l'Est*, 3 Jan. 1867.
85 Hector Langevin, *Le Canada, ses institutions, ressources, produits, manufactures, etc., etc., etc.* (Quebec: Lovell et Lamoureux 1855), p. 96.

Lawrence was an interprovincial organization – even more in the era of railroads than in that of the canal.[86]

Thus, the need for economic viability dictated some form of central authority and prevented Quebec's independence from being complete:

The more provinces there are gathered together, the greater will be the revenues, the more major works and improvements will be undertaken and consequently, the more prosperity there will be. What Lower Canada was unable to do on its own, we have done together with Upper Canada; and what the two Canadas have been unable to do together will be done by the confederation, because it will have markets and sea ports which we have not had.[87]

The British North American provinces had been endowed with resources enough. If they worked together to develop them, they could enjoy abundance, material progress, and even economic power.[88] But if they failed to co-operate, if they remained separate and isolated, then their economies would be weak, and inevitably they would become dependent on the United States, the prosperous neighbour to the south. 'But we know that where there is economic dependence there will also be political dependence. ... '[89]

There were strong reasons, then, why Quebec's independence could not be complete, why the nationalist longing for separateness had to compromise with the practical need for viability. But if some form of association with the rest of British North America was necessary, the degree of unification must be the minimum required to make Quebec viable. In the spring of 1867, on his way home from London, where he had helped write the BNA Act, Cartier told a welcoming crowd at a station-stop in the Eastern Townships that his main preoccupation had always been to protect the French-Canadian nationality, language, and institutions. 'That is why I was careful to make sure that the federal government would receive only that amount of power which was strictly necessary to serve the general interests of the Confederation.'[90] This meant, as E.-P. Taché had explained in 1864, that Ottawa would have enough power 'to do away with some of the internal hindrances to trade, and to unite

86 *L'Union des Cantons de l'Est*, 8 Aug. 1867.
87 *Contre-poison*, pp. 48–9.
88 Taché, *Des provinces*, pp. 10–11; *Le Courrier de St-Hyacinthe*, 23 July 1867; *Réponses aux censeurs*, pp. 3–4; Achintre and Labelle, *Cantate*, pp. 2–3, 8; Cauchon, *L'Union*, p. 3; Henry Lacroix, *Opuscule sur le présent et l'avenir du Canada* (Montreal: Senécal 1867).
89 *La Revue Canadienne*, II (1865), p. 103. See also Fournier, pp. 2–3, who argued that as long as Canada was economically dependent on overseas trade, she would be politically at the mercy of the U.S., unless she had her own all-British rail link with an ice-free port in New Brunswick or Nova Scotia. See also Cauchon, *L'Union*, pp. 34–5.
90 *L'Union des Cantons de l'Est*, 23 May 1867.

the Provinces for mutual defence', but that the provinces would remain the agencies to which the 'majority of the people' would look for the protection of their 'rights and privileges' and 'liberties'.[91]

Perhaps this arrangement was not *ideal*; perhaps, even, Confederation was only 'the least bad thing in a very bad world.'[92] The French-Canadian leaders, after all, had not been alone at the constitutional conferences, and French Canada's own needs and aspirations had had to be reconciled with 'our condition of colonial dependence and the heterogenous elements which make up our population.'[93]

Nevertheless, it had to be admitted that, despite Rouge protestations to the contrary, the old union could not have continued longer,[94] that the only alternative to Confederation would have been Rep by Pop,[95] and that, whatever degree of central authority there might be in the confederation, the patriotism of French-Canadian leaders could be relied on to promote the interests of their nationality, just as their patriotism had already won so much for French Canada in the making of the confederation.[96]

And what, then, in the final analysis, had they won? According to Bleu propaganda, Confederation was to be seen as an 'alliance' or 'association' of nations, each in its own autonomous province, and co-operating for the

---

91 Taché was speaking at the Quebec Conference. In Browne, pp. 127–8.

92 Quoted in Waite, 'The Quebec Resolutions and', p. 297. See *Le Courrier du Canada*, 11 Nov. 1864.

93 *Le Courrier de St-Hyacinthe*, 22 Nov. 1864. The opposition tried to stress the weakness and isolation of the French-Canadian delegates to the constitutional conferences as a reproach to them. Eg., *Le Pays*, 13 Oct. 1864. But Confederationists thought it only reasonable to take realities into account. Eg., *La Minerve*, 25 Feb. 1865; *La Gazette de Sorel*, 1 Sept. 1866.

94 *La Gazette de Sorel*, 23 June and 23 July 1864, 14 Jan. 1865; *Le Courrier du Canada*, 24 June 1864; *Le Courrier de St-Hyacinthe*, 8 Nov. 1864; *L'Union des Cantons de l'Est*, 4 Apr. 1864; *La Minverve*, 9 Sept. and 30 Dec. 1864; *Le Journal de Québec*, 15 Dec. 1864; Cauchon, *L'Union*, p. 19; *Contre-poison*, p. 7; the pastoral letters of Bishops Cooke and Larocque, in *Nouvelle constitution*, pp. 58–9, 68.

95 *La Minerve*, 28 Dec. 1864; *La Gazette de Sorel*, 30 July 1864; Louis-François Laflèche and Bishop Baillargeon, quoted in Walter Ullmann, 'The Quebec Bishops and Confederation', in the *CHR*, XLIV, 3 (Sept., 1963), reprinted in G.R. Cook, ed., *Confederation* (Toronto: University of Toronto Press 1967), pp. 53, 56, 66.

96 *Le Courrier du Canada*, 22 June 1864; Bishops Baillargeon and Cooke in *Nouvelle constitution*, pp. 54–5, 60; E.C. Parent to J.I. Tarte, Ottawa, 4 Sept. 1866, in PAC, Tarte papers (MG 27, II, D16). Just as they had promoted French-Canadian interests at the constitutional conferences, Quebec's sixty-five MPs would watch over French Quebec's interests at Ottawa. For they would be sent to Ottawa as representatives of Quebec, the French-Canadian province, and their responsibility would be toward that province and its autonomy. See Bonenfant, 'L'Idée que les Canadiens français,' p. 317; *Le Courrier de St-Hyacinthe*, 22 July 1864.

common welfare.[97] And this 'alliance with your neighbours',[98] this *federal alliance* among several peoples',[99] was to be regulated by the terms of a treaty or pact drawn up freely among them. Even the imperial authorities, according to Cartier, in preparing and passing the British North America Act, had accepted that they were only giving the official stamp of approval to an interprovincial compact. 'They understood ... that the Quebec plan was an agreement among the colonies, which had to be respected, and they respected it.'[100] Confederation had, thus, been achieved because four separate colonies had formed 'a pact' among themselves.[101]

And in the federal alliance thus formed, Quebec was to be the French-Canadian country, working together with the others on common projects, but always autonomous in the promotion and embodiment of the French-Canadian nationality. 'Our ambitions,' wrote a Bleu editor, 'will not centre on the federal government, but will have their natural focus in our local legislature; this we regard as fundamental for ourselves.'[102] This was, no doubt, an exaggerated position, like the statement of de Niverville in the Canadian legislature, but what it exaggerated was the general tendency of the Confederationist propaganda. It underlined the Quebec-centredness of French Canada's approach to Confederation, and the degree to which French Quebec's separateness and autonomy were central to French-Canadian acceptance of the new régime.

---

97 *La Gazette de Sorel*, 25 Feb. 1865; *La Minerve*, 1 July 1867. It was perfectly clear, of course, what Quebec's nationality was considered to be. It was French-Canadian. But what nationalities were to be attributed to the other provinces was never certain. French Canadians were aware of distinctions among the English, Scottish, and Irish nationalities (above, p. 40), and they may have seen the other provinces as having unique national characters determined by their respective blends of these various elements. But they were always vague on this point. Cartier, however, did suggest a similar distribution of religious characteristics when he said (in the legislative debate on the Quebec resolutions) that Ontario would be Protestant, Quebec Catholic, and the Maritimes pretty evenly divided between the two denominations (e.g., in Tassé, p. 422).

98 *L'Union des Cantons de l'Est*, 4 July 1867.

99 *Contre-poison*, p. 8. Also, p. 10.

100 *L'Union des Cantons de l'Est*, 23 May 1867.

101 *Le Journal de Québec*, 4 July 1867. See also the Bishop of St-Hyacinthe, in *Nouvelle constitution*, p. 65. J.-C. Taché had assumed, in 1858, that a confederation would necessarily be brought about by an intercolonial pact. See his *Des provinces*, p. 139.

102 *Le Courrier de St-Hyacinthe*, 10 July 1866. We shall find this point of view adopted not infrequently by French-Quebec journalists in the first decades after Confederation.

III

CONFEDERATION
AND MINORITY
RIGHTS

I F we have been correct so far in our interpretation of French-Canadian opinion on the question of Confederation, then our readers have a right to be somewhat surprised. For in what we have seen of French-Canadian reasons for approving the new régime, there was nothing at all of bilingualism, biculturalism, or the establishment of French-Canadian rights outside the province of Quebec. Everything, on the contrary, seemed to indicate that Quebec alone was to be the arena of French-Canadian national life, that within the federal alliance, Quebec was to be the French-Canadian country. Even the action of French Canada's federal MPs was to be directed toward fostering the interests and the autonomy of Quebec. For they were thought of as representing the province itself rather than individual Canadian citizens whose ridings happened to be located in Quebec.[1] Moreover, the inclusion in the constitution of a section (133) guaranteeing certain rights to the French language at Ottawa was perfectly consistent with this view, for even if Confederation was only an *association* of a French-Canadian province with a number of English-speaking ones, the *federal* institutions in which Quebec's representatives would participate would appropriately be bilingual.

But what about the French-Canadian nationality outside Quebec? Was it to have no official status in the new dominion? Were the French and Catholic minorities of the other provinces to be without national and religious rights?

Certainly, polemicists claimed to want minority rights – at least when they spoke in broad and general terms. 'But we would not want,' they claimed, 'any system which did not protect, in the same degree, the full rights of both minorities and majorities; nothing durable can be built unless it is based on

---

1 Even the critics of Confederation agreed with its supporters in viewing the federal Parliament in this way. Eg., *L'Ordre*, 23 June 1864.

justice.'[2] When the terms of the constitution were known, the opposition criticized it, among other reasons, for failing to give adequate protection to the minorities; they rejected Section 93, which gave Ottawa certain powers to protect some minority school rights, on the grounds that 'it is ridiculous for Catholics to have to appeal a decision made by one Protestant assembly to another assembly which is equally Protestant.'[3] Accordingly, government supporters, in their praise of the new constitution, included the claim that it protected 'all rights acquired by and granted to the Catholic minorities which the Protestants in the local governments might want to disturb.'[4]

It is not clear that such statements should be taken very seriously. The circumstances in which they were made were often suspicious. Thus, we find La Minerve, for example, calling for minority rights, but going on to say that these would be in the interests of the English Lower Canadians. Indeed, the matter had been raised by the Montreal Herald, which feared for the status of Anglo-Protestants in an autonomous Quebec. In magnanimously supporting the principle of minority rights, La Minerve was calling attention to these fears, which confirmed that the province of Quebec was indeed going to be autonomous and under French-Canadian control.[5]

Also suspicious was the fact that the very people who spoke of guarantees for minority rights, at one moment, argued, at others, that no guarantees could be effective anyway. Thus, the author of Contre-poison, who boasted on one page of the guarantees provided by Section 93, argued on another that under any system of majority rule guarantees were ineffective, 'because tomorrow's majority could always undo what yesterday's majority had done, by the changing even of a single vote!'[6] This was, after all, the whole French-Canadian argument against legislative union: that no matter what guarantees were provided by the constitution of such a union, they could always be nullified by the majority. The whole point of having an autonomous province of Quebec was that in such a province French Canadians would be the majority and, hence, would not need guarantees of minority rights.

Finally, we are justified in wondering just how far Lower Canadians were even aware of the existence of minorities who might stand in need of constitutional guarantees. We have already seen that the Acadians, in

---

2 Cauchon, L'Union, p. 45. Also, La Minerve, 6 Oct. and 6 Dec. 1864; La Gazette de Sorel, 14 Jan. 1865.
3 Confédération couronnement, p. 18. See also L'Ordre, 7 Nov. 1864.
4 Contre-poison, p. 14. Also, La Revue Canadienne, IV (1867), p. 233; Le Journal des Trois-Rivières, 22 Feb. 1867; Réponses aux censeurs, pp. 45–6, 60–1.
5 La Minerve, 6 Oct. 1864.
6 Contre-poison, p. 9.

particular, had always lived very much apart from the French Canadians, that their communities, on the eve of Confederation, were scarcely visible and without spokesmen to give them prominence, and that for their own part, they knew virtually nothing about the French Canadians. It is hardly surprising, therefore, that the French of Lower Canada knew practically nothing about them.

For a great many French Canadians, the last known fact about the Acadians was the expulsion. Indeed, during the 1860s, the translation by Pamphile Lemay of Longfellow's *Evangeline*, and the publication by the *Revue Canadienne* of Napoléon Bourassa's novel of the expulsion, *Jacques et Marie*, probably reinforced a traditional impression that the Acadian population had been dispersed once and for all in the eighteenth century. This impression should have begun to weaken at least as early as 1857, when J.-C. Taché wrote of the Acadian survival in *Le Courrier du Canada*.[7] The publication of Rameau de Saint-Père's *La France aux colonies* in 1859, and his tour of Canada and the Maritimes the following year, should further have increased awareness of the Acadians. Nevertheless, the emotion which French Canadians continued to express every time they were retold of the Acadian fact suggested that this fact continued to be little known in general. Thus, in October, 1864, the *Journal de Québec* published a letter from a man who had just visited the Maritimes, and introduced it by speaking of the pleasure its readers would feel on learning that the Acadian nation had survived its great ordeal.[8] The *Gazette de Sorel*, publishing the same letter a week later, commented that the traveller had been surprised to find Acadians still living and even prospering in the Maritimes. 'Our readers,' affirmed the paper, 'will no doubt be as delighted as we were ourselves to learn of these things. ... '[9] The revelation, in any case, did not reach all Lower Canadians, for when *Jacques et Marie* was published in book form two years later, the *Journal des Trois-Rivières* hoped it would help to 'revive the memory' of the Acadians, that it would 'perpetuate among us the memory of a race whose name must never perish.'[10] Strange language to use about a nationality that was alive and flourishing at that very moment!

Whether the continued existence of the Acadians was known to the French Canadians or not, they were virtually ignored by them when it came to guaranteeing minority rights in Confederation. At the Quebec Conference,

---

7 It was in the series of articles that were published in 1858 as the pamphlet *Des provinces.* ... See pp. 17, 22–3, 24, etc. Taché admitted that the discovery of Acadian survival had brought 'des larmes d'attendrissement et de joie' to his eyes.
8 *Le Journal de Québec*, 1 Oct. 1864.
9 *La Gazette de Sorel*, 8 Oct. 1864.
10 *Le Journal des Trois-Rivières*, 9 Oct. 1866.

the first draft of the resolution dealing with education (perhaps prepared and certainly approved by the French-Canadian ministers) simply said that education would be a provincial jurisdiction, and provided no guarantees for minority school rights. It was an English-speaking Lower Canadian, McGee, who proposed an amendment the next day to provide guarantees – but only for the Catholic and Protestant minorities of Upper and Lower Canada, and not for the other provinces.[11] A more general guarantee was not included until the London Conference of 1866–7, when the final BNA bill was drawn up – and its inclusion owed far more to the lobbying of the anglophone Archbishop of Halifax than to any initiative by a French Canadian.[12]

Archbishop Connolly's mission to London offers a fine opportunity to assess French-Canadian attitudes toward the status of the minorities. He met Cartier and Langevin often, working particularly with Langevin, whose family, he knew, was closely connected with the Church. Hector wrote about the meetings to his brother Jean and Edmond, both priests. His tone, at first, seemed benevolent:

What he wants is to obtain for the Catholics of the Atlantic Provinces advantages equal to those which the new constitution will guarantee for the respective minorities of Upper and Lower Canada. He has spoken to me about this matter on several occasions and at length. I told him he could be sure there would be no opposition from Mr Cartier or from myself, that on the contrary, as Catholics, we'd be happy to see our co-religionists of the lower Provinces obtain the advantages in question, but that he could not and must not expect that we would propose the thing ourselves. He must arrange for it to come from one of the delegates from the maritime Provinces, our role being necessarily limited to *seconding* a motion which must originate within the maritime delegation.[13]

There was an ambivalence here, which would run through the whole Quebec attitude toward the minorities. On the one hand, Langevin was a Catholic, and must therefore consider any guarantee of Catholic rights to be desirable. On the other hand, he was a representative of Lower Canada, and this was not a Lower Canadian but a Maritime concern. Clearly, the concept of Confederation as an alliance of distinct provinces was in Langevin's mind. Quebec was one thing, the Maritimes another, and Catholic school rights in the Maritimes, while they had Quebec's full support, must not prevent the provinces from having the control of their own affairs.

Connolly was not satisfied with Langevin's attitude. Relations between the two men turned sour: Langevin wrote deprecatingly about the arch-

---

11 In Browne, *Documents*, pp. 81–2.
12 Ibid., p. 262.
13 Hector to Jean and Edmond Langevin (London, 19 Nov. 1866), in Quebec provincial archives (APQ), Collection Chapais, Langevin papers, box 4 (AP-L-12-4).

bishop's personality to his brothers;[14] Connolly came more and more into opposition to the French-Canadian position, ultimately advocating federal control of education.[15] Finally, on 28 December, Langevin reported to his brothers that Connolly had seen and appeared to be pleased with the final draft of the school rights clause.[16] Yet Connolly himself had written to Lord Carnarvon only four days before to complain that the delegates had not adequately protected the welfare of the Catholic minorities![17]

Langevin's and Cartier's coolness toward the Maritime Catholics did not arouse the anger of their Lower Canadian constituents, whose concern for minority rights never really extended beyond the minorities of Upper and Lower Canada. From the beginning, Rouge criticism had been thus limited: 'But what will become of the Upper Canadian Catholics, toward whom you claim to be sympathetic?'[18] And the Bleu response, even after the contents of Section 93 were known, was similarly restricted: 'By these four clauses, the two minorities, Catholic and Protestant, of Upper and Lower Canada are put on exactly the same footing.'[19] Nor should there be anything surprising about this limitation. The unique association made possible by the Union of 1840 had given the Upper Canadian minority a special place in the thoughts of Lower Canadians.

But not *that* special!

In fact, what first raised the Ontario Catholic question was an attempt to protect the Protestants of Quebec, who, for the first time in their history, were about to become a minority in a province governed by a non-British, non-Protestant majority. To allay their fears and win their support for Confederation, their representative in the ministry, A.T. Galt, had promised some pretty radical guarantees.

Quebec's legislative council could itself be seen by some as a gift to the English. As a non-elected body, it would make possible representation by community instead of by population.[20] Far more important, though, were the regulations on constituency boundaries for the legislative assembly, which Galt proposed in the summer session of 1866. The government's original bill on the local institutions of Ontario and Quebec had provided that boundaries

---

14 Hector to Jean and Edmond Langevin (London, 4 Dec. 1866), in Ibid.
15 More on this episode can be found in the excellent discussion of it in Andrée Désilets, *Hector-Louis Langevin, un père de la confédération canadienne* (Quebec: Presses de l'Université Laval 1969), ch. 5.
16 Hector to Jean and Edmond Langevin (London, 28 Dec. 1866), in APQ.
17 In Browne, *Documents*, p. 216.
18 *Le Pays*, 23 July 1864. Also, 13 Nov. 1866.
19 *Le Courrier du Canada*, 8 Mar. 1867. Also, *La Minerve*, 11 Nov. 1864, and 23 July 1866; *Le Journal des Trois-Rivières*, 16 Nov. 1866; Cauchon, *Discours*, p. 8.
20 See, eg., *L'Ordre*, 18 July 1866; *La Minerve*, 17 July 1866.

of Quebec ridings could be changed by a three-quarters majority of the assembly. Galt's amendment provided that changes could be made on straight majority vote, except for twelve 'English' ridings, whose boundaries could not be changed without the additional approval of a majority of their own MPPS.

While these proposals were being discussed, the legislature was also preoccupied with a government bill which Langevin had presented, guaranteeing certain educational privileges to the Quebec Protestants. These included not only the assurance of a proper share of subsidies, but also the appointments of two deputy-superintendents of education for Quebec, appointments which would appear to create two separate departments of education – one Catholic and one Protestant.

The Galt and Langevin proposals provoked a universally hostile reaction among French-Canadian MPPS and journalists. They had been told by the Conservative leaders that Quebec was going to be a French-Catholic province, a French-Canadian homeland. And now, here was the government proposing to dilute the French-Catholic character of the province by awarding exorbitant privileges to the Anglo-Protestants. The Galt proposal, for example, not only diminished French Canadians' control over their own province, it insulted them into the bargain:

Was it possible to create distinctions more humiliating for the immense majority of Lower Canada and more insulting to our honour and our dignity – and could it be possible that our representatives would give them their approval?[21]

It was possible, indeed, and the Galt proposal was passed by the legislature, though the papers of the Bleu politicians condemned them for it:

We severely blame the French-Canadian Conservative MPPS who by their vote approved the arbitrary proviso of Mr Galt; ... we don't think it's too much to say that public opinion will not vindicate them.[22]

The most charitable thing that could be said was that if the government had not rushed the measure through so quickly, if French-Canadian MPPS had been given the chance to consider it, they would not have voted for it. 'More than one member of the Conservative Party would have seen it in a very different light.'[23]

Perhaps this condemnation by their own papers impressed Bleu MPPS, for

21 *Le Journal de Québec*, 4 Aug. 1866.
22 *Le Courrier du Canada*, 6 Aug. 1866.
23 *Le Journal des Trois-Rivières*, 10 Aug. 1866. The opposition, naturally, could claim greater foresight, for *L'Ordre* had warned on 18 July 1866 that Cartier was going to go too far in reassuring the Protestants about their constituency distribution.

when it came to the Langevin bill, the government found itself confronted by a full-scale rebellion of its French-Canadian back-benchers. Educational autonomy was, of course, a particularly sensitive issue for French Canadians, and without it, they felt, 'Confederation would not be possible'. But excessive guarantees of autonomy for the Protestants would undermine complete provincial control of education and thus sap the basis of Confederation itself.[24] It was not surprising, therefore, that when Langevin introduced his bill in the summer of 1866, it should have been condemned for giving 'exorbitant privileges' to the Protestants, and he himself branded a traitor to Catholicism.[25]

Naturally, those who condemned Confederation in any case were forward in criticizing the Langevin bill. *Le Pays* reminded its readers that when the Protestants had asked for the appointment of separate Catholic and Protestant school superintendents in 1865, the French-Canadian press had opposed them, but that now it was Langevin, the self-styled champion of the clergy, who was giving them just what they had asked for.[26] In giving the Protestants what amounted to their own department of education, 'they insult us by putting constitutional barriers between the two faiths in Lower Canada, and this in defiance of the Catholic majority. ... '[27] *Le Canadien*, wavering on the general issue of Confederation, agreed at any rate that Langevin's bill was 'unjust and anti-national' because it weakened French Canada's power to ensure that its province would have a Catholic educational system.[28]

But on this issue, government supporters were as rebellious as the opposition. They too condemned Langevin's bill for offering 'extraordinary privileges' to the Protestants[29] and for offering insult as well as injury to the French Canadians. Why, they wanted to know, did the Protestants show so much unwarranted mistrust of the French Canadians as to even want such guarantees?

I cannot refrain from saying that this conduct on the part of the Lower Canadian Protestants is an insult to us as Catholics and as French Canadians, and I hardly know how the government could accept all that in silence.[30]

Joseph Cauchon, writing to the *Journal de Québec* from his parliamentary seat, warned that the naming of two deputy superintendants would lead to 'a

24 *Le Journal de Québec*, 21 Jan. 1865.
25 *Le Canadien*, 1 Aug. 1866.
26 *Le Pays*, 4 Aug. 1866.
27 Ibid., 7 Aug. 1866. Also, 11 Aug. 1866.
28 *Le Canadien*, 3 Aug. 1866.
29 *Le Journal de Québec*, 6 Aug. 1866.
30 *Le Journal des Trois-Rivières*, 7 Aug. 1866.

system of spying, mistrust, and unbearable hostility'. He went on to describe his own feelings:

Never have I taken up my pen under the weight of such painful feelings. It is my painful duty to blame those men with whom I have worked to the best of my ability in the great cause of confederation; and at the same time I feel crushed under the weight of the humiliations to which our nation and history have been subjected.[31]

Cauchon was not alone in his feelings. According to his newspaper, the Galt and Langevin bills 'are causing profound sadness and lively dissatisfaction at Quebec.' Indeed, the mail indicated that the same angry feelings were to be found throughout the region.[32] It was no wonder, for Langevin's bill was seen as imposing a burden and a sacrifice on the majority of the Lower Canadian population. It was even feared that a Protestant deputy-super-intendency might be used to subject Catholics to Protestant rule:

We Catholics, who are the great majority of the Lower Canadian population, are making a big enough and painful enough concession by allowing the minority to be on the same footing as ourselves; we should at least have the right to demand that we not be exposed to being under its control.[33]

It was particularly painful to think that Quebec would have to assume this burden of minority rights, when Ontario showed no sign of taking a similar burden upon itself. In answer to a question from A.-A. Dorion, just after the introduction of the Langevin bill, John A. Macdonald had admitted that the government had no intention of presenting a similar measure to deal with Catholic school privileges in Upper Canada. And when, during the first week of August, such a bill was presented by an Upper Canadian private member, Robert Bell, reaction of other Upper Canadian MPPs was far from encouraging. George Brown was reported to be furious,[34] and Alexander Mackenzie was said to have turned quite red with anger.[35]

This double standard was hardly acceptable to French Canadians. 'This is a crying injustice,' they complained: 'the fanatics won't concede anything. They refuse to one side a constitutional guarantee which it very badly needs, while granting it to the other side, to which it is useless.'[36] Protestants appeared to think 'that the French Canadians are obliged to make all the

---

31 *Le Journal de Québec*, 2 Aug. 1866.
32 Ibid., 6 Aug. 1866. See also 7 Aug. 1866, and *Le Pays*, 9 Aug. 1866.
33 *Le Courrier du Canada*, 3 Aug. 1866.
34 *Le Courrier de St-Hyacinthe*, 7 Aug. 1866.
35 *Le Journal des Trois-Rivières*, 7 Aug. 1866.
36 *Le Pays*, 31 July 1866.

sacrifices for the sake of Confederation.'[37] It seemed that 'the Catholics of Lower Canada are giving up everything, even their principles and national dignity ... the Upper Canadian Protestants won't yield anything.'[38] It was clear that Lower Canada was to be subjected to the rule of its minority. 'Lower Canada is being sacrificed, its population humiliated, insulted, and treated really as an inferior race.' Thus the *Union Nationale*. 'Everywhere we see two weights and two measures.'[39] And through all this complaining and sense of outrage ran the idea that minority rights were a sacrifice made by the majority, a burden to be imposed on Quebec but not on Ontario. 'Since we are being insulted by the erection of constitutional barriers between the two faiths in Lower Canada, in defiance of the Catholic majority, why treat Upper Canada in a different way ... ?'[40]

This rather negative attitude toward minority rights was shared by Bleu papers as well as those of the opposition. The *Courrier du Canada*, a newspaper that had close associations with Langevin himself, urged French-Canadian MPPS to refuse support to the Langevin bill unless it were voted on simultaneously with the Bell measure.[41] The *Journal de Québec* agreed, and went on to make this interesting observation on the whole question of minority rights: if the Protestants had made no excessive demands of Lower Canada, the Catholics would have made none of Ontario; but once the former had demanded extraordinary privileges, simple equity pushed the latter to do the same.[42] 'The Catholics themselves admit that if the federal pact had been strictly observed, they would have no demands to make.' But the pact had not been adhered to. 'If you give the Protestants of Lower Canada exceptional privileges, we also have the right to demand them.'[43] The best situation would thus appear to have been what was originally proposed to the Quebec Conference by the Canadian ministers: strict provincial control of education, with no minority guarantees.[44]

The Bleu MPPS could not remain unresponsive to the uproar in their constituencies. Led by Joseph Cauchon, they informed Cartier that they would oppose the Langevin bill unless the government put it forward together

---

37 *Le Journal des Trois-Rivières*, 27 July 1866.
38 *Le Pays*, 3 Aug. 1866. Also, 2 Aug. 1866.
39 *L'Union Nationale*, 4 Aug. 1866.
40 *Le Pays*, 7 Aug. 1866. Also, 2 and 4 Aug. 1866; *L'Ordre*, 3 Aug. 1866.
41 *Le Courrier du Canada*, 6 Aug. 1866.
42 *Le Journal de Québec*, 6 Aug. 1866.
43 Ibid., 7 Aug. 1866. See also *Le Journal des Trois-Rivières*, 7 Aug. 1866; and *L'Ordre*, 15 Mar. 1867.
44 See *Le Journal de Québec*, 28 July 1866.

with the Bell proposal as one single measure. Faced with this back-bencher defiance, and realizing how adamant were the Grits on this matter, the government decided to back down, and withdrew the Langevin bill, even though this meant the resignation of Galt, who had committed himself too far to the Lower Canadian Protestants.

To this situation, the reaction of the French-Canadian press was a universal Hurrah! Though Upper Canadian Catholics were left without the guarantees they had just been demanding, papers of both parties claimed to have won a great victory. The government's 'fortunate about-face', claimed the Rouges, was attributable to the pressure exerted by Dorion. 'The honours of this victory must be accorded to the opposition.'[45] Bleu papers, however, claimed the honours for their own party, for Cauchon and the back-benchers, who had stood up for their nationality, and for the ministers themselves, who had withdrawn their bill when they saw that the stubborn Ontario Protestants would not let Bell's proposal pass.[46]

Whoever deserved the credit, the significant thing was that this withdrawal of guarantees was a victory for French Canada. The Langevin bill 'required compensations to be made in order to be acceptable to Lower Canada.'[47] The guarantees it had offered Quebec Protestants had been 'onerous' for the Catholics,[48] and even Cartier's organ, La Minerve, had to admit that their withdrawal was not a bad thing: 'It wasn't fair that the Catholics should have had to give without receiving.'[49]

But to call the failure of the Bell and Langevin bills a victory was to say that one really did not want minority guarantees at all:

In any case, why legislate at all in the field of education, since the plan of the Quebec conference didn't commit us to anything? The Upper Canadian Catholics weren't asking for anything and the rights of the Lower Canadian Protestants were sufficiently safeguarded by the present law.[50]

If the Protestants had demanded nothing, the Catholics would have kept quiet too. What we criticized the government for, explained the Pays later on, was having promised guarantees to the Lower Canadian Protestants without doing the same for the Ontario Catholics.[51] Bleus, embarrassed by the whole

45 Le Pays, 9 Aug. 1866.
46 Le Courrier de St-Hyacinthe, 9 Aug. 1866. See also Le Journal des Trois-Rivières, 13 Aug.. 1866; and La Gazette de Sorel, 1 Sept. 1866.
47 Le Courrier de St-Hyacinthe, 18 Aug. 1866.
48 Ibid., 21 Aug. 1866. Also, 23 Aug. 1866.
49 La Minerve, 9 Aug. 1866. Also, Le Journal des Trois-Rivières, 10 Aug. 1866.
50 Le Courrier du Canada, 8 Aug. 1866.
51 Le Pays, 13 Nov. 1866.

affair, hoped that the Ontario Catholics would now keep quiet and be satisfied with their situation under the educational act of 1863. If not, why then *La Minerve* was ready to condemn the 'exaggerated pretensions of the Upper Canadian Catholics'.[52] Hector Langevin agreed that Ontario Catholics' demands for constitutional guarantees were exaggerated pretensions. 'They were asking for more than they could or should have had,' he wrote to his brother, Jean.[53] But it was the chief opposition organ that best summed up everybody's feelings:

But they preferred that there be no concession of privileges to any religious minorities in the proposed constitution. If the government had given nothing to the Protestant minority of Lower Canada, you would not have seen us asking for guarantees for the Catholic minority of Upper Canada.[54]

The history of the Langevin bill must raise serious doubts about the significance of French-Canadian declarations that they wanted or expected the new constitution to guarantee special rights to their compatriots and co-religionists in provinces other than Quebec. Indeed, everything about it is consistent with the view of Confederation seen in the last chapter – the view that made it acceptable to French Lower Canadians. Confederation was to be an association of national states, called provinces, united in a federal alliance (within the British Empire, of course). And in that alliance, the province of Quebec was to be the national state of the French Canadians. That province, as *the* French-Catholic province, might well be concerned to support French Catholics in other parts of the federation, but such support must never involve the acceptance of principles that would expose or endanger the autonomy or the French and Catholic character of Quebec itself.

There were, perhaps, several flaws in this vision of Confederation, but one was particularly distressing. The fact was that, despite the failure of the Langevin bill, the Quebec minority had already shown itself capable of exerting a remarkable influence, and of diluting considerably the French and Catholic character which that province was supposed to have. When the smoke cleared in July, 1867, the English language was officially entrenched in Quebec by the BNA act (it was the only province under the Act to have two official languages instead of one); and the Galt provisions had gone into effect, protecting the boundaries of ridings where the minority were numerically strongest.

52 *Le Courrier de St-Hyacinthe*, 11 Aug. 1866; *La Minerve*, 8 Nov. 1866.
53 Hector to Jean Langevin (Ottawa, 7 Aug. 1866), in APQ, Collection Chapais, Langevin papers, box 4 (AP-L-12-4).
54 *Le Pays*, 17 Nov., 1866.

The Lower Canadian minority had two particular sources of strength: the support of other Anglo-Protestants, who formed the majority in Confederation as a whole, and hence, in the federal Parliament; and the economic influence which they wielded within Quebec itself.[55] The problem was that French Quebec needed this minority, just as it needed Confederation itself, to provide economic development and hence render viable the French-Canadian province. Yet this very need made necessary the concession to the minority of privileges which diluted the French-Canadian character of the province.[56]

Interestingly, what French Canadians feared was that the Anglo-Protestants would acquire the same sort of autonomy within Quebec that *they* had sought within Canada. 'So there we have one legislature within another,' complained Cauchon about the twelve-riding proviso, 'and God knows where all this will end.'[57] In education, the Protestants seemed to want the same thing: 'a state of things which would make of them a body apart, a state within the State.'[58] This was an appropriate way to view a confederation, but within Quebec itself, it could only destroy the integrity of the French-Canadian province.

These fears were so widespread that Cartier's organ found it necessary to reassure people. There was no need to worry, it explained, since these minority guarantees would soon become irrelevant:

Laws and constitutions are made with a view to the future. Well, the future is ours, all ours, in Lower Canada. With each census we can see new conquests. The English are moving back toward Upper Canada.[59]

More and more French Canadians were moving into the hitherto-English Eastern Townships, and soon they would replace English Canadians all over the province. The twelve counties would lose their English populations, and constitutional privileges would lose all significance, thanks to the vitality of the French-Canadian race and to provincial autonomy, which would enable Quebec to promote the work of French-Canadian colonization.

Meanwhile, the present minority was very much with them. The withdrawal of the Langevin bill in August of 1866 led the Provincial Association of

---

55 *L'Ordre*, 3 Aug. 1866, 10 Aug. 1866.
56 It was no coincidence that during the period of our study, Quebec finance ministers were always anglophones.
57 *Le Journal de Québec*, 2 Aug. 1866. Also, *Le Pays*, 9 Aug. 1866.
58 *Le Courrier de St-Hyacinthe*, 23 Aug. 1866. This very expression, 'un état dans l'état', was used by *La Minerve* to describe French Canada's position within Confederation. See also *Le Journal de Québec*, 3 Aug. 1866; and *Le Pays*, 7 Aug. 1866.
59 *La Minerve*, 4 Aug. 1866.

Protestant Teachers of Lower Canada to petition the Queen for the inclusion of its promised guarantees in the new constitution.[60] Protestant concern about the aborted bill led Cartier to make promises which may have reassured the minority, but which aroused the suspicion and anger of his own followers.[61] That fall, though he had resigned from the ministry, A.T. Galt went off to the London Conference; and when the British North America Act appeared, Section 93 included protection not only for minority school systems existing by law at the time of Confederation, but also for those 'thereafter established by the Legislature of the Province.' And in case anyone wondered which province that really referred to, Conservative Party bosses made it clear to candidates for the job of first Quebec premier that a condition of getting the job was an undertaking to put through the legislature a bill giving Protestants the privileges they would have got in 1866 by the ill-fated Langevin bill. Joseph Cauchon, to whom the position was first offered, refused to comply with this condition, and he was passed over in favour of P.-J.-O. Chauveau.[62]

It took Chauveau more than a year to get his bill ready, and when it finally appeared, there was little enthusiasm for it in the French-Canadian press. Ironically, the clearest support came from a Rouge newspaper, which, while admitting that this was just the old Langevin bill done over,[63] approved it, nevertheless, as based on generous principles and likely to settle, once and for all, an issue which would otherwise have led to a constant, bitter and unfortunate conflict.[64]

Papers which usually supported the Conservative government turned cold on this question. Some reported the legislative debate without comment,[65] passed it over entirely in embarassed silence,[66] or reluctantly approved the principle of Protestant rights while calling for amendments to protect

---

60 In Browne, *Documents*, pp. 198–9.
61 *La Minerve*, 12 Nov. 1866. See *Le Journal de Québec*, 15 and 24 Nov. 1866; *Le Journal des Trois-Rivières*, 27 Nov. 1866; *Le Courrier de St-Hyacinthe*, 18 and 23 Aug. 1866; *Le Pays*, 16 Aug. 1866.
62 Recounted in *Le Journal de Québec*, Mar.–Apr. 1869. Also, see Marcel Hamelin, *Les premières années*, pp. 11–12. Cauchon, of course, was remaining true to the role he had played in the summer of 1866. Interestingly, Chauveau, who accepted the conditions in 1867, had criticized the Protestants in print in 1865 for their complaints against the Lower Canadian school system (of which he was superintendent). See his *Observations sur l'Assemblée tenue à Montréal pour former une association dans le but de protéger les intérêts des protestants dans l'Instruction Publique* (Montreal: Senécal 1865).
63 *Le Pays*, 23 Mar. 1869.
64 Ibid., 25 Mar. 1869.
65 *La Gazette de Sorel*, 31 Mar. 1869, et seq.
66 *Le Journal des Trois-Rivières*, Mar.-Apr. 1869.

Catholics against possible injustices.[67] *Le Nouveau Monde*, preoccupied with the Catholic interests it was founded to represent, was willing to be fair to the Protestants, 'but not to the point of sacrificing principles.'[68] It brought itself to accept the bill, in the end, because, by keeping a denominational basis for Quebec's schools, it did contain and affirm 'the Christian idea of education'.[69] Besides, it would set an example that Ontario might follow in the treatment of its minority.[70]

But the hostile chorus was far louder than this weak expression of acceptance. Chauveau's bill was 'even more odious than Mr Langevin's was.' Indeed, it was a threat to the French-Canadian nationality.[71] It violated the BNA Act – or at least the spirt of the act – which had provided that the privileges of minorities should remain what they had been at the time of Confederation. 'Well, then, the school bill grants the Protestants several favours to which the constitution does not give them any right. ... '[72] It was all very well to satisfy the needs of justice, but this was going too far:

In the present case it was necessary to satisfy the demands of a minority concerning its rights by the concession of a legitimate privilege. Our ministers have given more than that; they've even infringed on the rights of the Catholics in order to satisfy the Protestants.[73]

This was, perhaps, the most outrageous thing about the bill: it had been imposed, it was being imposed, upon the government and upon the province by a too-powerful minority. That English-Protestant minority had prevented a patriotic French Canadian, Joseph Cauchon, from becoming premier of the French-Canadian province. It had negotiated with the government over the preparation of this bill, treating as the very equal of the government, and had even been strong enough to threaten the government's survival.[74] These were hardly the right conditions for winning acceptance of this sort of bill:

In the first place, we don't at all see the point of the generosity which the government has felt obliged to show toward the Protestant minority of Lower Canada in the matter of education. ... After all, when the Protestant minority, which is supposed to be so

67 *Le Pionnier de Sherbrooke*, 26 Mar. 1869. See also *Le Journal de Québec*, Mar.-Apr. 1869. Cauchon opposed the bill at first, but supported it after Chauveau had accepted minor amendments.
68 *Le Nouveau Monde* (Montreal), 20 Mar. 1869.
69 Ibid., 29 Mar. 1869.
70 Ibid., 22 Mar. 1869.
71 *Le Courrier de St-Hyacinthe*, 28 Mar. 1869. Also, 23 and 25 Mar. 1869.
72 *Le Courrier du Canada*, 24 Mar. 1869. Also, 22 Mar. 1869.
73 *L'Union des Cantons de l'Est*, 1 Apr. 1869.
74 *L'Ordre*, 20 Mar. 1869.

rich, demands that every last cent of its taxes be spent on *its* schools only, bickers constantly about its rights, so that in order to have peace we're forced to give in to it, is it showing any generosity? What need have we to be generous? Generosity is a slippery slope.[75]

Some might argue that the bill set an example of good will and ensured peace and harmony within the province of Quebec. But this was doubtful; 'the more tolerant and well disposed we are, the greater will be the demands made of us.' Meanwhile, there were places in the province where Protestants controlled municipal institutions. If the division of taxes were left to the civic employees at Montreal and Quebec, for example, 'one can foresee the result: the tax distribution will be enormously favourable to the minority.'

The minority, in short, was playing too prominent a role in this province which was supposed to be French and Catholic:

But everywhere and in every way the Protestants of Montreal insist on having their say. This isn't the first time they've shown themselves recalcitrant. They did everything they could to get the law on fire marshals repealed, because the government had the good sense to name a French Canadian to the post conjointly with an Englishman.[76]

In the county of Richmond and Wolfe, it was reported in the summer after the passing of the school bill that Stoke Township had decided to publish its official documents in English only, despite the fact that almost half the township's population was French-Canadian and did not understand English.[77] In Sherbrooke, the new Presbyterian minister proposed to undertake a campaign of preaching in French to convert the French Canadians.[78] Was this the way to promote that French-Catholic repossession of Quebec which *La Minerve* had promised in 1866? Was this, indeed, that Quebec, 'all ours', which Confederation was to have given the French Canadians – that Quebec in which, 'everything will be done by and for French Canadians, and in French'?

---

75 Ibid., 27 Mar. 1869. While not providing for two deputy-superintendents as the Langevin bill had done, the Chauveau bill divided the council of public instruction into a Catholic and a Protestant committee, the latter having power to separate to form a council apart. The minister of public instruction was to have two secretaries, one Protestant and one Catholic, the former assuming near-ministerial authority on matters concerning the minority. Protestant taxes were to go to Protestant schools, and where none existed, Protestants were to be exempt from taxation. Corporation tax was to be divided by population.
76 *L'Union des Cantons de l'Est*, 11 Mar. 1869.
77 *Le Pionnier de Sherbrooke*, 30 July 1869.
78 Ibid., 6 Aug. 1869.

The fact was that neither the way in which Confederation was sold nor the way in which it began was such as to make French Quebeckers think well of minority rights. But they had not yet begun to discover the French-Catholic minorities. That discovery would begin only months after the passing of the Quebec Protestant school bill.

IV

CONFEDERATION
AND THE
NORTH-WEST

URING the winter of 1868–9, George-Etienne Cartier and William McDougall, by lengthy negotiations at London, arranged for the transfer of the Hudson's Bay Company's territories north and west of Canada to the authority of the new dominion government. This transfer would have a double significance to the French Canadians. It would open up the prairie regions to Canadian settlement, and hence to their own; and it would bring them into contact with the French-Catholic Métis already living in those regions.

French-Quebec opinion was not well prepared for either of these effects. Certainly, it was not disposed to look on the North-West as a field of settlement for French Canadians. The very annexation of the North-West by Canada was viewed, indeed, with much doubt and scepticism.

These feelings could already be detected during the years 1864–7, for after all, the acquisition of the North-West had been part and parcel of the Confederation project. For the Rouges, it had been an important reason for opposing Confederation; they thought it 'ridiculous' to imagine that Canada could undertake the development of that vast desert when she was already so encumbered with debts and undeveloped lands.[1] The Bleus had not emphasized the project, and in 1865 Cauchon had observed that of all the aspects of the Confederation question, 'the plan to buy the North-West territory is perhaps the one which the press and the parliament treat with most indifference.'[2] French Quebeckers had little knowledge of those territories even at the time when the federal negotiators were busy about their transfer.

---

1 *Le Pays*, 6 July 1865. Also, *L'Ordre*, 14 Aug. 1865; *Le Canadien*, 7 July and 18 Sept. 1865; H.-G. Joly, *Discours sur la Confédération* (Quebec: Darveau 1865), pp. 20–2.
2 *Le Journal de Québec*, 14 Aug. 1865.

'These lands are little known to us,' wrote Cauchon, after Cartier's successful return from London in 1869.[3] And two years later Benjamin Sulte would remark that at the time the transfer was being arranged, French Canadians had thought of the North-West as 'a savage land, situated "at the end of the world", from which one only returns with the prestige of a great traveller.'[4]

This notion of a savage and distant country prompted the opposition, in particular, to express strong hostility toward the annexation. They thought it impossible that such a barren land could attract Canadian settlers, and feared the attempt to colonize it would involve the federal government in ruinous expenses. Why, even as the transfer was being arranged, the inhabitants of the North-West were appealing to Canada for charity to keep them from starvation as a result of a locust plague. 'In any case, the road that leads to prosperity can't run in this direction.'[5] Nor need one think that European emigrants would go where Canadians declined to settle. Like so many Canadians, they would continue to look for new homes in the United States.

Whatever they may say, the North-West territory is a desolate region, inaccessible during a large part of the year, with nothing to attract emigrants. When the American continent is all settled, so that there isn't even a square inch of land left available, maybe then people will head toward the Hudson Bay territory. Till then we cannot expect any emigrants.[6]

Far from wasting its money on costly expansion into such a worthless territory, Ottawa ought rather to be paying attention to the 'domestic well-being of the people', to the development of its own lands, which were certainly better suited than those of the North-West for colonization.[7]

This notion of the North-West as sterile, worthless, and foreign – particularly foreign to French Canadians, who saw their homeland in Quebec – was shared to a remarkable degree even by the supporters of the government. To be sure, they dutifully appeared to praise the transfer. At least it expanded the geographical extent of Confederation to impressive limits. 'Who would not feel proud of such a result? The authority of the Canadian government will extend over one of the vastest countries which

---

3 Ibid., 29 May 1869.
4 Benjamin Sulte, *L'Expédition militaire de Manitoba, 1870* (Montreal: Senécal 1871), pp. 49–50.
5 *Le Canadien*, 7 Sept. 1868. Also, 22 May 1868, 14 Apr., 2 June, 8 Oct., and 10 Nov. 1869; *L'Ordre*, 23 Sept. 1868; *Le Pays*, 31 Mar., 20 Apr., 2 June 1869.
6 *Le Pays*, 1 June 1869. Also, 31 Mar. and 20 Oct. 1869.
7 *L'Ordre*, 13 Apr. 1869. Also, *Le Pays*, 1 June 1869; *Le Canadien*, 22 May and 23 Sept. 1868, and 31 May 1869; L.-O. David, *Histoire du Canada depuis la Confédération, 1867–1887* (Montreal: Beauchemin 1909), p. 24.

exist in the world. Even our neighbours admit that we'll form a powerful empire.'[8]

Beyond these vague appeals to the sense of grandeur, however, even the Bleus were hesitant. By the time Parliament came to confirm the transfer agreement, in June of 1869, they were expressing the hope that Quebec's MPs would not support any expensive plans for rapid development of the territory.[9] 'Let's not bite off more than we can chew,' they warned.[10] Having the territory in reserve was fine, but any idea, for example, of building a railway across it was simply not to be thought of.[11]

The fact was that government supporters also thought of the North-West as a sterile and inhospitable land that could not support settlement. That was why this acquisition 'must for a long time remain of rather dubious utility to us.'[12] The publication in Quebec of the *Esquisse sur le Nord-Ouest de l'Amérique* by Bishop A.-A. Taché of St Boniface did not make people more sanguine. For although its English translator considered that the work made the country 'highly attractive to the emigrant',[13] French-Canadian reviewers saw it in a different light: 'Reading this work will cool the zeal of settlers intending to go and establish themselves in the North-West. Bishop Taché does not draw a very agreeable picture of these regions.'[14] There were better things, therefore, for the government to do with its money and its energy than to undertake a vain effort to settle the prairies. 'We're ready to believe that this North-West is a good acquisition for the Dominion, but that doesn't mean that our first efforts shouldn't be directed toward conserving our population and enlarging our own settlements.'[15]

Cartier's followers, therefore, do not seem to have looked toward the North-West as a field for settlement, especially not for French Canadians. And yet, there is a popular tradition in Canadian historiography that Cartier both wanted and expected French Canadians to participate fully in the

---

8 *Le Courrier de St-Hyacinthe*, 16 Apr. 1869. Also, *La Minverve*, 15 Apr. and 26 May 1869; *Le Journal des Trois-Rivières*, 13 and 16 Apr., 4 June 1869; *Le Journal de Québec*, 29 May 1869; *Le Nouveau Monde*, 1 and 17 Apr. 1869; *Le Pionnier de Sherbrooke*, 16 Apr. 1869.

9 *Le Journal des Trois-Rivières*, 22 June 1869.

10 *Le Courrier de St-Hyacinthe*, 15 June 1869: 'Qui trop embrasse mal étreint.'

11 *Le Journal de Québec*, 12 June 1869; *La Revue Canadienne*, II (1865), p. 568.

12 *Le Nouveau Monde*, 17 Apr. 1869. Also, 6 Apr. 1869.

13 A.-A. Taché, *Sketch of the North-West of America* (Montreal: Lovell 1870), translator's preface.

14 *Le Journal de Québec*, reprinted in *Le Nouveau Monde*, 4 Nov. 1869.

15 *L'Union des Cantons de l'Est*, 12 Aug. 1869. Also, *Le Nouveau Monde*, 16 Nov. 1869.

colonization of the prairies.[16] It is an attractive idea, for it enables us to look on North-West development as a model of Canada itself – a beautiful and harmonious partnership in which English and French Canadians are able to work together in a fruitful enterprise which gives satisfaction to all.

To support this view, it is possible to point out that it was Cartier who negotiated the transfer of Rupert's Land from the Hudson's Bay Company to the dominion government. He certainly attached importance to the transfer, and after his return from London, he exclaimed, during an after-dinner speech in Montreal: 'The West is the future.'[17] Even more, he specifically mentioned in public speeches that the North-West would be a place where Canadian surplus population might go. At Sherbrooke, for example, he told a crowd that the new territories 'will offer the people of this country the chance to emigrate to the West, if that seems desirable to them, instead of pouring into the United States.'[18] Speaking in the House of Commons a couple of years earlier, Cartier had said that annexation of the North-West 'will increase the importance of the whole country, not just of Ontario, and the representatives of Quebec know it.'[19]

Again, it would be Cartier who would negotiate with the delegates from the Red River provisional government in 1870, and who would author the Manitoba Act, establishing official bilingualism in the new province. Two years later, during the federal election campaign, he would boast to voters in his own riding that he had given Manitoba 'a government copied directly from Quebec's'.[20]

Finally, more general arguments can be made to suggest there was an expectation of French-Canadian participation in prairie development. During the Confederation Debates of 1865 in the Canadian legislature, speakers (including Cartier) several times spoke of equality and fair dealing between French and English Canada as the basis of Confederation – at least in the sense that it had been necessary to get agreement from both Upper and Lower Canada in order to create it. Even if that agreement did not involve equal status for French and English cultures and institutions in the four original

---

16 Eg., in the recent, popular biography by Alistair Sweeny, *George-Etienne Cartier* (Toronto: McClelland and Stewart 1976); or Ralph Heintzman, 'The Spirit of Confederation: Prof. Creighton, Biculturalism, and the Use of History', in the *CHR*, LII, 3 (Sept., 1971); Brian Young, 'The Defeat of George-Etienne Cartier in Montreal-East in 1872', in the *CHR*, LI, 4 (Dec., 1970); H.B.M. Best, 'George-Etienne Cartier and the North-West' (paper read to the Canadian Historical Association at its 1970 annual meeting); etc.
17 Tassé, p. 558.
18 Reported in *Le Pionnier de Sherbrooke*, 16 Apr. 1869. See also Tassé, p. 609.
19 Tassé, p. 558.
20 Tassé, p. 706.

provinces, it could well be expected to imply such a thing in the West. The four provinces of 1867 were already settled before Confederation, and entered the new régime each with its identity already established. In establishing the French language in Quebec but not in the others, for example, the fathers of Confederation only recognized these already-existing identities. But was not the North-West a new and empty territory, not yet settled, not yet developed? Furthermore, it was paid for by tax money collected from *all* Canadians, and could, therefore, be considered as much the property of French Quebeckers as of English Ontarians. Surely, then, it is reasonable to assume that French settlers were expected to have as much a part in the development of the West as English settlers, and that Cartier and other federal leaders anticipated a French-Canadian presence on the prairies?

It may seem a reasonable assumption, but the evidence for it is circumstantial at best, and is perfectly consistent with a very different interpretation of Cartier's expectations. That he wanted Canada to take over the West is clear, but he had other motives than a desire to see French Canadians settle there. He was, after all, deeply involved with the Grand Trunk Railway, which wanted to build a line to the North-West. He was an MP from Montreal, which would profit immensely by the extension of its railway network into that territory, whether the territory itself were settled by English Canadians, British emigrants, or anyone else. He was the political leader of Quebec, which needed commercial development to provide jobs for people who would otherwise have to emigrate to New England. When he told the House of Commons, therefore, that development of the North-West would benefit Quebeckers as well as Ontarians, he meant it literally: it would benefit *Quebeckers*. The North-West represented a great commercial empire; its settlement by a huge population (wherever that population came from) would produce goods and provide a market for products that would be shipped back and forth over a Montreal-based railroad system, to build up the St Lawrence ports and create the prosperity of Quebec. It would be a repetition, on a much greater scale, of the process which had built Montreal up to its present condition. 'It is the settlement of the West,' Cartier told a Quebec City banquet, and referring to Upper Canada as the West, 'which has caused the prosperity of Montreal.'[21]

Indeed, Cartier's commercial dreams did not stop with the prairies. Not only did he negotiate the transfer of Rupert's Land to Canada; not only would he negotiate with the delegates of the Red River government; but he was also the man who would handle the negotiations to bring British Columbia into Confederation in 1871. He would be the one to offer the British Columbians a

---

21 Tassé, p. 642.

railroad from Canada to the Pacific when they had not asked for it, and he would ram the deal through a reluctant House of Commons – though the conditions of British Columbia's entry did not involve any provision for the 'French fact'. There was no need for such provision, for British Columbia interested French Canada not as a place to live, but because it meant the extension of Quebec's commercial empire to the Pacific – and beyond! Cartier's newspaper explained in 1869 the real reason for his interest in the West:

The North-West ... means greatness and wealth; it's the empire of commerce; it's the last link between Europe and Asia, it's the road which leads to the gold of Australia, the shawls of Cashmere, the diamonds of Golconda, the silks of China, the spices of Malabar and the Moluccas, etc. By an immense effort, we'll eventually put Victoria into daily communication with Montreal, and the nations of the world, in order to trade, will have to land at our port. ...

Our statesmen and all the inhabitants of this country must never forget that the future is in commerce, the commerce of the West. ... [22]

From this point of view, it little mattered who settled the West, as long as they produced wealth to be shipped to the world via Montreal. Indeed, Cartier had told the Commons in 1867 that he expected European emigrants to be settlers of the territory.[23] But he also had more than a suspicion that Ontarians would play a major part too. In fact, the reason he had given for opposing annexation of the North-West before Confederation had been based on the assumption that Ontarians would be the ones to fill the country.[24] Here Cartier was in agreement with the newspapers of both political parties, which argued that if, despite its unfriendly climate and soil, the prairie region ever were settled, it would be by Ontarians. 'Upper Canada

---

22 *La Minerve*, 26 May 1869. *La Revue Canadienne*, VII (1870), p. 457, expressed the same idea in an article on B.C.'s future entry into Confederation.

23 Tassé, p. 557. See also *Le Journal de Québec*, 14 June 1865, and 29 May 1869.

24 A well-known quotation from a letter by A.K. Isbister has Cartier telling the Colonial Secretary in 1859 that 'as head of the Lower Canadian party, any proposal of this kind would meet with his determined opposition – as it would be putting a political extinguisher upon the party and the Province he represented, and, if carried out, would lead to the dissolution of the Union.' That is, the North-West would inevitably be an extension of Upper Canada, and would too much increase that section's weight in the Union. See, eg., W.L. Morton, *Manitoba: A History* (Toronto: University of Toronto Press 1957), p. 107. Of course, once Confederation had come, giving French Canadians autonomy in their own province of Quebec, Cartier could support the acquisition of Rupert's Land for other reasons, telling the House, 'Je n'ai jamais voulu consentir à ce que la province d'Ontario devint seul propriétaire de cette immense région. ...' (Tassé, p. 625).

alone will profit,' they complained,[25] 'ensuring its preponderance even more than now.'[26] It was no wonder that Ontario had been the chief source of support for the annexation, 'considering that Ontario alone will profit directly from it. ...'[27]

As for the one or two statements Cartier made about Quebeckers (he did not say French Canadians) being able to settle on the prairies if they wanted – well, after all, these were only statements of fact, but they did not mean that Cartier either wanted or expected a French-Canadian movement to the prairies. In 1872, when a St Boniface priest was sent to Ottawa to get help in organizing French-Canadian settlement in Manitoba, Cartier brushed him off with empty words. 'Mr Cartier,' wrote the priest, in a disappointed report to Archbishop Taché, 'ta ta ta, fine fine, we've got to make a French province of Manitoba. The Ontarians will skip over it and go on to Saskatchewan, ta ta ta.'[28]

There is no real reason, therefore, to suppose that either Cartier or any significant body of French-Canadian opinion wanted or expected a movement of French-Canadians to the prairies. If the newspapers ever mentioned such an idea, it was either to make fun of it or else in the same tone which Cartier used to the St Boniface priest.[29] In the summer of 1869, when Ottawa passed an act for the temporary government of Rupert's Land and appointed William McDougall as governor, there was no complaint in Quebec – even from the opposition – about the absence from the act of any provisions for bilingualism, or about the appointment as governor of a man associated with anti-French-Canadian positions. Far from criticizing the government for its failure to entrench French-Canadian rights in the territorial constitution – something the opposition could be expected to do if it had the slightest notion of encouraging French-Canadian settlement in the region – Le Pays even applauded the nomination of McDougall, which, it said, would be well viewed by all persons without bias.[30]

---

25 Le Pays, 2 June 1869. Also, 22 Aug. 1865, 28 June and 27 Nov. 1869.
26 L'Ordre, 18 Aug. 1865. Also, L'Union Nationale, 5 and 19 Sept. 1865; Le Pays, 13 Apr. 1869.
27 Le Courrier de St-Hyacinthe, 12 June 1869. Also, Le Nouveau Monde, 1 Apr. 1869.
28 J.-B. Proulx to A.-A. Taché (Ottawa, 5 June 1872), in Archives Deschâtelet (Scolasticat St-Joseph, Ottawa), microfilms of St Boniface archiepiscopal papers, mfm #310.
29 Le Canadien, 1 Apr. 1868; Le Courrier de St-Hyacinthe, 12 June 1869.
30 Le Pays, 30 June 1869. Also, Le Journal des Trois-Rivières, 8 June 1869; L'Union des Cantons de l'Est, 10 June 1869; Le Nouveau Monde, 5 June 1869. Even though the act of 1869 was only meant to be temporary, and hence is not a sure guide to the long-range intentions of the government, it would have been only natural for newspapers, especially opposition papers, to comment on the absence of bilingual provisions in it. If there had

In this absence of expectation of French-Canadian colonization on the prairies, we can see a continuation of the attitudes of 1864–7. Quebec alone was the French-Canadian homeland. To go west would be to go abroad. Attitudes like these, after all, do not change overnight – or even in two years of Confederation.

If French Quebeckers did not look on Rupert's Land as part of their country, neither did they look on the French-Catholic Métis as part of their own nationality. Certainly, they had been told something of the Métis. French-Canadian missionaries had been working in the North-West since 1818, and they had often enough, no doubt, appealed to Quebec's charity on behalf of a population composed 'almost exclusively of French Canadians or their descendants'.[31]

Nevertheless, the French of the North-West had been living apart from those of Quebec since the eighteenth century; neither the fur trading connection before 1822 nor the activity of missionaries since 1818 was such as to encourage the notion of a common nationality between the Métis and the French Quebeckers. Missionaries were expected to live in savage lands and among savage peoples, and if their appeals for charity mentioned the Canadian origins of the Métis, they could not omit their Indian origins as well, nor the difficulty of converting them from buffalo-hunting semi-nomads into the sort of people French Canadians were. As late as 1876 the Société de Colonisation de Manitoba was still complaining that in Quebec 'we are still asked if there are many savages in and around Winnipeg, if they are to be feared, and if there is much danger of being scalped by them.'[32]

Reactions to the federal plan for takeover of the North-West and to the beginnings of the resistance at Red River also reflected a view of the territory's population as savages rather than the sort of people with whom Quebec could identify itself. Opposition newspapers quite passed over the opportunity to

---

been any expectation that French-Canadian settlement in the West was to be provided for, then people would surely have asked about the act's silence, and the opposition would have taken advantage of the situation to criticize the government, while the ministerial press explained that this act was only temporary and that protection for French Canadians would appear in the West's permanent constitution.

31 A.-A. Taché, *Lettre de Mgr Taché, Evéque de St-Boniface, donnant à Mgr de Montréal le récit des malheurs de son diocèse depuis deux ans* (n.p., n.d.), p. 9. Note also L.-F. Laflèche, *Mandements de Mgr Laflèche*, vol. 1, circulaire 5 (5 Aug. 1869), in the Archives de l'Evéché de Trois-Rivières.

32 Société de Colonisation de Manitoba, *A nos compatriotes des Etats-Unis et du Canada: émigrez à Manitoba* (n.p., n.d.), p. 1. For a missionary account of the un-Canadian life in the North-West, see A.-A. Taché, *Vingt années de missions dans le Nord-Ouest de l'Amérique* (Montreal: Senécal 1866).

criticize the government for not consulting the wishes of the westerners (apparently agreeing that they were not civilized enough to warrant consultation), and only expressed the fear that it would be necessary to 'repulse the savage tribes' before colonization could begin.[33] *La Minerve*'s first report of the stopping of McDougall referred to the Métis as 'those who had come to scalp the new lieutenant-governor'.[34]

Politically embarrassed by the resistance, Conservative papers had, of course, no reason to give prominence to it or to the Métis. They passed it off, at first, as a small misunderstanding, which had been settled immediately, allowing McDougall to proceed to Winnipeg in triumph.[35] Obliged, at last, to admit that reports from the North-West told of McDougall being turned back to Pembina and one of his party, Provencher, being taken prisoner, they affected to mistrust those reports on the grounds that they came from American newspapers – the Americans having an interest in stirring up trouble at Red River.[36]

Even when the authenticity of reports from Red River had been ascertained, Quebec newspapers continued to pay little attention to them. Weeks or even months might go by with no mention of the uprising in their columns.[37] What was published showed little concern for or sympathy with the Métis. They were still seen as Indians, like those warring in the U.S. West,[38] who, once calmed down, would return to *the hunt*.[39] As late as April, 1870, *Le Courrier du Canada* was still referring to them as the 'ferocious mixed-bloods' of the North-West.[40]

Ferocious or tame, Indians or not, the Métis were readily characterized as 'rebels' or 'insurgents' by the Quebec press.[41] Their defeat was desired for the

---

33 *Le Canadien*, 22 May 1868.

34 *La Minerve*, 15 Nov. 1869.

35 Ibid. Also, *Le Courrier de St-Hyacinthe*, 19 Nov. 1869.

36 *La Minerve*, 18 and 19 Nov. 1869; *Le Courrier de St-Hyacinthe*, 26 Nov. 1869; *Le Courrier du Canada*, 19 and 24 Nov. 1869; *Le Journal des Trois-Rivières*, 19 Nov. 1869.

37 *L'Union des Cantons de l'Est* mentioned the uprising for the first time on 9 December, and not again till mid-January. See also, eg., *La Gazette de Sorel* or *Le Courrier de St-Hyacinthe* in November and December. Both papers devoted almost all their attention to the fall session of the Quebec parliament. But the silence about Red River continued into 1870. See *La Gazette de Sorel*, January, 1870; *Le Pionnier de Sherbrooke*, Jan.-Feb., 1870; *Le Nouveau Monde*, Jan., Mar., 1870; *Le Pays*, January, 1870.

38 *Le Canadien*, 8 Oct., 8, 9, 10 Nov. 1869; *Le Pays*, 20 Oct. 1869.

39 *Le Journal de Québec*, 9 Dec. 1869; *La Gazette de Sorel*, 27 Nov. 1869.

40 *Le Courrier du Canada*, 18 Apr. 1870.

41 Eg., *Le Journal de Québec*, 4 and 9 Dec. 1869; *La Gazette de Sorel*, 24 Nov. 1869; *Le Courrier du Canada*, 24 Nov. 1869 (in which the insurgents were accused of setting up a republican constitution), 6 and 27 Dec. 1869; *Le Nouveau Monde*, 27 Nov. 1869.

sake of 'the honour of the fledgeling Canadian diplomacy,'[42] and when they were thought to have been put down by a band of loyal (English) Canadians in December, *Le Courrier de St-Hyacinthe*, for one, was ready to express pleasure: 'The insurgents are dispersing, and the loyal subjects are organizing. Everything seems to be returning to normal.'[43] When this proved to have been wishful thinking, *Le Journal de Québec* blamed Ottawa for sabotaging McDougall's efforts and preventing a decisive suppression of the resistance.[44]

In their less hostile moods, papers spoke of the Métis as deluded and needing only to be brought round to a right way of thinking.[45] *Le Pays*, for its part, considered that 'Lower Canada ... looks with considerable indifference on the events taking place in the North-West',[46] and it may well have been right, for a Fort Garry correspondent wrote to *Le Nouveau Monde* in December to complain that French-Canadian newspapers had too little to say about the events at Red River, and that what little they did say was to blame the Métis.[47]

During the first months of the Red River uprising, then, French Quebeckers do not seem to have identified themselves with or felt much sympathy for the Métis. They certainly do not seem to have looked on them as representatives of the French-Canadian nationality in the West. They noted that Assiniboians of all races and religions supported the uprising,[48] and, when they had got over condemning them and started to look calmly for the motives of the uprising, they saw none that concerned French-Catholic rights in particular. The Assiniboians simply wanted local self-determination – 'out and out independence', according to some,[49] the right to be consulted, according to others, to say No to Canada and to remain a separate British colony, like Newfoundland. No-one denied this right to the Newfoundlanders, after all. Then why should the government behave in such a bullying way toward the Assiniboians? 'Leaving aside its cod-fish, Newfoundland has

---

42 *L'Ordre*, 25 Nov. 1869. This reference to Canadian diplomacy reinforces the conclusion that French Canadians looked on the North-West as essentially *foreign* to Canada. *Le Pays*, also, on 27 Nov. 1869, referred to the uprising as a test of Canada's 'politique extérieure'.

43 *Le Courrier de St-Hyacinthe*, 21 Dec. 1869.

44 *Le Journal de Québec*, 30 Dec. 1869.

45 Eg., *La Minerve*, 22 Dec. 1869; *Le Journal des Trois-Rivières*, 26 Nov. 1869; *Le Pionnier de Sherbrooke*, 26 Nov. 1869.

46 *Le Pays*, 27 Nov. 1869.

47 *Le Nouveau Monde*, 31 Dec. 1869.

48 Eg., *Le Nouveau Monde*, 27 Nov. 1869; *Le Courrier de St-Hyacinthe*, 25 Nov. 1869.

49 *Le Courrier du Canada*, 27 Dec. 1869.

less population than the North-West, and if it is thought right to respect the wishes of the former, why not respect those of Messrs Métis and Indians?'[50]

Naturally, the opposition laid most stress on government policy as having provoked the uprising, on Ottawa's failure to consult the local population. Bleus tended rather to blame certain bad and fanatical individuals from Ontario, who, by their irresponsible behaviour in the period preceding the annexation, had prejudiced the local population against Canada. 'Those gentlemen are, by their recklessness, their intriguing, their dishonesty toward the Métis, the cause of all the prejudices which the latter harbour against Canada.'[51] In any case, everyone agreed that the federal government ought to keep calm, be reasonable, try to persuade the Métis by soothing talk, and at all costs avoid a costly and extemely difficult military campaign to 'subdue the rebels and drive back the Indians'.[52]

All these attitudes toward the events at Red River continued to express themselves during the first months of 1870. Papers continued to go for long periods without even mentioning those events, to condemn the idea of insurrection,[53] to complain of the 'rather arbitrary conduct' of the Assiniboians,[54] and to protest that the 'origin of Riel's power is very questionable.' Fenians, Americans, annexationists were among the leaders of the uprising. 'It's a far cry from that to the interests of the French nationality and the Catholic religion.'[55] No wonder that Assiniboians still complained about the 'feebleness with which the Métis cause has been defended by the Catholic press'![56]

Lower Canadians still saw the uprising not as a French-Catholic struggle against English Protestantism but as a defence of local self-determination. Government and opposition papers were fundamentally in agreement about

---

50 *Le Pays*, 27 Nov. 1869. Also, 20 Oct., 26 Nov., 28 Dec. 1869; *Le Pionnier de Sherbroóke*, 26 Nov. and 31 Dec. 1869; *Le Courrier de St-Hyacinthe*, 25 Nov. 1869.

51 *La Minerve*, 22 Dec. 1869. Also, *Le Courrier de St-Hyacinthe*, 27 Nov. and 3 Dec. 1869; *Le Nouveau Monde*, 6 Apr., 16 Nov., and 31 Dec. 1869; *La Gazette de Sorel*, 4 Dec. 1869; *L'Ordre*, 31 Dec. 1869.

52 *Le Pays*, 19 Nov. 1869. Also, *L'Ordre*, 20 and 30 Nov. 1869; *Le Courrier du Canada*, 9 and 20 Dec. 1869; *Le Nouveau Monde*, 16 Nov. 1869; *L'Union des Cantons de l'Est*, 9 Dec. 1869.

53 Eg., *La Minerve*, 15 Jan. 1870; *Le Journal de Québec*, 25 Jan. 1870; *Le Courrier de St-Hyacinthe*, 28 Apr. 1870.

54 *Le Journal de Québec*, 11 Jan. 1870.

55 *L'Opinion Publique* (Montreal), 7 Apr. 1870. Also, 12 Feb. 1870; *La Gazette des Familles Canadiennes* (Quebec), 28 Feb. and 1 June 1870.

56 *L'Ordre*, 13 Jan. 1870. Also, *La Minerve*, 25 Apr.; *Le Journal de Québec*, 11 Mar.; *L'Union des Cantons de l'Est*, 20 Jan.; *L'Opinion Publique*, 1 Jan. and 23 Apr. 1870.

this, the main difference between them being that the latter were more willing to see the Assiniboians' attitude as legitimate, and analogous to that of Newfoundland or Prince Edward Island, [57] while the former were rather more impatient that the Métis should be so 'ticklish about their national honour'. [58] It was true, they claimed, that irresponsible and fanatical Ontarians had provoked the troubles and continued to aggravate them; [59] nevertheless, it had to be recognized that the Métis 'have never for one instant stopped considering the four provinces as one single hostile, aggressive, and despotic power. ... Lower Canadians were foreigners to them as much as the inhabitants of the other provinces.' [60] The whole Red River population – 'French Canadians and English alike' – were participating in the uprising, [61] because they all agreed with John Bruce's statement: 'To us, Canada is just a foreign power.' [62]

These initial attitudes toward the Red River uprising and toward the Métis – hostility, indifference, or bare tolerance – came gradually to change during the course of the uprising. Even before the end of 1869, in fact, a new note had been sounded. As early as November there appeared, here and there, a complaint that Ontario newspapers were interpreting the uprising in a very perverse manner. One Toronto paper had accused the Catholic clergy of encouraging the insurgents, and had even claimed that the Sisters of Charity were taking an active part in the uprising. The purpose of these accusations seemed to be to besmirch the Catholic element at Red River as much as possible. [63] Nor was it only the Catholic element that was singled out for attack by the Ontario press. 'The French-speaking Métis are considered as barbarians by the English element in Canada; it feels neither pity nor a sense of justice toward them, because of that belief.' [64] In short, Ontarians seemed to be singling out the French-Catholic group to blame for the uprising. Apparently they aimed at 'the exclusion of the French-Canadian element, ostensibly in the interest of peace, but in reality so that Ontario can enjoy its

---

57 *Le Pays*, 5 and 8 Feb., 9 Mar., 26 Apr. 1870; *L'Ordre*, 3 Feb. 1870.
58 *Le Courrier de St-Hyacinthe*, 7 May 1870. Also, *L'Union des Cantons de l'Est*, 14 Jan. 1870.
59 *Le Courrier de St-Hyacinthe*, 10 and 12 Mar., 7 May 1870; *Le Journal des Trois-Rivières*, 11 Jan.; *L'Union des Cantons de l'Est*, 14 Jan., 17 Mar., 2 June; *Le Pionnier de Sherbrooke*, 24 Mar.; *L'Ordre*, 13 Jan., 3 Feb., 12 Apr. 1870.
60 *La Minerve*, 8 Apr. 1870.
61 *La Gazette de Sorel*, 20 Apr. 1870. Also, *L'Union des Cantons de l'Est*, 31 Mar. and 7 Apr.; *Le Nouveau Monde*, 21 Feb. 1870.
62 *Le Courrier de St-Hyacinthe*, 5 Feb. 1870.
63 *Le Nouveau Monde*, 27 Nov. 1869. Also, 19 Nov. and 31 Dec. 1869.
64 *L'Ordre*, 31 Dec. 1869.

conquest without anyone else disputing its right to complete control of that territory.'[65]

William McDougall's return to Ontario in January helped spread the view of the uprising as a French-Catholic rebellion. In a speaking and writing campaign, McDougall accused 'foreign Jesuits', including 'Ritchot & Co.' as well as 'Bishop Taché and his co-conspirators' of launching the 'armed insurrection' in order to establish the North-West as a 'French Catholic Province'.[66] These, and other charges by the frustrated almost-governor of Rupert's Land were duly noted in Quebec, where the press reacted by calling them 'unjust and furious attacks',[67] and attributing them to the 'fanaticism which inspires Mr McDougall against the French Canadians'.[68] He had always been obsessed with the idea that Catholic priests were trouble-makers and revolutionaries,[69] and 'He is the one who started the cry in Ontario that we wanted to establish a "french domination" at Red River! Always appeals to fanaticism!'[70]

While French Quebeckers had tended to see the uprising as the combined work of all races at Red River fighting for local self-determination, McDougall's campaign suggested that Ontarians saw it as a French-Catholic attempt to overthrow British institutions:

Just because a French Canadian is the head of the movement, and because the names of a few priests have been mixed up with it, some of our compatriots in Ontario are under the impression that this whole rebellion was worked up in the interests of Lower Canada and the Catholic clergy.[71]

---

65 *Le Pays*, 27 Nov. 1869. See also *La Minerve*, 22 Dec. 1869.
66 William McDougall, *The Red River Rebellion* (Toronto: Hunter, Rose and Co. 1870), pp. 7, 40, 46, 50.
67 *La Gazette de Sorel*, 9 Feb. 1870.
68 Ibid., 26 Feb. 1870.
69 *Le Courrier du Canada*, 7 Feb. 1870.
70 *La Gazette de Sorel*, 26 Feb. 1870. Also, *Le Journal des Trois-Rivières*, 11 Jan. 1870; *L'Opinion Publique*, 26 Feb.; *L'Ordre*, 8 and 10 Feb. 1870.
71 *La Minerve*, 8 Apr. 1870. In 1874, French Canadians were to hear evidence that confirmed their notion of Ontario opinion, when Archbishop Taché testified to the select committee of the House of Commons on the amnesty question. Taché told the committee that Ontario volunteers in the 1870 expeditionary force seemed to have been motivated by 'une haine contre la race française toute entière'. See Canada, Parliament, House of Commons, *Rapport du Comité spécial sur les causes des troubles du territoire du Nord-Ouest en 1869–70* (Ottawa: Taylor 1874), p. 140. Benjamin Sulte, who had participated in the expedition, wrote in 1871, in his *Expédition militaire*, p. 43, that most of the Ontario volunteers had been 'trop disposés à exercer des représailles contre les catholiques et les français de Manitoba.' It is not necessary to speak of 'fanaticism' in explaining why so many Ontarians held French Canada in general and Quebec in particular responsible for what

Ontario's reaction to Thomas Scott's execution seemed an irresistible manifestation of this view, and it forced Quebec to respond energetically. The initial Lower Canadian reaction to the execution was far from justifying it.[72] Most papers referred to it as 'most regrettable',[73] or as an 'abhorrent murder', which 'we blame as energetically as possible.'[74] Yet, the furious reaction in Ontario – the 'indignation meetings' and the raging editorials – could not be ignored; they drew Quebec willy-nilly into an alignment with Scott's killers. 'Their newspapers have long ago made clear to us the cause of their indignation,' complained the *Journal de Québec*. 'There are inhabitants of French origin out there, and that upsets Upper Canada's plans.'[75] Clearly, Scott's death was not the real cause of the Ontarians' concern. 'All that is only a pretext to call for the expulsion of the French from the North-West.'[76] Worse than that, Ontario's anger seemed to be directed at Quebec itself, for

---

they considered a serious rebellion. Ontarians were naturally struck by the prominent role which the French-Catholic element played at Red River. (It was true that the French Métis generally took the initiatives in the uprising, with the more or less willing support of their English cousins.) Moreover, many Ontarians looked upon the opening of the North-West not only as a great opportunity for the establishment of their own people, but as a great work of national and human progress, which would build up the wealth and population of Canada, provide homes for great numbers of people and produce food for the world's hungry. Now that work of progress was being sabotaged, and when Ontarians saw the French name of the uprising's leader, when they saw the name of a French-Catholic priest among the spokesmen of the provisional government, when they recalled how French Lower Canadians had for so long opposed the annexation of the North-West, it was natural that many of them saw the uprising as a French-Canadian enterprise aimed at stopping what the *Globe* had called, in 1863, 'the wheels of Anglo-Saxon progress toward the setting sun'. A tradition coming from the days of the Glorious Revolution and of Jacobitism suspected the Catholic Church of being a friend of absolutism, an enemy of progress and freedom. And certainly, in Canada, the French-Catholic element did appear to be backward and unprogressive. The agricultural crisis in Quebec, the fact that the French Métis had remained much more dependent on the buffalo hunt than the English Métis, much less adapted to agriculture – these things convinced Ontarians of the backwardness of the French and made them ready to suspect them of trying to stop a great work of progress – especially when everyone, Ontarians and Quebeckers alike, had been expecting that it would be Ontarians who would first benefit from the annexation by becoming the settlers of the prairies.

72 *La Gazette de Sorel*, 27 Apr. 1870, and *Le Courrier du Canada*, 16 Apr. 1870, without justifying the killing, pleaded, in the first case, that there were extenuating circumstances, and, in the second, that even if unjust and unwise, the killing had still to be accepted as the act of a *de facto* government.

73 *Le Courrier de St-Hyacinthe*, 11 Apr. 1870.

74 *Le Journal des Trois-Rivières*, 18 Apr. 1870. Also, *L'Opinion Publique*, 7 Apr., *Le Journal de Québec*, 9 Apr., *La Gazette des Familles Canadiennes*, 1 June 1870.

75 *Le Journal de Québec*, 11 Apr. 1870.

76 Ibid., 12 Apr. 1870.

its papers had an unpleasant habit of including 'our ministers among Scott's murderers'.[77] It appeared, then, that what motivated Ontarians was not so much a desire to punish murderers as a desire to punish French Catholics. 'How much hatred there is in these Anglo-Saxons' souls against everything which is French and Catholic!'[78]

But as Quebeckers became increasingly convinced that Ontarians were anxious to repress the Métis not because they were rebels but because they were French Catholics, it became inevitable that Quebec, *the* French-Catholic province, would come to take up a position in favour of the Métis:

In any case, these indignation meetings in Ontario, this determination to make a war out of the affair ... must teach us Lower Canadians that the inhabitants of Ontario want to see a policy adopted that will undermine French influence in the North-West.

Ah, but on that point the Province of Quebec will have only one answer: to protect and assist our brothers out there.[79]

A counter-influence was necessary to defend against Ontario extremism, 'and the French press of Lower Canada must, sooner or later, begin preaching a more conciliatory behaviour toward our compatriots of the North-West.'[80]

It was thus Ontario's conduct – or at least Quebec's view of it – that began to push originally unsympathetic French Canadians into a pro-Métis position. Quebeckers had not wanted to be involved in a fight, claimed the *Courrier de St-Hyacinthe*. 'However, the English papers are dragging us into this difficulty; we must speak up.' It was the Ontario papers that 'would have people believe that the French Canadians are somehow partisans of Riel. ... '[81] It was they who were 'anxious to make a question of nationality out of this.'[82] It was they who were demanding a military expedition in the most disquieting terms:

The *Globe* wants to send English Upper Canadians only; the Toronto *Telegraph*, no doubt completing the thought of its colleague, makes no secret of its sanguinary design: the extermination of the French Métis at Red River. There are already too many Frenchmen, according to it, in the province of Quebec. ...

---

77 *Le Journal des Trois-Rivières*, 18 Apr. 1870.
78 *L'Union des Cantons de l'Est*, 14 Apr. 1870. Also, *Le Courrier du Canada*, 8 Apr.; *Le Pionnier de Sherbrooke*, 15 Apr.; *Le Pays*, 8 Apr.; *L'Ordre* , 14 Apr.; *Le Nouveau Monde*, 14 Apr.; *Le Courrier de St-Hyacinthe*, 16, 19, and 21 Apr.; *L'Opinion Publique*, 23 Apr.; *Le Journal de Québec*, 5 and 9 Apr. 1870.
79 *Le Journal des Trois-Rivières*, 18 Apr. 1870. Also, 21 Apr. 1870.
80 *La Gazette de Sorel*, 20 Apr. 1870.
81 *Le Courrier de St-Hyacinthe*, 23 Apr. 1870.
82 *Le Pays*, 11 Apr. 1870.

The whole French press, consequently, is justifiably upset: the Lower Canadian population is very alarmed.[83]

By the late spring of 1870, the Métis of the North-West, who had been almost unknown to French Quebeckers a year before, and had been condemned by them as savages and rebels six months before, were being found, thanks to Ontario extremists, to be civilized French-Catholic compatriots,[84] whose struggle for local self-determination was becoming a question of 'our position' in the North-West[85] and even of the place of 'the French race in Canada'.[86] Ontario reactions to the Manitoba bill encouraged the transition: 'The fanatical Upper Canadian press is calling the measure execrable and refuses to see anything in it but the triumph of clerical and French manoeuvring. That's a good sign for us.'[87]

This was not to say that Quebeckers now felt the Métis to be French Canadians like themselves. Rather, they were 'our friends' whose destruction would 'humiliate' Quebec because of the friendship she bore them.[88] Ontarians had accused Quebeckers of inspiring and directing the Métis movement; accordingly, they began to feel a certain protective friendship toward it. But their attitudes were still ambivalent. True, if they accepted Confederation peacefully, the Métis could become good friends to the French Canadians; but 'if Riel's so-called provisional government should refuse to accept Canada's liberal terms,' then it would be necessary to use 'the ultimate resource of arms'.[89] Thus the Bleus. Rouge editors, unwilling to go to such extremes, were ready to wash their hands of the Métis. 'Let's get back our money as quickly as possible, and let the Company take back its territory as quickly as possible also.'[90]

By the time the Manitoba Act was passed, some Quebeckers seem to have started thinking of the North-West, not as an extension of their homeland,

---

83 *L'Opinion Publique*, 28 Apr. 1870. For more examples of Quebec reacting to Ontario, see *Le Journal de Québec*, 10 and 15 Feb.; *Le Courrier de St-Hyacinthe*, 11 Feb.; *Le Courrier du Canada*, 25 Feb.; *Le Nouveau Monde*, 10 Mar. and 12 Apr.; and Pamphile Lemay's poem in *L'Union des Cantons de l'Est*, 21 Apr. 1870.

84 *Le Pays*, 8 Apr. 1870; *Le Courrier de St-Hyacinthe*, 23 Apr. and 7 May; *Le Journal des Trois-Rivières*, 18 and 21 Apr.; *L'Union des Cantons de l'Est*, 14 and 21 Apr. 1870.

85 *L'Opinion Publique*, 12 May 1870.

86 *Le Pays*, 11 Mar. 1870.

87 *L'Opinion Publique*, 12 May 1870. Also, *La Revue Canadienne*, VII (1870), p. 618.

88 Pamphile Lemay in *Le Courrier de St-Hyacinthe*, 21 Apr. 1870.

89 *L'Opinion Publique*, 28 Apr. 1870. Also, *Le Pionnier de Sherbrooke*, 6 May; *Le Nouveau Monde*, 14 Apr.; *Le Courrier de St-Hyacinthe*, 7 May 1870.

90 *Le Pays*, 8 Apr. 1870.

but as a second French-Catholic province which would become a special ally of the French-Catholic province of Quebec in the general Confederation. It was natural for Quebeckers to think in these terms, because ever since 1864 they had thought of Confederation as an alliance. They had looked on the federal Parliament, moreover, as a sort of House of Provinces, in which various combinations of provincial interests would have to be balanced against each other. In particular, it would be necessary for Quebec to seek allies in Ottawa against her traditional rival, the more populous province of Ontario. In 1864–5, Nova Scotia and New Brunswick had been looked to for this purpose.[91] Later, the admission of new provinces was often considered a way to balance Ontario's power in the federal legislature. Thus, *La Revue Canadienne* would see the admission of British Columbia as a great aid to French Canadians, 'since the numerical inferiority of our representation will probably receive important support from most of the MPs from the new province.'[92]

The acquisition of Rupert's Land was seen in the same light. By joining Confederation, its population would become the 'political allies' of the other provinces.[93] But within the general federation, whose side would they be on: Ontario's or Quebec's? The assumption that Ontarians rather than Quebeckers would settle the prairies led, at first, to the conclusion that the North-West would strengthen Ontario's hand at Ottawa. Thus, the *Courrier de St-Hyacinthe* thought it important that Newfoundland should enter Confederation at the same time:

To maintain the equilibrium between Quebec and Ontario, our MPs should ... uphold the line of conduct adopted by the government concerning Newfoundland. The annexation of that island will balance that of Rupert's Land and prevent the western provinces from getting the ascendancy over the eastern ones.[94]

The events of 1869–70 changed this equation. Quebeckers now discovered that the North-West had not been waiting for Ontarians to give it a population; it already had a population – a French-Catholic population apparently determined to preserve its identity and institutions. By its resistance that winter, and by the negotiations which led to the Manitoba Act, that population had unexpectedly provided for Manitoba to become not a mere extension of Ontario but a bilingual province – perhaps even another

91 Cauchon, *L'Union*, p. 48; Bonenfant, 'Le Canada et les hommes', p. 579.
92 *La Revue Canadienne*, VIII (Apr., 1871), p. 320.
93 *L'Union des Cantons de l'Est*, 9 Sept. 1868. Also, Sulte, *Expédition*, p. 49.
94 *Le Courrier de St-Hyacinthe*, 12 June 1869.

French and Catholic province![95] This was a great and unlooked-for windfall for Quebec:

Let's admit frankly what a lot of people are saying in private: this madness has served us well. If Mr McDougall had been prudent, the French population of the North-West would have found itself badly off in the political organization we were intending to provide. Without asking whether Riel was right in principle to act as he's done, let us at least note that the result is magnificent. The French and Catholic elements are safe in the North-West.[96]

But unexpected or not, the institution (or maintenance) of a French Manitoba would be a great support for Quebec within the Canadian confederation, 'a considerable reinforcement against any operation that might be tried against us in the future'.[97] Just as, during the winter of 1869–70, the tendency of Ontarians to pick out the French-Catholic element at Red River for blame and harassment had been felt as an attack on *all* French Canadians – and particularly on the French-Canadian province of Quebec – just so the success of the French-Catholic Métis was a success for French Canada and for Quebec. The Métis could now become, for Quebeckers, 'precious auxiliaries in the Canadian confederation'.[98]

If French-Quebec newspapers, therefore, acclaimed the passing of the Manitoba Act, it was not because its guarantees for the French language and Catholic schools made the prairies receptive to French-Canadian settlement, but because the act as a whole gave satisfaction to French Canada's friends and allies, the Métis; because it ensured their own, separate survival. 'We wanted the people of Red River ... to have institutions that could guarantee their religious and national autonomy, that would shelter them and save them from any unhealthy absorption that was intended.'[99] It was enough that the Métis felt they now had those institutions. Quebec newspapers did not bother to discuss the significance of the two sections in the Manitoba Act most closely touching the position of their nationality in the West – the establishment of French language and Catholic schools. Some, indeed, did not even report that such sections had been included.[100] The important thing was that their friends

---

95 Eg., *L'Ordre*, 7 May 1870.
96 *Le Courrier de St-Hyacinthe*, 12 Mar. 1870.
97 *L'Opinion Publique*, 28 Apr., 1870.
98 *La Gazette de Sorel*, 16 Feb. 1870.
99 *L'Ordre*, 7 May 1870.
100 Eg., *Le Journal de Québec*, 4 May 1870; *Le Journal des Trois-Rivières*, 16 May; *Le Courrier de St-Hyacinthe*, 7 May; *Le Courrier du Canada*, 4 May; *L'Union des Cantons de l'Est*, 2 June; *Le Pionnier de Sherbrooke*, 13 May; *Le Pays*, 4 and 9 May 1870.

and protégés at Red River had been satisfied, and that peace and tranquillity could now be restored.[101]

Whatever peace and tranquillity were restored in the spring only lasted till the arrival of the expeditionary force at Red River. Reports that Ontario volunteers were running about looking for Riel or Lépine to hang, had shot a Catholic missionary in the street,[102] and threatened to kill Bishop Taché himself,[103] rearoused Quebec's protective attitude toward the Métis. These volunteers seemed to have only one desire: 'to carry out an act of vengeance against the French and Catholic population.'[104] So, too, the Ontario settlers who followed them also seemed only to have gone 'to make harangues against Catholicism or against French preponderance in the North-West.'[105] And when Elzéar Goulet was murdered, how did the Ontario press react? 'A French Métis; that's one miscreant the less, adds the Daily Telegraph.'[106] Where, now, were the demands for justice that Ontarians had raised after the death of Scott? French Canadians wanted to hear the same for Goulet:

Unless the culprits are pursued vigorously and punished severely, unless Upper Canadians express a unanimous and energetic disapproval of this act of barbarism, there will be a dark feeling of dissatisfaction among the whole French and Catholic population of the Dominion. ... [107]

---

101 This rejoicing at the return of peace without a close examination of the details of the terms of peace was another sign that French Canada was still involved *only indirectly* in the Red River affair. Throughout the winter and spring, in fact, French-Quebec papers, pre-cisely because they were not closely and directly involved with the Métis, were able to appeal regularly to logic, legality, and calm in the handling of the uprising. They opposed force on the grounds that conciliation would be more effective. See, eg., *Le Courrier de St-Hyacinthe*, 16 Apr. 1870; *Le Journal des Trois-Rivières*, 18 and 21 Apr.; *Le Courrier du Canada*, 18 Apr.; *Le Pionnier de Sherbrooke*, 15 Apr.; *Le Pays*, 25 Apr.; *L'Ordre*, 3 Feb.; *Le Nouveau Monde*, 12 Apr. 1870. The same lack of engagement is, perhaps, to be seen in the ease with which papers accepted the idea that the Manitoba expeditionary force was a purely *imperial* force, or that it was being sent as a *peace* force only, to protect the Métis at their own request. Eg., *Le Courrier de St-Hyacinthe*, 28 Apr. and 3 May; *Le Journal des Trois-Rivières*, 11 Apr. and 5 May; *L'Ordre*, 5 May; *Le Nouveau Monde*, 3 May 1870, etc., etc.

102 *La Revue Canadienne*, VII (1870), p. 696.

103 *Le Journal de Québec*, 7 Oct. 1870. Also, *Le Courrier de St-Hyacinthe*, 13 and 20 Sept. 1870.

104 *Le Canadien*, 15 Mar. 1871.

105 *La Revue Canadienne*, VIII (1871), p. 800. Also, *Le Canadien*, 5 Oct. 1870; *Le Nouveau Monde*, 29 Dec. 1871.

106 *Ontario et Manitoba: la vérité* (n.p., n.d.), p. 5. Also, *Le Journal des Trois-Rivières*, 6 Oct. 1870; *Le Journal de Québec*, 23 and 28 Sept. 1870; *Ontario et Manitoba*, p. 2.

107 *L'Opinion Publique*, 13 Oct. 1870. See also *Le Franc-Parleur* (Montreal) 6 Oct. 1870.

Ontarians' silence about the death of Goulet seemed clear proof that their aims in the North-West were entirely anti-French and anti-Catholic. Their anger about the killing of Scott was provoked not by the act itself, but by the fact that he had been English and his executioners French.

And still, as during the winter of 1869–70, it was to what Ontarians did, to what Ontarians said, that Quebeckers responded. It was the renewal of Ontario demands for the arrest of the killers of Scott that led Quebec newspapers, in the early spring of 1871, to draw their readers' attention once more to the evil doings of Ontarians at Red River. Here were English Canadians still making a fuss about Scott, but ... 'They didn't get so excited when the Ontario volunteers massacred French Métis under the very eyes of their officers.'[108] And these misdeeds were still being perpetrated. Ontarians were still running a 'reign of terror' at Red River;[109] the clergy was regularly subjected to their abuse;[110] 'Scarcely two days go by together without some one of our people being beaten or chased by them.'[111]

Yet Manitoba and the Métis question had by this time fallen rather into the background of French-Quebec consciousness. Papers tended not to speak of them, unless provoked by Ontarians or Ontario press comment.[112] When they did speak of them, it was usually in the hope that things were calming down and that French Quebeckers would not have to be involved in any more conflicts regarding the West.[113] In 1872, when the Ontario government offered a $5,000 reward for the arrest of the killers of Scott, there were, to be

---

108 *Le Courrier de St-Hyacinthe*, 13 Apr. 1871. Also, *La Gazette de Sorel*, 19 Apr. 1871.

109 *Le Journal de Québec*, 13 Apr. 1871. Also, *L'Ordre*, 18 Mar. 1871.

110 *Le Monde*, 9 Jan., 3 and 4 Feb., 1871. (*Le Monde* was only *Le Nouveau Monde* under a new, temporary name. For a time it was also published as *Le Monde Canadien*. But it will henceforth be referred to here by its original name, *Le Nouveau Monde*.)

111 *Le Canadien*, 12 Apr. 1871. Also, *Le Journal de Québec*, 13 Apr.; *Le Courrier de St-Hyacinthe*, 21 Dec. 1871; *Le Nouveau Monde*, 8 July; *La Minerve*, 16 Oct. 1871.

112 Eg., note the absence of comment on Riel's role in organizing the Métis to resist a Fenian invasion in the fall of 1871: *Le Courrier de St-Hyacinthe*, *Le Journal des Trois-Rivières*, *La Gazette de Sorel*, *Le Franc-Parleur*, *L'Union des Cantons de l'Est*. *L'Union* even suggested that the Métis would have joined the Fenians but for the intervention of u.s. troops. *Le Pionnier de Sherbrooke*, 3 Nov. 1871, reported that Riel had rallied the Métis to the government, but seemed more interested in the effect of this news on the Toronto *Globe* than anything else. *Le Nouveau Monde*, *Le Franc-Parleur*, and *L'Union des Cantons de l'Est* all avoided discussing the behaviour of the Ontarians at Red River when it was raised in the spring of 1871. That April, when *Le Nouveau Monde* used the headline 'La Situation', it referred to the Paris Commune. *Le Pays*, for its part, had neglected the Métis problems ever since the outbreak of the Franco-Prussian war.

113 Even Riel's self-exile was praised as conducive to peace, to ending a crisis in which Quebec had been involved willy-nilly. See *La Revue Canadienne*, VIII (1871), p. 77. Also, *L'Union des Cantons de l'Est*, 24 Nov. 1870; *L'Evénement*, (Quebec), 27 Nov. 1871; *Le Courrier de St-Hyacinthe*, 30 Dec. 1871.

sure, protests in Quebec – but protests of a wearied sort. 'French Canadians are starting to be tired of these unseasonable demonstrations against their race which Ontario organizes on the slightest pretext.'[114] Indeed, so tired of all this did the Rouges seem to be that they did not even find it necessary to criticize the Liberal government of Ontario for what it had done. Some even defended it![115]

In the end, Quebeckers still couldn't take the Métis and the West all that seriously. 'We know how long a war can go on with these Indian races,' warned one paper, fearing that the Ontarians might push the Métis too far.[116] But at the same time, it seemed silly to give them a full-fledged provincial parliament. 'Just as in Spain, the Parliament is assembled and has begun to sit. ... There was a speech from the throne. ... Don't laugh; it may be more serious than we think.'[117] Why, Manitoba even had a sort of Indian counterpart of the House of Lords as well as a provincial police force and a court of Queen's Bench!

What a lot of big names for little things! That's local colour. We know that these savage peoples have big imaginations and that they like to call 'nation' a group of a few families. ... A few cases of beads would have satisfied them; it wasn't necessary to add all this menagerie.[118]

So, after a flurry of excitement, when Quebec seemed to be forced into the North-West affair by the accusations of Ontarians, attitudes returned, by 1871–2, to much what they had been at the outset. The Métis might be French and Catholic, and likely friends for the Quebeckers. But they were also half-savage, and their country was a wild and inhospitable one, which would not soon be settled, and which was already too much of burden on Canadian tax-payers.[119] Perhaps the Métis might have been forgotten altogether, if English-Canadian actions had not thrust them upon the consciousness and consciences of French Quebeckers again and again in the years that followed – and if events in the Maritimes had not added a whole new dimension of passion to the question of French and Catholic rights outside Quebec.

---

114 *L'Union des Cantons de l'Est*, 15 Feb. 1872. Also, *Le Pionnier de Sherbrooke*, 2 Feb.; *Le Journal de Québec*, 24 Jan.; *La Gazette de Sorel*, 14 Feb.; *Le Courrier du Canada*, 24 Jan. 1872.
115 *L'Evénement*, 29 Jan. and 14 Feb. 1872.
116 *Le Journal des Trois-Rivières*, 10 Oct. 1870.
117 *Le Franc-Parleur*, 6 Apr. 1871.
118 *L'Evénement*, 23 Feb. 1872. Also, 31 Jan., 14 Feb., 17 Apr., 3 May; *Le Nouveau Monde*, 21 Aug. 1872.
119 Hector Fabre, *Confédération, indépendance, annexion* (Quebec: L'Evénement 1871), p. 12; *Le Franc-Parleur*, 6 Apr. 1871; *Le Canadien*, 20 Jan., 3 Apr., 14 June, 25 Aug., 25 Sept., 9, 13, and 25 Oct. 1871.

V

LA QUESTION
MANITOBA-
BRUNSWICK

THE 1871 New Brunswick school law attracted very little attention, at first, in Quebec. Fewer than half of Quebec papers even mentioned it before the following year, and of those which did, most did so not in the spring, when the act was passed, but in July, when New Brunswick Catholics petitioned Ottawa for disallowance.[1] Even after that, the matter seemed of little account; in its year-end review of 1871, the *Courrier de St-Hyacinthe* observed that the year had brought French Canadians 'no great misfortunes to deplore', aside from the fact that Roman Catholics were being harassed by common school laws *in the United States*.[2] Many papers even failed to comment on Sir John A. Macdonald's January announcement that the government would not disallow the New Brunswick act.[3]

It was only when John Costigan brought the matter before the House of Commons in the spring of 1872 that French Quebeckers became fully aware of and concerned about it. What's more, the flurry of excitement which Costigan's motion provoked in the Quebec press died away when the Commons debate ended, and it was only when he came back to Ottawa with a new motion in May of 1873, that the New Brunswick school question regained prominence in Quebec.

Naturally, French Quebeckers sympathized with their co-religionists in

---

1 *L'Union des Cantons de l'Est*, 27 Apr. and 17 May 1871; *Le Pionnier de Sherbrooke*, 21 Apr., and *L'Ordre* commented on the bill itself, before reporting on the petition. But *Le Journal de Québec* (10 July), *Le Journal des Trois-Rivières* (27 July), *Le Nouveau Monde* (12 July) seemed to notice the affair only after the submission of the petition to Ottawa. *Le Pays*, though it carried regular dispatches from the *Moniteur Acadien* during the spring and summer of 1871, mentioned neither the bill nor the petition. *Le Courrier du Canada* was equally silent.
2 *Le Courrier de St-Hyacinthe*, 30 Dec. 1871.
3 Eg., *Le Franc-Parleur*, *L'Union des Cantons de l'Est*, *Le Pionnier de Sherbrooke*.

New Brunswick, considering the law 'unjust toward Catholics' because it deprived them of the right to send their children freely to the school of their choice and imposed upon them what amounted to an atheistic education.[4] At stake were 'religious rights, paternal rights, and the right of true freedom of conscience.'[5]

Beyond common sympathy with the New Brunswick Catholics, however, French Quebeckers were divided in their opinions. A minority, chiefly Liberals and extreme Ultramontanes, insisted that the New Brunswick school law must be disallowed because it was unconstitutional. 'Consider the Constitution from whatever angle you like; you'll never find anything in it but this: the rights of minorities are guaranteed against infringements by majorities. ... '[6] Section 93 of the BNA Act prohibited the abolition of school rights held by a minority at Confederation; the New Brunswick Catholics had had schools of their own which had been receiving tax support since 1858; therefore, the 1871 law was unconstitutional.[7]

Nevertheless, the Conservative majority seemed willing – at least in 1872 – to accept Macdonald's interpretation of the BNA Act. No New Brunswick law, he maintained, had ever established a separate school system with a legal right to tax support. Therefore, Catholic schools which did not conform to provincial government regulation were not covered by Section 93, whose wording only covered rights held 'by law' at Confederation. In his commons speech against the 1872 Costigan motion, Cartier not only supported Macdonald's interpretation but went so far as to say that the fathers of Confederation had never intended to give constitutional protection to Catholic schools in New Brunswick. 'In all our discussions on the subject of Confederation,' he said, 'there was never any question of the rights of Catholics in that province.'[8] It had to be admitted, therefore, that Ottawa had no right to disallow the act of 1871.[9]

---

4 *Le Courrier du Canada*, 1 May 1872; *La Minerve*, 11 May 1872; *Le Courrier de St-Hyacinthe*, 30 Jan. 1872; *La Gazette de Sorel*, 25 May 1872 and 17 May 1873; *La Revue Canadienne*, IX (1872), p. 479.

5 Pastoral letter of the Quebec bishops in council, quoted in *Le Courrier du Canada*, 16 June 1873. Also *Le Courrier de St-Hyacinthe*, 15 July 1873.

6 *L'Evénement*, 19 Feb. 1872.

7 *Le Journal des Trois-Rivières*, 6 Jan. and 8 Feb., 1872; *Le National* (Montreal), 23 May; *Le Nouveau Monde*, 3 Jan. 1872.

8 Tassé, pp. 734–5. It will be remembered that the Catholic character of some schools in New Brunswick was the result only of the autonomy which, in practice, the 1858 public school law left to local school boards.

9 *Le Journal de Québec*, 22 May 1872; *Le Courrier de St-Hyacinthe*, 16 May; *La Minerve*, 27 May; *L'Union des Cantons de L'Est*, 8 May; *Le Courrier du Canada*, 22 May; *Le Canadien*, 29 May 1872.

This was not a happy admission to have to make, for French Quebeckers did remain sympathetic to the Catholic cause. Was there no way out of the difficulty? Even if Macdonald and Cartier were right in saying that the text of the BNA Act did not give the desired guarantees, was it not at least consistent with the general spirit of Confederation that such minority rights should be protected?[10] This notion seems to have been behind an amendment to the Costigan motion proposed by P.-J.-O. Chauveau. Instead of disallowance, Chauveau asked for an address to the imperial parliament calling for an amendment to the BNA Act to introduce the desired protection for Catholic schools. This pleased the Bleu press, and there was widespread hope that the government would support the amendment.[11]

But the hope was to be disappointed. The ministry ended up giving its support to the much more innocuous amendment of Charles Colby expressing sympathy for the New Brunswick Catholics and a hope that their grievances would be redressed within their own province. To the opposition it appeared that the cabinet had surrendered to pressure from New Brunswick Protestants. 'The injustice is complete; the Catholic minority has been sacrificed by the Catholic Conservative leaders.'[12]

Nevertheless, most French-Canadian MPs supported the final amendment, and Bleu spokesmen saw important reasons for doing so. In the first place, compromise had practical advantages. To coerce the Protestant majority of New Brunswick would only create hostility, from which Catholics, as a minority, would be bound to suffer. Whatever happened at Ottawa, the ultimate administration of education in New Brunswick would depend on the provincial government, and if its 1871 law had been abolished through the obstinacy of Catholics at Ottawa, 'the resulting irritation would have been so great that the Catholics of that province, who are the minority, would have been unable to obtain an entirely satisfactory law for a long time.'[13]

But there was a much more important reason for limiting the federal role in this affair. If the position of the New Brunswick Catholics were to be settled through the intervention of the federal parliament, argued Cartier, a precedent would be set by which 'the fate of the Catholic majority of the province of Quebec would be at the mercy of the federal Parliament.' Quebec

---

10 *Le Courrier de St-Hyacinthe,* 10 Feb. and 25 May 1872; *La Gazette de Sorel,* 25 May; *Le Journal de Québec,* 22 May; *L'Opinion Publique,* 29 Feb.; *Le National,* 11 and 23 May 1872.
11 *L'Opinion Publique,* 30 May 1872; *La Minerve,* 27 and 31 May; *Le Courrier de St-Hyacinthe,* 25 May; *Le Journal de Québec,* 25 May; *Le Courrier du Canada,* 27 May; *Le Canadien,* 29 May 1872.
12 *Le National,* 1 June 1872. Also, *L'Evénement,* 31 May; *Le Nouveau Monde,* 3 June 1872.
13 *Le Courrier du Canada,* 7 June 1872. Also, 10 June; *La Minerve,* 1, 3, 5, 6 June; *La Revue Canadienne,* IX (1872), p. 480.

Protestants would be able to go to the Protestant-dominated federal parliament to upset the whole Quebec school system. Thus, the precedent of federal action in the New Brunswick affair, whether to disallow the provincial act or to procure a constitutional amendment in the provincial field of education, 'would throw us into the midst of all those dangers which we sought to avoid by Confederation.' Provincial control of education was a vital principle for French Canadians, claimed Cartier. 'I insisted very strongly on that in the discussions on the Union proposal, for I wanted the province of Quebec to have this right.'[14]

Cartier's arguments carried weight, and Bleu MPs and papers alike were willing to agree that 'it is in the interest of the province of Quebec that [Ottawa] not intervene in this affair. ... '[15] In fact, their attitude was still pretty much what Hector Langevin's had been at London in 1866: New Brunswick Catholics would have 'all our sympathy in the struggle they have just undertaken. ... Our voice is not strong, but we promise them to keep raising it on their behalf until they have obtained justice.'[16] But if one could raise one's voice in support of the Catholic cause, one could not support action that would threaten the autonomy of Quebec. To vote for the Colby amendment was a way of doing the former without doing the latter. It affirmed the rightness of the new Brunswick Catholic cause, but implied as well that the affair was, in the end, a New Brunswick concern.[17]

The New Brunswick legislature did not seem much affected by the resolution passed in the House of Commons. In 1872 it passed new legislation closing loopholes in the 1871 law. It was to ask for disallowance of this new legislation that Costigan proposed his next resolution at Ottawa in 1873. As they had done the year before, government supporters opposed federal intervention on the grounds that it might set a precedent 'authorizing the Protestant majority of the other provinces to come and demand changes in our own province.'[18] Who knew where it might not lead? – perhaps even to legislative union.[19] Even a compromise proposal that Ottawa should ask the imperial parliament to pass a declaration interpreting the BNA Act as

---

14 Tassé, pp. 752–3.
15 *Le Courrier du Canada*, 31 May 1872. Also, *Le Journal de Québec*, 22 May, 1 and 3 June; *L'Opinion Publique*, 30 May; *Le Courrier de St-Hyacinthe*, 16 May 1872.
16 *Le Pionnier de Sherbrooke*, 21 Apr. 1871.
17 This attitude can be seen as well in the tendency of papers to urge New Brunswick Catholics to fight on in their own behalf, and to refer to the matter always in the third person rather than the first – as *their* cause, *their* schools, and not ours. See, eg., *Le Pionnier de Sherbrooke*, 21 July 1871; *Le Journal de Québec*, 24 Jan. 1872; *Le Franc-Parleur*, 8 Feb. 1872; *L'Union des Cantons de l'Est*, 8 May 1872; Tassé, p. 734.
18 *La Minerve*, 24 Apr. 1873.
19 *Le Pionnier de Sherbrooke*, 23 May 1873. Also, *L'Union des Cantons de l'Est*, 21 May; *Le Courrier du Canada*, 16 May; *Le Courrier de St-Hyacinthe*, 17 May and 3 June 1873.

protecting the Catholic schools of New Brunswick was opposed by Hector Langevin:

It would be invoked against Lower Canada any day when there would be a wish to infringe upon our rights. It should not be asked from England & if asked the answer would be that we have no right to interfere in the constitutional rights of the Local legislature.[20]

Naturally, New Brunswick Catholics had the right to expect support from Catholic MPs at Ottawa, but the latter 'are not obliged, when all is said and done, to go on killing themselves over an impossibility. Their first responsibility is to see to the general welfare of the Confederation, and the representatives of Quebec must protect above all the interests of Quebec.'[21]

Despite these reasons for hesitation, the majority of French-Canadian MPs voted for the Costigan motion in 1873 and against the government. On the other hand, the fear of toppling the ministry, which led even the bishops to call for circumspection, overcame their zeal, and the issue was dropped (despite the best efforts of the Liberals) when Macdonald announced that the government would pay for an appeal to the courts to test the New Brunswick laws.

The excitement aroused by the Costigan motion had scarcely had time to subside, when French-Quebec emotions were stirred up anew by the arrest, in September, 1873, of the French Métis, Ambroise Lépine, for the 1870 killing of Thomas Scott. Lépine had been a member of the Red River provisional government in 1870, and when he was charged with the murder of Scott, Quebec's immediate reaction was to demand a complete and general amnesty of all participants in the Red River uprising. Indeed, French Quebeckers had never doubted that Ottawa was committed to such an amnesty,[22] and ever since 1870, demands that it be granted had been a regular response to news of anti-French or anti-Catholic activities in the West. Thus, the misbehaviour of Ontario volunteers in Manitoba brought the accusation that the federal ministers 'have ended up by giving in to the blind fanaticism of Upper Canada, and refuse to keep their just promise [to grant a general amnesty].'[23] Archbishop Taché gave assurances that the promise had been

---

20 Hector Langevin, telegram to the Bishop of Rimouski (Ottawa, 19 May 1873), in APQ, Langevin papers, box 5 (AP-L-12-5).
21 *La Minerve*, 24 Apr. 1873.
22 *L'Opinion Publique*, 8 Sept. 1870, reported that the amnesty was already on its way to Manitoba. See also, *L'Union des Cantons de l'Est*, 8 Sept. 1870.
23 *Le Canadien*, 7 Oct. 1870. Also, 4 Nov.; *Le Franc-Parleur*, 29 Sept. 1870; *Le Courrier de St-Hyacinthe*, 21 Dec. 1871.

made to him in person, and he urged French Canadians at Ottawa to put pressure on the government for its fulfilment.[24]

The certainty that an amnesty had been promised undoubtedly contributed to the intensity of the shock expressed when Lépine was arrested. 'We are clearly on the verge of a terrible crisis,' warned the *Franc-Parleur*, 'and the time has come for decisive action to do justice to an insulted and betrayed people.'[25] That the absence of an amnesty had permitted Ontarians to harass French-Catholic Métis with impunity, and that it was a *French* Métis who had been arrested now, made the granting of the amnesty particularly important to all French Canadians. 'On that point there can only be one opinion in Lower Canada,' claimed a leading Bleu paper.[26]

So much did Lépine's arrest provoke Quebeckers, that some papers which, in 1870, had condemned the 'rebellion' or 'insurrection' of the Métis now spoke of the 'so-called insurrection',[27] claimed there never had been a rebellion at Red River, and asserted, on the contrary, that the Assiniboians had acted in legitimate self-defence against illegal aggression by Canada.[28]

The excitement aroused by the arrest of Lépine was intensified by the election of Louis Riel to the House of Commons, his arrival at Ottawa in the spring of 1874, registration, and expulsion from Parliament. The whole affair embarrassed French-Canadian Liberals, for it trapped them between their feelings as French Canadians and their partisan loyalty to the government. *L'Evénement* hoped Riel would let them avoid the issue by resigning, and wished piously that Macdonald would admit to having promised an amnesty, so that Mackenzie could grant it.[29] In the House of Commons, Wilfrid Laurier took a similarly ambiguous position, supporting the appointment of a select committee to investigate whether or not an amnesty had really been promised, and hoping this would eliminate the need to vote on Riel's expulsion from the House .[30] But the bulk of the French-Quebec press, not being Liberal, could make a stronger stand on the issue. It accused the federal

---

24 A.-A. Taché to L.-R. Masson (16 Dec. 1872), in Gagnon Collection, Montreal Municipal Library: Typed copies of Taché letters, entitled A.-A. Taché, *Correspondance, 1870–1881*, p. 7. Also, the telegram from Taché to Rev. J.R. Deux (Fort Garry, 17 Apr. 1873), on pp. 40–1. Rev. Deux was a code name for Father Ritchot.

25 *Le Franc-Parleur*, 14 Oct. 1873.

26 *Le Courrier de St-Hyacinthe*, 7 Oct. 1873. Also, 14 Oct.; *Le Pionnier de Sherbrooke*, 24 Oct.; *L'Opinion Publique*, 2 and 9 Oct.; *Le Canadien*, 17 Oct.; *La Gazette de Sorel*, 4 Oct; *Le Courrier du Canada*, 13 Oct. 1873.

27 *Le Courrier de St-Hyacinthe*, 14 Oct. 1873.

28 *Le Courrier du Canada*, 13 Oct. 1873.

29 *L'Evénement*, 6 and 15 Apr. 1874.

30 Laurier's Commons speech of 15 Apr. 1874 is in Ulric Barthe, ed., *Wilfrid Laurier on the Platform* (Quebec: Turcotte et Menard 1890), pp. 22–3.

ministers of betraying Riel and delivering him up to Anglo-Protestant fanaticism by allowing the vote which expelled him.[31] This was a 'crying injustice', and it showed the need for granting immediately the long-promised amnesty.[32]

The hearings of the Commons select committee on the amnesty question served to provoke Quebec anger even further. The evidence revived memories of the aggressiveness of Ontarians, and of the way in which French-Catholic Métis has been harassed or persecuted by them. Especially telling was the testimony of Archbishop Taché, who recalled how Ontarians had begun picking on the Métis long before the fall of 1869, and how they had continued to persecute French-Catholic Manitobans after 1870.[33] Nor was Taché's account of his own role in the events of 1869–70 without its effect. 'One senses,' commented Joseph Cauchon, 'that this man of superior worth, brought back from Rome to pacify the North-West, was shamefully deceived by a government that needed his services and his influence.'[34]

The committee's final report seemed to confirm the 'bad faith' of the federal government in its dealings with both Taché and the Métis. 'The testimony presented to the North-West committee shows clearly that, from beginning to end, the French Métis have been shamefully betrayed by the Conservative leaders. They've been gulled and bamboozled mercilessly and unceasingly.'[35] Thus the Liberals, while Bleus in turn accused the Liberals of 'betrayal' for not granting the amnesty which, before coming to office, they had condemned the Conservatives for withholding.[36]

By the summer of 1874, then, Quebec's emotions were running high on the amnesty question. Even as the committee's report was being prepared, A.-A. Dorion wrote to Mackenzie to warn him of the need for action:

The sympathy for Riel and his companions is getting stronger and stronger in Lower Canada and it will soon be a difficulty in the way of any Government. It is I know [a]

---

31 *Le Journal des Trois-Rivières*, 20 and 23 Apr. 1874.
32 *Le Pionnier de Sherbrooke*, 24 Apr. 1874. Also, *Le Franc-Parleur*, 14, 17, 21, and 24 Apr.; *Le Journal de Québec*, 18 Apr.; *Le Nouveau Monde*, 13 Apr.; *L'Opinion Publique*, 23 Apr.; *L'Union des Cantons de l'Est*, 23 Apr. 1874.
33 Canada, Parliament, House of Commons, *Rapport du Comité spécial sur les causes des troubles du Territoire du Nord-Ouest en 1869–70* (Ottawa: Taylor 1874), pp. 8–9, 11–12, 28–9. Note also pp. 156–7. Taché's impact on Quebec opinion was increased by the publication, at this time, of his pamphlet, *L'Amnistie* (Montreal: Le Nouveau Monde 1874), which told the same story as his testimony. See, eg., p. 59.
34 *Le Journal de Québec*, 25 Apr. 1874. Also, 18 Apr. 1874.
35 *Au Pilori* (Quebec: L'Evénement 1874), p. 9.
36 *La Minerve*, 17 Apr. 1874; *Le Franc-Parleur*, 21 and 24 Apr. 1874. But see also *L'Union des Cantons de l'Est*, 20 Aug. 1874.

difficult question to deal with, but I hope you will find some means of disposing of it finally, otherwise it will constantly revive whether by the reelection of Riel or by the several trials to take place – and which I suppose will have no other result than to inflame [the] public mind.[37]

Dorion was right. The trial and conviction of Ambroise Lépine that October did further inflame the public mind. Lépine was seen in Quebec as an innocent victim, 'the representative of vanquished right struggling against brute force!'[38] His so-called trial was a scandal before world opinion; 'we're going to be considered, the Upper Canadians as frenzied sectarians of near-Iroquoian savagery, and we Lower Canadians as a bunch of imbeciles who don't understand anything about anything.' There must be not a commutation of sentence nor even an amnesty – 'because innocent people don't need amnesties' – but a complete halt to these fanatical persecutions of the Métis.[39]

When, in January 1875, the Governor-General commuted Lépine's death sentence to two years' imprisonment and loss of political rights for life, Quebec was far from satisfied. This was only another form of death – a 'juridical death' – that was being inflicted. 'The form of execution is less brutal, but it produces the same result.'[40] The three French-Canadian ministers at Ottawa must remind Mackenzie 'that an amnesty was necessary, that only such an act of justice and unqualified clemency for Lépine would satisfy the interests they are supposed to represent. ... '[41]

In light of this reaction to the commutation of Lépine's sentence, it is hardly surprising that Mackenzie's February proposal for an amnesty that excluded that three Catholic members of the provisional government[42] was not well received in Quebec. To be sure, Liberal Party faithful tried to express satisfaction,[43] but others were less easily pleased. Archbishop Taché published a new pamphlet to show that Riel and Lépine had been covered by the promise of amnesty, and wired to L.-R. Masson that he was 'not satisfied[;]

---

37 A.-A. Dorion to Alexander Mackenzie (Montreal, 10 June 1874), in PAC, Mackenzie papers on microfilm (M-197), pp. 529–30. See also, *L'Opinion Publique*, 9 Apr. 1874, and *Au Pilori*, p. 3.

38 *Le Journal de Québec*, 29 Oct. 1874.

39 *Le Franc-Parleur*, 6 Nov. 1874. Also, *La Minerve*, 28 Oct.; *Le Pionnier de Sherbrooke*, 30 Oct. and 6 Nov. 1874. See also the comment on the arrest of André Nault, in *Le Nouveau Monde*, 30 May 1874.

40 *Le Franc-Parleur*, 28 Jan. 1875.

41 *Le Courrier de St-Hyacinthe*, 28 Jan. 1875. See also *Le Journal des Trois-Rivières*, 25 Jan., 18 Feb.; *La Minerve*, 5 Jan. 1875; *Correspondances parlementaires; session fédérale de 1875* (Lévis: L'Echo 1875), p. 8.

42 The Irish member, who had participated in the 1871 Fenian raid, was banished for life, while the two French Métis (Riel and Lépine) were exiled for five years.

43 *L'Evénement*, 22 Jan. and 10 Feb. 1875.

amnesty promised not banishment.'[44] Conservative and Ultramontane papers were no more satisfied than he. This 'shadow of an amnesty',[45] they complained, was a 'disgraceful and dishonourable compromise'.[46] Mackenzie had shown himself to be 'more cruel than an Iroquois chief,'[47] and even the Liberal Le National had to admit the amnesty was not really satisfactory, though it tried to shift the blame for this from Ottawa to Westminster.[48]

Doubtless, there was a great deal of political point-scoring in all these complaints. Each party talked about the amnesty to make the other look bad. But the point was that this was thought to be an effective subject for such polemics in Quebec. For French-Quebec attitudes had come a long way from the indifference or hostility toward the Métis which had been expressed in 1869–70. The cause of the Métis was now being seen as a French-Canadian, a Quebec cause. A party which, in power, failed to deliver the amnesty could be accused of betraying French Canada and Quebec itself. In the 1874 election campaign, Quebec Liberals had attacked the Conservatives in this way, and had promised that they would grant an amnesty if elected. But once in office, complained the Bleus, these Rouge ministers had given in to their Grit colleagues, 'and they have thus made themselves guilty of betrayal toward the Métis and toward Lower Canadians, to whom they had promised to fight to the end for a complete and general amnesty.'[49] Clearly, both parties could be blamed, and that they were blamed showed that the amnesty itself had an importance for Quebec opinion. As early as November, 1874, the Conservative Courrier de St-Hyacinthe called for an end to quibbling about blame and a beginning to real action. It had to be admitted that both parties had acted badly. 'Sir John A. Macdonald, to avoid displeasing the Orangemen, whose grand master he used to be, shamefully abused Mr Cartier's good faith and betrayed the interests of the Conservative Party of the Province of Quebec.'[50]

---

44 A.-A. Taché to Masson (Feb., 1875), in Montreal Municipal Library, Correspondance, p. 77. The pamphlet was A.-A. Taché, Encore l'amnistie (St-Boniface: Le Métis 1875).
45 Le Courrier de St-Hyacinthe, 13 Feb. 1875.
46 Correspondances parlementaires, p. 9.
47 Le Franc-Parleur, 17 Feb. 1875. Also, Le Journal des Trois-Rivières, 15 Feb. 1875; Le Courrier de St-Hyacinthe, 11 and 18 Feb.; Le Courrier du Canada, 10 Feb.; L'Union des Cantons de l'Est, 18 Feb.; Le Pionnier de Sherbrooke, 19 Feb.; Le Nouveau Monde, 9 and 10 Feb. 1875.
48 Le National, 10 Feb. 1875.
49 Le Courrier de St-Hyacinthe, 13 Mar. 1875. Also, Le Franc-Parleur, 27 Feb.; L'Union des Cantons de l'Est, 28 Jan. 1875; Les Rouges et les Bleus devant le pays (Montreal 1875), pp. 2, 6, 7, 8–9, 10; Correspondances parlementaires, pp. 8–10.
50 Le Courrier de St-Hyacinthe, 14 Nov. 1874. Also, 30 Jan. 1875; Les Rouges et les Bleus devant le pays, p. 7.

While the dispute over the amnesty raged, the New Brunswick schools question was not forgotten. In fact, the first matter kept people aware of the second, for in both cases French Canadians saw persecution of people with whom they associated themselves. The harassment of Lépine and Riel reminded them that the New Brunswick Catholics were still suffering too. 'The wind of persecution is blowing through both of these provinces. In one, it's a war of religion; in the other, it's a race war.'[51]

The distinction made in that last statement between the *racial* issue in Manitoba and the *religious* issue in New Brunswick should be noted. From the beginning of the affair, and at least till the end of 1874, Quebeckers saw the New Brunswick issue as a religious and not a racial or linguistic one. They referred to the suffering New Brunswickers as their *co-religionists*, and not as their compatriots.[52] As in the 1860s, they seemed little aware even of the existence of an Acadian population, and if they did refer to it, it was in the third person, as a race distinct and separate from the French Canadians.[53] In his 1873 House of Commons speech, which is said to have been significant in swinging votes on the Costigan motion, Honoré Mercier spoke of his cause not as an Acadian one, but as 'the cause of the 100,000 Catholics of our sister province ... the cause of 1,500,000 Catholics from across the Dominion, who are represented by us in this house.'[54]

Quebec newspapers spoke of the fact that Catholic parents were required by their religion to give their children a Catholic education, and that to force them to send their children to 'atheistic schools' was unjust.[55] The New Brunswick school laws thus not only deprived Catholics of their religious liberty, but also constituted 'a persecution of the Church of God and ... banning of the teaching of the truth brought to the world by Jesus Christ.'[56]

---

51 *Le National,* 1 Oct. 1873. In the fall of 1873 Manitoba and New Brunswick were mentioned together as reasons for bringing down the Conservative government, and in the 1874 election campaign they were spoken of together again. See *La Gazette de Sorel,* 15 Oct. 1873; *Le Courrier de St-Hyacinthe,* 18 July 1874; L.-O. David, *Histoire du Canada depuis la confédération,* p. 80.

52 Eg., *La Gazette de Sorel,* 17 May 1873; *Le Journal des Trois-Rivières,* 23 Apr. and 23 July, 1874; *Le Courrier du Canada,* 16 June 1873; *Le Courrier de St-Hyacinthe,* 15 July 1873; *Le Franc-Parleur,* 28 Apr. 1874; *L'Evénement,* 22 July 1874; *La Minerve,* 4 Aug. 1874.

53 Only once, on 29 Feb. 1872, did *L'Opinion Publique* associate the Acadians and the French language with the school question. *Le Journal de Québec,* 24 Jan. 1872, mentioned the Acadians, in the third person, as a 'nationalité distincte', and as late as 25 Aug. 1874, *Le Franc-Parleur* was still informing its readers that there did exist an Acadian community in the Maritimes: 'un peuple à part et désirant vivre à part, au milieu des siens.'

54 Quoted in Robert Rumilly, *Honoré Mercier et son temps* (2 vols.; Montreal: Fides 1975), I, 83.

55 *Le Pionnier de Sherbrooke,* 21 Apr. 1871; *La Gazette des Familles,* III (1871–2), p. 208.

56 *Le Nouveau Monde,* 20 May 1873. Also, 15 May 1873; *La Gazette de Sorel,* 17 May; *Le Courrier de St-Hyacinthe,* 15 July; *Le Courrier du Canada,* 18 July 1873.

It was because this was essentially a religious issue that Ultramontane newspapers were the most uncompromising in discussing it, the most prolific in their commentaries, the most unwilling to condone compromises like the Colby amendment. In their eyes, the cause of the Catholic schools was nothing less than the cause of Truth.[57] The issues, as they discussed them, were not racial or linguistic, but lofty and philosophical: the jurisdictions of Church and State, the rights of parents and of the Church according to divine and natural law, the universal fight of the Church against secularism. They fought not as French Canadians but as Roman Catholics.[58]

This view of the New Brunswick affair began to change during the winter of 1874-5. The fall had brought the coincidence of two news reports that affected it: the trial of Lépine and the arrest of some Acadians (not just Catholics, but Acadians) for refusal to pay school taxes in New Brunswick. In both cases it appeared that not just the Catholic, but the French element was being singled out for persecution. Was it just a coincidence, then, that five days after announcing the Lépine verdict and the New Brunswick arrests in the same issue, the *Courrier de St-Hyacinthe* referred for the first time to 'les canadiens français métis et acadiens'?[59] or that only four days after reporting Chapleau's return from Manitoba, where he had defended Lépine, *La Minerve* made its first reference to 'our compatriots', rather than 'our co-religionists', in New Brunswick?[60]

The final crisis came in January with the violence at Caraquet. The villagers there were not just Catholics; they were Acadians, and the trouble in their community seems, more than anything else, to have made Quebeckers aware of their presence. Henceforth, the New Brunswick question, as Quebec understood it, would be not just religious, but linguistic or ethnic as well. It was now a matter of 'the Acadians of Caraquet',[61] of 'the French',[62] or even of 'the French Canadians of Caraquette'.[63] After this incident, Quebec newspapers would speak less of *co-religionists* in New Brunswick, and more of 'the French population'.[64]

---

57 *Le Journal des Trois-Rivières*, 1 Feb. 1872.
58 Ibid., 27 May 1872; *Le Franc-Parleur*, 16 May; *La Gazette des Familles*, 30 Aug. 1873. Note too *L'Opinion Publique*, 29 Feb. 1872.
59 *Le Courrier de St-Hyacinthe*, 29 Oct. and 3 Nov. 1874.
60 *La Minerve*, 13 Nov. 1874.
61 *Le Nouveau Monde*, 30 Jan. 1875.
62 Ibid., 3 Feb. 1875.
63 *La Minerve*, 15 Feb. 1875.
64 Eg., *Le Pionnier de Sherbrooke*, 5 Feb.; *La Minerve*, 25 Mar.; *Le Courrier de St-Hyacinthe*, 2 Feb. 1875.

The excitement of Caraquet was still in the air when John Costigan presented yet another motion to the House of Commons. This third resolution called for an amendment to the BNA Act, much as had the proposed Chauveau amendment of 1872. Like the earlier proposal, it provoked appeals to Catholic doctrine and calls for solidarity among Catholics in the defence of their New Brunswick co-religionists.[65] As in the past, these appeals were countered by articles emphasizing the responsibility of New Brunswick Catholics in their own cause,[66] and warning that federal action to obtain a change in the BNA Act now might open the way to future interference in Quebec's national autonomy. Liberals especially, now that their party had come to power, found much sense in this last argument, which the Conservatives had used in 1872 and 1873. After all, they claimed, 'in our desire to oblige this minority, we must not go so far as to ask the imperial government to put into question virtually all the guarantees which the constitution contains.'[67] Those who supported Costigan should remember that 'people who constantly stir up the religious question of the New Brunswick schools are digging the grave of Lower Canada's autonomy.'[68] The *non*-guarantee of minority rights had been, in a sense, a condition of French-Canadian acceptance of Confederation in 1867: 'in our own interest we enshrined in this constitution the inviolability of provincial autonomy.'[69]

Nor was this merely an argument of the party in power. The pro-Conservative *Journal des Trois-Rivières* expressed the same fear, and even the Quebec City Conservative organ was afraid that 'to help out in one province, we could expose the others to dangers or open the door to abuses.'[70]

Although this final Costigan motion was defeated, it had been discussed with more excitement than the first two. For the New Brunswick question was now firmly associated with the Manitoba question, and each reinforced the importance of the other. The Lépine commutation, the Caraquet affair, the Mackenzie amnesty, the Costigan motion – all these came virtually at once, were discussed side by side in the papers, until they became, in a sense, one single question: 'la question Manitoba-Brunswick'.[71] They were united

---

65 *Le Journal des Trois-Rivières*, 8 Mar.; *Le Courrier du Canada*, 17 Mar.; *Le Courrier de St-Hyacinthe*, 23 Feb. 1875; *Correspondances parlementaires*, p. 51.

66 *Le Journal de Québec*, 24 Feb. and 4 Mar. 1875.

67 *L'Evénement*, 1 Mar. 1875.

68 *Le National*, 13 Mar. 1875.

69 *Le Journal de Québec*, 18 Mar. 1875. Also, 24 Feb. and 4 Mar.; *L'Evénement*, 10 and 12 Mar. 1875.

70 *Le Journal des Trois-Rivières*, 8 Mar. 1875; *Le Courrier du Canada*, 1 Mar.; also, 8 Mar. 1875.

71 J.-B. Cauchemar, *L'Entente cordiale* (Montreal 1875), p. 26.

not only in time, but in significance: 'One is tempted to believe,' complained
Le Canadien, 'that there is an immense conspiracy against the French race in
the dominion. Trampled underfoot in Manitoba, crushed in New Brunswick,
we are threatened with annihilation.'[72]

As this last quotation suggests, there was coming to be an awareness in
Quebec of a French element in other parts of Canada, a sense that the element
was under attack, and a tendency to identify it with the French Canadians of
Quebec. After 1875, for example, the new awareness of the Acadians would
make Quebec papers sensitive to the existence of a language question in New
Brunswick, and lead them to complain of 'injustice to the French population'
when the New Brunswick government failed to publish official documents in
French.[73] As early as 1874, the tendency to identify other French-Catholic
groups with the French Canadians themselves had led to an attempt to
nominate Louis Riel as president of the national organization planned by the
great Montreal convention of St-Jean-Baptiste and related societies.[74]

This identification of the minorities with the French Quebeckers appeared
in the very language used to discuss them. In the past, the Métis and Acadians
had been referred to in the third person; by 1875, the first-person *we* and *us*
were appearing more and more frequently. 'We're despised ... we're trampled
underfoot, our most legitimate rights are not recognized. ... ' The cause of
the Métis was referred to as the cause of 'our nationality in Manitoba'. There,
as in New Brunswick, the majority sought to 'crush the French-Canadian
race and destroy its religion'. All French Canadians must face up to the threat:

Let us unite, otherwise we'll certainly fall victim to the most rabid fanaticism ever seen.
... Yes, once again, let us unite, and together let us call for justice. Let us put aside all
partisan spirit and work together to obtain our rights and our privileges.[75]

Partly because of this identification, the minority problems began to
produce frequent expressions of discontent with Confederation. Under the

---

72 *Le Canadien*, 3 Feb. 1875.
73 *Le Courrier de St-Hyacinthe*, 8 Mar. 1877. Also, *L'Opinion Publique*, 22 Mar. 1877.
74 *L'Opinion Publique*, 2 July 1874, and *Le Courrier de St-Hyacinthe*, 2 July 1874, gave two
    different accounts of the session. In any case, the attempt to nominate Riel failed.
75 *Le Franc-Parleur*, 15 Apr. 1875; C.J.L. Lafrance, *Nos divisions politiques* (Quebec: L'Evéne-
    ment 1873), p. 11; *L'Union des Cantons de l'Est*, 4 Feb. 1875; *Le Pionnier de Sher-
    brooke*, 6 Nov. 1874. Also, *L'Honorable J.A. Chapleau: sa biographie suivie de ses princi-
    paux discours* (Montreal: Senécal et Fils 1887), p. 54; *Le Nouveau Monde*, 22 and 30 Jan., 10
    Feb. 1875; *Le Courrier de St-Hyacinthe*, 8 Sept. and 29 Oct. 1874, 23 and 26 Jan., 2 and
    16 Feb., 11 Mar. 1875; *Le Journal des Trois-Rivières*, 4 Feb. 1875; *Le Canadien*, 30 Jan., 6
    and 17 Feb.; *L'Evénement*, 12 Mar.; *Le Courrier du Canada*, 26 Feb., 1875; *Correspon-
    dances parlementaires*, p. 11; etc.

existing régime, it was complained, 'we'll always be beaten by the majority on religious or national questions. ... ' Perhaps the problem was a 'clerical error or involuntary *omission*', which cause the letter of the BNA Act to fall short of its spirit. But in any case, 'it would be better to break up the confederation than to go on letting ourselves be mistreated in this way. ... ' The refusal to grant an amnesty, for instance, 'should be considered as proof that the English population does not possess that spirit of justice and conciliation which is necessary for the maintenance of Confederation.'[76]

As a matter of fact, this sort of complaint had been expressed as early as 1870, when it was claimed that Ontario agitation over the death of Scott 'could destroy the very existence of Confederation.' In 1872, Ontario's offer of a reward for the killers of Scott brought the warning: 'Confederation will become impossible before long.' And the failure to relieve the Catholic schools of New Brunswick was also said to be 'one of those affairs which could most easily break up the federal pact.'[77]

What was the meaning of these threats? And what was the significance of the growing tendency to identify with the minorities, which was behind them? Had Quebeckers entirely changed their notions since 1867? Had they ceased equating French Canada's future with Quebec's autonomy and come to see minority rights as essential to Confederation? It would be very rash to come to such conclusions.

In the first place, it should be remembered that rhetoric which cherished the minorities as compatriots and brothers, or which threatened that Confederation could not survive without respecting minority rights, could be very useful from a partisan point of view. A party out of office could score political points by criticizing the government for failure to protect the minorities. Bleus, furious at their 1874 electoral defeat, could speak of Rouge duplicity when the Liberals failed to take measures in office they had demanded in opposition. Liberals in opposition had already been able to criticize the Bleus for having accepted an inadequate federal arrangement or for failing to defend French and Catholic minorities. Things like the Costigan motions of 1872 and 1873 provided excellent opportunities, as well, for the Liberals to pose as

---

76 *Le Pionnier de Sherbrooke*, 24 Apr. 1874; *Le Courrier du Canada*, 1 Mar. 1875; *Le Courrier de St-Hyacinthe*, 29 Oct. 1874; *Le Nouveau Monde*, 4 Nov. 1874. Also, *Le Franc-Parleur*, 21 Apr. 1874; *Le Nouveau Monde*, 20 May 1873; *Le Pionnier de Sherbrooke*, 24 Apr. 1874; *Le Courrier de St-Hyacinthe*, 10 Nov. 1874; *L'Opinion Publique*, 22 Mar. 1877; L.O. David, *Histoire*, p. 51.
77 *Le Journal des Trois-Rivières*, 18 Apr. 1870; *L'Union des Cantons de l'Est*, 15 Feb. and 6 June 1872. Also, *L'Ordre*, 15 July 1871; *Le Journal de Québec*, 22 May 1872; *Le National*, 11 May 1872; *La Revue Canadienne*, IX (1872), p. 480.

champions of Catholicism, helping to rid themselves of the repugnant image of Rouge radicalism and anticlericalism.[78]

But beyond partisan rhetoric, what were the real feelings in Quebec, which political polemicists tried to exploit? If those polemicists thought they could make political hay by appealing to pro-minority sympathies, they must have recognized that such sympathies existed. But what was their nature, and their meaning?

These are not easy questions to answer, for by the mid-seventies there was a considerable amount of ambivalence in the expression of these feelings. If, for example, the first person was increasingly used in referring to the French-Catholic position outside Quebec, the third person was still frequent too.

One explanation for the evident ambivalence can be found in the notion that attacks on the minorities were only rehearsals or trials of strength that would eventually lead to an assault on the French-Canadian province itself:

Our turn will come in the period of persecutions which is beginning; we must expect it and prepare for it. ...

The enemy has begun by trying out his strength against the little provinces. The Catholic minority of New Brunswick has been the first victim, thanks to the cowardice of our leaders. Today it's the turn of the whole population of Manitoba and tomorrow it'll be ours.[79]

The motive of self-defence thus gave Quebec a direct stake in the outcome of the minorities questions. If she did not fight the enemies of Catholicism and of Frenchness in Manitoba and in New Brunswick, then she would ultimately have to face them at home. This was a sort of 'domino theory' of the minorities:

Today we are able to protect ourselves and protect our neighbours; if we lack courage, if our hearts fail us, we'll soon have what we'll have richly deserved; we'll be crushed in our turn because of our cowardice.[80]

But aside form this self-interested argument, one can find from an early date, and increasingly during the 1870s, the contention that Quebec, as *the* French-Catholic province, had an especial duty to defend French-Catholic groups, when they were endangered anywhere in Canada. Thus, when the

---

78 Eg., *L'Entente cordiale*, pp. 26–7; *La Minerve*, 1 Oct. 1873, 27 Feb. 1875; *Le Courrier de St-Hyacinthe*, 2 Feb. 1875; *Le Journal de Québec*, 4 Nov. 1874, 24 Feb. 1875; *Le Courrier du Canada*, 28 May 1873; *L'Evénement*, 14 Feb. and 3 June 1872; *Le National*, 11 May 1872, and 31 Oct. 1874; *Le Canadien*, 29 May 1872.

79 *Le Journal des Trois-Rivières*, 23 Apr. 1874. Also, *Le Pionnier de Sherbrooke*, 26 June 1874.

80 *Le National*, 29 Sept. 1873. Also, *Le Courrier de St-Hyacinthe*, as early as 10 Feb. 1872.

French Métis seemed to be singled out for harassment at Red River in 1870, we saw the response that 'the Province of Quebec will have only one answer: to protect and aid our brothers out there.'[81] Similarly, the crisis of 1872 was seen as a fight between 'New Brunswick, the persecutor, and Lower Canada, the defender of the oppressed'.[82] It was Quebec's role to uphold the cause of the minority:

They're counting on us; this is where the greatest part of the French and Catholic population lives, and naturally the minorities in the other provinces expect help from our influence.[83]

Quebeckers were thus 'the defenders of our faith in the confederation',[84] and because they had that role, the prime minister of their province must be seen as 'the principal representative of the Catholics in Confederation'.[85]

This view of Quebec as a province with a special mission to defend French and Catholic minorities in Canada not only explains the concern displayed for those minorities, but it does so in a way that is consistent with the autonomist approach of Lower Canadians toward Confederation in the first place. It enabled Quebeckers to express their natural sympathy for fellow French Catholics while retaining their fundamental belief that Quebec, after all, was the essential homeland of the French-Canadian nation.

It is not surprising, therefore, that this theme was repeated again and again. In his speech on the 1873 Costigan motion, Honoré Mercier asserted that it was most particularly the population of Quebec that demanded action on behalf of the New Brunswick Catholics, and he appealed especially to the Quebec MPs to do their duty by supporting the motion.[86] He might have added, as the *Courrier de St-Hyacinthe* was to say on another occasion, that the New Brunswick Catholics 'look to us to be their saviours.'[87] To defend the minorities, whether in the North-West or the Maritimes, was, in fact, Quebec's 'noble and lofty mission'.[88]

This interpretation of Quebec's interest in the minority questions is

---

81 *Le Journal des Trois-Rivières*, 18 Apr. 1870. Also, *La Revue Canadienne*, VIII (1871), p. 319.
82 *La Minerve*, 1 June 1872.
83 *Le Courrier de St-Hyacinthe*, 30 Jan. 1872.
84 *L'Union des Cantons de l'Est*, 6 June 1872.
85 *Le National*, 1 June 1872. Also, *La Gazette des Familles*, III (1871-2), p. 208.
86 In Rumilly, *Mercier et son temps*, I, 82, 84.
87 *Le Courrier de St-Hyacinthe*, 18 July 1874.
88 *Le Nouveau Monde*, 1 June 1874. Also, 17 Apr. 1874; *Le Canadien*, 8 Feb. and 17 Mar., 1875; *La Minerve*, 28 Oct. 1874, 22 Jan. and 11 Feb., 1875; *Le Courrier de St-Hyacinthe*, 8 Sept. 1874, 28 Jan. and 16 Feb. 1875; *L'Union des Cantons de l'Est*, 29 Oct. 1874; *Le Pionnier de Sherbrooke*, 29 Jan. 1875; *L'Opinion Publique*, 16 Dec. 1875.

consistent with a number of observations not yet fully considered. It would explain, for instance, why Quebeckers tended to become excited about the minorities only when attacks on the latter were brought forcibly to their attention, or when the minorities, having taken the initiatives in their own defence, appealed to Quebeckers for support. Because Quebec's role was that of defender of the oppressed, she was bound always to react rather than to take initiatives. Because she was not interested in the North-West for her own expansion, she had taken no steps in 1869 to ensure the entrenchment of the French fact there. Because she had not seen New Brunswick as part of her *own* country, she had not taken steps to ensure the position of French Catholics there. But when the Métis were attacked, and she along with them, when the New Brunswick Catholics appealed for help in restoring State support for their schools, then it was time for Quebec to react.

Because she was a *supporter* of the minorities rather than a sharer in their destinies, Quebec expected and urged them repeatedly to take action on their own behalf.[89] In 1874, while the New Brunswick schools case was before the courts, John Costigan feared that French-Canadian support would fall away unless a new initiative were taken by his Maritime co-religionists. He wrote to Bishop Sweeney of St John 'that a large number of Catholics, particularly among the French, will get discouraged if nothing be done this Session, and it will have a bad effect.'[90]

And yet, for the same reason, interest in the minorities seemed to fade away in periods when they were not embattled. Thus, while the Quebec press gave excited coverage to the various confrontations over the New Brunswick schools, it scarcely noticed the compromise solution by which the New Brunswick Catholics, without the knightly aid of Quebec, managed to improve their own situation.[91]

---

89 Eg., Cartier in Tassé, p. 734; *Le Pionnier de Sherbrooke*, 21 Apr. and 21 July 1871; *Le Journal de Québec*, 24 Jan. 1872; *Le Franc-Parleur*, 8 Feb. 1872; *Le Courrier de St-Hyacinthe*, 3 June 1873; *L'Opinion Publique*, 20 Aug. and 5 Nov. 1874; *L'Evénement*, 28 Oct. 1874 and 16 Apr. 1875; *Le Nouveau Monde*, 17 Apr. 1874.

90 John Costigan, letter to Bishop Sweeney (Ottawa, 3 May 1874), in PAC, John Costigan papers (MG 27, I, D5), vol. I.

91 *Le Courrier de St-Hyacinthe*, 24 Apr. 1875, reported that a compromise had been proposed but that its acceptance was doubtful. That August it failed to report the agreement at all. The same was true of *Le Courrier du Canada*. The pro-government *Journal de Québec*, 16 Aug., was pleased to report the 'règlement amiable' that would end the turmoil. The *Journal des Trois-Rivières* briefly reported the release of the Caraquet prisoners by the New Brunswick superior court (17 July 1876), though it made no comment. The previous summer it had been silent about the compromise agreement, as had *Le Franc-Parleur*, *L'Union des Cantons de l'Est*, *Le Pionnier de Sherbrooke*, and *L'Opinion Publique*. *Le Nouveau Monde* even insisted that the compromise attempt had failed, and that the New Brunswick Catholics were as badly off as ever (23 and 26 Apr., 6 and 19 Aug. 1875).

It is true that the 1876 Prince Edward Island election campaign, in which the introduction of common schools was a major issue, did provoke some anger in Quebec.[92] But when the island's common school bill was passed in 1877 without being disputed at Ottawa, Quebec newspapers let it go by without angry comment. In that same year, these newspapers, which had been so aroused when attacks had been made on French Catholics in the North-West, failed utterly to notice an amendment to the North-West Territories Act giving the French language the same official status in the Territories as it had in Quebec or Manitoba.[93] Nor, apparently, had they noticed in 1875, when the original territories act was passed with guarantees for a separate school system.[94] Good news, it seemed, was no news, as far as the minorities were concerned. Not their rights, but attacks upon their rights were what excited Quebeckers, calling them to play their role as defenders of the oppressed.

But if Quebec felt bound to protect the minorities against aggressions by Anglo-Protestant majorities, it followed that when those aggressions succeeded, Quebec suffered defeat. Thus, the treatment of Lépine was 'an insult ... to our province'.[95] The vote to expel Riel from the House of Commons had as its result 'to sacrifice the Province of Quebec.'[96] Quebec was 'humiliated' by its inability to nullify the New Brunswick school law,[97] and the refusal to grant a full amnesty to Riel and Lépine was a flouting of the earnest wishes of 'a whole province ... an entire people'.[98]

And if the province of Quebec suffered defeat, humiliation, and insult, at

---

92 *L'Union des Cantons de l'Est*, 24 Aug. 1876; *Le Courrier de St-Hyacinthe*, 22 Aug.; *Le Pionnier de Sherbrooke*, 1 Sept. 1876.

93 *Le Nouveau Monde* actually reported first, second, and third readings of the NWT bill without a single reference to the language provision. *Le Courrier de St-Hyacinthe* covered the session, but failed to mention the language provision, even in its May 3rd resumé of the session's work. The same was true of the *Union des Cantons de l'Est*, though its lead editorial on 3 May was about the session, whose debates it had covered right through. See also *Le Journal des Trois-Rivières*, *L'Opinion Publique*, and *Le Pionnier de Sherbrooke*, during the session and up to 4 May.

94 The provision for separate schools was mentioned by *Le Nouveau Monde* (20 Mar. 1875), together with a measure prohibiting distilleries in the territories, as very wise, and likely to produce excellent results. Other papers mentioned the territories bill without noting the separate schools provision (eg., *Le Courrier de St-Hyacinthe*, 27 Mar.; *Le Pionnier de Sherbrooke*, 9 Apr.; *Correspondances parlementaires*, pp. 55ff.), while still others, such as *Le Franc-Parleur* or *L'Opinion Publique*, failed even to mention the NWT bill, though they did deal with other aspects of the session.

95 *La Minerve*, 29 Jan. 1875.

96 *Le Journal des Trois-Rivières*, 23 Apr. 1874.

97 *L'Evénement*, 22 July 1874.

98 *Le Pionnier de Sherbrooke*, 29 Jan. 1875. Also, *Le Courrier de St-Hyacinthe*, 23 Feb. 1875.

whose hands was it done? Why, at the hands of her very partners in Confederation, her sister provinces, and above all, her old arch-rival, Upper Canada – Ontario.

Isn't it clear that this *banishment* is a tribute paid to Ontario fanaticism? And who pays this tribute if not Quebec, which asked for a complete amnesty?

The banishment is thus a victory for Ontario and a defeat for Quebec.[99]

Here we see how attitudes outlive the circumstances which give rise to them: the old tension and conflict which had made Upper and Lower Canada so uncomfortable under the Union carried over into Confederation itself, so that even events in the Maritimes or the prairies could be seen in terms of the old Canadas' struggle for dominance. Thus, we can see the 1871 New Brunswick school law blamed on the 'voracious fanaticism of those Upper Canadian gentlemen',[100] and the harassment of the Métis ascribed to Upper Canadian 'enemies of our race',[101] who wished to drive away the French and Catholic population of the North-West, in order to make that country over 'all English and Protestant'. They were driven not merely by blind prejudice, but by the expectation that an Anglo-Protestant West would side with Ontario and against Quebec in the federal councils at Ottawa. This would enable Ontario to 'dominate the confederation', to 'direct more easily the destinies of the Confederation along English and Protestant lines.'[102]

But we have already seen Quebeckers express the hope that a French-Catholic Manitoba would be *their* ally at Ottawa. Indeed, all the minorities could be useful supporters of the French-Canadian province, as Pierre Chauveau indicated in a speech of 1874: 'Within the limits of our Confederation, it is not impossible that the biggest Franco-Canadian province, Quebec, may one day owe its salvation to the Acadians of the Maritime Provinces or the Métis of Manitoba.'[103]

There was thus a double significance in the complaint that to accept the banishment of the French-Catholic Métis leaders was to 'force Quebec to submit to Ontario'[104] – and in each of the two senses it was a complaint against Confederation itself. First, by expelling the French-Catholic leaders, Ontario strengthened its influence in the West and hence at Ottawa, while Quebec,

---

99 *Le Courrier du Canada*, 10 Feb. 1875.
100 *L'Opinion Publique*, 29 Feb. 1872.
101 *Le Courrier de St-Hyacinthe*, 13 Feb. 1875.
102 *L'Opinion Publique*, 23 Oct. 1873.
103 Reported in *L'Opinion Publique*, 2 July 1874.
104 *Le Courrier du Canada*, 10 Feb. 1875. See also 15 Feb. 1875; *Le Courrier de St-Hyacinthe*, 21 Dec. 1871, 29 Oct. 1874, and 26 Jan. 1875; *Le Journal de Québec*, 4 Nov. 1874; *La Minerve*, 11 Feb. 1875; *Le Nouveau Monde*, 13 and 15 Apr., 1 June and 3 Nov. 1874, and 22 Jan. 1875; *L'Union des Cantons de l'Est*, 14 Feb. 1875.

losing an ally, was correspondingly weakened in the central organs of the dominion. Second, according to the Lower Canadian conception of Confederation, Quebec was allied with Ontario and the other provinces by the federal pact, bound to co-operate, to work together with them for the common good. Yet Quebec's responsibility as defender of the minorities obliged her again and again to fight against these other provinces. Could she long remain in a partnership in which she was continually obliged to engage in hostilities with her partners? As long as other provinces attacked their minorites, there would be a conflict between Quebec's responsibility to the partnership and her responsibility to the minorities. And as long as those attacks were successful, Quebec would feel beaten by her own partners and discontented with the partnership itself. Was this not the reason for the statements we have seen, that Confederation would break up if the minorities and their rights were not better respected?

While the Canadian minorities attracted French-Quebec attention mainly by their troubles, there was another minority that inspired a more constant interest: the Franco-Amerians. For a long time, of course, that interest had been negative – a desire to halt the emigration from Quebec and to bring home, if possible, those who had already gone to the United States. This desire had been based, in large part, on the assumption that those who went abroad would inevitably lose their language and their faith, and become detached from the French-Canadian nationality. Yet, at an early date, there began to appear indications that the French-Canadian identity was, in fact, being maintained in New England. Thus, in 1869, it was noted that the national holiday had been celebrated by a number of Franco-American communities. 'This shows,' commented a Sorel editor, 'that those who leave us form part of the élite of the Franco-Canadian nationality.'[105]

It began, in fact, to be recognized that emigration was a *fait accompli* which must be accepted willy-nilly, and that most emigrants, moreover, remained true 'to the faith and traditions of the homeland.' Rallied by their own newspapers, led by priests from Quebec, the Franco-Americans had proved able to 'keep intact, beyond our borders, the honour of the French-Canadian name, to carry on our apostolic mission and keep alive the traditions of our glorious past. ...'[106] Saint-Jean-Baptiste Societies had been founded throughout New England, and the 1871 Franco-American national convention at Worcester, Massachusetts, demonstrated the vitality of their patriotism.[107]

---

105 *La Gazette de Sorel*, 14 July 1869.
106 *Le Pionnier de Sherbrooke*, 25 June 1869.
107 *La Gazette de Sorel*, 4 Oct. 1871; *Le Courrier du Canada*, 4 Aug. 1871; *La Revue Canadienne*, x (1873), p. 525.

French Quebeckers followed with increasing regularity and increasing optimism the progress of French Canadianism and of Catholicism in the United States. By 1872, *L'Opinion Publique* carried a 'Bulletin américain' in every issue, and other papers too were on the look-out for Franco-American successes.[108] In 1874, at a time when the amnesty crisis was casting a shadow over the French-Catholic future in the Canadian North-West, some people were even predicting a French-Canadian takeover of parts of the U.S.:

Their development has been such during the last ten years, that they are on the way to Frenchifying certain states, Frenchifying the shores of the magnificent Lake Champlain, winning back by a peaceful invasion what was lost to us by the chance of arms. ... [109]

Optimistic interest in the Franco-Americans received much stimulus in June of 1874, when delegates from all over Canada and the U.S. met at Montreal to celebrate St-Jean-Baptiste day and to hold a national convention. Following from an invitation to the Franco-American patriotic societies to hold their annual convention back in the homeland that year, the affair always remained U.S.-oriented. Though delegates came from east and west, it was those from the south who received the warmest welcome. 'But those whom we welcome most of all are the delegates who have come from all parts of the United States. ... '[110] Thus *Le National.*

True, much of the interest in the Franco-American delegates was associated with a hope that they would discuss repatriation to Quebec. But while the convention did give some attention to repatriation, it gave much more to the keeping alive of the nationality in the U.S. itself.[111] So did *Le Nouveau Monde*, which welcomed the Franco-American delegates (apparently forgetting those from other parts of Canada), and hoped that this gathering would reinforce their determination to retain their nationality even on foreign soil.[112] Certainly, when Montrealers saw their bands and their societies marching proudly with banners flying in the St-Jean-Baptiste parade, and when they heard the enthusiasm of their convention oratory, they could hardly doubt that that determination was strong.[113]

---

108 *Le Bulletin de l'Union-Allet* (a monthly newsletter for old boys of the papal Zouaves) carried a regular report on the progress of Catholicism in the U.S. See also, eg., *Le Courrier de St-Hyacinthe*, 8 Sept. 1874; *Le Pionnier de Sherbrooke*, 17 July 1874.
109 *La Revue Canadienne*, XI (1874), p. 552.
110 *Le National,* 24 June 1874.
111 See account of Chauveau's speech in *L'Opinion Publique*, 2 July 1874.
112 *Le Nouveau Monde*, 22 June 1874.
113 Sixty-five out of eighty U.S. associations had come to the fête, and in the grand June 24th parade, they were the only ones from outside Montreal itself to be represented *en masse*, with marching bands and floats. See the report in *L'Opinion Publique*, 2 July 1874.

At all times, interest in the Franco-Americans was hardly to be wondered at. They were a people created by contemporary emigration from Quebec, not only akin to the Quebeckers, but transplanted Quebeckers themselves. And if, by 1875, French Quebeckers could speak of the Métis or the Acadians (people separated from them by history, geography, and more) as bound up in the French-Canadian national cause, how much more naturally could they speak of Franco-American cultural survival as 'the future of *our* race in the States'![114] So they sent both money and priests to their American compatriots, and P.J.O. Chauveau told them at the Montreal convention that 'our role toward you is the one that France, our old mother-country, played for us.'[115]

Such a role was at least partly that of protector; and indeed, the Franco-Americans had need of help against many of the same difficulties that afflicted the minorities in Canada. The problem of universal common schools, for example: 'Here we are up against an overwhelming Protestant fanaticism,' complained a Franco-Amerian to readers of a Quebec review.[116] And he could be sure of the same sympathies which had gone to the New Brunswick Catholics: 'It's certainly a sad commentary on liberty in the United States, this harsh necessity which weighs on Catholics to make enormous sacrifices in order to raise their children in the faith of their fathers. ... '[117]

The Franco-Americans, for their part, showed concern about the minority questions in Canada. Thus, the Massachusetts newspaper, *Le Travailleur*, reported at the beginning of 1875 that a public rally had recently been held at Worcester to demand a pardon for Lépine and an amnesty for all the Métis. Louis Riel, addressing the meeting, had thanked the French Canadians both of Quebec and of the States for their support. It was consciously that he had put the two groups together, for, he believed, 'we are moving toward the consolidation of all the elements of our race.'[118]

This notion of a pan-North-American consolidation of French Canadians must influence our appreciation of the concern felt by Quebeckers for the Métis and the Acadians. That concern, and the feelings of sympathy for and solidarity with those two groups, were not necessarily dependent on a common citizenship in the Dominion of Canada or on any understanding of the particular terms of Canadian confederation. For the same feelings were apparently felt with regard to French Canadians in the United States. The

---

114 *Le Courrier du Canada*, 11 Aug. 1875. Emphasis added.
115 Reported in *L'Opinion Publique*, 2 July 1874.
116 *La Gazette des Familles*, III (1871–2), p. 548.
117 *Le Courrier de St-Hyacinthe*, 5 Apr. 1870. Also, 7 Apr. 1870 and 30 Dec., 1871; *Le Nouveau Monde*, 25 Feb. 1875.
118 Reprinted in *Le Courrier de St-Hyacinthe*, 5 Jan. 1875.

limits of French Canada were wider than those of the dominion, 'from Acadia to the Pacific and on the shores of the majestic Lake Champlain as on the charming banks of the Mississippi.'[119] The decision of the 1874 convention to found a 'Union Canadienne-française de l'Amérique du Nord' was itself an expression of this idea.[120]

But if all North America was a place for French Canadians to stand, Quebec had still a special place. Here was the centre of the nationality, the metropolis of the French North American empire. For it was an empire, was it not? – formed of a French-Canadian province and a number of 'French colonies'.[121] How could it have been clearer than on 24 June 1874, when Montreal became 'the meeting place and the home of thousands of French Canadians, come from all parts of the American continent to fortify their patriotism and their religious and national faith in a common embrace, a family celebration'?[122] The province of Quebec was the 'impregnable bulwark of the nationality' to which the others had had to return to strengthen their French Canadianism.[123]

And so, after all this impassioned voyage among the minorities, we return to the preoccupation of 1864; the one place where French Canadians were a majority, whose autonomy must always be their basic hope: the province of Quebec.

119 *La Revue Canadienne*, x (1873), p. 525.
120 *Le Courrier de St-Hyacinthe*, 2 July 1874. Also, *Le Pionnier de Sherbrooke* , 3 July 1874;
    La Revue Canadienne, xi (1874), pp. 475, 554.
121 *La Revue Canadienne*, x (1873), p. 214.
122 Ibid., xi (1874), p. 475.
123 Ibid., p. 551. Also, *Le Courrier de St-Hyacinthe*, 27 June and 2 July 1874; *Le Franc-Parleur*, 3 July; *L'Opinion Publique*, 25 June and 2 July 1874; *Le Pionnier de Sherbrooke*, 29 Jan. 1875.

VI

THE
FRENCH-CANADIAN
PROVINCE

THE identification of French Canada with Lower Canada, which so much influenced French-Canadian attitudes toward Confederation, continued to shape opinions under the new régime. The Province of Quebec was seen as the geographical and political expression of the French-Canadian nationality, as a French-Catholic province and the French-Canadian homeland. The expression *French Canada* was still used to mean a geographic area, because that area, Quebec, was seen as essentially French-Canadian.[1] Thus: 'Lower Canada wants to remain French and Catholic, and will resist any attempt at fusion.'[2] Her French-Canadian character made Quebec unique in the confederation: 'Our national institutions, our customs, our civil laws are not the same as the civil laws and national institutions of the other Provinces of the confederation.'[3] Indeed, it was precisely because of the 'particular situation and exceptional interests of Quebec' that a federal rather than legislative form of union had been necessary in the first place.[4] The federal form had ensured that Quebec's parliament would be 'the epitome, the result, the last word, the essence of our liberties, and the very embodiment of our national, civil, and religious autonomy. All our deep-seated affections, all our dearest aspirations ... are focused on Quebec,'[5] In short:

The Province of Quebec is truly a New France, grand-daughter of the Church,

---

1 Eg., Honoré Beaugrand, *Jeanne la fileuse* (Fall River, Mass. 1878), p. 8.
2 *Les Rouges et les Bleus devant le pays*, p. 5. Also, p. 4.
3 *Le Courrier de St-Hyacinthe*, 8 Sept. 1874.
4 Wilfrid Laurier, speech in the Quebec legislature, 24 Nov. 1871, in Ulric Barthe, ed., *Wilfrid Laurier à la tribune* (Quebec: Turcotte et Menard 1890), p. 19.
5 *La Minerve*, 4 Dec. 1869. Also, *La Revue Canadienne*, xx (1884), p. 249; Oscar Dunn, *L'Union des partis politiques dans la Province de Québec* (Montreal: G.E. Desbarats 1874), p. 14.

governed by virtue of her mother's laws, having her own institutions and speaking a particular language which gives her a distinct national character.[6]

As these passages indicate, Quebec was made unique by far more than the French language and Catholic schools. Her political institutions and her special legal system opened to her people dimensions of French-Canadian life quite impossible for minorities, even in bilingual provinces like Manitoba. Only in Quebec could French Canadians say that 'we still keep alive the customs, the language, and the civil laws of our first mother-country. ... '[7] It was this civil code which secured Quebec's autonomy, which distinguished French Quebeckers 'from the other groups in the confederation and keeps alive among us the vital forces of the nationality.'[8]

Since Quebec was the particular homeland of the French Canadians, those who left it could be thought of as going into exile; and this was true of those who went to other Canadian provinces, as well as of those who left for the United States. 'If we sometimes take notice of the French-Canadians who emigrate to the United States or to the North-West,' wrote Benjamin Sulte, 'it's only to lament this abandoning of the native land.'[9] Indeed, a province like British Columbia was still to be thought of as a place for missions and hardships, for dedicated nuns, who left their homeland 'for a foreign country where they labour an often barren soil.'[10] No doubt the North-West, like New England and the Mississippi valley, contained French-Canadian colonies; nevertheless, to get to any of these places French-Canadians had to 'leave our country.'[11]

Because Quebec was the home of the French-Canadian nation, emigration from Quebec was frowned on as weakening that nation. For even if the emigrants managed to retain their language and religion abroad, their absence was a loss to Quebec: 'United all together, we can accomplish great things;

---

6 Philippe Masson, *Le Canada-Français et la Providence* (Quebec: Brousseau 1875), p. 52. Also, Charles Thibault, *Hier, aujourd'hui et demain: origines et destinées canadiennes* (n.p., 1880?), p. 10; *L'Opinion Publique*, 2 July 1874; *Le Pionnier de Sherbrooke*, 19 June 1874 (on the St-Jean-Baptiste); *Le Franc-Parleur*, 18 Apr. 1872 (article headed 'Canada français Province de Québec'); *La Gazette de Sorel*, 6 May 1871 (on Alsatian emigration); *L'Union des Cantons de l'Est*, 3 Mar. 1870; *La Vérité* (Quebec), 22 Sept. 1881; *La Revue Canadienne*, XVII (1881), p. 7, and XX (1884), pp. 375–6.

7 Oscar Dunn, *Pourquoi nous sommes français* (Montreal: La Minerve 1870), p. 8.

8 *Le Journal des Trois-Rivières*, 8 July 1886.

9 Benjamin Sulte, *Histoire des Canadiens-français, 1608–1880* (Montreal: Wilson et Cie 1882), VII, 155.

10 *La Revue Canadienne*, XIV (1877), p. 906: 'pour venir en pays étranger arroser de leurs sueurs une terre souvent ingrate.' Also, p. 845; *Le Courrier du Canada*, 2 Feb. 1872.

11 *La Minerve*, 26 June 1874. Also, *L'Evénement*, 3 Apr. 1880; Patrice Lacombe, *La Terre paternelle* (Montreal: Beauchemin et Valois 1871), p. 14.

dispersed to the four corners of the continent, our efforts are half paralysed.'[12] Ferdinand Gagnon took up this theme at Montreal in 1874, when he told the National Convention that French Canadians must become strong by concentrating themselves in Quebec. And Oscar Dunn told the same gathering:

How much strength, gentlemen, we scatter to the winds! And how much more powerful would we be if we were all grouped together in this province of Quebec, which is vast enough to hold a great nation and rich enough to support it. Our dispersion is our principal national problem.

It was inevitable that this should be so, for the first necessary condition of national life was for a people to have a defined territory. 'A homeland is a territory bounded by a frontier: let us choose what ours is to be.' Such a choice would produce palpable results, for in an electoral system of government, like the dominion parliament, concentrated numbers were all-important. Thus, Dunn told the minorities, 'If you were all with us in this province, your influence on Parliament would be direct and immediate.'[13]

Emigration from Quebec was thus a vital problem for the French-Canadian nationality, and the need to stop it, to retain the French-Canadian population within the borders of its proper homeland, underlay the great national projects of the post-Confederation decades.[14] The colonization movement, for example, popular, no doubt, because it fitted in with the agriculturalist leanings of leading intellectuals, had another obvious appeal in that it aimed, by filling the national territory with French Canadians, to ensure to the French-Canadian race 'the preponderance which it should have had its heart set on keeping in a land which it was the first to clear and settle.'[15] The settlement of Quebec's territory was, indeed, a national duty. 'In the colonization of the immense fertile areas which our Province contains is to be found, at least in part, the key to our future.'[16]

---

12 *L'Opinion Publique*, 25 June 1874.
13 Speeches reported in *L'Opinion Publique*, 2 July 1874. See also *Le Canadien*, 14 May 1873.
14 Marcel Hamelin refers to the fear of emigration as 'la hantise' (in *Les premièrs années*, ch. 3). *Le Pionnier de Sherbrooke* claimed, 28 July 1871, that emigration was the only real problem facing Quebec. See also Beaugrand, *Jeanne la fileuse*, p. 190.
15 *Le Canadien*, 3 May 1872 (letter from Bishop Langevin of Rimouski).
16 Ibid., 15 Jan. 1875. Also, *La Revue Canadienne*, XI (1874), pp. 548–54, and XVII (1881), p. 255; *L'Opinion Publique*, 25 June and 2 July 1874; *Le Pionnier de Sherbrooke*, 5 Feb. 1875; *Le Courrier du Canada*, 9 Aug. 1871; *L'Etendard* (Montreal), 13 May 1884; *Au Nord* (St-Jérome 1883), p. 3; E. Hamon, *Exil et patrie* (Montreal: Beauchemin n.d.), last act; Joseph Tassé, *Aux Canadiens Français émigrés* (Ottawa: Le Canada 1883), advertisement on back cover. *L'Union des Cantons de l'Est*, 24 Oct. 1867, considered colonization a matter of the first importance 'pour la conservation de notre autonomie nationale', and *Le*

Colonization, while attractive from an ideological point of view, was certainly not the only economic project that preoccupied Quebec's leaders after Confederation. Industrial development also attracted the attention and efforts of both politicians and journalists. But here too the motive of building up the French-Canadian population within its proper homeland was vital. Thus, in late 1871, the provincial parliament set up a select committee on industrial development, at the suggestion of the MPP for Bagot, who told the assembly that industrial jobs were the only means of keeping people from emigrating. *Le Courrier de St-Hyacinthe* applauded the move:

A certain number of our compatriots, finding no jobs where there is no manufacturing, emigrate to the manufacturing centres of the United States.

To keep these compatriots among us, we must develop our industry, so they can find here the sort of jobs they now seek abroad.[17]

In the same vein, the 1874 National Convention passed a resolution calling for the promotion of industrial development in Quebec on the grounds that 'the establishment of manufacturing in Lower Canada is indispensable for the public prosperity and the advancement of French Canadians in particular, as well as to bring back those who would like to repatriate themselves.'[18]

Along with colonization and industrial development went commercial expansion, and particularly the expansion to western Canada. *La Minerve* had explained in 1869 that construction of a Pacific railroad would be an extension of the St Lawrence transportation system, and would draw through the French-Canadian province the rich commerce of distant lands: the grains of the prairies and the splendours of the Orient. This was, after all, the natural conclusion of the reasoning that had supported Confederation itself. The CPR, by extending the commercial system of Quebec, would bring to that province the jobs and prosperity that would keep French Canadians within their own homeland:

Journal des Trois-Rivières, 29 Sept. 1868, claimed that the power to promote colonization was the most important of all the jurisdictions of the provincial government. The Société de colonisation du diocèse de Montréal, in its *Projet ... pour coloniser la vallée de l'Ottawa et le nord de ce diocèse* (Montreal: Imprimerie canadienne 1879), p. 3, wrote that the idea of colonization inspired exalted feelings of patriotism among French Canadians throughout the province; and the Curé Labelle wrote to Montreal's Archbishop Fabre in 1880: 'Cette œuvre de colonisation plaît à tout le monde. C'est la seule œuvre qui dans ma paroisse n'a rencontré aucune critique' (Montreal archiepiscopal archives: file on colonization).

17 *Le Courrier de St-Hyacinthe*, 12 Dec. 1871.

18 Reported in *L'Opinion Publique*, 2 July 1874. See also *L'Evénement*, 31 Jan. 1872; *Le Courrier de St-Hyacinthe*, 19 and 30 Dec. 1871; *L'Opinion Publique*, 5 Oct. 1871; *Le Journal des Trois-Rivières*, 15 July 1880; Beaugrand, *Jeanne*, pp. 172–3.

We'll export the products of British Columbia and Manitoba to the European markets and we'll import for them the manufactured products they'll need. Our shippers and importers will have all the profits.[19]

Indeed, the very logic of geography dictated that Quebec should be the beneficiary of western expansion:

We control the province which will be the natural outlet for the population of the North-West; the great enterprise of the Pacific railroad is only completed by the St Lawrence and its ports, and we must necessarily profit from our position.[20]

Thus, the Canadian Pacific Railway, which has been seen by so many English-Canadian historians and writers as a Canadian national dream, a moral as well as physical force binding all Canada together as a single nation, had in Quebec a particular importance for the *French*-Canadian nation. Not that French Quebeckers wanted to be bound with the West in any direct sense. Indeed, they asked, 'what have we to do in the West? doesn't our sphere of activity end at Ottawa?' But the *commerce* of the West was a different matter; it was 'the only traffic which can turn the North Shore and Northern Colonization Railroads into remunerative enterprises, while making the cities of Montreal and Quebec the entrepôts for the western trade.'[21] To obtain that commerce was thus, for the government of Quebec – for French Canadians – 'the only true provincial policy, the only true national policy.'[22]

The success of such a policy depended on obtaining control of the CPR by Quebec interests – or at least on obtaining its eastern terminus for Quebec. This was ultimately achieved when the Chapleau government sold the western part of its Quebec, Montreal, Ottawa and Western Railway to the CPR.[23] But it had always been an essential preoccupation. Indeed, so important had it seemed, that in the federal elections of 1874, the Bleus

---

19 *Le Courrier de St-Hyacinthe*, 14 Mar. 1872. Also 27 June 1872, and 25 Feb. 1875.

20 *La Revue Canadienne*, XVII (1881), p. 122. Also, *L'Union des Cantons de l'Est*, 6 June 1872; *La Gazette de Sorel*, 19 Aug. 1871.

21 Louis Beaubien, *Les Chemins de fer, nos communications avec l'Ouest* (n.p., n.d. – Quebec? 1875?), pp. 5, 32–3.

22 L.-G. Desjardins, *Discours ... sur la résolution relative à la vente de la partie ouest du chemin de fer Québec, Montréal, Ottawa et Occidental* (Quebec 1882), p. 28. Also *Le Courrier de St-Hyacinthe*, 27 June 1872; *L'Opinion Publique*, 12 Mar. 1870; *L'Union des Cantons de l'Est*, 16 July 1881; *Lettres au peuple* (Montreal: La Minerve 1873); J. Blanchet, *Discours de l'hon. J. Blanchet, secrétaire de la province de Québec, sur l'autonomie des provinces* (Quebec: A. Côté et Cie 1884), p. 27.

23 J.A. Chapleau, speech in the assembly, 28 Mar. 1882, in *L'Honorable J.A. Chapleau: sa biographie suivie de ses principaux discours* (Montreal: E. Senécal et Fils 1887), p. 198; Desjardins, *Discours*, p. 27.

confronted the Pacific scandal boldly by appealing to this interest. It was true that Sir Hugh Allan, the Montreal shipping tycoon, had committed a fault; true, he had given large sums of money to Conservative Party leaders in the last election campaign; true, too, that shortly after winning the elections the Conservatives had awarded the CPR contract to Allan's company. But after all, 'is it for Lower Canada, whose cause he was knowingly serving as well as his own, to complain?' No, no, those who opposed Allan opposed French Canada, and Quebec voters had only one choice: '"The Pacific railroad for Lower Canada with Sir Hugh Allan at its head!" With this slogan we'll defeat the enemies of Montreal, the enemies of Lower Canada, the enemies of our nationality. ... '[24]

The Bleus were able to use the issue of the railroad terminus more effectively in opposition. For Ontario, the arch-rival of Quebec, wanted the terminus for itself, and the decision to which the Mackenzie government leaned seemed to give too much to Ontario's desires at the expense of Quebec. 'Once more, alas,' lamented a Conservative polemicist, 'Lower Canada has been sacrificed in an outrageous manner!'[25]

But French Canada's interest in the railroad question was not left to the care of the federal government. The provincial government, by ensuring completion of the Québec, Montréal, Ottawa et Occidental, guaranteed that the CPR line would come down at least to Montreal. In this, it was acting as the national government of French Canada, so that the Q, M, O & O could be considered 'a national property and a national enterprise', a monument, even in its very sale to the CPR, to 'the wisdom, prudence and patriotism of the statesmen of the French-Canadian nationality.'[26]

The important point in the above quotations is the way in which they all identify the material interest of Quebec with the interest of the French-

---

24 *Lettres au peuple*, p. 6. Of course, this was base political interest exploiting national aspirations, and it did not save the Conservative government. But the very use of this tactic by Bleu propagandists is significant. It surely requires a very strong national feeling to tolerate a party's appeal to overlook public corruption for the sake of the nation – and a conviction among party strategists that such a strong national feeling exists to induce them to make such an appeal. Yet Liberal strategists seem to have shared the conviction, for they, at times, attempted to exploit national feeling in a similar way. Thus, an 1885 proposal by the federal government to subsidize construction of a railroad from Montreal through the Eastern Townships and U.S. territory to St John and Halifax angered Quebec City interests, which would be bypassed by such a line. But when the Quebec City newspaper, *L'Electeur*, expressed their anger on 12 June 1885, the loss of Quebec City businessmen had become a 'véritable calamité nationale', a turning of the back upon 'toute la partie française de la province de Québec'. And the complaint was headed 'LA PROVINCE ODIEUSEMENT SACRIFIÉE'.

25 *Les Rouges et les Bleus devant le pays*, p. 2.

26 Desjardins, *Discours*, p. 57.

Canadian nationality, and the government of Quebec as the French-Canadian government. In the first decades after Confederation, consciousness of these identities was continually turning French Canadians' attention away from the activities of other provinces and even from those of the federal parliament, toward the city where their peculiar destinies were being worked out. 'It is at Quebec, above all at Quebec, that the maintenance, the strength, and the future of our national autonomy can be ensured.'[27] The uniqueness of Quebec's nationality made her government unique too:

The differences of customs, spirit, aspirations, laws, language, and religion, which distinguish us from the peoples living beside us, are too great for us to be able to find political models and rules among them.[28]

Thus, for French Canadians, the only real political interest was centred on Quebec City. 'For us, the immediate interest is only in the province of Quebec, that is, in local politics.'[29] Even Ottawa could hardly attract attention away from Quebec: 'The Quebec legislature had hardly begun its session when all eyes were turned toward the provincial capital and firmly fixed upon it.'[30] This seemed to happen again and again when the federal and provincial sessions overlapped: 'For us, French Canadians, the Quebec legislature has a fascination against which the three or four hundred legislators who control our federal affairs cannot compete.'[31]

Given this attitude, it was not surprising that those who considered Quebec the proper homeland of the French Canadians should often look forward to its eventual separation from the rest of Canada and emergence as an independent French-Catholic state. This 'old French colony' aspired to become 'a nationality'.[32] Indeed, it was natural that French-Canadian patriotism should 'hope for national independence in the more or less distant future.'[33] For some – even for a Conservative newspaper like the *Courrier du Canada* – it was not simply a matter of hope; it was a certainty: 'We [French Canadians] are sure that one day we'll form an independent State in a second Europe.'[34] Oscar Dunn told the 1874 National Convention that this was the most important issue facing French Canadians:

The problem is to decide whether or not we want to be an independent people. ... If we

---

27 *L'Opinion Publique*, 13 Apr. 1871.
28 *La Revue Canadienne*, XVII (1881), p. 254.
29 Sulte, *Histoire*, VII, 155.
30 *La Revue Canadienne*, XVIII (1882), p. 186.
31 Ibid., XIX (1883), p. 121. Also, XVI (1879), p. 643; XVII (1881), p. 7; XX (1884), p. 248; *La Minerve*, 6 Apr. 1869; *La Vérité*, 15 Jan. 1888.
32 Hector Fabre, *Confédération, indépendance, annexion* (Quebec: L'Evénement 1871), p. 3.
33 Oscar Dunn, *L'Union des partis*, p. 25.
34 *Le Courrier du Canada*, 9 Aug. 1871.

want to be something on our own, and have a homeland which is really ours, then we must tighten our ranks; we must gather together on the same territory.[35]

Meanwhile, Quebec was part of the Canadian confederation, and her understanding of what that meant was shaped by the peculiar nature of French-Canadian patriotism. That patriotism had led Lower Canadians to accept Confederation in the first place as a means of separating themselves from Upper Canada, of 'freeing ourselves from her immediate authority'.[36] If the tactic had worked, it was because Confederation had been based on the principle of provincial autonomy; it had given each province the power to take care of its own interests. 'It's thanks to this institution that we are at present subordinate to nobody in our local affairs and that we enjoy our distinct autonomy.'[37] So distinct, in fact, was Quebec's autonomy, that her provincial secretary could describe her as 'a sovereign power within the jurisdiction granted to us by the act of union'.[38] And Chapleau, as premier, equated that autonomy with the spirit of Confederation itself: 'The programme of this government is essentially the continuation of the great idea which inspired the formation of the Canadian Confederation: the autonomy of our fine province within this great Dominion. ... '[39]

It seemed natural that provincial autonomy should be the essence of this régime, since Confederation 'was nothing but a treaty among the contracting parties. ... '[40] This 'federal pact'[41] had been made among provinces, and even though the imperial authority had been necessary to turn this 'interprovincial pact' into law, the fact remained that it was the agreement among the provinces which had given rise to the federal system:

The different provinces made a solemn pact among themselves; and from this pact among the provinces emerged the federal government, which is necessarily inferior to the powers that created it.[42]

---

35 In *L'Opinion Publique*, 2 July 1874. Robert Rumilly, in his life and times of Mercier, asserts repeatedly that Mercier always aspired toward the ultimate goal of Quebec independence. (*Honoré Mercier et son temps*, I, 44, 51, 54.)

36 *Le Franc-Parleur*, 25 Aug. 1870.

37 *La Revue Canadienne*, VIII (1871), p. 873. Also, *Le Courrier de St-Hyacinthe*, 12 Dec. 1871.

38 Blanchet, *Discours*, p. 9.

39 J.A. Chapleau, *Discours de l'hon. M. Chapleau prononcé à Ste-Thérèse, le 3 novembre, 1881* (Montreal 1881), p. 2. See also the speeches of Laurier and Mercier quoted in the *Report of the Royal Commission of Inquiry on Constitutional Problems* (Quebec 1956), I, 63–5. Also Dunn, *L'Union des partis*, p. 20.

40 *La Revue Canadienne*, XVII (1881), p. 42.

41 *Le National*, 23 May 1872.

42 *La Vérité*, 22 Mar. 1884. For other early references to the federal pact, see Richard Arès, *Dossier sur le pacte fédératif de 1867* (Montreal: Bellarmin 1967), pp. 28–9. While *La Vérité* here seems to infer from the idea of the pact that the provinces alone are sovereign in

This notion was reflected in a peculiar Quebec view of the Parliament of Canada, a body seen less as representing all the Canadian people, *as Canadians*, than as representing the provinces, which were the constituent members of the confederation. The job of a Quebec minister in the federal cabinet was thus to make sure that 'the just demands of the Province of Quebec will be heard in the Cabinet.'[43] Indeed, ministries themselves could be portrayed as properties awarded to provinces whose representatives were named to them. Some ministries in particular could give a province control of a great deal of patronage. Thus, for example, 'the Province of Quebec has a tremendous interest in having control of the militia.'[44]

Senators as well as MPs were seen as provincial representatives. In 1880 all but one of the French-Quebec senators supported Joseph Bellerose in complaining of 'the situation in which the province of Quebec is placed' by the absence of a French-Quebec senator in the cabinet. 'We representatives of the province of Quebec,' said Bellerose, were obliged to protest, 'by virtue of being the representatives of a province which is suffering from the culpable indifference of the government.'[45]

All these views of the nature of the relationship between French Canada and Quebec, provincial autonomy, the character of Confederation, and the significance of federal representation may have been held by many French Quebeckers. But they were not necessarily written into the BNA Act or shared by English Canadians. In fact, French Quebeckers were repeatedly confronted by contradictions between these views and the reality of Canadian practice. Federal interference in provincial affairs, for instance, brought complaints from Quebec from an early date. Thus, in 1869, Quebec's Conservative lieutenant-governor, Sir N.F. Belleau, wrote bitterly to Hector Langevin about the way Ottawa was interpreting the BNA Act 'to bring about federal centralization', and attempting to 'arrogate to yourselves powers

---

Confederation, Ottawa receiving only limited delegated powers from them, it should be recognized that this is not a necessary implication of the use of words like 'pact' or 'treaty' in discussing the origins of the B.N.A. Act. That that act was the result of an agreement among provinces is a patent fact, recognized in the act's opening section. The provinces could have agreed to form a legislative union, and it too would then have been the result of a pact. Most people, in using these words, simply meant to stress that Confederation could not have been obtained at the expense of what the provinces saw as their interests. Autonomy being a vital interest of Quebec, Confederation had required an agreement to maintain it.

43 *Le Pionnier de Sherbrooke*, 19 June 1874. Also *Le Courrier de St-Hyacinthe*, 8 Sept. 1874; *Les Rouges et les Bleus*, p. 1.

44 *La Minerve*, 28 Oct. 1878.

45 *Les Droits de la langue française méconnus: humiliante position de la Province de Québec* (n.p., n.d. – 1880?), pp. 1, 7.

which are more than doubtful'. Assuming, again, that federal MPs were representatives of their provinces, Belleau told Langevin that 'the federal cabinet minister who is MP from a Province must be careful not to diminish local powers, or allow them to be diminished, by exaggerated interpretations of the constitution. ... ' There were cases, claimed the governor, in which federal authorities said they saw ambiguities in the constitution, but where the provincial government saw none at all. In such cases, the powers in question should automatically be left to the provinces.[46] La Minerve had already made the point in a comment on duplication of federal and provincial actions to deal with a disputed election in a Quebec riding:

Our provincial legislature has to safeguard its autonomy, rights and privileges. Others will be ready enough to deprive it of them, without it going to the trouble of sacrificing them itself. ...

Quebec must never allow interference in her affairs by Ottawa, 'an authority which is completely foreign to her in this matter.'[47]

Because of Quebec's relationship with the French-Canadian nationality, centralization was inevitably seen from a racial point of view. 'To be a decentralizer is the duty of every French Canadian who loves his nationality.'[48] But on the other hand: 'The federal régime has no raison d'être for the English and Protestant population. ... '[49] It should never be forgotten that there were people who hated everything French, and who, therefore, 'detest the [Quebec] government as an institution in which the French Canadians are in the majority.' Their 'secret desire is for legislative union and the abolition of local government.'[50] French Canadians, therefore, must always be on their guard, 'and not let the centralizers trample on the rights of our province.'[51]

It has been argued that provincial autonomy was, in fact, a preoccupation of the Liberal but not the Conservative Party in the first decades of Confederation, and moreover, that Ontario was more actively concerned with it than Quebec.[52] Nevertheless, the frequency and the seriousness with which threats to provincial autonomy were complained of in Quebec suggest

---

46 Sir N.F. Belleau to Hector Langevin (Quebec, 7 Apr. 1869), in APQ, Collection Chapais, Langevin papers, box 7 (AP-L-12-7). This letter is also discussed by Andrée Désilets in Hector-Louis Langevin, pp. 221–3.
47 La Minerve, 21 Jan. 1869. Also, 4 Dec. 1869; Le Pays, 2 and 12 June 1869.
48 La Revue Canadienne, XVIII (1882), p. 253.
49 Dunn, L'Union des partis, pp. 15–16. Also, La Minerve, 28 Jan. 1875; Le Courrier de St-Hyacinthe, 6 Apr. 1875.
50 La Minerve, 6 Feb. 1878. Also La Vérité, 8 July 1882.
51 La Revue Canadienne, XX (1884), p. 249. Also p. 183.
52 Eg., Ramsay Cook, Provincial Autonomy, Minority Rights and the Compact Theory (Ottawa: Queen's Printer 1969), pp. 12ff.

that the matter was of real concern there too. And certainly, it was not only Rouges who raised the cry. Could one expect that the Bleus, having used the virtue of provincial autonomy to sell the Quebec Resolutions, would forget that virtue once the BNA Act was passed? Not according to the *Courrier de St-Hyacinthe*. 'As Conservatives,' it claimed in 1872, 'we must be in favour of provincial rights and against centralization.'[53] And not according to J. Blanchet, minister in the Conservative provincial government in 1884:

Now if we consider the actions of the different Conservative governments which have held office in Quebec, we'll see that they have never neglected an opportunity to assert provincial rights, to make the most of them, and even to get them confirmed by the courts.[54]

It was a Bleu who, in 1884, proposed repeal of Ottawa's liquor licensing law as an infringement on provincial rights, and Wilfrid Laurier, in supporting his motion in the Commons, was able to observe that both parties' papers in Quebec were against Ottawa's measure. 'All the newspapers declare,' he said, 'that it is an infraction of provincial rights.'[55] By 1886, when Honoré Mercier made provincial autonomy the basis of his national programme, the *Journal des Trois-Rivières* saw nothing original in the idea. 'Perfect,' it exclaimed. 'But this is precisely the doctrine asserted by the present Conservative administration, not only in the legislature but even before the Privy Council, in the recent celebrated licensing case.'[56]

So strong was Quebec's attachment to autonomy that even when, for partisan reasons, politicians and journalists were obliged to support measures that seemed centralizing, they attempted to justify them from a Quebec provincial point of view. Thus Blanchet admitted that Ottawa's Conservative government had shown centralizing tendencies in disallowing Manitoba railroad legislation, but argued that the disallowance had been in Quebec's interest, since the Manitoba legislation had provided for railroads that would have drained traffic away from the St Lawrence route.[57] Even if other provinces had sometimes to be kept somewhat in check, the important thing was to 'make our province respected. There is what our policy must be; it is the only national policy.'[58]

---

53 *Le Courrier de St-Hyacinthe*, 16 May 1872.
54 J. Blanchet, *Discours*, p. 10.
55 In Barthe, ed., *Wilfrid Laurier à la tribune*, p. 184.
56 *Le Journal des Trois-Rivières*, 8 July 1886. Marcel Hamelin points out the agreement between the two Quebec parties on the need for autonomy in *Les premières années*, p. 301. On the licensing issue, see Rumilly, *Honoré Mercier et son temps*, I, 216–19.
57 Blanchet, *Discours*, p. 27.
58 *La Minerve*, 16 July 1872, quoted in Dunn, *L'Union des partis*, p. 14.

This tendency can also be seen in Bleu statements about dual representation, or the election of a single man to represent a constituency both at Quebec and at Ottawa. While Liberals opposed the practice on the grounds that provincial autonomy could only be guaranteed by a complete separation of personnel in the federal and provincial spheres, and urged that Quebec should abolish the dual mandate, as other provinces had done,[59] Bleus went so far as to hold that the very overlapping of spheres would serve to protect Quebec's independence. After all, it was perfectly legitimate for one man to defend the interests and autonomy of his province both in its provincial capital and at Ottawa.[60] Why should one assume, as the Liberals did, that such a person would act as Ottawa's agent in the provincial assembly?[61] Belleau's letter to Langevin suggested, indeed, that the opposite should occur. Who would be better able than an MPP to know the needs of his province and to represent them in the federal parliament? Cartier himself argued in the Commons that if the double mandate were abolished, the 'provinces would then become dependents of the federal government, whereas in reality they constitute distinct governments.'[62]

When, in time, the Bleus came to support abolition, they were able to maintain that their main concern had not changed. J.A. Chapleau had accepted Cartier's argument in the first session of Quebec's legislature, but became convinced within a few years that the presence of federal MPs in the Quebec assembly was harmful to the latter's independence. He was an example of a Bleu who changed his vote on the dual mandate because he remained constant in his adherence to provincial autonomy.[63]

In fact, the Bleus were soon able to accuse the Liberals of centralizing actions too. When, for example, the Mackenzie government established the Supreme Court of Canada in 1875, the Bleu press (though it scarcely noticed the North-West Territories Act passed in the same session) came angrily to life. 'One thing is certain,' it charged, 'that the Supreme Court, as now organized, is going to move us toward legislative union and the destruction of our law codes.'[64] This court would destroy 'Quebec's French autonomy',[65]

---

59 Nova Scotia and New Brunswick abolished the system in 1867; Ontario did so in 1872 – under a Liberal government.

60 *Le Courrier de St-Hyacinthe*, 10 Oct. 1871.

61 Eg., Wilfrid Laurier in the provincial assembly in 1871, in Barthe, pp. 9–18, especially 16–17.

62 In Tassé, p. 554. This is not to suggest this was the only argument used by the Bleus. See Hamelin, p. 289.

63 J.A. Chapleau, speech in provincial assembly, 3 Dec. 1870. In *L'Hon. J.A. Chapleau: sa biographie suivie de ses principaux discours*, pp. 47–8.

64 *Le Courrier du Canada*, 24 Mar. 1875.

65 *L'Union des Cantons de l'Est*, 8 Apr. 1875.

for it would take from the provinces a great part of their jurisdiction over justice, and would submit Quebec's unique civil laws, along with the destinies of her citizens, 'to judges who will be strangers, for the most part, to their language, customs, habits, and usages, to the origins and numerous commentators of their law codes, and to the practices of their courts.'[66]

These fears seemed to be realized in the following years. 'From the moment it came into existence, this court has been centralizing; its decisions have constantly sanctioned the encroachments of the Ottawa government and deprived the provinces of rights which had been thought to be indisputable.'[67] And who were responsible for this 'demolition of our provincial institutions and anglicization of our French laws'?[68] Who had set up this court whose establishment the Conservatives had always opposed?[69] Why, the Liberals! It was they who had given it 'an almost absolute power to centralize at will, as indeed, it has done ever since. ... '[70]

The Bleus found a more spectacular provincial rights affair in 1878, when the Liberal lieutenant-governor, Luc Letellier de Saint-Just, dismissed his Conservative premier, Charles-Eugène Boucher de Boucherville, although the latter still enjoyed the confidence of the assembly. When Letellier invited the Liberal leader, Henri-Gustave Joly de Lotbinière, to form a government, the Bleu majority were furious. They accused the lieutenant-governor of having carried off a *coup d'état*, of trying to rule against the wishes of the people's elected representatives. He had violated 'the liberty of the people' and the principles of reponsible government.[71]

He had done more than that. Boucherville and his majority had been elected by the people of Quebec; Letellier had been appointed by Alexander Mackenzie's federal government. 'And so he wants go govern Lower Canada against its will, in the interest of Mr Mackenzie.'[72] It seemed clear, in fact, that the whole *coup d'état* had been 'secretly planned by the Ottawa government'[73] to suppress Quebec's individuality and turn it into a mere 'branch of the Ottawa Liberal government.'[74] This was an insult to the 'honour of our

---

66 *Les Rouges et les Bleus*, pp. 65–6. Also, *Correspondances parlementaires*, p. 5; *La Minerve*, 1 Apr. 1875; *Le Nouveau Monde*, 19 Mar. and 3 Apr. 1875; *Le Pionnier de Sherbrooke*, 2 Apr. 1875.
67 *La Revue Canadienne*, XVIII (1882), p. 61.
68 *La Vérité*, 21 Jan. 1882.
69 G. Amyot, *Adresse à MM. les électeurs du comté de Lotbinière* (n.p., n.d.), p. 12. Also, *La Vérité*, 7 July 1883.
70 Blanchet, *Discours*, p. 10. See also *La Revue Canadienne*, XVII (1881), pp. 565–6.
71 *Le Coup d'état, ou le renvoi du cabinet de Boucherville* (Quebec: Le Canadien 1878), p. 15; A.J. Chapleau, *Nos Libertés* (n.p., n.d), eg., p. 2.
72 Amyot, p. 6.
73 *Le Journal des Trois-Rivières*, 7 Mar. 1878.
74 *Le Pionnier de Sherbrooke*, 26 Apr. 1878.

homeland and the rights of our nation',[75] an attack upon the 'honour, independence and well-being of Lower Canada'.[76] It must, therefore, be opposed:

> No, we must not be governed in Quebec by the will of the Ottawa ministers; Lower Canadians will not suffer themselves to be thus deprived of their dearest liberties; they will not blindly give up the only serious guarantee they have for their most precious institutions.[77]

The Letellier affair raised the question of the lieutenant-governor's proper role. Bleus had already expressed views on this matter in 1869, when Ottawa disallowed a provincial law giving MPPs the same parliamentary immunities as imperial MPs. The central government had argued that while the BNA Act had expressly authorized it to model the privileges of federal MPs on those of Westminster, it had given no such authorization to the provinces. To this *La Minerve* replied that such privileges were granted to advisers of the Queen in deference to the dignity of Her Majesty, and that they ought, therefore, to be granted as well to those who advised her at the provincial level as to those who advised her at the federal and imperial levels. 'Now our local Parliament exists and functions in the name of the Queen. Through the agency of this Parliament, half the business of a country is administered and all the laws which govern it are made.'[78] This implied that the lieutenant-governor stood in the same way with respect to the provincial parliament as the governor general to the federal parliament and the Queen herself to the parliament of the empire; each was 'the Crown' within his own jurisdiction. *La Minerve* made the point more explicitly in its reaction to the 1878 *coup d'état*: 'England, in her benevolence, wanted us to have a Lieutenant-Governor who would be the symbol of her power and her maternal authority, while the Ottawa government thought above all to give us an officer who would be its strong right arm.'[79] But in this Ottawa had misunderstood the constitution. 'The constitution established two concurrent powers in Canada, each with specific, designated functions.'[80] It could hardly be said, then, that the central figure in one of these two concurrent powers was only an agent, an emanation of the other; and for Letellier to have behaved as if he were nothing more than

---

75 Amyot, p. 9.
76 *Le Nouveau Monde*, 27 Apr. 1878.
77 Ibid., 5 Mar. 1878. Also, 4 Mar.; *Le Pionnier de Sherbrooke*, 8 and 15 Mar. and 5 Apr.; *Le Courrier de St-Hyacinthe*, 7, 14, and 19 Mar.; *La Minerve*, 8 and 9 Mar. 1878.
78 *La Minerve*, 4 Dec. 1869. For the whole story of these privileges, see Marcel Hamelin, pp. 291–3.
79 *La Minerve*, 5 Mar. 1878.
80 Ibid., 6 Mar. 1878.

the agent of the federal government was grossly to have distorted the limits of the constitution.[81]

If Quebec's autonomy had repeatedly to be fought for, so did its French-Catholic character. In fact, the Anglo-Protestant minority and its culture seemed much more present than the Confederationists had led people to expect in 1864–7. By 1870 the language question was causing particular annoyance, and *Le Canadien* was urging French Quebeckers to defend their rights by insisting on being spoken to in their own language.[82] The problem was particularly acute in the Eastern Townships, where the anglophone population was especially numerous. In 1871 the new municipality of Lennoxville decided to publish its rules and proceedings in English only. To the *Pionnier de Sherbrooke* this sort of decision seemed to imply that Anglo-Quebeckers thought 'French Canadians had no business being in this part of the country.'[83] But the Townships weren't the only place where the French language had its difficulties. Jules-Paul Tardivel complained that in the provincial capital itself the post office insisted on dealing in English only with him, 'the owner of a French newspaper in an essentially French town.' Telegraph companies also used English, and messages in French were garbled or not delivered at all – right here in the French-Canadian province! 'How long will we tolerate these things?'[84]

But there was more to tolerate. English and Protestant Canadians seemed to get far more than their fair share of public positions in this French-Catholic province. Surely it was 'an injustice' that when the municipalities of Sorel, Drummondville, and Arthabaska set up a company to build a road through their region, all the directors were English.[85] Certainly it was not right that

---

81 The following year Bleus moved to have the now-Conservative federal government fire Letellier to punish him for his *coup d'état*. Now it was the turn of the Liberals to use the same language the Bleus had used the year before: the lieutenant-governor, once in office, is the head of the Quebec government, and for Ottawa to interfere with him is to interfere with the domestic affairs of the province, to wreck provincial autonomy. (Eg., speech of Wilfrid Laurier, in Barthe, pp. 99–100.) But the Bleus carried the day with the argument that Letellier's firing would be the very 'consecration of our provincial independence'. It was Letellier himself who, acting on behalf of the federal government, 's'est rendu coupable d'immixtion indue dans l'administration des affaires bas-canadiennes' (*La Minerve*, 18 June 1879). Undoubtedly both parties were defending their own partisan interests, but significantly, both had to argue in such a way as to be seen to defend provincial autonomy.
82 *Le Canadien*, 3 Jan. 1870.
83 *Le Pionnier de Sherbrooke*, 15 Dec. 1871.
84 *La Vérité*, 11 Aug. 1881.
85 *Le Pionnier de Sherbrooke*, 18 Mar. 1870.

when a new postal inspector was appointed for Quebec City, it should turn out to be an English Ontarian, imported to the French-Canadian capital despite an abundance of eligible French Quebeckers![86] But then, it was consistent with the fact that the Anglo-Protestant element was over-represented on the bench and even in the legislature of Quebec.[87] It was even rumoured, in 1875, that the Liberals intended to appoint an English Canadian, Luther Holton, as lieutenant-governor. Such an appointment, though, would be 'opposed to our national dignity and must not be allowed to go through without protest.'[88] After all, Quebec was assentially a French-Canadian province, and the English could not reasonably 'claim the right to promote one of their people to this dignity.'[89] It would be a serious blow to French Canada:

Let us not, in our own stronghold, expose our particular autonomy and destroy those advantages we possess by cowardly concessions to the foreign element which, as the minority, has the right to be respected but not to be preferred to the first honours and dignities of the Crown.

Let us keep the province of Quebec French and Catholic.[90]

Though Quebec did not get an English lieutenant-governor, it did get a Protestant premier when Letellier appointed Joly to the post in 1878 *coup d'état*. For Bleus, this was a 'humiliation of the Catholics'[91] and another reason for condemning Letellier's action:

Swiss by origin, a foreigner by birth, Protestant in religion, so much an enemy of our nationality that he has called for the suppression of our patriotic and religious demonstrations, Mr Joly certainly makes a strange leader for a population which is all Catholic and all French.[92]

Of course, both Holton and Joly were Liberals, and the Bleu press had partisan motives for attacking them. What is of interest to us is that these particular reasons were given in the attacks; they appear to have fallen within the range of normal and acceptable ideas in the 1870s. Indeed, on the popular level, hostility toward a too-public manifestation of the minority group was sometimes shown by outright violence. In the summer of 1871, for instance,

86 *L'Electeur*, 9 Nov. 1889.
87 Ibid., 7 Aug. 1885.
88 *L'Union des Cantons de l'Est*, 4 Mar. 1875.
89 *Le Courrier de St-Hyacinthe*, 2 Mar. 1875.
90 *L'Union des Cantons de l'Est*, 4 Mar. 1875.
91 Ibid., 28 Mar. 1878.
92 *Le Journal des Trois-Rivières*, 18 Mar. 1878.

an attempt by the apostate ex-priest, Chiniquy, to preach in French in Quebec was interrupted by an angry crowd.[93] That same summer, a franco-phone Protestant, who attempted to distribute Bibles and speak to militiamen in the Lévis military camp, was roughly thrown out by offended Catholic soldiers. English-language papers claimed that a mob of them had actually tried to kill him. That there had been any violence at all was flatly denied by the *Journal de Québec*. But even if a few potatoes had been thrown at him, commented *Le Nouveau Monde*, hadn't this 'Swiss pedlar' provoked it all himself? 'What right had Mr Muraire to attempt to pervert people who had not invited him, and whom he knew to be of a different faith? Wasn't this a real insult to them?'[94] The appearance of the Salvation Army on the streets of Quebec in 1887 was apparently seen as a similar sort of insult, for it also provoked mob anger; and when one of the members of the crowd was arrested for throwing stones at the Salvationists, *La Vérité* protested angrily. No doubt an official tolerance of the different cults was necessary in a country such as Canada. But for 'this scandalous and grotesque organization' to parade openly and noisily through the streets of the Catholic capital, deafening and outraging its citizens, was certainly beyond all limits of toleration.[95] Here, as in the Muraire and Chiniquy affairs, the source of the anger seems to have been the fear that Protestants, not content with living and worshipping in their own way, were attempting to impress the character of their own religion upon the very public life of what was to have been a Catholic province.

French Quebeckers could hardly feel that they were being unfair in their attitudes toward their province's minority:

We are the immense majority, and we only ask to live quietly on the little bit of territory we have gained by the sweat of our brow and the blood of our martyrs. You others are just the minority, and a very small minority. ... [96]

Indeed, this minority was well protected by the guarantees of the BNA Act, by the support of an Anglo-Protestant majority at Ottawa, and by its possession of the lion's share of economic power and honours in Quebec. It was the French Quebeckers who were on the defensive. 'Let us affirm our rights, and

---

93 *Le Nouveau Monde*, 18 July 1871. Chiniquy repeatedly attracted such violence over the years. See, for example, *Le Nouveau Monde*, 11 Nov. 1884; *Le Pionnier de Sherbrooke*, 20 Nov. 1884.

94 *Le Nouveau Monde*, 18 July 1871. Also *Le Journal de Québec*, 15 July; *Le Courrier du Canada*, 19 July 1871.

95 *La Vérité*, 1 Oct. 1887.

96 *L'Opinion Publique*, 18 Jan. 1872. Also, *Le Pionnier de Sherbrooke*, 11 Aug. 1876.

our supremacy where we have it, with a spirit of moderation and justice, but with enough energy to make sure we are respected.'[97] Failure of the Anglo-Protestants to respect the rights of the Quebec majority could lead to the break-up of Confederation, for 'we'll soon break loose from our bonds and seek a new arrangement which will shelter us from your fanaticism.'[98] After all, since Confederation had been acceptable in the first place precisely because it created a French-Catholic province, it was natural that if, because of its minority, the French-Catholic character of the province were seriously threatened, Confederation would cease to be acceptable.

The privileges, prevalence, and influence of the Quebec minority were particularly provoking when contrasted with the position of French-Catholic minorities elsewhere. And the comparison was one that must necessarily spring to mind again and again. How could one contemplate the New Brunswick school law, for example, without being reminded of what school privileges Protestants enjoyed in Quebec? Some people, indeed, hoped that Quebec's liberal example would serve as a model for other provinces, so that even New Brunswick would be influenced by it to restore Catholic school rights.[99] These hopes, however, proved groundless, and the observation was a bitter one:

It makes us wonder why we Lower Canadian Catholics are so tolerant, so generous toward the Protestant minority in this province, when our co-religionists in the other provinces are so badly treated, so persecuted by the Protestant majorities.[100]

Why, indeed, should French Quebeckers 'treat with generosity people who oppress our co-religionists in every part of the confederation where the latter are in the minority'?[101] This sort of complaint is reminiscent of the debate over the Bell and Langevin school bills in the summer of 1866. For the wording and the context are such that it is at least a matter of ambiguity whether what is being complained of is that French Catholics do not have rights, or that English Protestants do have them. As in 1866, the granting of privileges to a minority seems to be felt as a burden, detracting from the proper independence of a province. But if Quebec had to bear such a burden, why not the others? 'If

---

97 *La Gazette de Sorel*, 3 July 1872.

98 *L'Opinion Publique*, 18 Jan. 1872.

99 Eg., George Cartier, in Tassé, p. 374; *Le Courrier de St-Hyacinthe*, 30 Jan. 1872; *Le Courrier du Canada*, 22 May 1872; *Le Pionnier de Sherbrooke*, 21 Apr. 1871.

100 *L'Ordre*, 15 July 1871. Also, *L'Union des Cantons de l'Est*, 6 June 1872; *Le Nouveau Monde*, 3 June; *Le Journal des Trois-Rivières*, 25 Jan. 1872.

101 *Le Pionnier de Sherbrooke*, 11 Aug. 1876. See also *Le Courrier de St-Hyacinthe*, 15 June 1869, comparing minority school rights in Quebec and Nova Scotia.

they have the right to have their schools, we also claim to have the same right.'[102]

But why did the double standard exist? Was it not the result of Quebec's weakness, and of the great power of the Anglo-Protestant element in Canada? Was it not clear that 'if Protestants were treated like the Catholics of New Brunswick, they'd stir up heaven and earth, and God knows where it would end.'[103] But Quebec, on the other hand, did not seem able to stir up heaven and earth with any success when it came to defending French-Catholic minorities. The same weakness which obliged her to accept such a strong Anglo-Protestant presence on her own territory also brought about failure when she tried to fulfil her role as champion and protector of those groups. Thus, once again, each defeat for a minority was a defeat for Quebec iself: 'There you are: Quebec wants the amnesty, Ontario doesn't, Quebec gives in and that's all there is to it.'[104] A curious summing-up of the amnesty issue, which makes no reference to the Métis! And yet, a natural and frequently repeated approach, for clearly, Quebec's ability to defend the minorities was a sign of her own independence, prestige, and influence in Confederation, and was thus discussed in the same way – in the same breath, the same thought – as the share to be assigned Quebec in the division of the debt of the old United Canadas,[105] or the relative comfort and prestige of the postings assigned to the Quebec and Ontario units in the Manitoba expeditionary force.[106] In each case, Quebec's prestige, influence, and interest were at stake, just as they were even in the question of the CPR terminus. That matter, too, was lumped together with the amnesty and the New Brunswick schools, as in this Bleu condemnation of Mackenzie's handling of it:

The Rouges must have thought the best way to follow up their hateful and outrageous conduct in the two great national and religious questions of the amnesty and the New

---

102 *Le Pionnier de Sherbrooke*, 1 Sept. 1876.

103 *La Gazette des Familles*, III (1871–2), p. 208. Also, *Le Pionnier de Sherbrooke*, 1 Sept. 1876. It might be said that when Quebec granted Protestant separate school rights, she was giving less, in a sense, than other provinces, when they set up Catholic separate schools. For in so far as Quebeckers believed in a religious basis for education, it was consistent with their own ideology that schools should be organized separately on a Catholic and Protestant basis. But where, in other provinces, people had adopted the ideology of non-sectarian (not to say secular) education – of non-denominational schools equally open and inoffensive to all – it was a departure from this ideological position to support special schools for one denomination.

104 *Le Courrier du Canada*, 15 Feb. 1875. Also, *L'Union des Cantons de l'Est*, 28 Apr. 1870; *Le Pionnier de Sherbrooke*, 29 Jan. 1875.

105 *Le Franc-Parleur*, 25 Aug. 1870; *L'Opinion Publique*, 13 Oct. 1870.

106 *Le Franc-Parleur*, 29 Sept. 1870.

Brunswick schools was to sacrifice the material interests of the province of Quebec by voting for Mr Mackenzie's unjust policy on the Pacific railroad.[107]

All these matters seemed but aspects of the general question of Quebec's situation – the situation of French Catholicism – in the confederation:

Mr Mackenzie's assassins threaten to lynch Lépine; Riel is no longer protected by the law; the New Brunswick Catholics are thrown into jail while atheistic schools are forced on them; Ontario takes the military college away from Quebec; Ottawa doesn't subsidize any [rail]roads except Ontario's. A vast conspiracy against Catholic interests seems to be organized throughout the country.[108]

That Quebec's claim for public works or railroad subsidies should be described here as *Catholic interests* underlines once more the way in which French Canada's religion and nationality were identified with that province. In the first decades of Confederation, in fact, French Quebeckers continued to see the provinces as the embodiments of national or religious principles:

But as everyone knows, Ontario is the great protector of fanaticism and Protestant interests, while the French Canadians [the context indicates they mean Quebeckers] must always act as vigilant sentinels to preserve and defend 'their religion, their language and their laws.'[109]

Once more, then, we find ambivalence in the attitudes we are trying to understand: on the one hand, a feeling that Quebec was the province, the homeland, the politcal and geographical expression of the French-Canadian nationality; on the other hand, a belief that it was Quebec's duty and her glory to protect French Catholicism beyond her borders. But why, we may ask, did it seem important to protect French Catholicism in the other provinces? Did French Canadians see their own population as expanding outside of Quebec? Was it to make the West, for example, safe for their own settlement that they needed to protect the Métis and maintain the provisions of the Manitoba Act? This is what we must answer next.

107 *Correspondances parlementaires*, p. 55. Also, *Les Rouges et les Bleus*, p. 3.
108 *Le Courrier du Canada*, 3 Feb. 1875. Also, *Le Courrier de St-Hyacinthe*, 13 Mar. 1875.
109 *La Revue Canadienne*, VIII (1871), p. 319.

VII

FRENCH CANADA
IN THE WEST

I N what we have seen of French-Canadian attitudes
toward the annexation of Rupert's Land, and in the
patriotic identification of French Canada with the
province of Quebec, there has been nothing at all that would lead us to expect
a French-Canadian movement to settle the prairies. And, as it happens,
Quebeckers showed far less readiness than Ontarians to move to other parts
of Canada in the first decades of Confederation. During the 1870s, the
increase in the proportion of the Ontario-born who were living in other
provinces was twice as great as for Quebec-born. In the 1880s and 1890s, the
proportion for Ontarians was three times what it was for Quebeckers.[1]

This is not to say that Quebeckers did not move at all away from their
province. We know that emigration to the United States was a major problem.
u.s. figures indicate that more than 82 per cent of these French-Canadian
emigrants settled north of Florida and east of the Mississippi, that is to say, in
the part of the country which was closest to Quebec.[2] The same pattern can be
seen within the dominion. Most of those Quebeckers who did move to other
parts of Canada settled in the neighbouring provinces of Ontario and New
Brunswick – and of these, most went to the counties that bordered on
Quebec.[3]

---

1 To reach this conclusion, one can calculate, for each census year, the number of people born
   in a given province who were living in another part of the dominion. The increase in a
   province's extra-frontier population from one census to the next is then considered as a
   percentage of that province's population at the beginning of the decade.
2 u.s. Bureau of the Census, *A Century of Population Growth* (Washington: Government
   Printing Office 1909), p. 226.
3 For the decade 1871–81, 69 per cent of Quebec's emigrants to other parts of Canada went to
   Ontario and New Brunswick. For the period 1881–91, the figure was 53 per cent.
   Within New Brunswick itself, the 1871 census showed that 84 per cent of the Quebec-born

However, while French Quebeckers did establish themselves in places which were close to home, where the French fact had no official or constitutional status, they did not seem willing to settle on the prairies, where that fact was enshrined in fundamental law. By 1881, there were already 19,125 Ontarians living in Manitoba, but only 4,085 Quebeckers. The next decade saw Manitoba's Ontario-born population increase to 46,620, while the Quebec-born figure rose to only 7,555. And in the 1890s, while the Ontario-born population increased by another 20,946, the Quebec-born was enlarged by only 937.

Why were Quebeckers so much less represented than Ontarians among the prairie settlers? Was it because they had farther to go to get from their province to the West? Was it too costly a move for them? Did the federal government not give them sufficient encouragement or aid? Did it neglect them in favour of other groups?

Distance itself does not seem to have been a decisive factor. For one thing, Nova Scotians, who had much farther to go than Quebeckers, migrated to Manitoba at about the same rate. [4] What's more, it would appear that a greater proportion of English Quebeckers than of French made the move, though the distance was the same for both. [5] In any case, distance could be overcome to

population was living in the three border counties of Victoria, Restigouche, and Gloucester. During the next decade, the increase in the Quebec-born population of those three counties amounted to 86 per cent of the increase in the Quebec-born population for all of New Brunswick, and in the 1880s their share was 87 per cent. In Ontario, the increase in the Quebec-born population of the border counties, Prescott, Russell, Glengarry, Carleton, Nipissing, Renfrew, and Ottawa City, amounted to 70 per cent of the increase in the Quebec-born population for the province in the decade 1871–81. In the following decade, the increase for these counties was 72 per cent of the province-wide increase. If we include Cornwall and Stormont, which do not touch Quebec directly but which are adjacent to and form a block with those that do, then the figure becomes 83 per cent. During the 1890s, the increase of Quebec-born in the border counties alone *exceeded* the increase for Ontario as a whole. This meant that while the Quebec-born population was growing in this area, it was declining in more westerly regions. In fact there was a decrease of 921 just for the three counties of Essex North, Kent, and Simcoe East.

4 Between the censuses of 1881 and 1885, Manitoba's Quebec-born population increased by an amount equivalent to 0.1 per cent of Quebec's 1881 population, while her Nova Scotia-born population increased by a number equivalent to the same proportion of Nova Scotia's 1881 population.

5 Sometimes Quebec newspapers even seemed to suggest that the movement from Quebec was virtually all English. Thus, *Le Canadien*, 23 Feb. 1889: 'Tout fait prévoir un vaste mouvement d'émigration au Nord-Ouest, le printemps et l'été prochain. ... La province de Québec fournira aussi son contingent. Il paraît qu'une cinquantaine de familles irlandaises et écossaises du seul comté d'Argenteuil se préparent à partir.' While we know that, in fact, some French Quebeckers did go to Manitoba, the census does indicate that a greater proportion of non-French Quebeckers went. Thus, between 1880 and 1885, for

some extent. Railroad companies, eager for passengers, offered specially reduced fares to Manitoba-bound settlers. In the United States especially, competing companies showered the organizers of Manitoba settler groups with bargain-rate offers. 'The railroad companies are fighting for our immigrants' business,' wrote one such organizer to the Archbishop of St Boniface in 1877.[6] But in the early 1880s the CPR also advertised a special Montreal-to-Winnipeg fare for settlers.[7] In fact, with the help of special rail fares and the homestead system, a man from the Montreal area could get to the prairies and acquire 160 acres of land for half of what it would cost him to acquire the same amount of land in a northern Quebec colonization area – land, moreover, which, unlike the Manitoba homestead, would have to be laboriously cleared of bush before it could be brought into agricultural production.[8] Yet, in the decades after Confederation, these northern Quebec areas received far more attention from Quebec colonizers and far more settlers than did the North-West.[9]

---

instance, the Quebec-born population of Manitoba increased by 1,891, while the French-origin population increased by 1,241. Of the latter, 29 were from France. If we suppose that the remaining 1,212 represent the increase in French Quebeckers, we are left with 679 'English' Quebeckers (including all origins other than French as 'English'). But these 679 represent 0.2 per cent of Quebec's 1881 non-French population, while the 1,212 represent only half as large a fraction (0.1 per cent) of Quebec's 1881 French-origin population. And yet, the 1,212 is certainly an overestimate of the increase in French Quebeckers in Manitoba, since we know that a significant part of Manitoba's French-origin population came from the United States or the North-West Territories. In May, 1876, 605 Franco-American settlers had come to Manitoba in organized groups. Between May and July of 1877, Albert Lacombe alone brought 600 more, and by April, 1878, the federal agent, Charles Lalime, had brought 423. See A.-G. Morice, *History of the Catholic Church in Western Canada* (Toronto: Musson Book Co. 1910), pp. 121, 151.

6 Albert Lacombe, letter to Archbishop A.-A. Taché (Montreal, 7 Feb. 1877), Archives Deschâtelets: St Boniface archiepiscopal papers, mfm no. 505.

7 In the early 1880s, the usual second-class fare on the CPR from Montreal to Winnipeg was $17. (See *Le Nord-Ouest canadien*, n.p., n.d. – 1884? – p. 10.) But a special rate of $15 was offered to emigrant-settlers. (See, eg., the advertisement headed 'A Winnipeg pour $15.00' in *L'Etendard*, April-May, 1884.)

8 After taking care of his $15 settler's ticket on the railroad, the Manitoba pioneer had to pay a $10 registration fee for his homestead. In Quebec, the settler had to pay 30 cents per acre for land – $48 if he wanted 160 acres, though the usual grant was only 100 acres. Nor was transportation a negligible factor even here. The rail fare to Temiskaming from as near as Ottawa was $5.50. See, on these costs, a pamphlet of the Montreal and Ottawa dioceses colonization societies, *Au Nord* (St-Jérôme 1883), p. 8; also, F.C. Innes, 'The Land Use and Settlement of the Quebec Clay Belt' (unpublished master's thesis, Dept of Geography, McGill University, 1960), p. 68.

9 The division of attention between the Ottawa valley and Manitoba in the colonization files of the Montreal archiepiscopal archives tells the story. The former, naturally enough, nearly monopolized the attentions of the Montreal diocese colonizers. What's more, the pio-

Nor does it appear that French Canadians were hindered from settling on the prairies by any federal government discrimination against them. It was not till 1874 that Ottawa received any request for aid from a French-Canadian group, and by April of 1875 it had granted the Société de colonisation de Manitoba a free block of land for French-Canadian settlement in Manitoba.[10] The federal government published and distributed French-language pamphlets promoting prairie lands,[11] subsidized the movement of Franco-Americans to the Canadian West,[12] sent a special agent, Charles Lalime, to New England to promote such a movement,[13] and paid the expenses of agents which the Société de colonisation de Manitoba also sent for the same purpose.[14]

Ontarians do not seem to have waited for government initiatives to aid their colonization. They were quick to form colonizing companies or societies, or to raise public subscriptions to promote the westward movement. 'The emigration which comes to us from Ontario,' observed Manitoba's French-language newspaper, 'is organized there by public subscription, and at Toronto alone the Red River settlers' support fund amounts to $30,000'[15] But Ontarians did not see western settlement only as a charitable work. Their businessmen were quick to get in touch with Ottawa about western opportunities,[16] and by 1877, the Surveyor-General was reporting that while

---

neer counties of Pontiac, Ottawa, Argenteuil, Chicoutimi, and Saguenay increased in population by 31,315 in the 1870s and 21,242 in the 1880s. The entire French-Canadian population of Manitoba at the end of that second decade was still only 11,000.

10 J.-C. Taché, the Deputy Minister of Agriculture, letter to the Minister of the Interior (Ottawa, 6 Nov. 1874), PAC: Dept of the Interior papers, Dominion Lands Branch, file no. 165914. In addition to a basic reserve for settlement, the society received a special bonus of free land for each settler established. This bonus was eventually replaced by a cash payment.

11 Eg., Thomas Spence, Manitoba et le Nord-Ouest canadien (Ottawa: Dept of Agriculture 1875); Province de Manitoba et Territoire du Nord-Ouest (Ottawa 1878); Le Manitoba et les Territoires du Nord-Ouest (Ottawa 1881); Canada, Dept of Agriculture, Esquisse générale du Nord-Ouest du Canada (Trois-Rivières 1886); T.A. Bernier, Le Manitoba, champ d'immigration (Ottawa 1887); M.J. Blais, Le Manitoba (Ottawa: Imprimerie de l'Etat 1898); etc.

12 Ottawa paid $17 per settler – two dollars more than the CPR's special Montreal-to-Winnipeg rail fare. See Albert Lacombe to A.-A. Taché (Ottawa, 6 Mar. 1876), and Lacombe to Taché (Ottawa, 21 Feb. 1877), in Archives Deschâtelets: St Boniface archiepiscopal papers, mfms no. 477 and 507.

13 Dom Paul Benoit, Vie de Mgr Taché, Archevêque de St-Boniface (Montreal: Beauchemin 1904), II, 298.

14 Albert Lacombe to A.-A. Taché (Ottawa, 21 Feb. 1877), Archives Deschâtelets: St Boniface archiepiscopal papers, mfm no. 507.

15 Le Métis (St Boniface), 15 June 1871. See also W.L. Morton, Manitoba: A History (Toronto: University of Toronto Press 1957), p. 157.

16 Eg., James Graham to George-Etienne Cartier (Toronto, 10 May 1869), PAC, Cartier papers, correspondence.

five English-Canadian companies had applied for and received grants of land for settlement in Manitoba, only one French-Canadian group had done the same: the Société de colonisation de Manitoba.[17]

It was significant that the Société de colonisation de Manitoba was not a Quebec but a western organization. Its guiding spirit was Archbishop Alexandre-Antonin Taché, who was, as a matter of fact, the fount and origin of almost every attempt to bring French Canadians to the West in the decades after 1870. Having lived all his adult life as a missionary in the North-West, Taché was dedicated to his Métis and Indian charges there. This led him, for a long time, to oppose all settlement of the prairies, as white settlement, he foresaw, would have devastating effects on the native peoples. When, however, it became apparent to him that Canadian takeover and colonization were inevitable, he began to hope that a French-speaking Catholic group could at least be brought from Quebec. Such a group would provide a shield for his original flock, a buffer between them and the sharpest thrust of modernism brought by the Anglo-Protestants of Ontario; it might give them a little more time and help to make the necessary transformation of their own life pattern from hunting to farming.[18] In an 1869 sermon at St-Hyacinthe, the then-bishop reminded his listeners of their long tradition of assistance to the northwestern missions, and suggested they could continue that tradition by sending settlers. 'You may not find material fortune there,' he said; but this giving of aid would pay spiritual dividends – 'a happiness which only religion can give.'[19]

From the first, then, the promotion of French-Canadian settlement on the prairies took the form of appeals for help from the French-Catholic West. By such appeals Taché persuaded men like Joseph Royal, Joseph Dubuc, and T.-A. Bernier to come to provide secular leadership for the French-Manitoban community.[20] With such a motive Taché organized the Société de colonisation de Manitoba.[21] In the same spirit he organized a St Boniface

---

17 PAC: Department of the Interior records, file no. 13765. Also, file no. 44447. In 1878, fourteen more townships were granted to an Ontario-based company, and by 1882, of 104 grants made under a special promotion scheme, not one was to a French-Canadian applicant.

18 A.-A. Taché, 'Letter from the Bishop of St Boniface', in S.J. Dawson, *Report on the Exploration of the Country between Lake Superior and the Red River Settlement* (Toronto 1859), pp. 44–5. Also, Bishop V.-J. Grandin, quoted in Marcel Giraud, *Le Métis canadien*, p. 957.

19 *Le Courrier de St-Hyacinthe*, 29 July 1869.

20 Edouard Lecompte, *Un Grand Chrétien: Sir Joseph Dubuc* (Montreal: Imprimerie du Messager 1923), pp. 96, 107; Cornelius J. Jaenen, 'Glimpses of the Franco-Manitoban Community' (Manitoba centennial lecture, University of Winnipeg, 26 Feb. 1970), p. 6; Rumilly, *Mercier et son temps*, I, 129.

21 Benoit, *Vie de Mgr Taché*, II, 300.

lobby, working through his brother, the deputy minister of agriculture, to get federal government help, and sent to Quebec and New England colonizing agents like T.-A. Bernier or the priests J.-B. Proulx, C.-A. Beaudry, and Albert Lacombe to stir up, organize, and promote the movement of western settlement.[22]

Again and again, discussions of western settlement in the Quebec press were stimulated by letters to the editors from Manitoba or by visits of Franco-Manitobans to Quebec.[23] Sermons in Quebec pulpits were the results of appeals by Taché to his Quebec colleagues[24] or of visits from the St Boniface priests.[25] The men of St Boniface wrote prefaces or 'letters' in the books of travel or adventure prepared by Quebeckers,[26] and almost all of the French-language pamphlets promoting western settlement (aside from those done by the federal government) were written or published by the St Boniface group.[27] Even Quebec MPS were used by Taché as his agents. Thus, when

22 Lacombe to Taché (Montreal, 21 Feb. 1876), Archives Deschâtelets, St Boniface papers, mfm no. 475. Also Lacombe to Taché (Fall River, Mass., 15 Feb. 1877, and Ottawa, 21 Feb. 1877), mfms no. 506 and 507; Jaenen, Glimpses, p. 7. Note the role of Taché's brother in PAC: Dept of the Interior, Dominion Lands Branch, file no. 165914, on the Colonization Society of Manitoba. Benoit also claims (II, 295) it was Taché who secured Lalime's appointment as federal agent. Again according to Benoit, Taché was responsible for the founding of a sort of sub-society at Montreal. Lacombe reported to Taché in a letter from Montreal, 22 May 1876, that 'notre bureau s'organise' (Deschâtelets, St Boniface papers, mfm no. 486), but traces of this bureau's activities are hard to find.

23 Eg., Le Canadien, 29 Mar. 1871; La Gazette des Familles, v (1873–4), pp. 271–3; La Vérité, 24 April and 3 July 1886; L'Opinion Publique, 9 July 1874.

24 Benoit, Vie de Mgr Taché, II, 196–7, 284–6, 383–4; Montreal archiepiscopal archives: correspondence from St Boniface: Taché-Bourget (22 Mar. and 21 May 1872, 28 Dec. 1874, 7 June 1876, 2 Jan. 1886); to the clergy of Quebec, June, 1874 and 8 Mar. 1894. Also, circular of 189- from Taché to the clergy of Trois-Rivières (Archives Deschâtelets, Trois-Rivières episcopal papers, mfm no. 2).

25 Eg., Montreal archiepiscopal archives, St Boniface correspondence: Bourget to Taché (Montreal, 5 Mar. 1874, and 26 May 1876); and in the colonization file, Lacombe to Bourget (Montreal, 27 Apr. 1880), and Beaudry to Fabre, 4 Mar. 1888. At the Archives Deschâtelets, in the St Boniface papers: Lacombe to Taché (Quebec, 28 Dec. 1872, 16 Apr. 1880, and Montreal, 3 Mar. 1876, and 14 Apr. 1880 – mfms no. 335, 611, 476, 611); Lacombe to Archbishop Taschereau (1 Apr. 1876); Lacombe to the priests of the Montreal diocese (5 Apr. 1884), mfm no. 750; Lacombe to the clergy of Quebec (19 Mar. 1876), mfm no. 478.

26 Eg., T.-A. Bernier in part III of J.E.T. Barrette, Récit d'aventures dans le Nord-Ouest, etc. (Montreal: W.F. Daniel 1881); or the impact of Dubuc, Royal, and Larivière in N.-E. Dionne, Etats-Unis, Manitoba, et Nord-Ouest: notes de voyage (Quebec: Brousseau 1882), p. 40.

27 Eg., T.-A. Bernier, Manitoba, champ d'immigration (Ottawa 1887); Georges Dugas, Manitoba et ses avantages pour l'agriculture (n.p., n.d.); Albert Lacombe, Un Nouveau

L.-R. Masson of Terrebonne rose in the Commons in 1875 to ask for federal aid for French-Canadian prairie settlement, he was acting in response to a prompting by Taché. Indeed, Taché continued to urge Masson to 'insist that they do something to aid French-Canadian emigration; it's our only hope of salvation.'[28]

Quebeckers did not respond enthusiastically to these appeals from the West. To be sure, they were usually polite, and willing to make a gesture. They might admit that the soil of Manitoba was fertile,[29] or announce that Quebeckers should not remain 'quiet spectators of what the Province of Ontario does to colonize this fertile territory.'[30] But such positive statements were invariably qualified, usually by the observation that French Canadians might go to the West *instead of emigrating to the United States.*[31] Indeed, why should French Canadians leave Quebec at all? It had jobs and resources for everyone. But if people really must leave, then why not go to Manitoba instead of the States?[32] It was in this spirit that *Le Courrier de St-Hyacinthe* advised its readers not to leave western settlement all to Ontario:

It's always sad to see any of our compatriots, our brothers, abandoning their native land and expatriating themselves, but instead of seeing them head for the United States … we'd be glad to see them go toward the North-West.[33]

One thing that made Quebeckers cool toward the idea of prairie settlement was the survival of that same pessimistic opinion about the value of western land and climate which had made them wary of the project to annex the North-West in the first place. More than a decade after the annexation, Joseph Royal complained that Quebeckers were ignorant of the richness and potential of the land:

The lack of knowledge about the wealth or the value of the interior country meant that

---

champ de colonisation: la vallée de la Saskatchewan (n.p., n.d.); Société de colonisation de Manitoba, *A nos compatriotes des Etats-Unis et du Canada, émigrez à Manitoba* (St Boniface? 1876?); Elie Tassé, *Le Nord-Ouest* (Ottawa: Imprimerie du Canda 1880); *Le Nord-Ouest canadien; brochure compilée par un colonisateur de neuf ans d'expérience* (n.p., 188-); etc.

28 Masson to Taché (22 Jan. 1876), and Taché to Masson (3 Feb. 1876), in A.-A. Taché, *Correspondance, 1870–1881* (typed copies of the originals, in the Gagnon Collection, Montreal Municipal Library).
29 *La Minerve,* 12 May 1873.
30 *Le Courrier de St-Hyacinthe,* 17 July 1873.
31 In the same article in *La Minerve,* 12 May 1873.
32 *La Minerve,* 20 May 1873. Also, 6 Oct. 1886.
33 *Le Courrier de St-Hyacinthe,* 17 July 1873.

people attached very little importance to ... the West. A land of furs, a region for adventure, an almost legendary country – Canadian policy had no business with it.[34]

A belief that the West was a barren and inclement land was, in fact, a natural consequence of the religious connection between it and Quebec since 1818. From the beginning, missionaries' reports to Quebec were discouraging,[35] partly, no doubt, because they usually accompanied appeals for charity. In 1866, Bishop Taché referred to his twenty years in the North-West as 'twenty years of devotion and sacrifice.'[36] Both the missionaries and their flocks had to put up with great hardship. 'Often,' wrote Taché, 'the poor missionaries of the diocese of St Boniface have had to deprive themselves, to tighten their belts seriously, in order to feed people whose relations live here in ease and abundance.'[37]

Not only did this type of description encourage countributions to missionary collections, but it also served, before the 1860s, to dampen any enthusiasm for Canadian expansion into the North-West, thus helping to put off the evil day for the native peoples. But after 1870, when changed conditions made the missionaries want settlers from Quebec, they were hampered by their own earlier efforts. Albert Lacombe explained the predicament in a letter of 1876:

There's one thing in this country [Quebec] that badly hurts our Manitoba colonization work, and that is that people often fling in my teeth the accusation that not many years ago Mgr Taché and some of his priests were continually writing and speaking against the advantages which they now claim Manitoba offers. Your Lordship, I've just received a letter this morning from someone in a huff, saying: 'If this emigration hasn't been a success, it's because Mgr Taché did everything he could, in the beginning, to prevent people from going there (no doubt in the best of intentions) but when one has run down a region so much, with its soil, climate, means of subsistence, &c &c, one must not be surprised to see the current of emigration headed elsewhere.'[38]

---

34 *La Revue Canadienne*, XVII (1881), pp. 42–3. This view of a wild and savage North-West was no doubt strengthened when Albert Lacombe spoke to the 1874 National Convention about 'my savages and Métis' (in *L'Opinion Publique*, 2 July 1874), or when Bishop Laflèche complained in the *Journal des Trois-Rivières*, 5 Aug. 1880, that the Métis still rebelled against the sedentary life.

35 Eg., J.-N. Provencher's account, *Mémoire ou notice sur l'établissement de la mission de la Rivière-Rouge* (Rome 1836).

36 A.-A. Taché, *Vingt années de missions dans le Nord-Ouest de l'Amérique* (Montreal: Senécal 1866), p. 2.

37 A.-A. Taché, *Lettre ... donnant à Mgr de Montréal le récit des malheurs de son diocèse depuis deux ans* (Montreal? 1861?), p. 9.

38 Lacombe to Taché (Montreal, 6 Apr. 1876), in Archives Deschâtelets, St Boniface papers, mfm no. 480.

Lacombe urged Taché to produce a new publication to counteract the negative influence of his 1869 *Sketch of the North-West of America.*[39]

Often, the old negative attitudes, instead of being dissipated, were reinforced by new reports from the West. In 1874, Lacombe asked Taché for verification of a report circulated in Quebec that grasshoppers had destroyed the crops and pastures of Manitoba, whose population was faced with great distress.[40] The archbishop's answering telegram was discouraging: 'Emigrants with means to support themselves may come. Poor people ought not to come this year.'[41] And Lacombe reported what effect such communications had on Quebec opinion:

The bad news from Manitoba concerning torrential rains, floods, lack of work, etc., is making a very bad impression on the minds of people who have always been pessimistic about out work and our settlements in that country.[42]

The impression was made even blacker when several French Canadians, having tried farming in Manitoba, returned to the East to report failure. 'The return of some of our emigrants,' wrote Lacombe in 1877, 'is doing a lot of harm to our movement in general and causing me many set-backs in particular.'[43]

Even more than by these attitudes, western settlement was hampered by the whole feeling of Quebec patriotism which was the subject of the last chapter – the feeling expressed by Conservative journalist Arthur Dansereau when he wrote that 'it is well known that the French Canadians have no other

39 Lacombe to Taché (Montreal, 14 Apr. 1880), in Archives Deschâtelets, St Boniface papers, mfm no. 611. Also, letters quoted in Benoit, *Vie de Mgr Taché*, II, 198–9.
40 Lacombe to Taché (Ottawa, 30 July 1874), in Archives Deschâtelets, St Boniface papers, mfm no. 419.
41 A.-A. Taché, telegram to J.-C. Taché (St Boniface, 1 Aug. 1874), in Archives Deschâtelets, St Boniface papers, mfm no. 419.
42 Lacombe to Taché (Montreal, 10 July 1877), in Deschâtelets, St Boniface papers, mfm no. 522. Also, letters dated Montreal, 21 Feb. 1876, and 16 July 1877 (mfms no. 475 and 523).
43 Lacombe to Taché (Salem, Mass., 11 June 1877), in Deschâtelets, St Boniface papers, mfm no. 520. Also, letters dated Fall River, 15 Feb. 1877, and Worcester, 10 Mar. 1877 (mfms no. 506 and 509). Ontarians had been able to escape much of the negativism that characterized Quebec attitudes because of their relative isolation from the North-West in the early period. From the early 1820s to the late 1850s, the English-speaking element in the North-West had practically no regular contact with Canada. Thus, while French Quebeckers had been hearing for decades that the North-West was a hard land where survival required 'that dedication which only Catholicism can inspire', the first serious word Ontarians heard about the territory's potential was Professor Hind's reference to it as a 'Paradise of Fertility'.

homeland in the world than the Province of Quebec. ... '[44] And since Quebec, and only Quebec, was the French-Canadian homeland, 'any emigration at all, whether toward the United States or to the North-West, is a social calamity which all true patriots have the duty to fight by all legitimate means.'[45]

The prevalence of this attitude led Quebeckers to see the St Boniface colonizers as competitors against their own Quebec colonization movement. Thus, *L'Evénement*, arguing against a Conservative statement that a Pacific railroad was necessary for the future of colonization:

For our part, we think that public opinion is not eager to go looking for *the key to colonization* so far away. As long as it hasn't undone the lock that closes the gates to the colonization of the St Maurice, the Saguenay, etc., it will hardly be eager to pay out millions for the key to colonization in the North-West.[46]

And *La Vérité* answered the appeals from St Boniface by asserting that 'the province of Quebec needs all its people here to develop its resources and the wealth of its soil.'[47]

Thus, the St Boniface colonizers met not only apathy but outright opposition when they visited Quebec. 'The men of Quebec,' wrote J.-B. Proulx in 1872, 'seem to fear a public crusade on my part. ... '[48] From Montreal he reported that he had met 'discouraging words, indifference, senseless objections, at best a sort of cold encouragement.'[49] Albert Lacombe met the same reception among the Quebec clergy a few months later. 'It's terrible,' he complained, 'our French-Canadian priests show very little attachment to our cause. ... '[50] Nor did the situation seem to improve. In 1876, Lacombe was still lamenting that 'I met very little sympathy among the clergy for our migration [to Manitoba] movement.'[51] The Bishop of Sherbrooke even refused Lacombe permission to circulate a pro-Manitoba

---

44 Arthur Dansereau, letter to J.-A. Chapleau (Montreal, 5 Aug. 1885), in PAC: Chapleau papers (MG 27, I, C3). Also, Frédéric Gerbié, *Le Canada et l'émigration française* (Quebec: Darveau 1884), p. 150; Benjamin Sulte, *Histoire des Canadiens-Français*, VII, 155; Philippe Masson, *Le Canada-Français et la Providence*, p. 52.

45 *La Vérité*, 12 June 1886. Also, 3 July 1886; Masson, p. 53; Gerbié, p. 272; Dionne, *Etats-Unis, Manitoba*, p. 22.

46 *L'Evénement*, 29 Apr. 1872. Also, 5 Mar. 1875.

47 *La Vérité*, 12 June 1886. Also, 15 May and 3 July 1886; *Le Journal d'Agriculture* (Montreal), May, 1878, and Mar., 1880; *Le Pionnier de Sherbrooke*, 12 Aug. 1881; *Le Monde Illustré* (Montreal), 14 Nov. 1885; *La Revue Canadienne*, XXIII (1887), pp. 502–4.

48 Proulx to Taché (Ottawa, 5 June 1872), in Deschâtelets, St Boniface papers, mfm no. 310.

49 Proulx to Taché (Montreal, 11 June 1872), in ibid., mfm no. 310.

50 Lacombe to Taché (Quebec, 28 Dec. 1872), in ibid., mfm no. 335.

51 Lacombe to Taché (Montreal, 21 Feb. 1876), in ibid., mfm no. 475.

letter in his diocese. 'Since coming to Sherbrooke,' wrote the bishop, 'I've done everything I could to attract French Canadians to the Eastern Townships, and to keep the Catholic families already settled here.' Despite these efforts, Protestants still outnumbered Catholics in the diocese. Consequently, the bishop could not agree to 'encourage a movement of emigration from my diocese to Manitoba.'[52]

What the bishop feared at the level of the diocese, others feared at the level of the province. Quebec government leaders told Proulx in 1872: '"We are opposed on principle to the depopulation of our province. ... "'[53] Four years later, the premier, Boucherville, put it more strongly to Lacombe. 'Far from encouraging me in our emigration work,' reported the missionary, 'he assured me he'd do everything in his power to prevent the French Canadians of the Province of Quebec from emigrating to Manitoba.'[54] By 1880, the opposition was familiar. 'It's always the same old story,' wrote Lacombe, 'they're afraid of depopulating the province of Quebec to aid Manitoba.'[55]

Against the conviction that the Province of Quebec was the proper homeland of the French Canadians it was hard for the westerners to strive. Sometimes they tried to protest that 'Manitoba too is the homeland. On the banks of the Red River we can, just like the upright population which inhabits the St Lawrence valley, claim our rights as first occupants of the land.'[56] *Occupants of the land* was, in fact, a rather exaggerated expression, for the French-Canadian claim to a pioneering role in the West had been based on the work of missionaries and traders rather than farmers and settlers. What the St Boniface people could claim was that the West belonged to French Canada because 'our fathers, those intrepid *coureurs des bois*, went before us into the region and laid the groundwork there.'[57] French Canadians, they claimed, were no newcomers to the North-West:

One hundred and fifty-five years ago the Sieur de la Vérendrye and his sons crossed the immense prairies of the West to the foot of the Rocky Mountains, and took possession of them in the name of the King of France; for a century and a half our

52 Antoine, Bishop of Sherbrooke, to Lacombe (Sherbrooke, 27 Mar. 1876), in ibid., mfm no. 479.
53 Proulx to Taché (Ottawa, 5 June 1872), in ibid., mfm no. 310.
54 Lacombe to Taché (Montreal, 1 Mar. 1876), in ibid., mfm no. 476.
55 Lacombe to Taché (Quebec, 16 Apr. 1880), in ibid., mfm no. 611. Also, Lacombe to Taché (Montreal, 30 May 1876), in mfm no. 486 ('Il y a par ici quelques prêtres qu'on croirait des amis, qui sont loin de favoriser les intérêts de Manitoba'); Noël Bernier, *Fanystelle* (St Boniface, 1939?), p. 19; Benoit, II, 384; *Le Courrier du Canada*, 18 June 1879.
56 Bernier, *Manitoba, champ*, p. 16.
57 Barrette, *Récit d'aventures*, p. 17.

French-Canadian voyageurs have been crossing the prairies back and forth in every direction. ... No, the French-Canadians are not foreigners to the North-West![58]

But this was a weak argument after all, for Franch Canada's claim to Quebec had always been based, as we have seen, not merely on exploration but on real occupation. Why, if exploration, commerce, and missions could establish a real claim to a territory, then French Canada would be entitled to most of the United States as well! 'The Mississippi valley, the North-West and the western part of New England itself were all founded by us.'[59] What the St Boniface colonizers could say of Manitoba, Joseph Tassé could say, and more, about the western U.S.A. 'In this town [St Paul], as everywhere in Minnesota, French Canadians were the first to exploit the teeming forests and rivers, to labour the soil or to found cities and villages.'[60]

The Franco-Manitobans were obliged, therefore, to come to terms with the fact that Quebeckers considered their province the only real homeland of French Canadians, and with their refusal to encourage emigration from Quebec to the West. They announced that they would seek as settlers only those who already lived in or were about to leave for the United States.[61] And even here they ran into trouble, for they competed against the movement to repatriate Franco-Americans back to Quebec. Patriotic Franco-Americans, who still looked on Quebec as the homeland, sometimes objected to the presence among them of the St Boniface colonizers.[62]

58 Georges Dugas, *L'Ouest canadien* (Montreal: Cadieux et Derome 1896), p. 6. Also, Archbishop Taché's circular to the Quebec clergy, June, 1874, referring to Manitoba as 'un pays découvert par nos pères et arrosé par les sueurs de nos dévoués missionnaires' (Montreal archiepiscopal archives, St Boniface correspondence); the circular of 1871, quoted by Robert Rumilly in vol. 1 of his *Histoire de la province de Québec* (Montreal: Valiquette n.d.), pp. 191–2; *La Minerve*, 27 Mar. 1885.
59 *La Minerve*, 26 June 1874.
60 In *La Revue Canadienne*, VIII (1871), p. 82. Also, Tassé's *Les Canadiens de l'Ouest* (Montreal: imprimerie Canadienne 1878), pp. v–xiv; *L'Opinion Publique*, 19 June 1879; *La Revue Canadienne*, VI (1869), p. 322; VIII (1871), p. 319; X (1873), pp. 213, 521, 525; XI (1874), pp. 549–52; XIII (1876), p. 475. A propos of such claims to territory, the Quebec historian R.-L. Séguin asks ironically: 'Un Français va-t-il revendiquer l'Espagne pour sa patrie en alléguant qu'un empereur, du nom de Charlemagne, y a un jour chevauché bannière au vent?' In 'Doit-on mêler histoire et politique?' in the *RHAF*, XXII, 2 (Sept., 1968), p. 32.
61 Lacombe to the clergy of the Montreal archdiocese (Montreal, 19 Mar. 1876), in Deschâtelets, St Boniface papers, mfm no. 478.
62 Eg., Janson La-Palme to R.P. Harel (Lawrence, Mass., 14 June 1885), in the Montreal archiepiscopal archives, colonization file. *La Revue Canadienne*, XIII (1876), p. 475, claimed that the Franco-Americans still dreamed of returning to end their days on the banks of the St Lawrence.

When people in Quebec thought of colonization, then, their first thought was still of Quebec, and not of the West. In contrast to the coldness which met Proulx and Lacombe were the 'invaluable efforts' and the 'good will' which the curé Labelle received from the Montreal archdiocese and throughout the province.[63] 'This work of colonization pleases everyone,' wrote Labelle. 'It's the only work in my parish which has never been criticized.'[64]

The primacy of Quebec had always to be accepted by the St Boniface colonizers. 'Our idea,' they repeated again and again, 'is not to ask the peaceful and contented inhabitants of the province of Quebec to exchange a secure and advantageous position for the uncertainties and the risks of a distant emigration; but if there are any who *must* move and who are reluctant to undertake the heavy work of cutting timber, to those people, *Monsieur le Curé*, we ask you to indicate the province of Manitoba.'[65]

This much, at least, Quebec leaders might be willing to go along with.[66] Without encouraging western settlement in a general way, one might at least 'direct toward Manitoba those who cannot earn their living here.'[67] Perhaps, after all, that was better than emigration to the United States – though it was certainly not as good as having all French Canadians remain in Quebec:

We cannot advise our compatriots to leave the province; but as for those who are already determined to leave, we can only encourage them to go preferably to

---

63 Quoted in Rumilly, *Histoire de la province de Québec*, v, 251.
64 Antoine Labelle, report on colonization to Archbishop Fabre, 1880. In Montreal archiepiscopal archives, colonization file. See also G.A. Nantel, *Notre Nord-Ouest provincial* (Montreal: Senécal et fils 1887). The title itself is significant; so is the premise, that the natural and obvious place for French Canadians to settle is northern Quebec (eg., p. 11).
65 Circular of the bishops to the clergy of the ecclesiastical province of Quebec, 23 Oct. 1871, quoted in Rumilly, *Histoire de la province*, I, 191–2. Also, J.-C. Langelier, *Etude sur les territoires du Nord-Ouest du Canada* (Montreal 1874), p. iv; Elie Tassé, Le Nord-Ouest, letter of introduction and preface; Bernier, *Manitoba, champ*, pp. 7, 69, and 'Projet de rapport de la 6ᵉ commission de la Convention nationale sur la situation des Canadiens au Manitoba' (ms, Quebec, 26 June 1880, in the archives of the Collège Ste-Marie at Montreal); *Le Nouveau Monde*, 25 Feb. 1875.
66 That they did go along with it to some extent is seen in the fact that the circular letter from which the above was quoted, while it originated with the Bishop of St Boniface, was signed by all the bishops of Quebec. This has been taken by some historians to indicate that there was a real support in Quebec for Manitoba settlement, at least in the 1870s. However, the evidence we have seen – especially the letters of Proulx and Lacombe –suggests that the signing of this circular was probably a mere gesture, a token of good will on the part of the Quebec bishops toward their western colleague. It was this very circular, in fact, which the Bishop of Sherbrooke refused to allow Lacombe to distribute in his diocese.
67 *Le Pionnier de Sherbrooke*, 26 June 1874.

Manitoba, just as we are happy to see the French Canadians of the United States head in that same direction.[68]

Bishop Laflèche of Trois-Rivières expressed the same scale of priorities: 'The best thing for a French Canadian is to stay in his own country. ... As for those who are forced by harsh circumstances to leave the province of Quebec, it's to Manitoba that they ought to go.'[69]

But if the prairies needed more settlers, well then, let them come from elsewhere. 'It's to the West that European emigrants especially will go. As for us, we have the North!'[70] Let Ontario, too, send its population away if it wished to:

The province of Ontario is pretty well depopulating itself. Its farmers are emigrating *en masse* to Manitoba. ...

We don't want to advise our farmers who have land here to leave our province in order to go and open up new lands. We need all our population here.[71]

Indeed, if Ontarians emigrated to the prairies, while French Canadians remained in their own province, then Quebec could only benefit, both in terms of its political representation at Ottawa and in its economy:

The movement of emigration from Ontario to the North-West will continue to grow. It will assuredly balance what we in the province of Quebec will lose by emigration to the United States, which we can diminish in any case. When Quebec and Montreal are directly linked with the North-West by the Pacific railroad, when that line is being exploited, it is certain that those two cities will make rapid progress by their commercial relations with Manitoba.[72]

And here, having come to it by way of the question of settlement, we rejoin once again the main line of French-Canadian attitudes toward the prairie West. What we saw in the discussion about the territory's acquisition in 1869,

---

68 *L'Opinion Publique*, 10 May 1877.
69 L.-F. Laflèche, letter to *Le Canadien*, 14 Mar. 1889. Also, *Le Journal d'Agriculture* (Montreal), Mar., 1880; *L'Etendard*, 20 Feb. 1883; *L'Union des Cantons de l'Est*, 30 Aug. 1884; *Le Canadien*, 23 May, 13 and 20 June, 1873; *Le Nouveau Monde*, 25 Feb. 1875; *La Revue Canadienne*, XI (1874), p. 553; *Le Journal de Québec*, 2 May 1876; *Le Journal des Trois-Rivières*, 5 Aug. 1880; *L'Opinion Publique*, 2 July 1874 (Lacombe's remarks).
70 *Le Monde Illustré*, 14 Nov. 1885. Although federal aid to the Mennonites was criticized in 1875, Ottawa was at other times encouraged to promote European emigration to the Canadian West. Eg., *Le Canadien*, 4 May, 15 July, and 5 Aug. 1880; 12 June 1883.
71 *Le Courrier du Canada*, 18 June 1879.
72 *Le Canadien*, 3 Aug. 1881. Frédéric Gerbié suggested (in *Le Canada et l'émigration française*, p. 150) that French Canadians were particularly glad to see English Quebeckers move to the West, since it enabled French Quebeckers to take over their land.

what we saw in the promotion of Quebec's commercial and railroad interests, we see here once more. No matter who actually peopled the prairies, French Canada would benefit, as Montreal's mayor, Honoré Beaugrand, pointed out in 1887, by the 'continual tribute' carried by the railway, by 'the whole commerce of the North-West.'[73]

The failure of French Canadians to move to the West endangered the existence of their cultural institutions there. The Manitoba Act had established the French language and Catholic schools, but as the proportion of French to English population changed radically to the disadvantage of the former, these institutions came under attack. By 1874 the Winnipeg *Free Press* had launched a campaign against the dual systems of language and schools,[74] and Archbishop Taché was soon obliged to take to print in their defence.[75] By 1879 the pressure was so great that premier John Norquay was able to push through the legislature a bill to abolish the official status of the French language. Only the presence of a French-Canadian lieutenant-governor (Joseph Cauchon) kept the bill from being signed into law. But in the course of the affair, the Franco-Manitobans had broken with Norquay and found themselves without representation in the cabinet.

This crisis was followed with a natural interest but less than feverish excitement in Quebec. *La Revue Canadienne* described Manitoba as 'rather agitated' by the affair, it which 'the French minority of this previously all-French province has seen its dearest rights threatened.'[76] It was clear that Norquay's action constituted a 'declaration of war' against the minority,[77] and a 'persecution of our race in Manitoba.'[78]

As the last quotation suggests, Quebeckers had less difficulty in 1879 in identifying themselves with the embattled minority than they had had in the cases of the Métis or Acadians. While not many Quebeckers had moved to Manitoba since 1870, the few French Catholics who did live there were now mostly French Canadians from Quebec. Quebec newspapers, therefore,

---

73 Honoré Beaugrand, *De Montréal à Victoria par le transcontinental canadien* (Montreal 1887), p. 6. Also, pp. 3, 5; *Le Canadien*, 30 July 1881.
74 R.O. MacFarlane, 'Manitoba Politics and Parties after Confederation', in the *CHAR*, 1940, p. 48.
75 A.-A. Taché, *Denominational or Free Christian Schools in Manitoba* (Winnipeg: Standard Printing 1877).
76 *La Revue Canadienne*, XVI (1879), p. 644.
77 *Le Nouveau Monde*, 5 June 1879.
78 *Le Courrier de St-Hyacinthe*, 7 June 1879. Also, *La Minerve*, 3 and 17 June; *Le Courrier de St-Hyacinthe*, 7 June; *Le Canadien*, 6, 9, 16, and 21 June; *L'Evénement*, 11 and 14 June; *La Patrie* (Montreal) 9 June; *Le Journal des Trois-Rivières*, 9 June; *L'Opinion Publique*, 12 June; *Le Nouveau Monde*, 4 June 1879.

could easily use the first-person 'us' and 'our nationality' in discussing this case.[79] It was a question, they readily saw, 'of the future of our race in that vast territory.'[80]

Nevertheless, this never became the *cause célèbre* that the amnesty or the New Brunswick schools had been. It was too quickly resolved of its own accord, and never brought to Ottawa, where French Quebeckers would have had the chance to play their role of defenders of the minorities. Not that they were unready to play the part again. They expected the Franco-Manitobans, of course, to fight in their own behalf,[81] but would not be surprised if a successful resolution of the matter could only be obtained at Ottawa.[82] They would certainly give their help to the Franco-Manitobans in that case:

Naturally, they are assured of our sympathy and of our most loyal co-operation, and we are confident that this struggle, carried on by peaceful means, and with the aid of the laws and institutions of the country, will end to the shame of the perpetrators of fanaticism.[83]

Despite this proclaimed eagerness to fight the battle to a successful conclusion, Quebeckers showed (as they had done in the case of the New Brunswick schools) a tendency to overlook the happy outsome of the crisis. Thus, *Le Pionnier de Sherbrooke*, having declared that French Canadians would resist assimilation to the end, failed to note that the anti-French bill had not become law. Another paper, while reporting that Cauchon had refused to sign the bill, commented not that this ended the matter happily but that English Manitobans were narrow-minded and intolerant.[84] And two weeks later, still another paper continued to complain about Anglo-Manitoban fanaticism and its consequences: 'We have suffered losses which are probably irreparable, but we are not yet crushed.'[85] Apparently, French-Quebec opinion still considered the opportunity for its nationality to live in the West to be less important than the threats to it!

Because of this tendency, the 1879 crisis served to strengthen already-traditional resentments in Quebec, particularly resentments against the

---

79 *L'Union des Cantons de l'Est*, 13 June 1879.
80 *Le Courrier du Canada*, 9 June 1879. Also, *Le Nouveau Monde*, 31 May; *Le Canadien*, 2 June; *Le Journal des Trois-Rivières*, 5 June 1879.
81 *Le Courrier de St-Hyacinthe*, 7 June 1879.
82 *L'Union des Cantons de l'Est*, 13 June 1879 (quoting *La Minerve*); *La Minverve*, 5 June 1879.
83 *La Minerve*, 17 June 1879. Also, *Le Courrier de St-Hyacinthe*, 14 June 1879.
84 *L'Union des Cantons de l'Est*, 3 July 1879.
85 *Le Courrier du Canada*, 17 July 1879. The conclusion of the Manitoba crisis was obscured in the Quebec press by the session of Quebec's own parliament, by the federal move to fire Letellier de St-Just, and by the death of Prince Louis Bonaparte in Zululand.

Anglo-Quebeckers. Manitoba's treatment of its minority stood in bitter contrast 'to the situation in the province of Quebec, where the Franco-Canadian element is such a big majority and yet treats the Anglo-Canadian minority in such a different manner.'[86]

But what was the effect of this affair on the St Boniface colonization movement? Surely we should expect that harassment of the minorities, especially in the West, would be an important factor in discouraging French Canadians from going to settle on the prairies? In fact, at least one paper in Quebec did draw discouraging conclusions from the crisis. It was now too late, claimed *L'Opinion Publique*, to advise French Canadians to go west. The position of their nationality there was already wrecked:

The time to speak up was sooner. For five years English emigration has flooded Manitoba, and French emigration has been pretty well nil. It's too late. ... It's best to be realistic about the future and prepare for it. The North-West, founded and settled by the French, is destined, like the rest of North America, to be English.[87]

This attitude, however, was not shared by the rest of the French-language press. Far from being discouraged by what had happened, other papers expected and advocated a growing movement of French Canadians to Manitoba, not only in spite of, but even because of this crisis. With such a movement, French Canadians could regain their majority position in the Manitoba population, and thus ensure that their rights would be respected.[88] They must profit from the warning they had just received:

It's time for our compatriots in the province of Quebec to open their eyes and come to the rescue of their brothers in Manitoba, by helping in the colonization of the North-West.[89]

In fact, in the midst of the discussion of the Manitoba crisis, a new and interesting goal was proposed to French Canadians by one of their papers:

The Franco-Canadian element has, and must have, its place in the sun in our North-West. If fanaticism makes life too hard for it in Manitoba, it will have to take a

---

86 *Le Nouveau Monde*, 31 May 1879. Also, *La Patrie*, 10 June: *Le Courrier de St-Hyacinthe*, 7 June; *La Minerve*, 5 June 1879.
87 *L'Opinion Publique*, 19 June 1879. To say in this way that French-Canadian settlement in Manitoba should have been thought of five years earlier was completely to ignore the work of Taché, Lacombe, and the Société de colonisation de Manitoba, which had been formed precisely five years before.
88 *Le Courrier de St-Hyacinthe*, 7 June 1879. Also, *Le Nouveau Monde*, 9 June 1879.
89 *La Patrie*, 10 June 1879. It is important to note that even here the usual conditions were made. This was not a general encouragement to French Quebeckers to go to Manitoba, but only to those who would otherwise emigrate to the States.

part of the neighbouring territory, and instead of uniting with that province, form a separate province where it will be able to find a refuge from persecution. ... [90]

Here was the beginning, at least, of a new departure in the interpretation of Confederation. The notion that French Canadians should have a special province of their own in the West was consistent with the autonomist view of 1864–7, and with the old premise that the only real guarantee of national life was majority status within a provincial framework. But it was new in its implication of a French Canada properly at home outside of Quebec. In this, it undoubtedly reflected the new awareness of French-Catholic minorities which had been forced on Quebeckers by the events of the past decade.

During the 1879 Manitoba crisis we also find for the first time a tentative expression of a new view of the agreement which brought Confederation into being. It was *La Minerve* which, arguing that Manitoba could never get away with banning French, maintained not only that such a ban violated section 23 of the Manitoba Act, but even more, that it was a 'violation of the sworn pact between the two nationalities.'[91] What was this pact between two nationalities? Surely no-one had mentioned it before? When the Confederationists had spoken of a pact, a compact, or a treaty in the past, they had meant an agreement among provinces. And yet, those provinces had themselves represented or even embodied nationalities. Quebec, in particular, had represented the French-Canadian nation.

In the events of and following from the Red River uprising of 1869–70, two provinces seemed to be battling over the future of the North-West. They were the two provinces which, since 1791, had represented French and English Canada: Quebec and Ontario. Through them, it had appeared to be the two nationalities that were in conflict. Through them the two nationalities had seemed to come to an agreement about the West: Ontario had accepted the Manitoba Act, Quebec the expeditionary force.

But the people involved in the 1879 crisis were mostly, as we have seen, French Canadians from Quebec, from one of the original nationalities and provinces that had made the confederation in 1867 and the Manitoba compromise in 1870. By settling in Manitoba, they had, in a sense, detached their nationality from the province of Quebec, and it was perhaps not surprising, therefore, that in a polemic concerning their national status, *La Minerve*'s editorialist should have spoken of the confederation pact in terms of the nationalities and not of the provinces which had represented them in 1867.

---

90 *Le Nouveau Monde*, 13 June 1879.
91 *La Minerve*, 5 June 1879.

However it may have been, there was no theoretical discussion, only a brief passing expression, neither elaborated upon by *La Minerve* nor taken up by another paper. It was the germ of an idea whose time had not yet come. And yet, like the proposal to create a special, French-Canadian province in the West, it suggested what effect the minority affairs might eventually have upon French-Canadians' attitudes toward Confederation and their place in it.

VIII

THE

RIEL AFFAIR

THE future-foreshadowing phrases let drop by *La Minerve* or *Le Nouveau Monde* in the excitement of the Manitoba language crisis made no particular impression at the time. French Canadians continued reluctant to move or encourage each other to move to the West. Their attitudes toward Quebec and the place of their nationality inside and outside of it did not suddenly change.

These attitudes had the chance to express themselves in June of 1880, when the Quebec City St-Jean-Baptiste Society organized a national convention in imitation of the one Montreal had held in 1874. Though this reunion was smaller than the earlier one, and the press commentary somewhat less excited, the themes sounded were familiar. On the one hand, the manifestations of the continued strength of the French-Canadian identity in the United States were impressive, creating not only a confidence in the permanence of the Franco-American community but even a hope 'that the French Canadians are called to exercise an important influence in the public affairs of the whole continent.'[1] On the other hand, there was again an emphasis on homecoming which implied that Quebec was still the real homeland of all French Canadians. Indeed, the patriotism inspired by the gathering of French Canadians in the ancient capital of their nation caused Dominion Day to pass by unnoticed,[2] and inspired the expression of separatist hopes:

'A day shall come which is not yet come,' when the flag of independence by hall fly over the shores of the St Lawrence, as over those of the Seine; and to defend it against the attacks of the enemy, we will see ... our brothers come, as on the 24th of June,

---

1 *La Minerve*, 26 June 1880. Also, *Le Nouveau Monde*, 25 June 1880; *Le Journal des Trois-Rivières*, 24 and 28 June 1880.
2 *L'Union des Cantons de l'Est*, 3 July 1880.

1880, aroused by the noise of danger, just as even yesterday they were moved by the memory of Carillon and the Plains of Abraham.[3]

One group that had come to Quebec was the Acadians, and the idea of the national convention so much appealed to them that they decided to hold one of their own the following year in New Brunswick. There was nothing surprising about a French-Catholic group holding a local convention of its own – other, French-Canadian, groups had done so – but this one was certainly more than local. Yet nothing about it seemed to disturb the Quebec press. No-one seemed surprised when Hector Langevin was seated 'among the foreigners' observing the convention,[4] and when the Acadians rejected the Saint-Jean-Baptiste to choose another, distinctive national holiday for themselves, only *L'Union des Cantons de l'Est* expressed surprise or disappointment.[5]

The Acadian convention, in fact, caused little ink to flow in Quebec, and most of that was spent expressing surprised pleasure that an Acadian nation existed at all. 'The Acadian people is waking up,' commented *La Revue Canadienne*; 'it is taking stock of itself, affirming itself.' French Quebeckers could only be pleased to see the progress 'of this little people, which is brother to our own'.[6] Indeed, both the pleasure and the surprise were all the greater because, ever since the expulsion, a veil had hung over the history of the Acadians; 'for a century now, we've scarcely even heard their name pronounced.' Thus, the convention, which helped the Quebeckers to discover the Acadians, seemed also to announce a rebirth: 'Such is the moving spectacle we have just witnessed: it is the resurrection of the Acadian people.'[7] This comment indicated that, despite the presence of Acadians at Montreal and Quebec in 1874 and 1880, and despite the events of 1874–5, the discovery of their community by Quebeckers was still incomplete. The latter could still be surprised at the great numbers who attended the New Brunswick convention,[8] or even at the fact that the Acadians spoke proper French – that 'their French is the same as ours.'[9]

---

3 *Le Courrier de St-Hyacinthe*, 6 July 1880.
4 Ibid., 30 July 1881: 'au nombre des étrangers'.
5 *L'Union des Cantons de l'Est*, 27 Aug. 1881. The decision was reported without comment by *L'Opinion Publique*, 11 Aug.; *Le Nouveau Monde*, 25 and 29 July; *La Patrie*, 22 July; *Le Courrier de St-Hyacinthe*, 30 July 1881.
6 *La Revue Canadienne*, XVII (1881), p. 444. Also, *Le Courrier de St-Hyacinthe*, 30 July 1881.
7 *La Vérité*, 4 Aug. 1881.
8 *L'Union des Cantons de l'Est*, 30 July 1881; *Le Pionnier de Sherbrooke*, 29 July 1881.
9 *Le Nouveau Monde*, 23 July 1881.

And the connection between the two communities? They were related, no doubt, and indeed the Acadians and the French Canadians seemed to be moving closer together – but only in the same way as 'all the children of New France ... from British Columbia to Newfoundland, from the far North-West to New Orleans'.[10] Acadians were the 'brothers' of French Canadians, but it was a brotherhood of fellow French nations, each with its place 'among the nations under the sun'; the Acadians marched 'beside us' but not as part of us.[11]

But the Acadians were not the only minority group being discovered in the early 1880s. In 1883, Hector Langevin wondered if he weren't dreaming when he attended a French-Canadian convention at Windsor, Ontario – 'a festivity ... so French-Canadian in every respect, at a distance of almost 300 leagues from our old Quebec.' He had been amazed, moreover, to read in the census that there were as many French Canadians in Ontario as Acadians in the Maritimes.[12] Two years later Benjamin Sulte was still amazed at the size of the Franco-Ontarian community. 'Our people,' he wrote, 'form half the population in certain counties.'[13] Others, too, observed optimistically the vitality of the French Canadians, seen in the fact that 'not only are they not losing any ground in the province of Quebec, but they are gradually taking over neighbouring territory.'[14]

The position of French Catholics in the North-West gave less cause for exuberance. The tendency of French Quebeckers to emigrate only to areas close to home made for strength in Ontario but weakness in Manitoba. Unless these migration patterns changed, warned L'Etendard, the North-West would 'pass over completely to an element to whom our language, our religion and our customs are completely foreign.'[15] Even now, Orangemen were confidently announcing that French would be abolished in Manitoba within ten years. Franco-Manitobans must be 'vigilant'.[16] So, indeed, must all French Canadians:

The position of the French Canadians in the North-West must be the particular object of our concern. In view of the considerable proportion of the foreign element which daily swells the population of our territories, this is, perhaps, of all the parts of

---

10 *La Vérité*, 4 Aug. 1881.
11 *Le Journal des Trois-Rivières*, 8 Aug. 1881.
12 In N.-E. Dionne, *Fête nationale des Canadiens-Français célébrée à Windsor, Ontario, le 25 juin 1883* (Quebec: Brousseau 1883), pp. 39–41.
13 Benjamin Sulte, *Situation de la langue française au Canada* (Montreal: Imprimerie Générale 1885), p. 25.
14 *La Vérité*, 23 May 1885. Also, *Le Nouveau Monde*, 23 Oct. 1885.
15 *L'Etendard*, 20 Feb. 1883.
16 *L'Evénement*, 26 May 1883.

Canada, the one where our own element runs the greatest risk of seeing its influence neutralized. [17]

A year later came the North-West rebellion and the Riel affair.

From the outset, French Quebeckers displayed an ambivalent attitude toward the second Riel uprising. This was no longer 1869, when the Métis had been so largely unknown, and Riel himself was now a familiar figure, whom Quebeckers had defended in the amnesty affair. On the other hand, there was no question this time about the illegality of his actions. Rebellion was a serious crime, and this time Riel had no Father Ritchot to represent him or Bishop Taché to act as mediator between him and the federal government.

Certainly, Quebeckers had no doubt that the rebellion must be suppressed as quickly as possible. Whatever position they might take on the causes or the consequences of the action, none were prepared to condone the act of rebellion. 'The Roman Catholic Church has no sympathy for this insurrectionary movement,' stated one paper bluntly. [18] Riel himself was an 'agitator', whose return to Canada was 'deplorable'[19] – or else he was, at best, 'a poor madman'. [20] Conservative organs were not above blaming him again for his actions at Red River, for which they had been willing to forgive him in 1875! [21]

Questioning Riel's morality or mentality led some papers to question the legitimacy of Métis complaints. If they had been valid, after all, 'the natural and authorized defender of the Métis, Archbishop Taché, would long ago have taken up the cause.'[22] But even if their grievances were valid, the Métis had forfeited the right to sympathy by the act of rebellion. 'The revolt has made an evil cause of a just one,' and the rights which the Métis might have claimed with justice 'they have themselves wiped out by this revolt.'[23] Even the opposition press seemed to share this point of view. 'We have not the least symapthy,' declared *La Patrie*, 'for a revolt which, at the least, may well cost the lives of several of our own people.'[24]

This hostility toward the rebellion led Quebeckers to cheer on the

17 *L'Etendard*, 30 May 1884.
18 *Le Pionnier de Sherbrooke*, 2 Apr. 1885.
19 Ibid., 9 Apr. 1885. Also, *Le Courrier de St-Hyacinthe*, 21 May 1885; *Le Canadien*, 11 Jan. 1886.
20 *Le Nouveau Monde*, 31 Mar. 1885. Also, *La Minerve*, 30 Mar.
21 *La Minerve*, 30 Mar. 1885; *Le Nouveau Monde*, 31 Mar.
22 *Le Nouveau Monde*, 31 Mar. 1885. Also, 30 Mar.; *La Minerve*, 30 Mar. and 4 Apr. 1885.
23 *Le Pionnier de Sherbrooke*, 9 Apr. 1885. Also, *La Vérité*, 4 Apr.; *La Presse*, 24 and 27 Mar.; *Le Nouveau Monde*, 31 Mar. 1885.
24 *La Patrie*, 28 Mar. 1885. See also *Le Canadien*, 27 Mar.; *Le Courrier de St-Hyacinthe*, 31 Mar. and 23 Apr.; *L'Union des Cantons de l'Est*, 11 Apr. 1885.

Canadian expeditionary force throughout the campaign, and to take special pride in the French Canadians of the 65th (Montreal) and 9th (Quebec) battalions. Cheering crowds were reported to have turned out to their departures. 'Everywhere they have been acclaimed, everywhere they have been the object of the warmest sympathies.'[25] It was 'our gallant volunteers'[26] and congratulations to 'General Middleton and his valiant soldiers on their brilliant success'.[27] The French-Canadian soldiers were themselves said to be enthusiastic. Lt-Col. G. Amyot wrote to H.-G. Joly that the 9th battalion was determined to reflect credit on Quebec City, 'and to deserve the praises and the support which have been given it.'[28] And of the Montreal battalion it was reported: 'Great enthusiasm reigns among the volunteers.'[29]

And yet, the enthusiasm of the volunteers was not unalloyed with darker feelings. The surgeon of the 65th described these when he asked the minister of the militia not to send his battalion to the front:

You are, no doubt, aware that several of our principal officers are close friends and ex-classmates of Louis Riel, and that all our men look on the Métis as their compatriots and are not far from thinking that the demands of the Métis are made in the national interest and are as fair and just as those of our ancestors in 1837.[30]

An anonymous soldier's mother wrote to the minister in an angrier mood. She told him to call back the men of the French-Canadian battalions, who would be 'more in their place playing with clumps of snow than being put into a position where they have to refuse to fight against compatriots.'[31]

Thus, French Canadians were caught between their duty and their affections, between their minds and their hearts, or, as one pamphleteer put it, between patriotism and loyalty.[32] Dr Lachapelle expressed the dilemma when he assured the minister that 'the 65th Battalion will do its duty if it is ordered to march,' but that it might be wiser, considering public opinion, to send other battalions to the front instead. In any case, the French-Canadian volunteers deserved special praise for participating in this campaign, for

---

25 *La Minerve*, 4 Apr. 1885.
26 *La Revue Canadienne*, XXI (1885), p. 256.
27 Ibid., p. 316. Also, *Le Courrier du Canada*, 20 May; *Le Courrier de St-Hyacinthe*, 16 May; *Le Nouveau Monde*, 15 and 18 May; *La Presse*, 15 and 16 May 1885.
28 Lt-Col. G. Amyot to Henri-Gustave Joly de Lotbinière (first page, with date, missing), in PAC, microfilms of Joly papers, mfm no. M791.
29 *Le Courrier de St-Hyacinthe*, 2 Apr. 1885. Also 7 Apr.
30 E.V. Lachapelle to Adolphe Caron (Montreal, 28 Mar. 1885), in PAC: MG 27, I, D3, vol. 192.
31 Anonymous letter to Adolphe Caron (n.p., n.d.), in PAC: MG 27, I, D3, vol. 199.
32 Jules Deriares, *Riel: patriotisme vs loyauté* (n.p. 1885).

'many of them were sacrificing not only their interests, but even their feelings and sympathies, listening only to the call of duty,'[33]

The ambivalence of French-Canadian attitudes applied not only to the rebellion but to the Métis themselves and the degree of their relatedness to French Canadians. On the one hand, the Métis were still referred to as 'half-savage' people,[34] whose behaviour 'holds back settlement'.[35] Even if they loved the French Canadians, they still 'strongly love the savage life'.[36] Yet this very recognition of the Indian-like nature of the Métis, while defining a separateness between them and the French Canadians, was also a reason to sympathize with them, to excuse their conduct. Even a paper which heartily condemned the crime and the sin of rebellion could find in the difficulty of conversion from nomadic to sedentary life a reason to argue that 'the best way to pacify them would be to treat them justly.'[37] Their very savageness was a reason why 'we could call them misguided rather than actual rebels against the authority of the country.'[38]

In any case, the savageness of the Métis was much less mentioned in early 1885 than it had been in the winter of 1869–70. their Frenchness and Catholicism, on the other hand, were much more emphasized, while the existence of any English or Protestant element among them was entirely neglected.[39] Thus, even while condemning both Riel and the rebellion, Quebeckers could declare: 'The cause of the Métis is dear to us. They are too closely related to us by blood for us to be able to remain indifferent to their good or bad fortune. ... '[40] Indeed, for all their sense of the wrongness of the rebellion, many French Canadians could not help feeling a certain thrill at the thought of the 'cleverness' with which Riel had organized it. 'Who would

---

33 *La Revue Canadienne*, XXI (1885), p. 447. The ambivalence of the soldiers' attitude is seen in the rather unenthusiastic report of the 65th battalion's departure, given in *Le Monde Illustré*, 4 Apr. 1885. For more French-Canadian ambivalence, see the same paper, 11 Apr. and 16 May.

34 *La Patrie*, 16 May 1885. Also, 18 May.

35 *Le Canadien*, 14 June 1885.

36 Barrette, *Récit d'aventures*, p. 15. Also, *Le Monde Illustré*, 4 Apr. 1885; *Le Nouveau Monde*, 27 Mar. 1885.

37 *Le Nouveau Monde*, 27 Mar. 1885. Also, *La Presse*, 1 Apr.

38 *Le Nouveau Monde*, 2 Apr. 1885. Also, 7 Apr.

39 Even in the fall, when French Canadians complained about the contrast between the treatment meted out to Riel and that given his secretary, Jackson, 'an English Métis', they did not seem to notice the strangeness of an English Métis participating in what was supposed to be a French-Catholic uprising.

40 *Le Pionnier de Sherbrooke*, 9 Apr. 1885.

have thought,' they marvelled, 'that poor Métis would be able to force the government in this way to concede their just demands?'[41]

Sympathy for the Métis was reinforced, as had been the case in 1870, by Quebec's perception of the English-Canadian press. In the West, it was reported, the Franco-Manitobans and their leaders were being accused of financial and other involvement in the rebellion,[42] and in Ontario too, francophobe fanaticism had apparently been aroused by the rebellion. 'This fierce hostility is not new; but it has never manifested itself as openly, and with as much unanimity, as it has done since the beginning of the North-West troubles.'[43] Was it not, in fact, because of their French blood and Catholic religion – 'because of us'[44] – that the Métis were hated by the English Canadians? It was enough to arouse suspicions about 'Orange fanaticism, which would like to exterminate the French Métis of the North-West, and which must have fomented these troubles on purpose, in order to have a reason to deal severely with the hated race.'[45] Surely this was, after all, the real if secret reason for the abuse and mistreatment to which the Métis had been subjected by English-Canadian employees of the federal government?[46]

In the end, therefore, even those papers which, on one day, questioned the legitimacy of Métis grievances, found, on other days, reason to sympathize with them. *La Minerve* itself, the chief Conservative organ, admitted that 'the grievances of the Métis are serious,' and attributed the federal ministry's failure to satisfy them sooner to discrimination against French Catholics:

It would take much less time, no doubt, if it were a question of the Icelanders, Russian Mennonites, and other tribes imported at great expense – at our expense – into the Canadian North-West – that North-West which was discovered, founded, settled, peopled by the ancestors of those same *rebels* who are being treated so shabbily.[47]

All in all, then, during the spring of 1885, French Quebeckers seemed embarrassed, ambivalent, changing, in their attitudes toward the events in the North-West. They wanted the rebellion crushed, but felt sympathy for its perpetrators. They felt that insurrection was wrong, but that at least some of the Métis' complaints were justified, that if the Métis were to blame, so was

---

41 *La Revue Canadienne*, XXI (1885), p. 256. Also, *Le Monde Illustré*, 16 May 1885.
42 *Le Courrier du Canada*, 14 and 18 Apr. and 1 May 1885.
43 *La Patrie*, 15 May 1885.
44 *L'Etendard*, 1 Apr. 1885.
45 *La Vérité*, 4 Apr. 1885. Also, *La Patrie*, 15 May.
46 *L'Etendard*, 1 Apr. 1885; *L'Union des Cantons de l'Est*, 11 Apr.; *La Presse*, 1 Apr. 1885.
47 *La Minerve*, 27 Mar. 1885. Also, *La Revue Canadienne*, XXI (1885), p. 316; *L'Etendard*, 9 Apr.; *Le Monde Illustré*, 18 Apr.; *Le Canadien*, 8 Apr.; *La Patrie*, 30 Mar.; *L'Electeur*, 26 and 30 Mar. 1885.

the federal government. The former were certainly guilty, and had to be put down; but they were also victims of federal neglect, intolerance, and fanaticism, and that could not be forgotten.[48]

This ambivalence expressed itself in moderate statements after the rebellion was crushed and its leader under arrest. Riel, it was said, must certainly be charged and put on trial; but his trial must be a fair one, seeking impartial justice, and not vengence.[49] This would have to mean taking into account that Riel was insane. For French Canadians certainly seemed to believe that he was a 'maniac'.[50] They recalled that he had been confined in a Quebec asylum in the 1870s, and thought it likely that he was suffering now from a recurrence of the same derangement.[51]

Yes, we say it again, Riel is just a madman, a visionary entirely without responsibility for his acts. He is a moonstruck fellow whose sickly excitation naturally made a great impression on the minds of the primitive people who took him for a sort of prophet.[52]

This did not mean, of course, that he should be set free. 'We believe that the leader of the rebellion is a dangerous lunatic who cannot be treated with the full rigour of the law, but who must be put into a situation in which he cannot do any more harm or start up again with his wild escapades.'[53]

While Riel's madness was one reason why the full weight of the law could not be brought to bear upon him, so were the primitive nature of the Métis and the real grievances which had provoked them. While these were certainly not a justification of rebellion, they were at least extenuating circumstances. 'Let us remember,' urged *La Patrie*, 'that the unfortunate rebels of the North-West are half savage, that they've been scandalously persecuted, and that they believed they were fighting for the holiest of causes: their homeland.'[54] The feeling that neither Riel nor his followers could be entirely blamed for the rebellion, the one because of his madness, the others because of their primitiveness and suffering; a sense that Ottawa, because of its neglect or

---

48 *L'Etendard*, 1 Apr. 1885; *Le Courrier du Canada*, 31 Mar. and 15 May; *L'Union des Cantons de l'Est*, 11 Apr.; *La Patrie*, 13 May; *Le Monde Illustré*, 11 and 18 Apr.; *L'Etendard*, 31 Mar.; *Le Courrier de St-Hyacinthe*, 28 Mar.; *Le Canadien*, 31 Mar. 1885.
49 Eg., *La Presse*, 16 and 18 May; *Le Nouveau Monde*, 18 May; *Le Courrier du Canada*, 20 May; *La Vérité*, 23 May; *Le Courrier de St-Hyacinthe*, 28 July 1885.
50 *Le Courrier de St-Hyacinthe*, 21 May 1885. Also, 23 May.
51 *L'Union des Cantons de l'Est*, 30 May 1885.
52 *La Patrie*, 18 May 1885. Also, *La Presse*, 31 July.
53 *Le Pionnier de Sherbrooke*, 30 July 1885.
54 *La Patrie*, 16 May 1885. Also, *La Minerve*, 30 Mar.; *Le Pionnier de Sherbrooke*, 9 Apr.; *Le Nouveau Monde*, 27 Mar.; *Le Monde Illustré*, 4 Apr. 1885.

because of the irresponsible conduct of its agents, must take a share in the blame; the conviction that Riel's trial, in a way, 'will be the trial of the government'[55] – all this was reflected in the ambivalence and moderation which continued to characterize most French-Canadian comments in the late spring and early summer of 1885.

Unfortunately, it did not seem to Quebeckers that Ontarians shared their point of view. English Canadians seemed dominated by a 'pitiless pride of race.'[56] They insisted Riel be executed, no matter what the trial might reveal, and even threatened to lynch him 'if the authorities fail to give them prompt satisfaction.'[57] This perception of Ontario opinion could only serve to rearouse in French Canadians the passions of the 1870s – the feelings associated with the Lépine trial and the amnesty campaign. It reinforced the belief that Ontarians wanted to crush the Métis and hang Riel not so much because they were rebels as because they were French and Catholic. 'French Canadians remember. This year is just like 1837. At that time the English wanted to squash the French nationality in the East. Today the Saxon wants to clear out the West.'[58]

Nevertheless, such strong expressions of feeling were not widespread till after Riel's trial.[59] It was the announcement of the sentence that turned moderation and ambivalence into anger and outrage. 'Quebec is in an uproar,' reported La Patrie,[60] while La Minerve's editor sent off a fearful warning to the Bleu minister, J.-A. Chapleau:

Don't even ask me about Riel. People have gone wild from one end of the Province to the other. The Liberals will have their revenge ... if Riel is hanged. You have no idea of the violence with which even our best friends express themselves.[61]

This furore was probably a reflection of the virtual unanimity with which Quebeckers believed in Riel's madness and in the notion that the Métis' grievances ought to have been considered as extenuating circumstances in his

---

55 *La Revue Canadienne*, XXI (1885), p. 370. Also, *Le Monde Illustré*, 23 May; *La Presse*, 31 July; *L'Union des Cantons de l'Est*, 30 May; *Le Canadien*, 13 June 1885.
56 *La Revue Canadienne*, XXI (1885), p. 316.
57 *L'Union des Cantons de l'Est*, 13 June 1885. Also, *Le Courrier de St-Hyacinthe*, 23, 28, and 30 July 1885.
58 *La Patrie*, 28 July 1885. Also, *Le Canadien*, 17 June.
59 Even during the trial, *Le Nouveau Monde*'s writers were still referring to Riel as a 'vulgar ambitious man' who had cynically exploited the 'naïve credulity' of the Métis. See *L'Insurrection du Nord-Ouest, 1885* (Montreal: Le Monde n.d.), p. 3.
60 *La Patrie*, 28 July 1885.
61 Arthur Dansereau to J.-A. Chapleau (Montreal, 5 Aug. 1885), in PAC, Chapleau papers (MG 27, I, C3), Correspondence. See also, *La Presse*, 4 Aug.; *L'Union des Cantons de l'Est*, 8 Aug.; *Le Monde Illustré*, 15 Aug. 1885.

case. These factors were brought up again and again in the protests against the sentence. The federal government's own irresponsibility – and that of its agents – had aroused the Métis and even provoked the violence.[62] Riel himself was only a 'victim of his mad illusions'[63] and 'not responsible for his acts'.[64] How could the authorities hang a man 'who cannot be considered responsible since he is insane,'[65] and who, even in the midst of his trial, had given new 'unequivocal proof of the absolute derangement of his faculties'?[66]

Clearly, if Riel was condemned despite all this, then something must have been wrong with his trial. Could a group of six *Anglais* be considered a jury of Riel's peers? Had not the competence of the court been doubtful and the trial conducted in an irregular way? The implication was obvious: 'Riel was condemned even before being heard.'[67] This from a normally pro-government paper! Opposition organs were harsher:

Riel did not really have a trial. It was a sort of inquisition set up by the government, not for the purpose of enquiring into the guilt or innocence of the prisoner, but only in order to deliver up his head to the fanatics under the cover of a sham trial.[68]

Again and again, in editorials, in resolutions passed at public rallies, and in the petitions which thousands of French Canadians signed between August and November, similar complaints were made about the conduct of the trial, the choice of jury, and the fiercely prejudiced behaviour of the judge, who, it was said, 'does not belong in Canada, but would be more at home in Russia or at the court of the king of Dahomey.'[69]

The belief that the trial had been rigged was certainly strengthened by the contrast between Riel's treatment and that of his English-Canadian secretary, William Jackson, who seemed to have been found insane with scarcely any hearing at all and to have had no difficulty in escaping from custody and making off to the United States. 'The inconceivable ease with which they

---

62 *La Patrie*, 7 Aug. 1885; *La Vérité*, 7 Nov.; *L'Union des Cantons de l'Est*, 14 Nov.; *L'Elec-teur*, 5 Aug. 1885.

63 *L'Union des Cantons de l'Est*, 8 Aug. 1885.

64 *La Vérité*, 8 Aug. 1885.

65 *La Revue Canadienne*, XXI (1885), p. 506. Also, p. 569.

66 *La Presse*, 31 July 1885. Also, 4 Aug.; *La Minerve*, 3 and 5 Aug., 13 Nov.; *Le Courrier de St-Hyacinthe*, 4 and 15 Aug.; *Le Nouveau Monde*, 1 and 3 Aug., 15 and 22 Oct., 14 Nov.; *Le Courrier du Canada*, 4 and 6 Aug.; *L'Union des Cantons de l'Est*, 29 Aug. and 14 Nov.; *Le Monde Illustré*, 8 Aug.; *L'Etendard*, 8 Aug. 1885.

67 *Le Pionnier de Sherbrooke*, 6 Aug. 1885.

68 *L'Electeur* (Quebec), 4 Aug. 1885.

69 *Le Monde Illustré*, 8 Aug. 1885. Also, *La Presse*, 3 Aug.; *La Patrie*, 3 and 5 Aug.; *L'Eten-dard*, 8 Aug. 1885; *Epitome des documents parlementaires relatifs à la rébellion du Nord-Ouest* (Ottawa: Maclean, Roger 1886), pp. 244, 245, 256, 270, etc.

acquitted Jackson, and the fanatical and bloody relentlessness with which they condemned Riel, disgust us and dishonour the justice of the country.'[70] Surely there were racial implications in this contrast! They were pointed out by one of the petitions sent to Ottawa:

That the acquittal of Jackson, an English Métis, seriously compromised in the North-West troubles, declared to be without responsibility for his acts, without proof, without a trial, simply by a hasty agreement between the Crown and the court, is a revolting act of partiality, and a show of defiance not only toward our Métis compatriots in the North-West, but toward all French Canadians. ... [71]

Here was the key to the understanding of French-Canadian anger. The contrast between the treatments of Riel and of Jackson showed why Riel had been condemned; and it was apparently not because he was a criminal:

Why this difference between Riel and Jackson? Because Jackson is English while Riel is French-Canadian. ... It is only as a French Canadian that they want to hang him; as French Canadians we ask that he not be hanged. It is his nationality that they want to punish through him; it's his nationality that we want to defend.[72]

Riel's condemnation, then, had been arranged to satisfy English-Canadian francophobes. They were the ones who had turned the North-West affair into an anti-French campaign. 'It's in Ontario that it all began. It's in Upper Canada that people first considered the insurrection as a racial struggle, and, to put it frankly, as a means of getting rid of the Métis once and for all for the benefit of the Anglo-Saxon element.'[73] Even now, the people who demanded that Riel be executed were 'those who hate everything which is French-Canadian and Catholic.' For such people, 'Riel is only a name. It's the whole French-Canadian and Catholic population that they'd like to see dancing at the end of a rope!'[74]

It thus appears that what angered French Quebeckers was not so much the condemnation of the man Riel as the motives attributed to the people who condemned him. Just as in the 1870s, they reacted less to the actual situation of the Métis than to the English Canadians or Ontarians who opposed them. It was again because English Canadians were thought to have interpreted the rebellion as a French-Canadian enterprise, and to have made it the occasion for

---

70 Le Courrier de St-Hyacinthe, 15 Aug. 1885. Also, Le Nouveau Monde, 3 Aug.; La Presse, 3 Aug. 1885.
71 Epitome des documents parlementaires, p. 262.
72 L'Electeur, 7 Aug. 1885.
73 La Presse, 4 Aug. 1885.
74 L'Union des Cantons de l'Est, 14 Nov. 1885. Also, Le Nouveau Monde, 21 Sept. and 14 Nov.; Le Courrier de St-Hyacinthe, 15 Aug.; Le Canadien, 12 Nov. 1885.

attacks on French Canada, that French Quebeckers reacted in national terms. Undoubtedly, they exaggerated the degree of fanaticism in English Canada and distorted Ontario opinion in their newspapers.[75] Nevertheless, the image of an anti-French-Canadian wave sweeping through English Canada was held up repeatedly as Quebeckers commented on Riel's conviction and sentence. One of the Quebec battalions was reported to have been jeered and harassed in the streets of Winnipeg.[76] Ontario troops, on the other hand, were said to have been pillaging Métis homes.[77] L'Electeur even went so far as to accuse them of attempting 'the extermination of our Métis compatriots ... on the orders of their commanders'.[78] And along with this persecution of French people went persecution of the French language:

The fanatics of the North-West, having pushed the Métis to revolt, could hardly stop there. Now that they have brought such peril to those whose destruction they've aimed at, they are calling for the abolition of the French language in the North-West. ... Just to think of abolishing the French language is a proof of fanaticism, but to actually go about agitating for its abolition is both an absurdity and an insult to the French-Canadian nationality.[79]

It was not just Riel, therefore, who was being victimized by the English Canadians. What was being done to him 'is just what they intend to do to all our French Métis.'[80] The execution of Riel would thus be 'the triumph of Orangism over Catholicism', a victory for those who wanted to eliminate the French-Catholic element from the North-West.[81]

Papers of all parties, accordingly, urged their readers to petition, to agitate, to support the movement to have the sentence commuted and Riel saved. 'Let us plead,' advised the leading Bleu organ, 'let us petition, and we may yet

---

75 A serious study on English-Canadian opinion during the Riel affair has yet to appear. But even Jules-Paul Tardivel doubted that the declarations of fanatics were representative of what Ontarians really thought (*La Vérité*, 23 May 1885). Indeed, anyone who examines the Correspondence relating to the execution of Riel, 1885, in the Macdonald papers, North-West Rebellion, 1885 (PAC: MG 26, A, 1(a), vol. 108), will be struck by the number of letters from English Canadians calling for clemency. Certainly, some Quebec papers distorted the remarks made by the magistrate on sentencing Riel, representing them as much more cruel than they really had been. Compare, for example, *La Patrie*, 5 Aug., or *L'Electeur*, 3 and 4 Aug. 1885, with the transcript in *Epitome des documents parlementaires*, p. 225.

76 *Le Canadien*, 7 May 1885; *Le Courrier de St-Hyacinthe*, 30 July; George Beauregard, *Le 9ᵉ bataillon au Nord-Ouest* (Quebec: Gringas 1886), p. 23.

77 *Le Courrier de St-Hyacinthe*, 1 Aug. 1885.

78 *L'Electeur*, 10 Oct. 1885.

79 *Le Canadien*, 11 Aug. 1885. Also, 6 Aug; *Le Nouveau Monde*, 6 and 8 Aug. 1885.

80 *L'Etendard*, 8 Aug. 1885.

81 *L'Electeur*, 13 Nov. 1885. Also, *La Patrie*, 7 Aug.; *La Presse*, 4 Aug. 1885.

hope to save the unfortunate condemned man. ... '[82] Hope, indeed, was warranted both by the merits of Riel's case and by the encouragement of Conservative spokesmen. 'For our part,' proclaimed the *Revue Canadienne* in September, 'we are convinced that one way or another Riel will escape death, especially since new proofs of his insanity are brought forward every day.'[83] Every new delay by Ottawa was interpreted as a sign that the government would not, in the end, let Riel hang,[84] and only two days before the execution, *L'Union des Cantons de l'Est* still expressed confidence. 'Sir Hector's promise that Riel will not be hanged is going to be kept. ... Riel is mad, and we don't hang madmen in our country.'[85]

Yet Bleu leaders knew well enough that Riel was going to die, and they feared the impact his death would have on Quebec opinion. 'I may be sent home for my courage at the next electoral contest,' wrote Chapleau to Quebec's commissioner of Crown lands; and he added: 'Tomorrow the storm will rage. ... '[86]

Chapleau was right. Riel's execution unleashed the winds of fury throughout the province of Quebec, and the frustration of the previously encouraged hope made the fury all the greater. 'It is clear,' wrote Thomas Chapais, 'that the province of Quebec expected a measure of clemency. Its hopes have been deceived, and that is why it is agitated.'[87] Even *La Minerve* expressed frustration: 'The hopes of an entire race have been dashed. ... '[88] And the resulting uproar was universal. 'An electric current is running through Quebec,' wrote Chapleau, 'the force of which is not known even to those using it. ... It was generated in the sli[p] of a rope on the scaffold at Regina & it will end .... where?'[89] Not a single newspaper failed to join in the reaction of outrage. At Quebec, the Conservative *Courrier du Canada* called

---

82 *La Minerve*, 6 Aug. 1885. Also, 5 Aug. and 22 Oct.; *Le Courrier de St-Hyacinthe*, 8 and 25 Aug.; *L'Union des Cantons de l'Est*, 15 Aug.; *Le Nouveau Monde*, 15 Sept.; *L'Elec-teur*, 4 Aug.; *Le Courrier du Canada*, 10 Nov. 1885.
83 *La Revue Canadienne*, xxi (1885), p. 569. Also, *La Patrie*, 5 Aug.; *Le Courrier de St-Hyacinthe*, 15 Aug. 1885.
84 *Le Courrier de St-Hyacinthe*, 25 July and 12 Sept. 1885; *Le Courrier du Canada*, 29 July, 5 Aug., and 28 Oct.; *La Minerve*, 10 Sept.; *Le Nouveau Monde*, 15 Sept. and 22 Oct. 1885.
85 *L'Union des Cantons de l'Est*, 14 Nov. 1885. Also, *Le Courrier du Canada*, 10 Nov.
86 J.-A. Chapleau to W.W. Lynch (Ottawa, 12 Nov. 1885), in PAC, Chapleau papers, Correspondence (MG 27, I, C3).
87 *Le Courrier du Canada*, 17 Nov. 1885.
88 *La Minerve*, 17 Nov. 1885. Also, *L'Union des Cantons de l'Est*, 21 Nov.; *Le Nouveau Monde*, 16 Nov.; *La Patrie*, 17 Nov.; *L'Electeur*, 16 and 17 Nov. 1885.
89 Chapleau to Lynch (Ottawa, 21 Nov. 1885), in PAC, Chapleau papers, Correspondence (MG 27, I, C3).

November 16th a day of mourning and anger,[90] while at Montreal even the staunchest of bleu organs found it impossible to resist the storm. 'They've put cruelty in the place of justice,' it complained.[91] Not even twenty years after its opening, the great book of Confederation had been 'soiled by a stain of blood'.[92] Riel's execution had 'scandalized an entire people in a shocking manner.' The hand that passed the rope around Riel's neck had 'insulted a whole nation.'[93]

Clearly, Conservative spokesmen were in disarray, and they squirmed most uncomfortably as they looked for ways to avoid the blame for what they themselves had to condemn. Scapegoats had to be found; *La Minerve* suggested the 'hypocritical coteries who had wormed their way into the ranks of the Upper Canadian Conservative Party'. These 'agitators' had duped the honest Bleus and even taken in Sir John A. Macdonald. French Canadians ought to protest against their machinations – but to do so with calm and dignity. 'We are too much in the right to allow ourselves to get carried away.'[94]

But it wasn't enough to blame English-Canadian agitators. Why, after all, had the three French-Canadian ministers not resigned rather than allow Riel to be hanged? Had they not betrayed their nationality in order to hold on to power?[95] This question was asked so often and so pointedly that Chapleau fully expected, because of it, to be dragged 'from the Capitol to the Tarpeian Rock'.[96] Well might he have that fear, for the discomfiture among the French-Canadian Conservatives was so great that they were ready even to turn upon each other. Supporters of Langevin or the Ultramontanes, who had mistrusted Chapleau for some time, saw in him a potential whipping boy: 'May the blood of Riel and all the consequences of this terrible drama fall on the head of this renegade, this traitor, this Judas!'[97]

In the end, though, the Bleus could not escape responsibility; they had to find ways of defending the execution, or at least of taking away from it its racial significance. Within months, people who had predicted Riel would not be hanged because he was mad were denying his insanity.[98] Some who had

---

90 *Le Courrier du Canada*, 17 Nov. 1885.
91 *La Minerve*, 16 Nov. 1885.
92 Ibid., 17 Nov. 1885.
93 Ibid., 18 Nov. 1885.
94 Ibid., 16 Nov. 1885. Also 17 and 18 Nov.
95 *La Revue Canadienne*, XXI (1885), p. 697; *L'Union des Cantons de l'Est*, 21 Nov.; *La Patrie*, 16, 17, and 26 Nov. 1885.
96 J.-A. Chapleau to Gédéon Ouimet (Ottawa, 21 Nov. 1885), in PAC, Gédéon Ouimet papers (MG 27, I, F8), vol. I.
97 *L'Union des Cantons de l'Est*, 28 Nov. 1885. Also 12 Dec.
98 Eg., *La Minerve*, 11 Mar. 1886; *Le Pionnier de Sherbrooke*, 23 June 1886.

seen extenuating circumstances in the Métis grievances began to deny that such grievances had existed or to claim that if they had been real, they could have been satisfied by constitutional means.[99] And some who had questioned the fairness of the trial now began to claim that the government had 'wanted to be merciful and generous toward a condemned man in whom our population had shown (though wrongly) so much interest.'[100] In any case, it was argued, the execution had been necessary in the interest of law and order:

It is necessary, if we want to encourage immigrants to come and settle in our country, to show them that Canada is able to defend those who entrust their destinies to it. We must show that in the far North-West, just as in the old provinces, the Canadian government is strong enough to protect its people, to maintain order and to ensure respect for the law.[101]

Above all, supporters of the Conservative Party had to argue that Riel had *not* been the representative of the French-Canadian nationality in the North-West. *La Minerve* had begun making this point even before the execution, perhaps trying to prepare people for what was coming.[102] On the fatal day itself, *Le Courrier du Canada* attempted to mitigate the general anger with this comment: 'Riel on the scaffold does not represent the French-Canadian race in our eyes, nor even the Métis race.'[103] As the initial fury began to abate, some Bleu spokesmen began to grow bolder. Riel, they claimed, had not intended to defend the Métis' rights by organizing the rebellion. His real purpose had been to exploit the Métis in order to extort $35,000 from the federal government.[104] According to the Bleus, even the missionaries of the North-West considered Riel to be 'unworthy of public confidence. Riel did everything in his own personal interest.'[105] The purpose of such claims, of course, was to separate Riel from the Métis in the public mind. This would permit people to sympathize with or even admire the

---

99 Eg., *La Question Riel* (n.p., n.d.), first section, entitled 'Les griefs des Métis'; *Electeurs, attention, ne vous laissez pas tromper* (n.p., n.d.), p. 6; J.-A Chapleau, *La Question Riel: lettre aux Canadiens-français* (n.p., n.d.), arguing that all the Métis' grievances had been redressed before the outbreak of the rebellion.

100 *La Minerve*, 11 Mar. 1886.

101 Adolphe Caron, *Discours sur la question Riel* (n.p., 1886?), p. 2. This argument had been used by *Le Courrier de St-Hyacinthe* as early as 23 Apr. 1885 to defend the government against charges of having pushed the Métis to revolt, and again by *La Minerve* on 22 Oct. 1885, to hold within limits the agitation to save Riel's life.

102 *La Minerve*, 23 Sept. and 22 Oct. 1885.

103 *Le Courrier du Canada*, 16 Nov. 1885. Also, *Le Pionnier de Sherbrooke*, 23 June 1886.

104 Caron, *Discours*, p. 3; Joseph Tassé, *La Question Riel* (Ottawa? 1886?), p. 6.

105 *Le Véritable Riel* (Montreal: Imprimerie Générale 1887).

Métis, and to rejoice at the clemency shown them by the authorities, while blaming Riel who had tricked them into taking up arms against their own intentions. [106]

While using these arguments against the cause for which Quebeckers were agitating, Bleus also argued against the wisdom of agitation *per se*. French Canadians must avoid a racial division which would put them into 'a hopeless and unviable position'. [107] In a racial conflict, the French Canadians, being fewer than the English, must necessarily lose:

The protests against the hanging of Riel are unanimous; nevertheless, it would be dangerous to stir up feelings too much and to prolong the excitation indefinitely. ...

We are the minority in Confederation, and we must not allow an emotional impulse to compromise the future of our national cause. ... We must not ... put ourselves on a hostile footing with regard to the English population. That would mean civil war. ... [108]

Already, in the first weeks of agitation, angry reactions had been seen in the West. Archbishop Taché had been hanged in effigy, and Franco-Manitobans felt their community to be in danger. Taché was reported to have called on Quebeckers 'to halt their protest movement, not to isolate us from the other races, not to expose the Catholic group in the North-West to ruin.' And the Franco-Manitobans' newspaper warned that 'if we were purposely trying to ruin the French Canadians in the territories, we couldn't do it better than by continuing this agitation.' [109]

The Bleus' last defence, of course, was to play down the agitation by portraying it as a Liberal Party political manoeuvre. Even before the execution, *La Minerve* had begun accusing the Liberals of exploiting the Riel affair. [110] Afterwards, they continued to harp on the theme, with regard both

---

106 Tassé, *La Question Riel*, pp. 7ff.; Caron, *Discours*; *Rébellion du Nord-Ouest: faits pour le peuple* (n.p., n.d.); *Le Canadien*, 11 Jan. 1886. Riel's religious apostasy was particularly stressed to discredit him in the eyes of French Canadians; eg., in the anonymously written pamphlet, *Riel contre l'Eglise catholique*. Published fifteen months after his death, it contained what purported to be a letter, in Riel's handwriting, calling on an unnamed addressee to join in a revolt against the Church of Rome.

107 *La Minerve*, 23 Nov. 1885.

108 *Le Courrier de St-Hyacinthe*, 24 Nov. 1885. Also, *Le Pionnier de Sherbrooke*, 1 Apr. 1886; *Le Nouveau Monde*, 26 Mar. 1886; Chapleau, *Question Riel*; *Electeurs, attention*; J.-A. Chapleau, *Discours à l'occasion de la motion censurant le ministère pour avoir permis l'exécution de Louis Riel* (Montreal: Imprimerie Générale 1886); J.L. Archambault, *Conservateurs et libéraux: étude politique* (Montreal 1887).

109 In *Le Canadien*, 11 Jan. 1886. Also, *Le Courrier de St-Hyacinthe*, 16 Mar. 1886.

110 *La Minerve*, from time to time between 6 Aug. and 13 Nov. 1885. Also, *Le Courrier du Canada*, 10 Nov.; *Le Nouveau Monde*, as early as 30 and 31 Mar. 1885.

to the Liberals and to the Parti National.[111] At least one notable Liberal agreed with the accusation. Henri-Gustave Joly, the Protestant ex-Liberal leader and Quebec premier, quit the party because of the Riel affair. He could not accept, he wrote to Wilfrid Laurier, the way in which 'the Opposition is exploiting the Riel question', the way in which Liberal leaders were appealing to the 'national prejudices of the majority in our Province.'[112]

In the long run, the efforts of Conservative propagandists to retain French-Quebec support were largely successful; but the difficulties they faced were enormous. At first, as we have seen, the anger was so widespread that even loyal Bleu organs had to go along with it. It was only gradually that they fell back into line, and even then, the party seems never to have recovered all that it lost on 16 November 1885.[113]

---

111 *Le Courrier de St-Hyacinthe*, 24 and 26 Nov. 1885, 27 Mar. and 1 Apr. 1886; *L'Union des Cantons de l'Est*, 10 and 17 July, 11 and 25 Sept. 1886; *Le Pionnier de Sherbrooke*, 12 Oct. 1886; *Le Canadien*, 10 Apr. 1886; *Le Nouveau Monde*, 20 Mar., 9 July, and 13 Oct. 1886. A whole pamphlet, *Mémoires sur la coalition* (St-Hyacinthe: Le Courrier 1886), was devoted to demonstrating that Mercier had always sought to form a national coalition simply as a means of attaining power, that he had been prepared to use unscrupulous means in the past to form it, and that he was being similarly unscrupulous now.

112 H.-G. Joly to Wilfrid Laurier (Leclercville, 15 Nov. 1886), in PAC, Henri-Gustave Joly de Lotbinière papers, mfm no. M-792. It was, perhaps, an indication of Joly's correctness that *La Presse* accused him of joining the *pendards* and named him among 'our enemies'– i.e., the enemies of the French-Canadian nation (12 May 1886).

113 The old Conservative stalwarts, *La Minerve* and *Le Courrier du Canada*, friendly to the ministers, held firmest before the blast. While not, at first, denying the legitimacy of French-Canadian discontent, *La Minerve* always counselled moderation, tried to find non-Bleu scapegoats, and warned of the dangers of over-reacting. This last point was being stressed by 23 November, along with the insinuation that Riel's cause was only indirectly of concern to French Canadians. Subtly, *La Minerve* praised the protesting Quebeckers for their 'generosity, which makes us forget our own interests to defend those of others'. But it was the March 1886 tabling in the Commons of the medical commission's report on Riel that enabled *La Minerve* to pull out all the stops. Riel's sanity and wickedness; the government's fairness and generosity toward him; the Liberals' cynical exploitation of him – all these now became regular fare for the paper's readers. Stronger in its first reaction but almost as quick to return to the Conservative fold was the *Courrier de St-Hyacinthe*. On 19 November, it called for a 'war to the death against the ministers who betrayed us', and on the 21st it singled out Chapleau for blame. Perhaps the great *Champ de Mars* rally frightened the editor (Pierre Boucher de la Bruère), however, for on 24 November he retracted the editorial of the 21st and warned against the dangers of racial division. By the 26th he was accusing the Liberals of exploiting the sincerity of honest patriots and praising the Bleu caucus for its patriotism in criticizing its own leaders. By March, 1886, when the Landry motion was presented to the House of Commons, censuring the government for allowing Riel to be hanged, *Le Courrier* was ready to oppose the motion and praise even Chapleau for his patriotism, good faith, and brilliant oratory (27 Mar. and 1 Apr. 1886). Somewhat less easily reconciled were *Le Nouveau*

The embarrassment of Bleu polemicists was an indication of the seriousness of the impact which the Riel affair made on Quebec opinion. Though Wilfrid Laurier had denied, in a letter to Joly, that this was a national issue for French Canadians,[114] that was precisely what it really was. The basic assumption of the protests always was that Riel's execution had been an act of aggression by English Canadians against French Canada. That was why Quebec commentators were constantly preoccupied with English-Canadian motives and feelings. Even the execution itself seemed hardly more important than English-Canadian reactions to it. 'The 16th of November, 1885, will have been a day of ferocious rejoicing for the bloodthirsty fanatics of Ontario and the North-West.'[115] These fanatics were celebrating a victory over Riel and over the nationality he had represented:

Riel is dead, and the cursed city which has drunk his blood, the hordes of sectarians who called for it with foaming mouths and sinister, execrable cries are still plunged in an infernal orgy of fanaticism and hatred against everything French.[116]

But victory was not enough for them; they would go on. 'The blood of Riel

---

Monde (though it had been bought by Hector Langevin himself in 1884), Israel Tarte's Le Canadien, and Le Pionnier de Sherbrooke. They condemned the government to the end of 1885, then fell gradually back into line, though the Le Pionnier waited till the end of the censure motion debate to give its support back to the Conservatives. Of the usually-pro-government papers that gave the Conservatives particular trouble, most were Ultramontane or Church-supported. The Journal des Trois-Rivières, which declared itself to be Catholic and Conservative, was not quick to forgive the federal ministry for the execution. In March of 1886 it supported the censure motion (15, 22, and 29 Mar.). Influenced by Bishop Laflèche, however, it opposed Mercier in the summer and fall, defending the provincial Conservatives, who, it claimed, were not responsible for the hateful execution (5 Apr. and 9 Sept.). By the time of the federal election campaign, the editors were so shaken by Mercier's success that they were ready to support the federal Conservatives once more (10, 14, 21, 24 Feb. 1887). The independent Ultramontane papers, Tardivel's Vérité and Trudel's Etendard, went further, throwing their weight behind Mercier's national movement and continuing to attack the federal Conservatives even in 1887. One other hitherto-Bleu newspaper was a considerable loss to the party. The Union des Cantons de l'Est strongly condemned the decision to let Riel be hanged, singling out Chapleau for particular blame (12 Dec. 1885). It supported the censure motion and blamed its local MP for voting against it (3 Apr. 1886). On 10 July it expressed a preference for Edward Blake over Macdonald, and thereafter it supported the Liberals federally, though it did not throw its weight behind Mercier on the provincial level until 1887. Clearly, though, from an editorial point of view, the Riel affair was a turning point for this paper, losing its support to the Conservative party several years before it was finally sold, in 1890, to a group of Liberal party militants.

114 Laurier to Joly (Arthabaskaville, 17 Nov. 1886), in PAC, Henri-Gustave Joly de Lotbinière papers, mfm no. M-792.
115 L'Etendard, 16 Nov. 1885.
116 La Mort de Riel et la voix du sang (n.p., n.d.), p. 4.

does not satisfy them; they still want that of all the French Canadians.'[117] After all, wasn't it the hatred of French Canada which had brought about the execution – and the desire to 'satisfy the mindless fanaticism of the province of Ontario'?[118] Here was the real significance of the Riel affair: the motives of those who had hanged him:

> If Riel had not had French blood in his veins and if he had not been Catholic; if he had been English and Protestant – or even Turkish – there would never have been any question of hanging him. ...
>
> The province of Quebec was unanimous in asking that Riel not be treated any differently from an English prisoner accused of the same crime and put in the same circumstances. Several of our compatriots had no lively sympathy for the agitator – far from it – but they did not see why Riel should be an exception to the general rule simply because he was French and Catholic. ...
>
> The answer of the Upper Canadian and North-Western fanatics to the legitimate request of French Canada was this: 'Riel shall be hanged, mad or not. It's true that in England they no longer hang political criminals, but Riel must mount the scaffold because he is French and Catholic. ... '
>
> How, then, can one deny that the tragic end of Riel has been made a national question by the very rage of the fanatics and the incredible weakness of the cabinet?
>
> The truth is that our nationality has been humilated and scorned by the sectarians.[119]

The anger expressed in Quebec, then, was not incoherent or irrational. It followed a clear reasoning. The evidence indicated that Riel had been mad and therefore not responsible for his acts. Furthermore, the Métis had had real, serious, and neglected grievances which ought to have counted as extenuating circumstances in his case. If he was hanged despite his madness and despite these extenuating circumstances, it could only have been for one reason – a reason suggested by the violence with which some English Canadians apparently expressed themselves: 'Because he was French.'[120] This was a view which Conservative attempts to dissociate Riel from the Métis could do little to counteract. For even if Riel had not had Métis interests at heart, even if he had been an apostate, even if he had not been mad,[121] the important thing was the reason for which Ontarians had wanted him dead. And they had been

---

117 *La Patrie*, 26 Nov. 1885.
118 *Le Courrier de St-Hyacinthe*, 17 Nov. 1885. Also, *L'Electeur*, 16 Nov.
119 *La Vérité*, 21 Nov. 1885. See also *La Minerve*, 18 Nov.; *Le Nouveau Monde*, 17 Nov.; *L'Union des Cantons de l'Est*, 5 Dec. 1885.
120 *La Mort de Riel et la voix du sang*, p. 15.
121 It was hard to maintain the extreme Bleu position after Archbishop Taché entered the fray. Publishing both at St Boniface (under the title *La Situation*) and Quebec (*La Situation*

against him not because of his criminal responsibility but because he was a French Catholic; 'it's not the criminal they hanged at Regina, it's the Catholic.'[122]

But if Riel had been hanged because of his French Catholicism, then obviously it was all French Catholicism that had been attacked through him – and all French Catholics. 'The death of Riel is an impious declaration of war, an audacious defiance hurled at the French-Canadian race. ... '[123] The treatment of Riel was really intended for the whole French-Canadian people: 'We all know that they'd have liked to slit all our throats, to kill all of us French Canadians.'[124] This was why French Canadians must unite. It was because Riel's hanging had been an attack on all that all must resist, that henceforth there must be 'neither Conservatives nor Liberals nor Castors', but only 'PATRIOTS AND TRAITORS'.[125] There was no point in warning that such a unification would lead to a race war; Riel's execution was already an English-Canadian declaration of war against French Canada.[126]

In the protests against the hanging of Riel there may be seen some signs that French-Quebec attitudes toward Confederation had been changing since 1867. This change can, perhaps, be detected in the complaint that Riel's hanging had been part of a concerted campaign to deprive the French-Catholic element of its rightful place in the North-West. Had not the 'Orange vandals ... maintained a continual reign of terror in the North-West for more than fifteen years'?[127] Had they not been able to 'persecute the group of French Métis ... conspire to exterminate them by force of arms, and rob them

---

au Nord-Ouest), the highly respected prelate argued that the Métis had had legitimate complaints against the government and had asked Riel to represent them because of their complete confidence in him. Riel himself had been mad. The archbishop whose missionaries had been killed during the rebellion could not consider Riel a hero; but neither could he join Bleu propagandists in calling him an evil and vengeful schemer.

122 *Le Monde Illustré*, 28 Nov. 1885.

123 *Le Courrier de St-Hyacinthe*, 19 Nov. 1885.

124 *Le Canadien*, 17 Nov. 1885. Also, 16 and 19 Nov.; *Le Nouveau Monde*, 17, 19, 20, and 23 Nov.; *La Revue Canadienne*, xxi (1885), p. 696; *La Presse*, 16 Nov.; *La Patrie*, 16 Nov.; *L'Etendard*, 16 Nov.; *Le Pionnier de Sherbrooke*, 19 and 26 Nov. 1885; *Question nationale au Nord-Ouest* (Montreal: L'Etendard 1886), p. 2.

125 *La Presse*, 16 Nov. 1885.

126 Eg., *La Presse*, 23 and 26 Nov. 1885; *La Patrie*, 20 and 23 Nov. *La Vérité* had announced as early as 23 May that English Canadians had more to lose from exaggerated racial tensions than French Canadians, since such tensions would only break up the confederation, in which the English had a greater stake than the French. *L'Electeur* (16 Nov.) argued there would be no race war, since only the Tories were capable of starting one, while English-Canadian Liberals would support the French Canadians.

127 *Le Gibet de Régina* (New York: Thompson and Moreau 1886), p. 146.

of their heritage'?[128] Even now they were campaigning to do away with the French language on the prairies. It was clear what the end goal was:

How great would have been the progress of Canada if the development of our rich North-West had been opened fairly and impartially to participation by all honest Canadians, to an equitable competition by us all!

They have wanted to make the North-West essentially Anglo-Saxon in race and language, and to banish from it the entire French-Catholic element.

But, since the majority of the population already settled there was French and Catholic, they had to destroy it or expel it. ...

And that is the explanation for the series of crimes committed against our people.[129]

The hanging of Riel could thus be seen as a blow struck against the right of French-Canadians to participate in the development of the West, 'which they're making into an English land at our expense. ... '[130]

In what sense does this express a new attitude toward Confederation? In the sense that it seems to imply an expectation that French-Canadians should have had equal access to the West, should have been equally at home there with the English. We did not find such an expectation at the time when the North-West was annexed; and certainly, at the time of Confederation, French Canadians seemed to assume that their sphere of national activity would be found within the province of Quebec. This assumption seemed, also, to be working against the Franco-Manitoban colonizers between 1870 and 1885. The view of Confederation on which it was based was that the French-Canadian province (Quebec) was allied with a number of other provinces, each with its own national characteristics and autonomy. But in the complaints which we have just now read there seems to be a new emphasis – a notion of Confederation as alliance not just among provinces but between two races: 'they have the same rights and the same duties. Although their aspirations are different, they are equal to each other.' Unfortunately, certain Ontarians wanted to deny French Canada 'the equality to which it is entitled', and they had thus undertaken to exclude it from the North-West. Such an undertaking was fundamentally wrong, since 'the two races are destined to live a common life on the Canadian land, to have the same political institutions and be governed by the same men. ... '[131]

It is a common political cliché in Canada today that the Riel affair turned Quebec away from participation in western or general Canadian develop-

---

128 *Le Mot de la fin* (n.p., n.d.), p. 2.
129 *Question nationale au Nord-Ouest*, p. 14.
130 *Louis Riel, martyr du Nord-Ouest* (Montreal: La Presse 1885), p. 77.
131 *Le Courrier de St-Hyacinthe*, 23 July 1885. Also 30 July and 24 Nov.

ment, that it convinced French Canadians Confederation would not give
them the equal partnership with English Canada, the common sharing of the
country, which they had expected from it, and that this deception turned
them inwards so that *after* the Riel affair they became preoccupied with
Quebec alone. What we have seen here, however, suggests exactly the
opposite. Entering Confederation with an exclusive concern for Quebec,
French Canadians were brought by the Métis question to discover an interest
in the West. It was Riel and the Métis who turned their attentions *outwards*.
And after fifteen years of increasing concern for the Métis, stimulated by the
repeated difficulties of the latter since the Red River uprising, Quebeckers had
come to feel so closely involved with the West that some of them at least were
asserting a right to a share in it. This did not yet necessarily mean that the
prairies should all be bilingual; but at least French-Canadians should have 'a
little province of Quebec' set aside for them in the region. 'Let it be understood that we have the right, in the North-West just as on the banks of the St
Lawrence, to work to set up a French-Canadian state. ... '[132] Nevertheless,
the Riel affair, by bringing to such an intense pitch French-Canadian feelings
of concern about events in the West, helped move them *toward* a bilingual
theory of Confederation,

The belief that French-Canadians were being deprived of their rightful share
in the West, while it was significant as a step toward a new view of
Confederation, was not the principal basis of the Riel agitation in Quebec. The
hanging of the Métis leader provoked, in fact, strong expressions of a much
more traditional concern with Quebec itself.

To begin with, this crisis, like other minority affairs in the past, provoked
bitter comparisons between the privileged position of English Protestants in
Quebec and the intolerance and tyranny to which French Catholics were
subjected in other parts of Canada.[133] If the Métis were to be persecuted in the
West, why should Quebec have to bear the burden of *its* too-present
minority?

The province of Quebec is ours; it is our property, and let's tell the English we intend
to keep it. No concessions: absolute power in our own house, French governments
throughout.

No more English mayors in Montreal, and let's have the French flag on the city hall.
No more English MPs where our nationality is in the majority. ...

---

132 *La Patrie*, 7 Aug. 1885.
133 Eg., *L'Electeur*, 7 Aug. 1885; *Le Monde Illustré*, 22 Aug.

Reading in French of the minutes of municipal councils and the legislative assembly. ... [134]

The aftermath of Riel's execution brought more specific complaints. When the Huntingdon *Gleaner* objected, in early 1886, to the Church-aided expansion of French-Canadian settlement in the Eastern Townships, which, it claimed, was pushing out the old Protestant population, the *Union des Cantons de l'Est* told it to stop complaining about the majority and to follow the example of Ontario's Catholics, who 'respect the [local] laws and live in peace with everyone.' If English Protestants were leaving the Eastern Townships, it was only because of their insistence on having everything their own way, even when they were in the minority. [135] That fall, after the provincial elections, *La Vérité* noted that most of the 'hang-dogs' elected were either from English ridings or from those where 'the English element is strong enough to have tipped the balance toward the anti-French side.' This, argued the paper, was reason for the Conservative government to resign. [136] But such an argument seems to imply that in a Quebec election the English vote should not count. the English Quebeckers, apparently, were to be considered as a sort of resident foreigners, and not full citizens of the province.

If English Quebeckers were viewed in this way – and it is not so surprising that they should have been, given the 1867 promise that Quebec was to be a French-Canadian province – then it was natural for the hanging of Riel, interpreted as the killing of the French Catholic, to arouse anger about the condition of Quebec itself. The aggression against French Catholicism in the West underlined once again Confederation's failure to give French Catholics control of their own province.

But the Riel affair not only reminded French Quebeckers that their province's character was sapped from within; it showed it to be under attack from without. For in hanging Riel because of his French nationality, the majority struck also at the province which was that nationality's political and geographical expression:

The province of Quebec, which personifies the French nationality, was particularly

---

134 Jules Deriares, *Riel: patriotisme vs loyauté* (n.p., 1885), p. 7.
135 *L'Union des Cantons de l'Est*, 27 Mar. 1886. Also, *La Patrie*, 15 Mar.
136 *La Vérité*, 23 Oct. 1886. 'Hang-dog' is the nearest I can come to the French word 'pendard', used by Quebec nationalists for those who attempted to justify the Riel hanging or continued to support the Conservatives after it. 'Pendard' means rascal or rogue, but in using it the nationalists were playing on its relationship to the verb 'pendre', to hang. On 1 October, *La Vérité* had complained about another Protestant manifestation, the Salvation Army, whose parades in the streets of Quebec City had recently provoked a riot. See above, p. 127.

shaken and stupefied by the announcement of the gruesome event at Regina. It felt immediately that in putting Riel to death, they were trying to wound it in its most intimate feelings.[137]

Indeed, English-Canadians were accused of wanting to do worse than hurt Quebec's feelings. 'The rope which strangled him strangles and throttles the province of Quebec in the minds of the thousands of spectators who delighted in witnessing his death rattle. ... '[138] Thus, one could conclude, 'Riel has been sacrificed, and with him the province of Quebec.'[139]

The Riel agitation was concerned, therefore, not merely with the treatment of French Catholicism in the West. It was much more, as Henri-Gustave Joly wrote sadly to Wilfrid Laurier, an expression of the desire to have a distinct nationality in Quebec.[140] Both the autonomy of that province and its influence in the federal partnership had been diminished in the Riel affair.

We have seen in previous minority crises that one of the important functions of a strong Quebec was to protect French Catholics elsewhere. This notion manifested itself strongly in 1885. Already, by the beginning of April, *L'Etendard* was reminding its readers 'what role is assigned to us by the constitution, by the laws of equity, and by the demands of kinship, with regard to the minorities in the other provinces, especially those who are related to us by religion and origin.'[141] The Turcotte resolutions, presented to the Quebec assembly later that month, seemed to be based on the same notion. In presenting them, Arthur Turcotte was calling on the representatives of *Quebec* to express the sympathy which, he claimed, French-Canadians felt for the Métis.[142] Conservatives, while opposing this sort of resolution on the grounds that Riel and the Métis were a matter of federal rather than provincial jurisdiction and hence no legitimate concern of Quebec's parliament, nevertheless had to recognize the significance of the feeling which gave rise to it. 'As soon as some other French group in Canada complains of a wrong done to it,' observed *La Minerve*, 'this chivalrous feeling pushes us to embrace its cause with an ardour which our protégés themselves often do not show.'[143]

Quebec, then, had embraced the cause of Riel, 'the oppressed, the

---

137 *La Revue Canadienne*, XXI (1885), p. 697.
138 *La Mort de Riel et la voix du sang*, p. 4.
139 *La Presse*, 23 Nov. 1885. Also, 19 Nov.; *L'Electeur*, 21 Nov.; *Le Nouveau Monde*, 20 Nov.; *La Patrie*, 17 Nov. 1885, and 8 and 15 Oct. 1886.
140 Henri-Gustave Joly de Lotbinière to Wilfrid Laurier (Leclercville, 15 Nov. 1886), in PAC, Joly papers, mfm no. M-792. See also *La Vérité*, 12 June 1886.
141 *L'Etendard*, 1 Apr. 1885.
142 *L'Electeur*, 11 and 16 Apr. 1885.
143 *La Minerve*, 23 Nov. 1885. Also, *Le Courrier du Canada*, 16 and 17 Nov.

prisoner.'[144] It had embraced the cause of the 'poor Métis', who, 'without education, without experience,' had been easy victims of those who sought to injure, through them, the French Catholic element in the West.[145] It was natural that Quebec should have stood up for them; after all, they might not have been French Canadians exactly, but they were certainly related. And 'French-Canadians [in Quebec] feel for their cousins of the North-West the same interest which the English and the Scotch show for their compatriots and co-religionists in the Irish province of Ulster.'[146]

Yet, despite the unanimity of Quebec's population, despite their petitions, their rallies, their pleading, Riel had been hanged, Quebec had lost its battle, 'since they refused to listen to our supplications.'[147] The federal government, 'instead of listening to the just demands of the province of Quebec, gave in to the ferocious clamouring the Orangemen.'[148] The execution of Riel, therefore, represented the defeat of 'French influence' at Ottawa, the cancellation of Quebec's power to make its will prevail in the council of the federal partnership.[149]

Why had the voice of Quebec been so ineffective? The answer of the national movement which grew out of the Riel protest was that the province's Conservative leaders had been unwilling to use the provincial institutions to reflect the will of the people. The province of Quebec, as 'constitutional guardian of the religious and national rights [of French Canadians],'[150] ought to have been the natural defender of the Métis. The provincial government ought to have spoken out on behalf of Riel. It was no use for Conservatives to say that Riel's fate was a matter of federal jurisdiction, and that the province had no right to interfere in it.[151] 'Was this inviolable right not consecrated by the very hang-dogs of today, when, in 1874, Messrs Ross and Chapleau had both provincial houses give unanimous approval to a resolution calling for the commutation of Lépine's sentence?'[152] Why, then, had the Ross government refused to approve resolutions this time on behalf of Riel? Why had it refused to listen to the people of Quebec, 'to act as the representative of our

---

144 *Le Monde Illustré*, 15 Aug. 1885.
145 *L'Electeur*, 13 Nov. 1885.
146 *La Presse*, 17 Mar. 1886.
147 *Le Courrier de St-Hyacinthe*, 24 Nov. 1885.
148 *La Vérité*, 21 Nov. 1885.
149 *La Presse*, 19 Nov. 1885. Also, 17 and 23 Nov.; *L'Union des Cantons de l'Est*, 14 Nov. 1885.
150 Mercier's 1886 election manifesto, in *L'Electeur*, 2 July 1886.
151 Eg., *Le Nouveau Monde*, 13 Oct. 1886; *Le Journal des Trois-Rivières*, 11 Jan., 8 Feb., 29 Mar., 5 Apr., and 6 Sept. 1886.
152 *L'Electeur*, 26 Apr. 1886.

nationality'?[153] The answer was clear: the Conservative government at Quebec had allowed itself to be dominated by the Conservative government at Ottawa. It had become nothing more than 'the tool and the accomplice of the federal cabinet which hanged Riel.'[154]

The failure of the Quebec government to stand up and do its duty was thus a sign that it had permitted a serious infringement on provincial autonomy. This was certainly the claim of Mercier's programme, at any rate:

By its anti-patriotic attitude in the discussion of the Riel question, and more recently, by its withdrawal of resolutions in favour of an amnesty for the Métis, the provincial ministry has revealed to everyone its state of dependence [on Ottawa] ... which perverts the working of the constitution and threatens our public liberties.[155]

Thus, in the 1886 provincial election campaign, Mercier's supporters made it their principal argument that the Conservatives, by their conduct in the Riel affair, had shown themselves to be inadequate defenders of provincial autonomy.[156] 'The situation is serious,' warned their manifesto, 'for you are threatened in that which is most precious to you after your religion: in the autonomy of your province.' The Conservatives had brought about 'the annihilation of the local ministry and its subordination to the will and the policy of the federal ministers', whose aim was 'to impose upon the provinces, by little and by little, a régime of legislative union.'[157] As the elections approached, the nationalists became increasingly insistent that the Ross government was taking its orders directly from Ottawa,[158] that it was 'nothing but the tool of the Orange ministry of John A. Macdonald.'[159] This was why the provincial Bleus, like their federal counterparts, could be branded as 'hang-dogs'.[160] To vote for them would be to give 'a verdict approving of the crime of November 16'.[161]

And so the Riel affair, which had ostensibly been concerned with the position of French Catholics outside of Quebec, culminated in the election of

---

153 *La Patrie*, 8 Oct. 1886. Also, *L'Electeur*, 6 Feb.
154 *La Vérité*, 23 Oct. 1886.
155 In *La Patrie*, 16 Oct. 1886, and in *L'Electeur*, 2 July 1886.
156 *La Patrie*, 13, 21, 29 Sept., and 16 Oct. 1886.
157 In *L'Electeur*, 2 July 1886.
158 *L'Electeur*, 5 July 1886.
159 Ibid., 11 Oct. 1886.
160 Ibid., 31 Aug. 1886. From August until the elections, this paper printed each day, in bold-face type, in a prominent place on its front page, a section headed 'Remember, People', reporting briefly the events of the corresponding date in 1885 related to the Riel affair.
161 Ibid., 11 Oct. 1886. Also, *L'Etendard*, 25 Sept. and 14 Oct.

a government calling itself national, stressing the special position of Quebec itself, and dedicated above all else to defending that province's autonomy.[162]

French-Canadian attitudes toward western settlement after 1885 reflected the impact of the Riel affair to some extent. The view, for example, that Riel's execution represented a denial to French Canadians of the right to participate in the development of the West led naturally to the conclusion that it was unsafe for French Canadians to move to that region. 'I ask you,' wrote a Liberal pamphleteer in an open letter to Chapleau, 'what security one can have in a country whose Government authorizes the plundering of its inhabitants, ignores their requests, and hangs madmen!'[163] In 1887, the St Boniface colonizer, T.A. Bernier, listed this fear as one of the factors hampering his efforts to get Quebec settlers for Manitoba. 'We often hear people reproaching the Anglo-Saxon races,' he wrote, 'for wanting to take over the North-West and make it into English provinces.' Already the French element was almost completely drowned out in Manitoba, and would soon disappear completely; 'why, then, should we go there? several of our compatriots have asked.'[164] Bernier did not refer this specifically to the Riel affair, but a series of articles in La Vérité some months before had done so. Tardivel had said quite bluntly that 'recent events have hardly been of a nature to attract our compatriots to the North-West.' He went on: 'Those of our

---

162 Joly to Laurier (Leclercville, 21 Nov. 1886), in PAC, Joly papers, mfm no. M-792. Also, *La Vérité*, 2 Oct.; *La Patrie*, 13 Oct. 1886; *La Presse*, 26 Nov. 1885. In the provincial election campaign, the Riel affair was associated in Nationalist propaganda with other *provincial* interests. Thus, *L'Electeur* (7 July 1886) brought up the matter of the Quebec City bridge, claiming that the Ross government had, in this matter, 'played the game of our Ottawa enemies, and aided them in their anti-French enterprise.'

163 Ernest Tremblay, *Riel: Réponse à Monsieur J.A. Chapleau* (St Hyacinthe: L'Union 1885), p. 77.

164 T.A. Bernier, *Le Manitoba, champ d'immigration*, pp. 21, 29. Ironically, this fear had been largely fostered by the St Boniface colonizers themselves, starting long before the Riel affair. Their own fear of being swamped by Anglo-Protestant immigration had led them to put their appeals for Quebec settlers too often in the form of calls for help. 'What a misfortune it will be if we don't get any French-Canadian immigration!' Archbishop Taché had written to Mgr Bourget in 1872 (letter from St Boniface, 22 Mar. 1872, in Montreal archiepiscopal archives). In circulars, letters, speeches, and pamphlets, Taché, Bernier, Lacombe, and others, during the years that followed, kept referring to the danger that their community would be drowned in an Anglo-Saxon sea unless it were reinforced by Quebeckers. Eg., A.-A. Taché, circular letter to the Quebec clergy, June, 1874 (in Montreal archiepiscopal archives); Albert Lacombe, letter to Monsieur le Curé (Montreal, 19 Mar. 1876), in Archives Deschâtelets, St Boniface papers, mfm no. 478; *Le Nord-Ouest canadien; brochure compilée par un colonisateur de neuf ans d'expérience*, pp. 3–4; Bernier's letter to the *Echo d'Iberville* in Barrette's *Récit d'aventures*.

compatriots who are already settled in those vast territories have been mistreated, pushed into rebellion by the civil authorities; and then, instead of being given justice, they've been massacred, hanged, imprisoned.'[165]

Nevertheless, the significance of these articles is not as clear as it seems at first, for Tardival concluded:

In any case, these events have very little to do with the question which concerns us. Even if they had never taken place, we should still be just as hostile ... to any kind of emigration, whether it be to the North-West or to the South.[166]

In fact, La Vérité had been consistently opposed to any movement of French Canadians away from the province of Quebec ever since its founding in 1881. The Riel affair had done nothing to change its position. Indeed, there were some people who even saw that affair as a stimulus to French-Canadian settlement in the West. Thus, on the eve of his departure with the expeditionary force, Colonel Amyot of the 9th battalion wrote to Joly that one advantage of the campaign would be to better acquaint French Canadians with the prairies, so that some of them might decide to settle there.[167] Even in the fall of 1885, when Riel's neck was almost in the noose, the idea still seemed good. Le Canadien commented on Amyot's plan to settle his men in the West: 'The North-West offers our race a splendid future. It was discovered by la Vérendrye and by our people. This is now a fine and honourable opportunity for our soldiers to establish French-Canadian parishes there.'[168]

---

165 La Vérité, 24 Apr. 1886. Also 15 May and 3 July.

166 Ibid., 3 July 1886. The impact of Tardivel's 'recent events' argument is also considerably diminished by the motives which seem to have inspired his articles. They were a response to Le Manitoba, which had criticized the Quebec press for its failure to promote western settlement. Now Le Manitoba was a Conservative paper supporting Joseph Royal, who had voted in Parliament against Landry's censure motion. La Vérité, on the other hand, supported Mercier, the nationalist movement, and the censure motion. To bring up the Riel affair, therefore, in a response to the raising of the settlement question, was a way for Tardivel to score political points by attacking Le Manitoba in turn. Thus, he wrote: 'And what is even more deplorable, while we French Canadians are protesting with all our might against this infamy [the execution], the Royals and Girards, that is to say the political leaders of our Manitoba compatriots, assure us placidly that the Orangemen have done well, that we are wrong to agitate, that we should rather mind our own business, that the atrocious hanging of Riel is not even regrettable! And Le Manitoba complacently makes itself the echo of the Royals and Girards.' (La Vérité, 24 Apr. 1886.) See also La Vérité, 15 May and 12 June, for more expressions of the traditional Quebec patriotism.

167 Amyot to Joly (undated), in PAC, Joly papers, mfm no. M-791. The departure of the 65th battalion from Montreal brought a similar comment from Le Nouveau Monde (2 Apr. 1885).

168 Le Canadien, 12 Sept. 1885. Also 18 Sept. and 1 Oct.

Thus, even the Riel affair cannot really be shown to have turned French Canadians away from the West. On the contrary, the decade that followed saw more activity among western colonizers than the previous fifteen years.[169] What hampered their efforts after 1885 as before was the traditional notion that Quebec and Quebec alone was the true French-Canadian homeland. This Quebec patriotism, to which the Confederationists had appealed in 1867, still excluded any notion of a '*truly Canadian sentiment, aside from any question of race or religion*', still opposed any kind of 'amalgamation of the different races which inhabit this country.' French Canada must always maintain not only its language and traditions, but also its 'institutions and its distinct autonomy'. These were threatened by western appeals for French-Canadian settlers. The West simply was not part of the homeland; it was not even much better than the United States as a home for French Canadians:

The fact that the province of Manitoba and the North-West Territories are part of the same Confederation as we ourselves takes nothing away from the force of our argument.

For aside from the fact that this Dominion has absolutely no political stability, it doesn't make much difference to us, from the point of view of our national future, whether the scattered groups that we may form here and there are subject to Ottawa or to Washington. In either case they're bound to be overwhelmed by the other elements and without any real influence.[170]

The Riel affair, then, served to reinforce the traditional Quebec patriotism, to provoke new expression of the overriding concern of French Canadians for the integrity of their Quebec homeland.[171] At the same time, the affair

---

169 In fact, the census showed a greater increase in Quebec-born population in the North-West Territories during the 1890s than during the 1880s (although for Manitoba the increase declined). Figures on French origin are unreliable, because the 1891 census did not ask the usual question. In any case, the increased activity of the colonizers themselves can be seen in the increase in the number of brochures they put out after 1885. Eg., T.A. Bernier, *Le Manitoba: champ d'immigration*; M.J. Blais, *Le Manitoba* (Ottawa 1898); *Esquisse générale du Nord-Ouest du Canada* (Trois-Rivières 1886); J.B. Morin, *En avant la colonisation: la vallée de la Saskatchewan* (Joliette 1893); Morin's *Le Nord-Ouest canadien et ses ressources agricoles* (Ottawa 1894); Morin's *La Terre promise aux Canadiens-français: le Nord-Ouest canadien* (Ottawa 1897); etc.

170 *La Vérité*, 5 Nov. 1887 and 12 June 1886.

171 Even some of the polemics which seemed at first to be calls for an equal chance for French Canadians to participate in the settlement of the West can also be read in the light of the Quebec patriotism. The complaint, for example, that the North-West was being made into

brought to a climax fifteen years of increasing Quebec concern about the
harassed French Métis. This growing involvement with the Métis had
gradually led Quebeckers to feel that they – that French Canada – had
something important at stake in the West. The emotions they had been
investing in the protection of the Métis over the past fifteen years – the passion
they had committed to the defence of Riel – had been leading them toward a
new conception of their sphere of interests in the confederation. Ultimately,
some of them at least would be led to a redefinition of Canada itself – to a novel
view of the dominion as a bilingual, dual nationality.

'an English land at our expense' (above, p. 170) takes on a new sound when the preceding lines are read with it: 'Before the policy of Sir John A. Macdonald, the North-West
was French. Today, all our money, which could have been used for colonizing the
province of Quebec, is gone to the North-West, which they're making into an English
land at our expense. ... ' The complaint is that *Quebec's* money is being taken, *Quebec's* colonization is being neglected, and Quebec's *protégés*, the French Métis, are
being driven from a land (the North-West) which has belonged to them in the past. This
persecution of the West's own, indigenous French population would have been quite
enough on its own to arouse the anger of Quebec, without any desire on the part of
Quebeckers to settle in the West themselves.

IX

MANITOBA SCHOOLS
AND THE
RISE OF
BILINGUALISM

THE Riel agitation did not end with the 1886 provincial elections. During the 1887 federal campaign Liberals and Nationals again stressed the Riel affair, looking forward to 'the hour of national revenge',[1] and reminding voters that Macdonald had authorized 'the plundering of our compatriots and coreligionists of the North-West'[2] and sacrificed Riel 'to the Orange lodges'.[3] Conservatives, for their part, put some considerable effort into arguing that Riel had not been worthy of Quebec's sympathy, that he had pushed the Métis into unjustified rebellion for his own selfish purposes,[4] had been responsible for the murders of priests and the deaths of 150 soldiers, and even as far back as 1870 had shown his wickedness by causing 'the brutal and senseless shooting of Scott, who was laid still breathing into his grave.'[5] Whatever effect this arguing may have had on the election results,[6] it was still not the last of Riel. By the end of the decade polemicists were still contending whether he had been an impostor or the noble victim of 'a judicial murder',[7]

---

1 *L'Electeur*, 16 Nov.; 1886.

2 Ibid., 10 Jan. 1887. Also 10 Feb.

3 *Le Mot de la fin* (n.p., n.d.), pp. 7, 22. Also, *L'Etendard*, 4 Feb. 1887, and *La Vérité*'s interpretation of the election results, 26 Feb. 1887.

4 *Rébellion du Nord-Ouest: faits pour le peuple* (n.p., n.d.).

5 *Electeurs, attention, ne vous laissez pas tromper* (n.p., n.d.), p. 6. Also, *Elections de 1887: la vraie question* (n.p., n.d.); *Le Journal des Trois-Rivières*, 10, 14, 21, and 24 Feb., 1887; *Le Courrier de St-Hyacinthe*, 26 Feb. 1887.

6 The Bleus just barely managed to hold Quebec in 1887, but the gains which the Liberals made may well be attributable to other factors than Riel. See H.B. Neatby, *Laurier and a Liberal Quebec* (Toronto: McClelland and Stewart 1973), pp. 33–4.

7 *Le Courrier de St-Hyacinthe*, 20 Apr. 1889; *Le Journal des Trois-Rivières*, 23 Dec.; *L'Etendard*, 14, 17, and 23 Aug. 1889; Adolphe Ouimet, *La Vérité sur la question métisse au Nord-Ouest* (Montreal 1889), esp. pp. 188, 288–9, 397.

and Wilfrid Laurier could say, during the 1890 debate on the language question, that the agitation begun in 1885 still had not ended.[8]

Nevertheless, the most important continuing impact of the Riel execution was indirect. It came from the fact that the affair had increased English-Canadian sensitivity to the dangers of French-Canadian nationalism while at the same time calling forth new assertions of that nationalism.

Mercier, as we have seen, came to power by stressing the traditional concern for the autonomy of the French-Catholic province. His followers still spoke of Quebec as the homeland of the French Canadians,[9] and he responded by telling them: 'This province of Quebec is Catholic and French, and it shall remain Catholic and French.'[10] The autonomy of this homeland must not be weakened, for it was the key to French Canada's national future.[11] Provincial autonomy, claimed an 1890 Parti National brochure, was the 'first article of the national programme'. No sooner had Mercier come to power than he 'took up the fight for the province's rights.'[12]

Conservatives could not help being annoyed at the way in which Mercierites spoke of provincial autonomy. Autonomy was a splendid thing, they observed during the 1886 campaign. 'But this is precisely the doctrine championed by the present Conservative administration. ... '[13] The Liberals had attacked provincial autonomy in the past – witness the Letellier *coup d'état* – and even now, for the sake of gaining power, they seemed willing to endanger it by obscuring the boundary between federal and provincial powers in the Riel affair.[14] No, it was the Conservatives who had always been 'the true friends of the 1867 federal pact', the true friends of provincial autonomy.[15]

But if Mercier's conception of an autonomous French-Catholic Quebec was not original, he thrust it more jarringly than the Bleus had ever done upon the attentions of English Canadians – and this at a time when the Riel affair had already caused them to become nervous about the implications of French-Canadian nationalism.[16] Mercier's manner of campaigning, his

---

8 *Wilfrid Laurier à la tribune*, pp. 588–9. See also *Le Nouveau Monde*, 17 Feb. 1890.
9 Eg., *La Vérité*, 10 Sept. 1887, 15 Jan. 1888; *L'Electeur*, 9 Mar. 1892.
10 Mercier's speech at Quebec, 24 June 1889, quoted in Rumilly, *Honoré Mercier et son temps*, II, 94.
11 *L'Etendard*, 29 jan. 1887; *La Vérité*, 15 Jan. 1888.
12 *Elections provinciales, 1890: le gouvernement Mercier* (Quebec: Belleau et Cie 1890), p. 259.
13 *Le Journal des Trois-Rivières*, 8 July 1886.
14 *Le Courrier de St-Hyacinthe*, 11 Sept. 1886. Also, 25 oct. 1887; *Le Nouveau Monde*, 13 oct. 1886; *Le Journal des Trois-Rivières*, 11 Jan., 8 Feb., 29 Mar., 5 Apr., and 6 Sept. 1886.
15 *Le Courrier de St-Hyacinthe*, 24 Aug. 1889. Also 10 Dec. 1887.
16 Accepting the trial as legitimate, convinced of Riel's sanity not only by the testimony but also by the lucidity and rationality of his own final address to the court, English Canadians apparently tended to consider the execution a normal consequence of a valid

appointment of a priest as deputy-minister of colonization, his grand trips abroad and acceptance of high honours from the French government and the papacy[17] – these alone might well have worried English Canadians. But he took other initiatives as well.

Shortly after coming to office, Mercier began to organize an interprovincial conference at Quebec in an attempt to enhance the autonomy of the provinces. Praising the idea, Jules-Paul Tardivel warned that unless it succeeded in its aim, Confederation could not endure much longer.[18] As the delegates gathered at Quebec, L'Electeur referred to them as 'the foreign ministers', and published banner headlines of welcome and pictures of the Ontario delegation.[19] During and after the conference Mercierite publications emphasized its importance for provincial autonomy in general and Quebec in particular.[20]

Naturally, the Bleus would not admit that this 'Mowat-Mercier picnic' might serve any useful purpose.[21] How could one expect anything from a group of Liberals gathered together to complain (for example) about the federal veto power, when they themselves had been guilty of an 'immoderate use' of the veto between 1873 and 1878? The Liberals would do well to 'tune their fiddles before they begin the dance.'[22]

But while the Bleus may have been right in saying Mercier's conference achieved no concrete gains for the province, it was probably also true that the meeting helped build up an image of Mercier as a challenger of Confederation, and a man who aimed to loosen its bonds. What else could have been the effect of this comment from a pro-Mercier newspaper: 'Some people are afraid of seeing a weakening of the federal bonds. It's precisely because we want to see a weakening of those bonds, which are much too strong, that we

---

conviction. If Riel had been English, Scotch, or even Turkish, they felt, the execution would have taken place without any protest. The French Canadians seemed to be demanding that Riel should be saved – that he be made an exception – simply because he was French and Catholic. They seemed to be saying, in fact, that there should be two different laws in Canada: one for French Canadians and one for everyone else. Such a pretension surely implied a rejection not only of equality but also of any real cohesion in the Canadian confederation.

17 We have seen in our own time how nervous English Canadians can become when the French government makes a Quebec premier commander of the Légion d'Honneur, as it did Mercier.

18 Quoted in Rumilly, Histoire de la province de Québec, v, 265–6.

19 L'Electeur, 12 and 15 Oct. 1887, and following issues. Also, La Patrie, 19 Oct.; L'Union des Cantons de l'Est, 22 Oct. 1887.

20 Eg., La Vérité, 5 and 26 Nov.; L'Etendard, 21 and 28 Oct., 1887; Elections provinciales, 1890, pp. 260–3.

21 Le Nouveau Monde, 26 Oct. 1887.

22 La Minerve, 31 Oct. 1887. Also, La Presse, 21 Oct.; Le Pionnier de Sherbrooke, 27 oct.; Le Journal des Trois-Rivières, 24 Oct.; Le Courrier de St-Hyacinthe, 10 Dec. 1887.

approve most of the resolutions passed by the conference.'[23] But this sort of image could be a source of great danger if it provoked English Canadians into some sort of militant backlash. Bleu leaders, in fact, had feared such a backlash since the beginning of the Riel agitation.[24] It seemed certain to them 'that the coalition of French Canadians would provoke a union of English MPs against us. And as we are the minority, the province of Quebec would be crushed by the other provinces.'[25] French Canadians must stand up for their rights, of course; but their appeal should be to justice and right, not to race and nationality:

Is it wise, in an affair like that of the North-West, and in a Parliament like the one at Ottawa, where the other races outnumber us three to one, to raise so heatedly the question of nationality? Clearly not. How can we win at this game if the other races decide to do the same thing?[26]

By the beginning of 1887 it seemed these fears were already being realized. 'The agitation, which, thank heaven, has not been universal among us, has nevertheless provoked an opposite agitation in Ontario and Manitoba – an anti-French and anti-Catholic agitation.'[27]

The situation became worse after the passing of the Jesuits' Estates Act, for this act, more than anything Mercier had done before, helped convince English Canadians that French-Catholic assertiveness threatened both Canadian unity and the rule of law.[28] The angry agitation against the act could not fail to impress Quebeckers, whatever their party. Conservatives blamed Mercier for having provoked it by his own aggressiveness: 'Mr Mercier stuffed the preamble to the law with Latin and Italian in order to arouse the fanaticism of his Protestant confederates against the Conservative government in Ottawa.'[29] Rejecting this blame, Liberals still had to admit that the act had provoked a fearsome reaction against French Catholicism. Ontario's Anglo-Protestant press seemed to have 'declared an out-and-out war against Canadian Catholicism over the settlement of the Jeusits question.'[30] Every-

---

23 *La Vérité*, 26 Nov. 1887.
24 See Laurier LaPierre, 'Politics, Race and Religion in French Canada: Joseph Israel Tarte' (unpublished PH D thesis, Department of History , University of Toronto, 1962), p. 158.
25 *Le Nouveau Monde*, 26 Mar. 1886.
26 *Le Journal des Trois-Rivières*, 20 Dec. 1886.
27 *Electeurs, attention, ne vous laissez pas tromper*, p. 2.
28 See J.R. Miller's book, *Equal Rights: The Jesuits' Estates Act Controversy* (Montreal: McGill-Queen's University Press 1979). Also his article, 'D'Alton McCarthy, Equal Rights, and the origins of the Manitoba School Question', in the *CHR*, LIV, 4 (Dec., 1973).
29 *Le Nouveau Monde*, 5 Aug. 1889. Also, 26 Mar.; *Le Courrier de St-Hyacinthe*, 24 Aug. 1889; *La Presse*, 12 Oct. 1888.
30 *L'Union des Cantons de l'Est*, 23 Feb. 1889.

where, the 'Orange fanatics have been unleashed against the Pope, against the Church, against the religious orders, and against the French Canadians of the province of Quebec.'[31]

French Canadians had every reason to be frightened by the 'insults against the Catholics and the French Canadians' that were said to fill Ontario newspapers[32] – every reason to be frightened by 'this regrettable agitation which seems to threaten the peace and tranquillity of the country.'[33] Things had gone too far, and everyone could see the need to abandon appeals to race and religion. 'Appeals to prejudice and to religious and national fanaticism are always dangerous, because they tend to disrupt the harmony among the different races which inhabit this country. ... '[34] Confederation's very existence depended on this harmony. 'It is only by maintaining peace in the country, by maintaining harmony between the two races, that we can come to full development.'[35] All public-spirited men must desire 'peace and harmony between the races of this country.'[36] Mercierites as well as Bleus could see the need for racial harmony, the need for the present 'mistrust between the races, mistrust between the religions' to be replaced by 'good will and mutual respect'.[37]

In the long run, then, the Riel affair led to fears of racial conflict which French Canada would necessarily lose, and consequently, to a new insistence in French-Canadian rhetoric on the need for the two races, English- and French-Canadian, to live together in peace and harmony, to share Canada between them on friendly and equitable terms.

It did not take long to see just where the English-Canadian backlash was directed. Convinced that Canada could only survive if it had 'national unity' and a single Canadianism, that only these could check the disruptive influence of Mercierism, many English Canadians began to press for measures of unification. And since the maintenance of the French language and of Catholic

---

31 Ibid., 21 Sept. 1889. Also, 26 Jan.; *L'Electeur*, 18 Oct. and 7 Dec. 1889; *Elections provinciales*, 1890, p. 306; *Laurier à la tribune*, pp. 499–503, 567; *La Vérité*, 26 Feb. 1887; *Elections provinciales de 1892* (Quebec: Belleau et Cie 1892), p. 121.

32 *Le Nouveau Monde*, 26 Mar. 1889. Also, 5 Oct. 1888, and 9 Feb. 1889.

33 *Le Journal des Trois-Rivières*, 13 Jan. 1890. Also, *Le Courrier de St-Hyacinthe*, 18 July and 24 Aug. 1899; *La Presse*, 25 and 26 Oct. 1888, 30 Mar., 1, 20, and 26 Apr., 15 and 17 June 1889; *L'Electeur*, 18 Oct. 1889.

34 *Le Nouveau Monde*, 25 Oct. 1888. Also, 30 May 1887, 9 Feb. and 30 Mar. 1889; *Le Courrier de St-Hyacinthe*, 8 and 24 Aug. 1889.

35 *Le Journal des Trois-Rivières* (quoting Sir John A. Macdonald), 21 Oct. 1889. Also, 20 Dec. 1886; *La Presse*, 29 Mar. 1889.

36 *Le Courrier de St-Hyacinthe*, 5 Sept. 1889. Also, 26 Feb. 1887, and 24 Aug. 1889.

37 *L'Union des Cantons de l'Est*, 12 Oct. 1889.

separate school systems seemed to encourage French-Canadian separateness and prevent the growth of a community of feeling among Canadians, these institutions became, more than ever, the objects of criticism. In Ontario, attacks were directed against the use of French in schools and against the Catholic school system.[38] Similar attacks had begun in Manitoba by the summer of 1889.[39] That fall both Manitoba and the North-West Territories moved to drop the French language from their official gazettes.[40] And before the end of the year an appeal reached Quebec from Alberta's Bishop V.-J. Grandin, who complained that Catholic schools were being persecuted in the Territories.[41]

To the Bleus, at least, it was clear why all this was happening. In these attacks on the French language and Catholic schools, 'the English majority continues to give its answer to the useless and senseless provocations of the national movement and the so-called Catholic party!'[42] Having sown the wind of nationalism, French Catholics must now reap a whirlwind of 'fanaticism, intolerance, and prejudice'.[43] It all showed once again the need to establish peace and harmony between the two races. 'The two nationalities should live in perfect harmony, but in order to reach that goal they must not treat each other unjustly.'[44] They must realize that both races in Canada 'are equal before the constitution and before the law.'[45]

The war against French and Catholic institutions was accelerated at the

38 *Laurier à la tribune*, p. 503; *L'Union des Cantons de l'Est*, 23 Mar. 1889; *La Presse*, 26 Mar. and 31 Aug.; *La Patrie*, 28 Aug.; *Le Nouveau Monde*, 26 July; *L'Electeur*, 13 Nov.; *Le Courrier de St-Hyacinthe*, 31 Aug. 1889.
39 *Le Courrier de St-Hyacinthe*, 8, 13, 15, 20, and 22 Aug., 12 Sept.; 24 and 31 Oct. 1889; *L'Electeur*, 13 Nov.; *Le Journal des Trois-Rivières*, 5 and 10 Sept. 1889.
40 *L'Etendard*, 21 Sept. 1889; *L'Electeur*, 2 Nov.; *Le Courrier de St-Hyacinthe*, 22 and 24 Oct., 7 and 16 Nov. 1889.
41 *Le Journal des Trois-Rivières*, 19 Dec. 1889; *L'Union des Cantons de l'Est*, 28 Dec. Grandin's letter to the bishops of Quebec, dated 20 Nov. 1889, was published in 1891 under the title *Un Suprême appel: l'Evêque du Nord-Ouest supplie tous les amis de la justice de l'aider à protéger ses ouailles contre les tyrans d'Ottawa*.
42 *La Presse*, 14 Sept. 1889. Also, 14 and 20 Aug., 16 and 19 Sept.; *Le Courrier de St-Hyacinthe*, 8 Aug. 1889.
43 *La Minerve*, 5 Mar. 1890.
44 *La Presse*, 13 Feb. 1890. Also, *La Patrie*, 14 Feb.
45 *L'Electeur*, 18 Feb. 1890. These calls for harmony and equitable sharing between the races continued from the late 1880s through the 1890s. See, eg., *L'Electeur*, 8 and 27 Nov., 7 Dec. 1889; *L'Union des Cantons de l'Est*, 3 July 1890, 26 Mar. 1891; *La Presse*, 21 Feb. 1894; *Laurier à la tribune*, pp. 534, 544, 596, 604; *Elections provinciales de 1892*, pp. 120–1; Honoré Mercier, *L'Avenir du Canada* (Montreal: Gebhardt-Berthiaume 1893), p. 88; Honoré Mercier, *Réponse de l'hon. Honoré Mercier au pamphlet de l'Association des 'Equal Rights' contre la majorité des habitants de la Province de Québec* (Quebec 1890).

beginning of 1890. In the House of Commons, D'Alton McCarthy presented his bill to end the official use of French in the North-West Territories, since it was 'expedient in the interest of the national unity of the Dominion that there should be community of language among the people of Canada'.[46] Meanwhile, at Winnipeg, the Manitoba government was preparing legislation of its own to end both the dual school system and official bilingualism.

Quebec's reaction to the McCarthy bill set the tone of debate for the 1890s. It was called 'a declaration of war ... against the French race.'[47] To pass it would be 'an infamy' and a 'defiance of the French-Canadian nationality'[48] – an acceptance of 'domination and intolerance toward the French minority'.[49] It would bring about 'the complete anglicization of the North-West ... the complete exclusion from it of French-Canadian and Catholic influence.'[50] And that was only the beginning. 'The abolition of French in the territories ... is only the prelude to the general abolition throughout the dominion, not only of the official use of French, but also of the separate school system.'[51]

Such designs must not come to fruition. It was not by eliminating one of the races in Canada that you could bring about unity between them,[52] especially when this was done in opposition to 'the sense of equity of the 1877 Parliament',[53] when it meant that Parliament would be vilely taking back what it had given already (imagine it doing that with homesteads!)[54] and when it meant taking away 'a right which is solemnly established by law'.[55] French

---

46 Quoted in numerous common books, eg., O.D. Skelton, *Life and Letters of Sir Wilfrid Laurier* (2 vols.; Toronto: McClelland and Stewart 1965), I, 129. For reports on the presentation of the bill and progress of the debate, see, eg., *Le Courrier de St-Hyacinthe*, 25 Jan., 1, 20, and 22 Feb. 1890; *Le Journal des Trois-Rivières*, 27 Jan., 17, 20, and 27 Feb., 3 Mar.; *L'Electeur*, 13 and 15 Feb.; *La Minerve*, 22 Feb.; *Le Nouveau Monde*, 18 Feb.; *La Presse*, 14, 15, and 19 Feb. 1890.

47 *Laurier à la tribune*, p. 580.

48 *La Presse*, 13 Feb. 1890, and *La Patrie*, 14 Feb.

49 *L'Electeur*, 18 Feb. 1890. Also, 20 and 21 Feb.

50 *L'Etendard*, 11 Feb. 1890. Also, 20 Feb.

51 *L'Electeur*, 17 Feb. 1890. Also, *La Patrie*, 27 Jan.; *Laurier à la tribune*, pp. 585–6; *L'Etendard*, 26 Feb. 1890.

52 *Laurier à la tribune*, p. 589. It is interesting to note that this debate saw not only the rejection of a single Canadianism but also the refutation of one of the most common arguments against bilingualism: its expense. When McCarthy argued that it was too costly to translate documents into French, Sir Hector Langevin offered to pay the whole cost of translation for the North-West Territories out of his own pocket. See *La Minerve*, 19 Feb. 1890, and Hector Langevin, *Speech on the French Language in the North-West*, in the House of Commons, 13 Feb. 1890 (n.p., n.d.).

53 *L'Etendard*, 11 Feb. 1890.

54 *Le Journal des Trois-Rivières*, 10 Feb. 1890.

55 *La Minerve*, 16 Feb. 1890.

was secured in the territories both by federal law and by the terms upon which the North-West agreed to enter Confederation in the first place – in other words, by 'the fundamental law of that vast country'.[56] To abolish it, therefore, would be 'to admit that the most solemn guarantees, the most sacred rights of the minority are at the mercy of the first political intriguer who takes it into his head to remake the constitution according to his own whim. ...' It would be to treat French Canadians as a people without rights. 'Is there a caste of conquerors here and a caste of conquered slaves? Are we not all British subjects in the same right?'[57]

Certain characteristics of the above comments are to be noted. First, there seems to be, among French Quebeckers, greater concern for and closer identification with the people of the North-West than we have seen in the past. Second, there is a much greater readiness than in the past to see French Catholic rights as constitutionally guaranteed and irrevocable.

In the past, embattled minorities had been Acadians or Métis – not exactly French Canadians – but this time there could be no doubt that the targets of the attacks were 'our French-Canadian compatriots',[58] the 'French Canadians of Manitoba',[59] and even 'our own people'[60] or 'us'.[61] At stake in the West were '*our* institutions, *our* schools, *our* language.'[62] Not surprisingly, therefore, the western language and schools questions were debated more heatedly and more persistently than any previous minority question.

Moreover, while French Quebeckers had not even imagined there could be constitutional rights when the West was annexed, and had accepted readily enough that the constitution did not protect Catholic schools in the Maritimes,[63] they did not hesitate at all in 1890 to assert that actions taken against the French language and Catholic schools in the West were illegal or unconstitutional. Language and school rights were 'conferred by the

---

56 Ibid., 16 Feb. 1890.
57 *La Patrie*, 27 Jan. 1890. The need for harmony between two races of loyal British subjects was a natural theme for politicians who had to try to appeal to both. See, eg., Laurier's speech in *Laurier à la tribune*, Langevin's *Speech on the French Language in the North-West* and J.A. *Chapleau's Speech on the French Language in the North-West* (Ottawa: Brown, Chamberlain 1890).
58 *L'Electeur*, 13 June 1890. Also, 20 Feb.; *La Patrie*, 8 Apr.; *L'Union des Cantons de l'Est*, 17 July 1890 , 15 Sept. 1892, 16 Feb. 1893, 15 Oct. 1896; *Le Courrier de St-Hyacinthe*, 29 Aug. 1889, and 17 July 1890; *La Presse*, 22 June 1896.
59 *Le Courrier de St-Hyacinthe*, 12 Sept. 1889. Also, *La Presse*, 27 Aug.
60 *L'Etendard*, 19 Aug. 1889. Also, 23 Aug. 1892, *Le Courrier de St-Hyacinthe*, 19 Oct. 1895.
61 *La Minerve*, 28 Jan. 1890; *Le Courrier de St-Hyacinthe*, 12 Nov. 1896.
62 *La Minerve*, 5 Apr. 1890 (emphasis added).
63 See *Le Courrier de St-Hyacinthe* as late as 20 Feb. 1896.

constitution'.[64] To take them away was to 'violate the law and the constitution',[65] and to maintain them was to defend the 'integrity of the constitution.'[66] Accordingly, there was a spontaneous desire and expectation that Ottawa should 'disallow the iniquitous laws which deprive Manitoba's French Canadians and Catholics of their constitutional rights.'[67] Disallowance was, for the federal government, 'a responsibility which the constitution imposes upon it.'[68]

The readiness of Quebeckers in the 1890s to believe that the constitution guaranteed French language and Catholic school rights in Manitoba and the North-West Territories can be explained partly by the twenty years of history we have followed to this point. The increasing anxiety since 1869 to protect the Métis in their difficulties had – we saw it in the last chapter – convinced French Quebeckers that they had something important at stake in the West – had committed them firmly to French Catholicism there. And this emotional commitment was the more easily translated into a belief in constitutional rights because of the concern for peace and harmony between the races – yes, and even for Canadian unity – which had developed within the past few years. It might be desirable for Canada to form a single great nation, allowed *L'Electeur* in a generous moment, 'but that does not mean that this nation must not speak any other language than English.' On the contrary, unity could only be based on duality, on a recognition that both races 'are equal before the contitution and before the law.'[69]

But certainty about the immutability of western language and school rights was also based on the specific circumstances in which Manitoba and the North-West Territories had been established. The constitution of Manitoba, for example, was contained in a federal act, the Manitoba Act of 1870, which had been confirmed by the imperial British North America Act of 1871. Manitoba, therefore, was incompetent to amend it. 'It is not in the power of

---

64 *La Presse*, 27 Aug. 1889. Also, 23 Aug.

65 *L'Electeur*, 4 Aug. 1892. Also, 3 Aug. 1892, 6 Mar. 1893.

66 *La Presse*, 19 Sept. 1889. Also, 17 Aug.; *Le Courrier du Canada*, 4 Sept.; *Le Courrier de St-Hyacinthe*, 12 Sept. and 24 Oct. 1889, 17 and 22 July 1890; *Le Journal des Trois-Rivières*, 5 and 10 Sept. 1889, and 2 Oct. 1890; *La Minerve*, 28 Jan. and 20 Feb. 1890; *L'Etendard*, 2 Apr. 1890, and 30 Aug. 1892; *Le Nouveau Monde*, 9 Oct. 1888, 10 and 23 Aug. 1889, and 29 Oct. 1891; *La Patrie*, 11 Sept. 1889, 27 Jan. and 21 Feb. 1890; *L'Union des Cantons de l'Est*, 9 Apr. 1891; A.-A. Taché, *Ecoles séparées: partie des négotiations à Ottawa en 1870* (n.p., 1890), pp. 7–8.

67 *L'Union des Cantons de l'Est*, 17 July 1890. Also 9 Apr. 1891.

68 Ibid., 16 Feb. 1893. Also, *L'Etendard*, 8 Apr. 1890, and 30 Aug. 1892; *Le Courrier de St-Hyacinthe*, 26 Feb. 1891; *L'Electeur*, 3 Feb. 1891, and 4 Aug. 1892; *Le Journal des Trois-Rivières*, 2 Aug. 1890, and 16 Feb. 1891.

69 *L'Electeur*, 18 Feb. 1890. Also, *Le Journal des Trois-Rivières*, 23 Dec. 1892.

the Manitoba legislature to abolish the use of the French language and separate schools. The law which governs these matters is under the jurisdiction of the parliament at Ottawa.'[70]

But behind the Manitoba Act had been a more fundamental commitment: the agreement between the Canadian government and the Red River authorities, which had been the basis of the West's agreement to join Canada in the first place. This was an argument put forward repeatedly by Archbishop Taché. He maintained that Catholic school rights in Manitoba 'are not only the result of an act passed in Parliament, but are also part of an arrangement or treaty concluded between the Dominion of Canada and the inhabitants of Red River before the admission of our province into the confederation.'[71] In a number of articles and pamphlets, the archbishop described again and again the negotiations between the Red River delegates and the federal ministers, the insistence of imperial authorities that the Red River demands be met, and the inclusion of school and language rights among the conditions which Red River required to be satisfied before it would agree to Confederation.[72] These arguments did not fail to impress Quebeckers. Manitoba's Catholic schools and French language, they maintained, had been absolutely protected in the new province's constitution. 'It was on these conditions that the province of Manitoba was admitted into the Canadian confederation.'[73]

---

70 *Le Courrier de St-Hyacinthe*, 13 Aug. 1889. Also, *L'Etendard*, 13 Aug. 1889 and 7 Jan. 1890; *La Minerve*, 16 Feb. 1890; *La Patrie*, 14 Feb. 1890.

71 In *L'Etendard*, 7 Jan. 1890.

72 Ibid. Also, *Ecoles séparées*, pp. 1–4, 7; *Mémoire de Monseigneur Taché sur la question des écoles en réponse au rapport du comité de l'honorable Conseil Privé du Canada* (Montreal: Beauchemin et Fils 1894), pp. 25, 32, 33; *Une Page de l'histoire des écoles de Manitoba* (Montreal: Beauchemin et Fils 1894), pp. 6–7, 27–35.

73 *La Revue Canadienne*, XXVII (1892), p. 465. Also, *Le Courrier de St-Hyacinthe*, 31 Jan. 1895, and 20 June 1896; *L'Electeur*, 6 Mar. 1893; *L'Etendard*, 2 Apr. 1890; *Le Journal des Trois-Rivières*, 23 Dec. 1892; *La Minerve*, 16 Feb. 1890; *Le Nouveau Monde*, 7 Mar. 1893. The emphasis on the 1870 negotiations as the guarantee of French and Catholic rights sometimes led to a certain reinterpretation of the events of 1869–70, in which the resistance was no longer seen as the defence of the old buffalo-based way of life against a foreign invasion of settlement, but as a French-Catholic defence against an Anglo-Protestant threat. Eg., Taché, *Une Page de l'histoire*, pp. 18–19. It should be noted, as well, that all the arguments mentioned above with regard to the Manitoba schools question were also applied through the 1890s to the language and schools question in the territories. Eg., *La Presse*, 21 Feb. 1894; *L'Electeur*, 12 Jan. and 20 Mar.; *La Minerve*, 8 Feb. 1894; *La Revue Canadienne*, XXX (1894), pp. 118, 163; *L'Union des Cantons de l'Est*, 16 Feb. 1893, and 22 Mar. 1894; Taché, *Mémoire*, pp. 25–35, 41.

Belief in the constitutional protection of French and Catholic rights in the West could only be strengthened by the court cases fought over them. In 1890–1 Archbishop Taché had reluctantly agreed not to press for disallowance of the Manitoba school law, having been persuaded by Quebec leaders that the courts would declare it unconstitutional, or that, if they did not, Ottawa would act to remedy the situation.[74] This last promise, made by a leading federal minister, J.A. Chapleau, implied Ottawa's acknowledgement that the Manitoba Catholics had indeed been deprived of something to which they were legally entitled. Consequently, when the Judicial Committee of the imperial Privy Council ruled in 1892 that the Manitoba school law was constitutionally valid, French Canadians were not so much weakened in their conviction as angered by the judgement:

We consider it an injustice toward Roman Catholics, for it is obvious that the aim of the legislators who passed the Manitoba Act (which was afterwards sanctioned by an imperial statute) was to grant separate schools to the Catholics. This is a basic principle of Canadian legislation: it's what we have in Ontario and Quebec, and the federal parliament up till now has also declared itself favourable to the maintenance of separate schools in the North-West.[75]

It was hard to see, therefore, how the Privy Council could deliver so wrong-headed a judgement[76] – a judgement which set at naught all 'those so-called guarantees which the fathers of Confederation thought to have assured to the minorities',[77] and which would provoke a new round of 'the most terrible sort of strife, based on nationality, language, and religion.'[78] Nevertheless, rights were rights, and if the courts would not restore them, Ottawa must do so.[79] This contention was the subject of a second Privy Council judgement in early 1895. This time the Council found that Manitoba Catholics did have a legitimate complaint and that the federal government did have the power to remedy it – though it did not say what action, if any, Ottawa had to take.[80]

Despite their lordships' warning that the 'particular course to be pursued must be determined by the authorities to whom it has been committed by the

---

74 On this see Paul Crunican, *Priests and Politicians: Manitoba Schools and the Election of 1896* (Toronto and Buffalo: University of Toronto Press 1974), pp. 18–33.

75 *L'Union des Cantons de l'Est*, 4 Aug. 1892.

76 *Le Journal des Trois-Rivières*, 20 Dec. 1892, Also, 13 Dec.

77 *L'Electeur*, 4 Aug. 1892.

78 *L'Etendard*, 23 Aug. 1892.

79 *La Presse*, 3 Aug. 1892; *L'Electeur*, 3 Aug.

80 *Le Nouveau Monde*, 30 Jan. 1895; *L'Electeur*, 30 Jan.

statute'[81] – that is, by the federal government – French-Canadian commentators took the judgement as a definite confirmation that the constitution guaranteed Catholic separate schools in Manitoba. 'The imperial privy council declares that the rights of the Catholics have been ignored and trampled upon, and that they must be restored.'[82] Ottawa must act 'to carry out Her Majesty's judgement, rendered by the Sovereign's Judicial Council.' This did not involve any political decision by the federal government. 'It is only the High-Sheriff of the Queen, charged with a writ of execution of which it does not have the right to change the terms.'[83] It was the constitution that compelled action, as interpreted by 'the highest court in the empire'.[84] In 1896, when the Quebec bishops issued a pastoral letter to guide voters on the school question, they claimed that what they wanted was to give 'the Catholic minority of Manitoba the school rights which have been reconized by the Honourable Privy Council of Great Britain.'[85] And when the federal government produced first an order-in-council and then remedial legislation on this subject, its aim, according to its supporters, was, in compliance with the Privy Council's instructions, to 'impose upon [Manitoba] the respect of the constitution and of the minority's rights.'[86]

By 1896, then, French Quebeckers had acquired, first, an emotional concern about the treatment of the minorities; second, a desire for harmony and mutual respect between English and French; and third, a belief in 'constitutional' guarantees for minority languge and school rights, at least in the West. It was easy to go from these to generalizations about the nature of Confederation.[87] Confederation, it now began to be asserted, had been meant

---

81 The decision is most easily accessible in Lovell Clark, ed., *The Manitoba School Question: Majority Rule or Minority Rights* (Toronto: Copp Clark 1968), pp. 116–7. 'It is not for this tribunal,' said the judgement, 'to intimate the precise steps to be taken.' And Lord Watson added in a separate comment that the federal authorities 'may legislate or not as they think fit.' (Quoted in Crunican, *Priests and Politicians*, p. 43.)

82 *La Minerve*, 21 June 1895.

83 *La Presse*, 4 Mar. 1895. Also, *La Minerve*, 7 Jan.

84 *Le Courrier de St-Hyacinthe*, 23 Mar. 1895. Also, 20 Feb. 1896.

85 Published in *Le Courrier de St-Hyacinthe*, 19 May 1896; *L'Electeur*, 18 May; *Le Nouveau Monde*, 18 May; *La Patrie*, 18 May; *L'Union des Cantons de l'Est*, 21 May; etc.

86 *Le Nouveau Monde*, 22 Mar. 1895.; Also, *Le Courrier de St-Hyacinthe*, 31 Jan. and 2 Feb. 1895, 5 Mar. and 7 May 1896; *La Minerve*, 8 Jan. 1896; P. Bernard, *Un Manifeste libéral* (Quebec: Brousseau 1896), pp. 28–9, 33.

87 It will be apparent that expressions like 'guaranteed by the constitution' or 'constitutional guarantees' were used in vague and varied ways in these discussions of the 1890s. It was precisely this vagueness about what 'the constitution' was and what it contained that

to establish 'perfect equality of the two races before the law'.[88] The very 'stability of the constitution' depended on 'the peace and harmony which must exist between the two great races which form the Canadian confederation.'[89] But this required the preservation of the very rights which were in dispute during the 1890s:

The education of youth, in which religion and language occupy so large a place, was deliberately put out of reach of any attack, and never would Confederation have been accepted, nor will it ever be consolidated in a durable way, if this spirit of mutual esteem and tolerance ceases to prevail in all levels and all parts of the edifice.[90]

In short, bilingualism – or biculturalism – was the very basis, the *sine qua non*, of Confederation. It was not just a question of the Manitoba Act, but of 'a pact made in 1867 to guarantee equal rights to all in matters of education.'[91] Without such a guarantee, 'it is certain that Confederation would never have been adopted.'[92] Aside from separate schools, it had been 'the intention of the original federal pact to admit the official use of the two languages in each and every province of the confederation.'[93]

The novelty of this conception is evident. In 1867 French Quebeckers had seen their province alone as the home of the French-Canadian nationality, and looked to Confederation to separate it as much as possible from the others. But many were now coming to accept some notion of a Canadian nation based on equality between two races, each having guaranteed rights in *all* provinces. This view emerged from events in the intervening decades. It was only *after* French Quebeckers had discovered and become concerned about the French-Catholic minorities, only *after* they had tried to help the Métis, only *after* the Riel affair, the racial agitation of the late 1880s and the controversies of the 1890s – only *after* all this that the bilingual theory of Confederation could emerge. Only then could an Henri Bourassa appear on the scene.

---

permitted people to claim it guaranteed minority rights or perfect equality between English and French Canadians, and thus permitted the emergence of the bilingual theory of Confederation.

88 *La Patrie,* 27 Jan. 1890.
89 *Le Courrier de St-Hyacinthe,* 5 Mar. 1896.
90 *La Presse,* 21 Feb. 1894. Also, 3 Aug. 1892; *L'Electeur,* 13 June 1890 and 7 Mar. 1893; *L'Etendard,* 30 Aug. 1892; *Le Nouveau Monde,* 24 Feb. 1896; *La Revue Canadienne,* XXVIII (1892), p. 471; *L'Union des Cantons de l'Est,* 4 Aug. 1892, 25 July and 22 Aug. 1895; Taché, *Mémoire,* p. 35; Mercier, *Avenir du Canada,* p. 26.
91 *Le Nouveau Monde,* 7 Mar. 1893.
92 *La Revue Canadienne,* XXVIII (1892), pp. 464–5.
93 *La Patrie,* 21 Feb. 1890. It was unusual for so strong a statement to be made at such an early date. Such an assertion would have been more usual later in the decade. See also *L'Electeur,* 7 Mar. 1893; *Le Nouveau Monde,* 22 Feb. and 16 Apr. 1896.

More than anyone before him, Bourassa expressed the new ideas clearly, coherently, and systematically. To the English-Canadian nationalism of the time, his theory replied that it was possible for English and French Canadians to work together, but not on the basis of cultural unity. Confederation must be seen as an agreement between two nations – English and French Canada – to live together on terms of equality. The British North America Act, claimed Bourassa, was only the official sanctioning of this agreement. Its aim was to build a Canada

that would be French and English in each of its parts as well as in its whole – not French and English in the sense of some bastard fusion of the two races, in which they would lose their distinctive qualities and characteristics, but a fruitful alliance of the two races, each one remaining distinctly itself, but finding within the Canadian confederation enough room and liberty to live together side by side.[94]

Perhaps the BNA Act did not spell this out in so many words; but after all, only scribes and pharisees split hairs about the wording of texts. What counted was the 'spirit of Confederation', and it was clear that according to that spirit, French Canadians had a right to their language, schools, and religion 'throughout the entire confederation.'[95]

These ideas became increasingly current among Bourassa's contemporaries. The newspaper, Le Nationaliste, with which he was associated, proclaimed that the 'entire edifice of the Canadian confederation rests on the equality of the races,'[96] on the 'duality of origins, language, and religion of the Canadian people'.[97] Even school textbooks were influenced by this idea. Thus, a 1911 geography text:

By its political constitution, as Mr Henri Bourassa recently said, by its ethnic composition, and by natural law, Canada is an Anglo-French confederation, the product of the fruitful union of two great and noble races. It must remain, under the protection of the British Crown, the heritage of a bilingual people.[98]

In the light of such conceptions, Laurier's failure in 1905 to secure adequate protection for French language and Catholic schools in the new provinces of Saskatchewan and Alberta could only seem the violation of a contract 'which

---

94 Henri Bourassa, Pour la justice (Montreal 1912), p. 12.
95 Ibid., pp. 31, 33. Also, Henri Bourassa, Le Patriotisme canadien-français: ce qu'il est, ce qu'il doit être (Montreal: Revue Canadienne 1902), p. 8.
96 Le Nationaliste (Montreal), 12 Mar. 1905.
97 Ibid., 3 Apr. 1904.
98 Abbé Adélard Desrosiers and Abbé Fournet, La Race française en Amérique (Montreal: Beauchemin 1911), p. x.

was supposed to ensure the permanence of their separate school system for our compatriots in Ontario, New Brunswick, and the North-West Territories.'[99] Similarly, the Ontario Department of Education's Regulation 17, which, in 1912, virtually ended the use of French in Ontario schools, also seemed to betray a constitution which had guaranteed that French Canadians should be 'at home in Ontario as everywhere else in Canada.'[100]

The appearance of the bilingual theory of Confederation did not, however, mean the abandonment of older conceptions. Neither Bourassa nor any other French Quebecker was prepared to forget about provincial autonomy, or to deny that, whatever rights might be claimed elsewhere, Quebec would always be the homeland in a most particular sense. Only in Quebec, after all – that province which Bourassa described as the 'particular inheritance of French Canada'[101] – were French Canadians a majority. Only there could they control the government; only there were they in a position to build a society reflecting their own distinctive national characteristics and aspirations.

Quebec, therefore, always continued to be referred to as the French Canadians' special country. Even the editors of Le Nationaliste referred to it as 'the French Province of the Dominion'.[102] Poets still described the banks of 'the Great River' as 'our country',[103] and pamphleteers still advised their compatriots to 'remain in our dear province, which is fertile enough to support all its children.'[104] Those who left Quebec, even for a province as near as Ontario, might wish for cultural privileges. 'But as they have committed themselves to Ontario, the best thing for them to do is to face their situation bravely and work vigorously and persistently for the improvement of their lot.'[105] It was still population – the majority in each province – that must ultimately determine cultural rights. That was why Wilfrid Laurier rejected a proposal in the Commons in 1905 to make French official in the new provinces of Saskatchewan and Alberta:

By virtue of what principle or what law would you give the French population of the

---

99 La Revue Canadienne, LVII (1909), p. 133. ALso, Le Nationaliste, 12 Mar. and 23 Apr. 1905.
100 Jules Tremblay, Le Français en Ontario (Montreal: Nault 1913), p. 33. Also, p. 23–4, 25–8; La Revue Canadienne, LXIII (1912), pp. 442–4; Charles Langelier, Etude historique: la Confédération, sa genèse, son établissement (Quebec: Le Soleil 1916), p. 43.
101 Bourassa, Le Patriotisme canadien-française, p. 3.
102 Le Nationaliste, 16 Oct. 1904.
103 Albert Ferland in La Revue Canadienne, LVII (1909), p. 477.
104 Denys Lanctot, Avenir des Canadiens-Français (Montreal 1902), p. 11.
105 La Minerve, 24 Oct. 1887.

North-West Territories the privilege of permanently establishing its language in the constitution? ...

My answer to this question is that I DO NOT RECOGNIZE ANY RIGHT OF PARLIAMENT TO IMPOSE THE FRENCH LANGUAGE ON THE NEW PROVINCES. [106]

Even *Le Nationaliste* seemed at least partly to accept this, for its first criticism of the 1905 autonomy bills was not concerned with language or school rights but with the boundaries of the new provinces. Given the distributions of the French and English populations, an east-west boundary would have created 'one English province and one largely French province.'[107] The actual north-south line divided the French-Catholic group and left it weak in both the new provinces. This 'unnatural and anti-French-Canadian geographic division ... destroys forever the French influence in Saskatchewan.'[108]

Control of provinces was essential because provinces were still seen as the basis of the Canadian edifice. One had only to recollect the way in which the régime had been founded:

Representatives of *four* provinces – Upper Canada, Lower Canada, Nova Scotia, and New Brunswick – met in a convention at Quebec to discuss a plan for federation. *Each one* had certain rights and privileges which had been granted to it by the metropolis, and, within the limits of its juridiction, and as long as these rights are not withdrawn, each one was and still remains sovereign. [109]

The provinces were thus 'the constituent power' of the confederation,[110] and their autonomy remained the basis of the whole system. This was as necessary for Quebec now as in 1864 – and for the same reasons. Thus, a strong central government could still be seen as 'the common enemy'.[111]

---

106 *La Langue française dans l'Alberta et la Saskatchewan* (n.p., n.d.), p. 13. Just as Laurier argued that the majority in the new provinces was entitled to decide on language matters, so French Quebeckers too appealed to their demographic position to justify their contention that Quebec was a French-Canadian country. Eg., *Laurier à la tribune*, pp. 614–16; *L'Union des Cantons de l'Est*, 30 Mar. 1889, and 4 Aug. 1892; Honoré Mercier, *Réponse au pamphlet de l'Association des 'Equal Rights'*, pp. 59–60, 84; L.-O. David, *Le Clergé canadien: sa mission, son œuvre* (Montreal 1896), p. 40; *Canada: la province de Québec, pays de langue française* (Quebec 1918), pp. 5, 10, 11, 13; *La Vérité*, 10 Sept. 1887, 15 Jan. 1888.
107 *Le Nationaliste*, 5 Feb. 1905.
108 Ibid., 26 Feb. 1905.
109 *L'Etendard*, 22 Oct. 1887. Also, 29 Sept. 1887; *La Presse*, 21 Feb. 1894; *La Vérité*, 16 Apr. 1892; *Canada: la province de Québec*, pp. 15–16.
110 *L'Electeur*, 2 Feb. 1895.
111 *La Revue Canadienne*, XXIV (1888), p. 271. Ottawa was not only the common enemy of Quebec's own political parties; it was the common enemy of the provinces, as shown by Manitoba's defence of provincial rights in the matter of railroads. See pp. 198, 270.

Indeed, the feeling for Quebec's autonomy appeared even to strengthen toward the end of the century, for some writers now began to refer to separatism no longer just as a vague dream but as something French Canadians ought actively to prepare themselves for. 'The province of Quebec belongs to us French Canadians; this is what we must love, develop, strengthen, and prepare for independence.'[112] Yes, it was an 'imperious duty to prepare for the complete and definitive independence of French Canada, for therein, and only therein, is our salvation.'[113] This was not only French Canada's duty; it had always been her inevitable destiny and her heart's innermost desire.[114]

We can see, therefore, a persistence of traditional attitudes toward Confederation and provincial autonomy at the end of the nineteenth and beginning of the twentieth century. Provincial affairs still usually predominated in the press – even (for example) during the debate on the 1890 McCarthy bill and at a time when the Manitoba school and language laws were being passed. Federal MPs were still referred to not as representatives of their constituencies but as delegates of their provinces or of the cultural or national groups which the provinces embodied. Thus, there were men who 'represent the French and the Catholics in the cabinet' – this referring to the Quebec ministers at Ottawa.[115] This was a notion which the Liberals naturally exploited after Laurier became their federal leader: 'for our province and our race, he has a particular quality' because of 'the honour he reflects upon them. ...'[116]

This provincial approach to things could even be seen in the discussion of minority affairs. Thus, loss of rights by French-Catholic minorities was still particularly hard to bear because Quebec was obliged to be so liberal with its Anglo-Protestants. Quebeckers, commented one paper with bitter irony, 'continually pamper the English minority of Quebec with righteous generosity and delicate attentions.'[117] After all, what Manitoba Catholics wanted was what 'the Protestants have here even though they're only a minority in the province of Quebec.'[118] Were the English, then, to 'keep for themselves alone

---

112 *La Presse*, 20 Mar. 1894.
113 *La Revue Canadienne*, LVII (1909), pp. 137–8.
114 Jules-Paul Tardivel, *Pour la patrie* (Montreal: Cadieux et Derome 1895), pp. 7–8, 9–10, 150; Denys Lanctot, *Avenir des Canadiens-Français*, pp. 9–10, 13. The increasing prominence of separatism was reflected in the pains which someone like Laurier took to repudiate it. (Eg., *Laurier à la tribune*, pp. 546–7.)
115 *L'Electeur*, 26 Mar. 1895.
116 Ibid., 6 Feb. 1891. Also, *L'Union des Cantons de l'Est*, 26 Mar. 1891.
117 *Le Nouveau Monde*, 22 Aug. 1889.
118 *La Presse*, 3 Aug. 1894. See also 21 Feb. 1894; *La Revue Canadienne*, XXX (1894), p. 174; Tremblay, *Français en Ontario*, p. 30.

the guarantees they have obtained?'[119] It was certain that if Quebec were to abolish its minority's language and schools as Manitoba had done, Ottawa would disallow the act in an instant.[120]

The capacity of the western language and school questions to provoke concern about Quebec's own identity can also be seen in the reappearance of the 'domino theory' we noted in chapter v. This is particularly apparent in the case of McCarthy's 1890 language bill. The preamble, with its contention that unilingualism was necessary for the sake of national unity, was 'a declaration of war against the French language not only in the North-West but in the whole dominion.'[121] This was undoubtedly why Bleu and Rouge leaders alike could accept Sir John Thompson's amendment, which dropped the threatening preamble but authorized the territorial council, after holding elections, to end the use of French in its own proceedings and records.[122] But fear of the domino effect was provoked throughout the decade. Manitoba's abolition of Catholic schools would soon be copied by other provinces, it was feared, after which 'they'll descend upon Quebec to force a legislative union on us, and then the name of Mr McCarthy will go on to posterity while that of the French race goes down to oblivion.'[123] The rise of the Protestant Protective Association in Ontario showed that the wave of intolerance was moving eastward from Manitoba. 'Isn't it obvious that the current is rushing straight toward the province of Quebec?'[124]

Like the western minority problem, western railroads and development were also still seen in a provincial light: they were advantageous for the commerce they brought to Quebec ports – 'a continual tribute which will increase with the whole commerce of the North-West.'[125] As for settlement, it was still, as it always had been, the westerners themselves who took the

---

119 *L'Union des Cantons de l'Est*, 16 Mar. 1893. Also, 23 Mar. 1889, 22 Mar. 1894; *L'Electeur*, 27 Nov. 1889; *La Minerve*, 25 Feb. 1890; *Laurier à la tribune*, p. 567.

120 *L'Electeur*, 7 Mar. 1893. Also, 7 Dec. 1889; *Le Courrier de St-Hyacinthe*, 28 Sept. 1889; *La Minerve*, 5 Apr. 1890; Taché, *Mémoire*, p. 39; Mercier, *Réponse au pamphlet*, especially pp. 59–60.

121 *La Minerve*, 20 Feb. 1890. Also, *L'Electeur*, 17, 18, and 20 Feb.; *Le Journal des Trois-Rivières*, 27 Jan.; *La Patrie*, 27 Jan. and 21 Feb. 1890; *Laurier à la tribune*, p. 614.

122 *Laurier à la tribune*, pp. 614–16; *La Minerve*, 20 Feb. 1890; *L'Electeur*, 25 Feb.; *Le Nouveau Monde*, 24 Feb.; *La Presse*, 21 and 22 Feb.; *Le Courrier de St-Hyacinthe*, 4 Mar. 1890.

123 *L'Electeur*, 3 Aug. 1892.

124 Ibid., 23 Jan. 1894. Also, 13 Nov. 1889, 6 Mar. 1893, and 15 Jan. 1894; *La Presse*, 13 and 14 Sept. 1889; *Le Nouveau Monde*, 24 Feb. 1896; *La Revue Canadienne*, LVII (1909), p. 135.

125 Honoré Beaugrand, *De Montréal à Victoria par le transcontinental canadien* (Montreal 1887), pp. 5–6. Also, *Le Canadien*, 8 Feb. 1889; *L'Electeur*, 10 Jan. 1887; *La Presse*, 9 Mar. 1888; *Elections de 1887: la vraie question*, p. 21.

initiatives;[126] and their appeals became increasingly desperate as Quebec continued not to respond. We do not wish to depopulate Quebec, wrote Bishop Grandin in his *Ultimate Appeal*, by taking away those who are not already planning to emigrate to the United States; 'but without weakening your province, at least give us the crumbs from your table.'[127] Some Quebeckers were willing at least to go this far; but all the concern about western school rights did not change old priorities when it came to migration:

The best thing for a French Canadian is to stay in his own country, where there is still so much good land covered with rich forest and only awaiting men of stout heart and good will to exploit it. As for those who are forced by hard circumstances to leave the province of Quebec, it is to Manitoba that they ought to turn.[128]

Many, however, were not even willing to go this far. To them, the arrival in Manitoba of French Canadians with enough capital to establish themselves meant 'just so much capital and population lost to our province.'[129] It was more satisfying to see English Quebeckers make the move – or Ontarians, who might depopulate their own province to Quebec's advantage.[130]

---

126 Eg., note how the matter was raised in *Le Courrier de St-Hyacinthe*, 4 July 1889; *Le Journal des Trois-Rivières*, 19 Dec. 1889; *L'Union des Cantons de l'Est*, 8 Mar. 1890. Public meetings continued to be organized by men sent from St Boniface for the purpose (eg., Abbé Beaudry, referred to in the *Union des Cantons de l'Est*, 16 Mar. 1889, or in *Le Courrier de St-Hyacinthe*, 4 July 1889 – or Father Nolin, author of a long letter in the *Courrier de St-Hyacinthe*, 11 June 1889). Again, in this post-Riel period, brochures encouraging western settlement continued to be the work of westerners: eg., M.J. Blais, *Le Manitoba* (Ottawa: Imprimerie de l'Etat 1898), T.A. Bernier, *Le Manitoba: champ d'immigration*; Georges Dugas, *Manitoba et ses avantages pour l'agriculture* (n.p., n.d.); Albert Lacombe, *Un Nouveau champ de colonisation: la vallée de la Saskatchewan* (n.p., n.d.); J.-B. Morin, *En avant la colonisation: la vallée de la Saskatchewan*; Morin, *Le Nord-Ouest canadien et ses ressources agricoles*; Morin, *La Terre promise aux Canadiens-Français: le Nord-Ouest canadien*.

127 Grandin, *Suprême appel*, p. 4; *Le Journal des Trois-Rivières*, 19 Dec. 1889.

128 Bishop Laflèche, in the *Union des Cantons de l'Est*, 16 Mar. 1889. For the same set of priorities see *Le Courrier de St-Hyacinthe*, 11 June 1889, 6 May 1890, 24 Jan. 1891, and 28 Feb. 1895; *Le Canadien*, 14 Mar. 1889; *La Minerve*, 6 Oct. 1886; *La Revue Canadienne*, xxiv (1888), p. 406; C.-E. Rouleau, *L'Emigration: ses principales causes* (Quebec: Brousseau 1896), p. 146.

129 *L'Union des Cantons de l'Est*, 30 Mar. 1889. See also Louis Beaubien, *Discours: agriculture et colonisation* (Montreal: Senécal et Fils 1894), p. 18.

130 *Le Canadien*, 23 Feb. 1889. One does, however, begin to see some expressions of regret that more had not been done in the past to settle French Canadians in the West, since a more numerous community might not have had to endure a Riel affair or loss of language and school rights. Eg., *Le Nouveau Monde*, 22 Aug. 1889; *La Minerve*, 5 Apr. 1890; *Le Courrier de St-Hyacinthe*, 22 Oct. 1889; A.-B. Routhier, *De Québec à Victoria* (Quebec: L.-J. Demers et Frère 1893), p. 105.

On the other hand, there does seem to be in this period – indeed, during all the 1880s and 1890s – an increasing acceptance of settlement in the United States and confidence in the possibility of French-Canadian national survival there. Though some articles (often inspired by Manitoba colonizers) still complained of unemployment, poverty, and assimilation in the States,[131] many more spoke of prosperity,[132] the successes of French Canadians in American public life,[133] and the manifestations of national vitality among the Franco-Americans. They had their own schools,[134] continued to speak French,[135] and worked energetically to organize conventions and societies to promote their national interests.[136] Living under a free and tolerant constitution,[137] and reinforced continually by emigration from Canada, they appeared destined to take over and gallicize considerable portions of the United States. Already New England was being transformed into a New France. 'The Yankees are all headed toward the West; French Canadians are replacing them.'[138]

This growing predominance of French Canadians in the northeastern United States represented, in effect, an expansion of Quebec itself. Unlike those who went to Manitoba, separating themselves by a thousand miles from their native province, emigrants to New England remained next door, as it were, in geographical contact with Quebec. Their movement was 'simply the normal extension of a people which is little by little pushing its advance guard

131 Eg., *Le Courrier de St-Hyacinthe*, 24 Jan. and 22 July 1890.

132 *L'Electeur*, 29 Nov. 1890; Joseph Tassé, *Les Canadiens de l'Ouest* (Montreal: Imprimerie Canadienne 1878); N.E. Dionne, *Etats-Unis, Manitoba et Nord-Ouest*, pp. 21–2; Honoré Beaugrand, *Jeanne la fileuse*.

133 *Le Courrier de St-Hyacinthe*, 20 Sept. 1884, and 17 Jan. 1885; *Le Nouveau Monde*, 26 Oct. 1888; *La Presse*, 24 Oct. 1888, and 27 Mar. 1890; *L'Union des Cantons de l'Est*, 15 Sept. 1892; *L'Electeur*, 11 Nov. 1889, and 1 Apr. 1890.

134 *Le Courrier de St-Hyacinthe*, 7 July 1881; *La Presse*, 24 Apr. 1889.

135 *L'Electeur*, 2 Feb. 1891; *La Presse*, 9 Nov. 1888; Tassé, *Les Canadiens de l'Ouest*, p. xxix; E. Hamon, *Les Canadiens-Français de la Nouvelle-Angleterre* (Quebec: N.S. Hardy 1891), pp. 33–4, 75.

136 *Le Pionnier de Sherbrooke*, 12 Aug. and 2 Sept. 1881; *L'Union des Cantons de l'Est*, 23 and 30 July 1881, and 2 June 1885; *La Revue Canadienne*, XVIII (1882), pp. 377–80; *La Minerve*, 3 Aug. 1885; *Le Courrier de St-Hyacinthe*, 4 July 1889; *L'Electeur*, 23 Oct., 6, 11, and 14 Nov. 1889; *La Presse*, 15, 18, and 25 June 1888; *Le Nouveau Monde*, 26 Oct. 1888; Desrosiers and Fournet, *La Race française en Amérique*; Hamon, *Les Canadiens-Français de la Nouvelle-Angleterre*, pp. 22–8, 5off., 113–7.

137 *L'Electeur*, 13 Nov. and 7 Dec. 1889.

138 Ibid., 12 Nov. 1889. Also, *La Revue Canadienne*, XXVII (1891), pp. 42ff., 513–21; Joseph Tassé, *Aux Canadiens français émigrés* (Ottawa 1883), p. 13; J.-B. Proulx, *Le Curé Labelle et la colonisation* (Paris 1885), pp. 11–12.

toward the south.'[139] Like the movement of French Quebeckers into those parts of Ontario and New Brunswick which bordered on Quebec, this expansion into contiguous parts of the u.s. enabled French Canadians to remain 'united on a consolidated territory' rather than being 'dispersed among heterogeneous groups and assimilated to the other races'.[140] In a sense, Quebec was being enlarged to include the surrounding areas; 'the East of America' was becoming a larger French-Canadian homeland.[141] This would soon be true even in a political sense, 'for within twenty years [the Franco-Americans] will have become our compatriots once more. ...' Annexation might be a preliminary step, but not the last. For 'once the United States have engulfed the whole of North America, then their dismemberment will begin, and from that ephemeral confederation will be born a number of independent republics, of which not the least will be a New France.'[142] French Canadians would ultimately control 'an independent state formed by a part of the present dominion together with a fragment of the American bloc. ...'[143]

Meanwhile, they were having to fight for cultural rights in the United States just as in Manitoba and the North-West. There was a 'school question in the United States', brought on, like Manitoba's by the desire to replace free Christian schools by compulsory non-sectarians ones.[144] Franco-Americans too had to fight for the rights of their language, in schools, in public life, and even within the Church.[145] Melting-pot pressures for Americanization, the

---

139 Hamon, *Canadiens-Français*, p. 127. Also, *La Vérité*, 12 June 1886.

140 Edmond de Nevers, *L'Avenir du peuple canadien-français* (Paris: Henri Jouve 1896), pp. 424–5.

141 Edmond de Nevers, 'Les Anglais et nous', in *La Revue Canadienne*, XLII (1902), p. 12. See also, *La Revue Canadienne*, XL (1901), p. 478; XXXIX (1901), p. 493; LVII (1909), pp. 106–16 and 296–301.

142 Lanctot, *L'Avenir*, p. 13. Also, *La Vérité*, 8 Oct. 1887.

143 G. Bourassa, *Conférences et discours* (Montreal: Beauchemin 1899), p. 171. Also, N.H.E. Faucher de St-Maurice, *La Question du jour: resterons-nous français* (Quebec: Belleau 1890), pp. 135–6; Hamon, *Canadiens-Français*, pp. 125–50; *La Revue Canadienne*, XXVII (1891), p. 521, and XL (1901), p. 493. This idea of a Greater Quebec reflected the continued belief that national survival depended less on laws or constitutional rights than on demographic strength. The same belief shows up in the argument that French Canadians must colonize northern Ontario before Manitoba, so as to form a continuous belt of settlement from Quebec westward. See, eg., Routhier *De Québec à Victoria*, p. 107; Association catholique de la Jeunesse canadienne-française, *Le Problème de la colonisation* (Montreal: ACJC 1920), p. 90.

144 *La Revue Canadienne*, XXVIII (1892), pp. 324ff., 513ff.; *Le Courrier de St-Hyacinthe*, 21 Mar. 1889; *Le Nouveau Monde*, 9 Feb. 1889.

145 Robert Rumilly, *Histoire des Franco-Américains* (Montreal 1958), pp. 129–30; *La Vérité*, 8 Oct. 1887; *La Presse*, 2 Apr. 1890; *L'Electeur*, 29 Mar. 1890, and 2 Feb. 1891.

hostility of Americans toward autonomous cultures, obliged Franco-Americans to struggle to keep alive their nationality.[146] And this they did with an attitude not unlike that of the Franco-Manitobans. 'They were conscious of not being intruders on American soil: "We've been here longer than the Irish; it's they who are the foreigners." '[147] Their rights were based on natural law, Church law, and the spirit of the American constitution itself – 'the principles of liberty which are so dear to the Americans'.[148] Indeed, Franco-Americans, in demanding French and Catholic rights, 'have the constitution for them, and the liberty which protects them under the shelter of the stars and stripes.'[149]

In their struggles, Franco-Americans could count on support from Quebec, for Quebec was their motherland, to which they showed their attachment by their determination to maintain their nationality.[150] Thus it was Quebec that sent most of the priests and teachers to the New England francophone parishes.[151] And it was Quebec's premier, Mercier, who told the provincial legislature: 'For the French Canadians of the United States, we are the mother country. We have the rights and duties of the mother country.'[152] He backed up these words by granting Quebec government subsidies to Franco-American organizations, participating in Franco-American conventions, and using an 1891 audience with the Pope to ask for the appointment of a French-Canadian bishop in New England.

These attitudes toward the Franco-Americans and their rights must affect our conclusions about the Canadian question. For they do seem to indicate that the French-Canadian expectation of linguistic and scholastic rights was not based solely on the conditions or institutions of the Canadian confederation. Even where there was no argument to be made about racial equality, the BNA Act, or a binational compact, there was still an expectation of a French-Canadian national life and of French-Canadian rights. Comments about justice, natural law, or the American spirit of liberty suggest a general

---

146 Hamon, *Canadiens-Français*, pp. 39–40, 65–86; *L'Electeur*, 31 Oct. 1889; *La Revue Canadienne*, XL (1901), p. 478.
147 Rumilly, *Histoire des Franco-Américains*, p. 150.
148 Hamon, *Canadiens-Français*, p. 117. Note also Henri Beaudé, *Le Français dans le New Hampshire* (n.p., 1919), p. 17.
149 *L'Electeur*, 10 Mar. 1890.
150 Ibid.
151 G.F. Theriault, 'The Franco-Americans of New England', in Wade and Falardeau, *Canadian Dualism*, p. 400; Hamon, *Canadiens-Français*, p. 62; Rumilly, *Franco-Américains*, p. 44.
152 In Rumilly, *Franco-Américains*, p. 121.

principle of respect for ethnic life and aspirations, a spirit of tolerance and equity.

As a matter of fact, arguments for minority rights even in Canada did not always depend on interpretations of the BNA Act or the meaning of Confederation. As in the U.S., so in Canada French Canadians were not newcomers, and they were not unwilling to assert the right of first exploration or settlement to justify minority demands. Thus, French had rights in the North-West as the 'language first used to evangelize the savages of the country'[153] and in Ontario as 'the first civilized language to echo by the Great Lakes and in the forests of this sister province.'[154] Such rights were also referred to the terms of the 1760 capitulation, early post-Conquest precedents and custom, and the law of nations.[155] Church law was said to guarantee language rights,[156] and of course, so was natural law. Thus, Manitoba Catholics held their right to separate schools 'from nature',[157] and French belonged in Ontario schools by 'natural law, historic right, political right, and true national interest.'[158] So, in Canada as in the States, we find the demand for French-Catholic rights based on a broad principle of equity, tolerance, and right.

This is certainly not to suggest that the demand for rights in Canada was based on such a principle alone. We have seen clearly enough the emergence of a constitutional theory which made bilingualism or biculturalism an essential basis of Confederation itself. But that theory did not represent the whole of what French Canadians thought about the place of their nationality in Canada or in America. It shared a place in their minds with a more traditional Quebec nationalism as well as with a general concern about rights in the continent as a whole. In other words, we must recognize a certain ambivalence or ambiguity in the attitudes we are seeking to identify.

This ambivalence shows up in the matter of Quebec support for the minorities. Quebeckers certainly liked to think that minorities benefited from

153 Elections provinciales de 1892, p. 154. Also, L'Electeur, 15 Jan. and 3 Feb. 1890; La Minerve, 30 Jan. 1890; Le Courrier de St-Hyacinthe, 7 Nov. 1889, and 17 July 1890; L'Electeur, 20 Feb. 1890, 6 Mar. 1893, L'Union des Cantons de l'Est, 3 Dec. 1896; Le Nationaliste, 12 Mar. 1905; Georges Dugas, L'Ouest canadien (Montreal: Cadieux et Derome 1896), pp. 5–6; Lewis Drummond, The French Element in the Canadian North-West (Winnipeg: The North-West Review 1887), p. 14.
154 Langelier, Etude historique, p. 37. Also, Tremblay, Français en Ontario, pp. 9–16.
155 L'Etendard, 29 Aug. 1889; Tremblay, Français en Ontario, pp. 9–16.
156 [J. Sasseville], Dialogue entre un Acadien et un Canadien-Français (Quebec: L.-J. Demers et Frère 1889), pp. 18–19.
157 Le Journal des Trois-Rivières, 7 Dec. 1892.
158 La Revue Canadienne, LXXI (1916), p. 555. Also, LXIII (1912), p. 443; Desrosiers and Fournet, La Race française, p. x.

their aid and could depend on it. [159] The minorities themselves, however, were apt to take a different point of view, and to complain that Quebeckers did not really care about them and were all too ready to let them down in a pinch. [160] The fact was that Quebeckers still did expect the others to take the initiatives on their own behalf, and they awaited those initiatives before doing anything themselves. Thus, as the North-West schools question began to be raised, Jules-Paul Tardivel warned western Catholics that their failure to stand up for themselves by supporting the Riel agitation had 'weakened as much as possible' the support that Quebec could give them now. [161]

However, once minority initiatives had made them aware of the problems, most Quebeckers were ready to proclaim themselves their supporters. Thus, a plea from *Le Manitoba* that Quebeckers should be on guard against proposed anti-French and anti-Catholic measures in the West brought this response: 'Our colleague can be certain that he'll find in our province courageous combatants for the defence of the dearest rights of our brothers out there.'[162] Quebeckers, after all, were 'those who, by the constitution and by circumstances, ought to be protecting them. ... '[163] Quebec's MPs at Ottawa were particularly bound by this duty. [164] But, to provide a really solid support for the minorities, Quebec must be strong:

Those who are protected by the strong are not oppressed, and if the province of Quebec were rich and strong, nobody in the confederation would dare to touch the

---

159 *Dialogue entre un Acadien et un Canadien-Français*, p. 9; *Le Courrier de St-Hyacinthe*, 19 Apr. 1890; *La Revue Canadienne*, LVII (1909), pp. 106, 116.

160 *Dialogue entre un Acadien et*, p. 9. Acadian disappointment and resentment at the Quebec attitude is a major theme in Martin Spigelman's 'The Acadian Renaissance and the Development of Acadien-Canadien Relations, 1864–1912' (unpublished PHD thesis, Dept of History, Dalhousie University, 1975), eg., pp. 147, 256–8, 368–75, 383, 436ff. Western feelings of betrayal by Quebec are explored in Robert Painchaud, 'French-Canadian Historiography and Franco-Catholic Settlement in Western Canada, 1870–1915', in the *CHR*, LIX, 4 (Dec., 1978), while Gilbert-L. Comeault indicates that Quebec action was often independent of the appeals or even the real needs of the Franco-Manitobans, which Quebeckers often failed to understand, in his paper, 'Les Franco-Manitobains face à la question des écoles', given to the 1978 annual meeting of the Institut d'Histoire de l'Amérique Française.

161 *La Vérité*, 5 Nov. 1887. The tendency of Quebeckers to wait for these affairs to be brought to them, as it were, is probably reflected in the very skimpy coverage newspapers gave to the Manitoba schools question in 1890 and 1891. After the Privy Council decisions, however – especially the second one – the question came to dominate the Quebec press.

162 *Le Courrier du Canada*, 3 Sept. 1889. Also, *La Minerve*, 24 Feb. 1890.

163 *La Revue Canadienne*, XXVIII (1892), p. 478. Also, *La Minerve*, 5 Apr. 1890.

164 *L'Electeur*, 7 Mar. 1893. Also, 15 Jan. 1894; *Le Courrier de St-Hyacinthe*, 17 July 1890; *L'Etendard*, 19 Aug. 1889; *L'Union des Cantons de l'Est*, 15 Sept. 1892; Bernard, *Manifeste libéral*, pp. 42–3, 220.

schools of the North-West or speak of expelling French Canadians from the places they occupy.[165]

So, then, it came back to Quebec, its strength, influence, and autonomy. Between the old Quebec patriotism and the new Canadian biculturalism there was a tension, a balance, but ultimately an interdependence. Some might still fear that to protect minority rights effectively might endanger provincial autonomy;[166] others might find it necessary to explain that restrictions of provincial autonomy on behalf of minorities need not always be dangerous for Quebec;[167] nevertheless, when it came down to it, it was no longer a question of choosing between provincial autonomy and minority rights at all, for in fact, they went together. Each implied the other. In forming the confederation, after all, the provinces had insisted on autonomy in order to protect their respective nationalities. It followed that they must respect each other's nationalities:

The confederated nations did not unite for the purpose of fusion; on the contrary, each one of them was careful to preserve its autonomy; each one of them insisted on having its nationals or co-religionists respected. In a word, the basis of a confederation is the respect of minorities.[168]

Of course, Quebec's case was the clearest. We have seen it in the fear that elimination of French rights in the West was only the first stage in a campaign whose ultimate goal was legislative union. Obviously, this was where the PPA's reasoning led:

If a Catholic is unworthy of making a good policeman, then *a fortiori* a Catholic people is incapable of governing itself. So down with our legislature, all our provincial institutions, our civil laws, our schools, our traditions, our language!'[169]

But if French Quebeckers had insisted on governing themselves, on having their own autonomous province, it was for the sake of promoting the French-Canadian nationality. For the sake of that nationality, declared Bourassa, Cartier had insisted on and obtained a federal structure, 'in opposition to the principle of 'fusion', of legislative union, advocated by Sir John Macdonald.'[170] But if the basis of Confederation was provincial

---

165 *La Presse*, 20 Mar. 1894. Also, *La Revue Canadienne*, LVII (1909), p. 137.
166 *L'Electeur*, 25 Feb. 1890, 4 Aug. 1892; *La Patrie*, 23 Mar. 1895; *Laurier à la tribune*, pp. 614–16.
167 Taché, *Mémoire*, p. 32; *Le Nationaliste*, 12 Mar. 1905.
168 *La Revue Canadienne*, XXVIII (1892), p. 469. Cf. *Le Nationaliste's* reference to Canada (3 Apr. 1904) as a 'federation of distinct races and autonomous provinces'. See also *L'Union des Cantons de l'Est*, 1 Mar. 1890.
169 *L'Electeur*, 15 Jan. 1894.
170 Bourassa, *Pour la justice*, p. 12.

autonomy, and if the *raison d'être* of provincial autonomy was the protection of Quebec's nationality, then it surely followed that the sharers of Quebec's nationality should have 'a right to equality throughout the whole of this confederation'.[171] To attack the minorities was to work against the very aim of Confederation, just as much as to attack provincial autonomy:

If their elements of national individuality were certainly the heritage which the contracting parties [provinces] intended to protect above all against outside enemies, then at the very least they have the right to see that heritage respected first of all by the co-signatories of the pact.[172]

Thus, as the idea of bilingualism, or cultural duality, emerged toward the end of the nineteenth century, it was not seen by its advocates as an alternative to the traditional conception of Confederation as an alliance of autonomous provinces with distinct identities, but as a corollary of it. This is what gives the air of ambivalence or ambiguity to the attitudes we have been examining.

The emergence of these new attitudes was not unconnected with the political process by which the Liberals came to replace the Bleus as the dominant political party in Quebec. An important first step in both these changes was the appropriation by the Liberals of the principle of provincial autonomy. Having protested at first that provincial autonomy had always been *their* policy,[173] the Bleus ultimately reacted to Mercier by rallying to the federal government and institutions. Since Quebec was now Liberal, Bleus must turn to Ottawa, where their party still ruled. And since Mercier rocked the federal boat by demanding more autonomy for Quebec, Bleus responded by defending the present constitutional arrangements. This constitution, they claimed, contained precious advantages for Quebec, and Quebeckers ought to oppose any change in it.[174] Nor should Quebec seek conflict with Ottawa, as Mercier did:

Mr Mercier has become a political radical in the full sense of the word, since he is undermining our written constitution and seems to desire, between the federal and provincial governments, a continuous state of war and dispute, from which our province only stands to lose. For we must not forget that the *status quo* contains all the guarantees we could want for the happiness, liberty, and independence of the French-Canadian population.[175]

---

171 Ibid., p. 32.
172 Lionel Groulx, 'Ce Cinquantenaire', first published in *L'Action Française*, July, 1917, reprinted in the *RHAF*, xxi, 3a (1967), p. 669. See also *L'Etendard*, 29 Jan. 1887; *La Minerve*, 28 Jan. 1890; *Le Nationaliste*, 3 Apr. 1904.
173 Above, pp. 181–2.
174 *Le Courrier de St-Hyacinthe*, 26 Feb. 1887; *Le Nouveau Monde*, 1 Apr. 1889.
175 *La Presse*, 12 Oct. 1888.

French Canadians, the Bleus began to assert, were part of a 'heterogeneous people' whose different groups should be 'working together in common agreement for the general prosperity'.[176] They must, therefore, place emphasis on the common government, and participate fully in *common* political movements, of which the federal Conservative Party was the archetype.[177] The Bleus claimed, in fact, that the Ottawa Conservatives – the government of Sir John A. Macdonald – were French Canada's best friends. As proof of this, they stressed Macdonald's decision not to disallow the Jesuits' Estates Act,[178] and pointed out that English-Canadian 'fanatics' criticized him for being under the influence of the French Catholics.[179] Moreover, Bleu newspapers began to quote Macdonald's statements and manifestos at great length.[180] In short, they countered Mercier's Quebec nationalism by rallying to Confederation, which they identified with the central government.

The effect of this strategy (in so far as it had a positive effect) was to encourage people to look to the *federal* government to act in the interest of French Canada. This would certainly affect the discussion of the Manitoba school question. While we saw that in the 1870s French Quebeckers had been reluctant for Ottawa to intervene on behalf of New Brunswick's Catholics, we find them in the 1890s demanding and expecting such intervention in the West.

The belief that Manitoba's 1890 legislation had exceeded the limits of the province's jurisdiction reinforced the tendency to look to Ottawa because it implied the need for disallowance. 'The Martin law was manifestly unconstitutional; the federal government should have disallowed it. ... '[181] The failure to disallow caused 'the federal government to bear the odium of this unjust legislation.'[182]

Once the time had passed within which disallowance was possible, and once the Privy Council had declared the school law to be valid, Ottawa was looked to for remedial action. The federal government must produce 'special legislation to ensure Manitoba's Catholic minority the separate schools which

---

176 *Le Courrier de St-Hyacinthe*, 2 July 1889. Also 11 Sept. 1886, and 25 Oct. 1887.
177 *Le Journal des Trois-Rivières*, 20 Dec. 1886.
178 *La Presse*, 21, 26, and 28 Jan., 1 and 4 Apr., 23 Aug. 1889.
179 *Le Courrier de St-Hyacinthe*, 24 Aug. 1889; *Le Nouveau Monde*, 5 Aug. 1889.
180 Eg., *Le Nouveau Monde*, 9 Feb. 1891; *Le Courrier de St-Hyacinthe*, 15 Oct. 1889, 12 Feb. 1891. Note also *Le Nouveau Monde*, 13 Oct. 1888. This emphasis on the federal government and federal party fits perfectly, of course, with the Bleu insistence, at the same time, on the need for harmony and co-operation between the two races.
181 *L'Etendard*, 30 Aug. 1892.
182 *L'Union des Cantons de l'Est*, 9 Apr. 1891. Also, 17 July 1890.

were promised them, as was perfectly well understood, when that province entered the union.'[183]

The notion of federal responsibility for minority rights was emphasized in the motion which Joseph Israel Tarte presented to the House of Commons in 1893, to censure the government for its handling of the Manitoba schools issue. In supporting it, Tarte expressed many of the ideas we have seen emerging in the 1890s: the need for mutual tolerance and respect between the races, the idea that Confederation had sought to ensure that tolerance by a pact which guaranteed minority rights, and the idea that the West's entry into Canada had been dependent on specific guarantees of French-Catholic rights. Because equality between the races and religions was the very 'basis' of the constitution, 'the Manitoba legislature had no right to abolish the French language and Catholic schools', and once it had done so, Ottawa had the duty to intervene.[184] Thus, concluded Tarte's journalistic commentators, it was the federal ministers who were 'the cause of the present agitation. If they had acted as statesmen, if they had faced up to the constitution and forced Manitoba to respect the law, then we would not be having our present troubles.'[185]

The second Privy Council decision made federal action inescapable – at least as it was interpreted in Quebec. It was in the interest of both parties, in fact, to interpret the judgement in this way: it enabled the Bleus to reassure their French and Catholic voters while encouraging their Tory colleagues to act; and it enabled the Liberals to embarrass their opponents. In any case, by interpreting the judgement as a clear statement that Catholic schools were constitutionally guaranteed, both sides focused attention on Ottawa as the enforcer of these guarantees. Thus: 'The question of the rights and powers of the federal parliament is now settled; it only remains for it to do its duty.'[186] The responsibility was not avoided by the federal order-in-council of 1895, which called on Manitoba to restore the lost school rights. For if Manitoba failed to comply, there could be 'only one possible result: the intervention of Parliament.'[187] When Manitoba's refusal was announced, therefore, the reaction was predictable:

There is great excitement here and all eyes are turned toward Ottawa. Catholics are

---

183 *L'Electeur*, 3 Aug. 1892. Also, *La Presse*, 3 Aug.; *L'Union des Cantons de l'Est*, 11 Aug. 1892.
184 *L'Electeur*, 6 and 7 Mar. 1893.
185 *Le Nouveau Monde*, 7 Mar. 1893. Also, *L'Union des Cantons de l'Est*, 16 Feb. and 16 Mar. 1893, 17 May and 21 June 1894; *L'Electeur*, 7 Mar. 1891.
186 *La Minerve*, 7 Jan. 1895.
187 Ibid., 14 June 1895.

convinced that the federal government will intervene, and they even prefer that the redress of their grievances should be the work of the central power rather than of the local legislature, which could have subjected them to constant vexations.[188]

The federal remedial bill was the logical outcome of these expectations. Through that bill Bleus claimed to be carrying out the federal duty 'to do justice, and to protect the minorities against majorities, be they Catholic or Protestant.'[189]

The Liberals were able to exploit this expectation of federal action as long as the Conservatives were in power at Ottawa. The Bleus could be made to look bad, first of all, by their failure to obtain disallowance. They had 'allowed the law and the constitution to be violated without saying a word.'[190] After the second Privy Council decision they had issued an order-in-council which was merely an attempt to 'decoy' the minority by 'dilatory means' in the face of clear instructions from 'the highest court in the empire' about what the constitution required.[191] As for remedial legislation, Liberals proclaimed the need for it. They would even support the Conservative ministry 'if it would only make up its mind to give justice to the Catholic minority of Manitoba' by effective action.[192] But the 'so-called remedial bill'[193] which the Tories presented to Parliament in 1896 was nothing but a 'legislative hoax'[194] which left itself open to every sort of sabotage by unco-operative Manitobans.[195] It represented a failure of Ottawa to carry out its duty as defender of the minority.

The effect of all this was to help bring about the changes we have seen in French-Canadian views of Confederation. First, the more the Liberals succeeded in making the Conservatives look guilty for their failure to restore Catholic schools in Manitoba, the more they reinforced the belief that the constitution contained guarantees for those schools. The Liberal approach, after all, was that the Conservatives were failing to act according to the constitution. Conversely, the more people became persuaded that the constitution guaranteed minority rights and that the federal government ought to be enforcing it, the more the Conservatives, who controlled that

---

188 *Le Courrier de St-Hyacinthe*, 14 June 1895.
189 Ibid., 5 Mar. 1896. Also, 15 Feb., 21 and 31 Mar., 16, 21, and 30 Apr.; *La Presse*, 4 and 23 Mar. 1896; Bernard, *Manifeste libéral*, pp.68ff.; *La Minerve*, 14 Apr. 1896.
190 *L'Electeur*, 4 Aug. 1892.
191 Ibid., 23 Mar. 1895. Also, *La Patrie*, 23 Mar.
192 *L'Electeur*, 15 Apr. 1895. Also, 20 Apr.
193 *La Patrie*, 9 Apr. 1896.
194 *L'Union des Cantons de l'Est*, 2 Apr. 1896. Also, *L'Electeur*, 17 Apr.; *La Patrie*, 16 Apr. 1896.
195 *L'Union des Cantons de l'Est*, 20 Feb. 1896.

government, must appear reprehensible. But also, the effect of all the factors which encouraged the expectation of federal action – from Bleus' rallying to Ottawa in the time of Mercier to Liberals' criticizing the federal Conservatives for not acting – was to make cultural rights seem no longer dependent on the provinces alone (as in the view of the 1860s) but on the confederation itself. This made possible the emergence of the theory that French-Catholic institutions were guaranteed not only in Quebec but throughout the dominion.

The Conservatives, however, were not to profit from the remedial action which they did eventually take. Their long delays and evasions, which had enabled the Liberals to criticize them so often, had hurt their credibility among Catholic voters. They had missed chance after chance to do something, from 1890, when Sir John A. Macdonald had instructed Manitoba's lieutenant-governor not to refuse to sign the infamous bills into law,[196] till 1896, when they introduced remedial legislation so late and so ineffectively as to indicate clearly that they did not really intend it to pass.[197] Especially after the 1895 Privy Council decision, the Liberals were able to mock their opponents for their delays, and to conclude from them that they did not intend to remedy the situation. After five years of stalling, they complained, and in spite of the clear instructions of the Privy Council, things were still at the same point as in 1890.[198] The vulnerability of the remedial bill itself to Liberal criticism also hurt the Conservatives. Since it failed to ensure that Catholic schools would receive their share of provincial grants, or some equivalent, Liberals could oppose the bill as 'vague, incomplete, unjust, and in reality [giving] nothing at all to the Manitoba Catholics.'[199]

The Bleus also suffered from the English-Canadian company they kept. Already in the 1880s Mercierites had begun claiming that Sir John A. Macdonald was an Orangeman – a member of the 'Black Degree'[200] – and sworn 'to work for the annihilation of the Catholic religion in Canada and consequently of the French-Canadian race, which professes it.'[201] Other English-Canadian Conservatives were much more embarrassing to the Bleus: D'Alton McCarthy, and William Meredith, the Ontario Conservative leader

---

196 *La Patrie,* 24 Mar. and 8 Apr. 1890.
197 *L'Electeur,* 17 Feb. 1896; *La Patrie,* 9 Apr.
198 *L'Union des Cantons de l'Est,* 7 Feb. 1895.
199 David, *Le Clergé canadien,* p. 64. Also, *L'Electeur,* 7 Mar. 1896; *L'Union des Cantons de l'Est,* 13 Feb., 19 Mar., and 30 Apr. 1896.
200 *L'Etendard,* 22 Feb. 1889. See also 15 Feb. 1890, where Macdonald's Orange sympathies are said to be manifest in his support for the incorporation of the order.
201 *L'Electeur,* 13 Oct. 1885. Also, 16 Nov.

who had been attacking French and Catholic schools in that province since the late 1880s.[202] McCarthy, a president of the Ontario Conservative Association and prominent Tory MP, had been a leader of the anti-Jesuit agitation, had led the attack against the French language in the North-West, and was accused of having stirred up the hornets' nest of anti-separate school legislation in Manitoba in 1889, when 'Sir John sent [him] to Manitoba to arouse the fanaticism of the Protestants.'[203] It was this intolerant Ontario wing, which even a leading Bleu had described as 'a collection of factions led by Meredith and McCarthy',[204] that seemed to rule the Conservative Party, while the servile Bleus bowed to their Orange allies and let slip chance after chance to aid the Manitoba minority.[205] Could one really trust such a party to follow through with effective remedial action, when even during the 1896 election campaign its Anglo-Protestant leader told a Winnipeg audience 'that it was a lie to claim that the Conservatives favoured the re-establishment of separate schools'?[206]

The Liberals, on the other hand, had been looking more and more like defenders of French and Catholic rights, ever since Mercier won ultramontane support for the formation of his government and went on to appoint the Curé Labelle deputy minister, correspond with and receive great honours from the Pope, make a flamboyant appearance at the great 1889 Baltimore convention of American Catholicism, and settle the Jesuits' estates question.[207] It certainly helped at the federal level also to have in Laurier a French-Catholic leader, who upheld the Catholic theory of education,[208] could be reported to have attended mass all over the country, and was praised by a Catholic bishop as 'the first among the Canadians'.[209]

---

202 Ibid., 20 Feb. 1890; *L'Union des Cantons de l'Est*, 23 Mar. 1889.

203 *L'Union des Cantons de l'Est*, 24 Aug. 1889. Also, *L'Electeur*, 18 Oct. and 30 Nov. 1889, 25 Mar., 11 Apr., and 6 May 1891; 23 Jan. and 21 Nov. 1894. While there were Liberals involved in the anti-Jesuit agitation, and while the Manitoba government itself was Liberal during this period, the role of Conservatives seemed most prominent, and it was that party's image that suffered from identification with the anti-French and anti-Catholic agitation. See J.R. Miller, '"This Saving Remnant": Macdonald and the Catholic Vote in the 1891 Election', in the Canadian Catholic Historical Association, *Study Sessions*, 1974, pp. 36–7.

204 *L'Union des Cantons de l'Est*, 21 May 1896.

205 *L'Electeur*, 26 Mar. 1895; *L'Union des Cantons de l'Est*, 14 Mar.

206 *L'Electeur*, 16 May 1896. Also, 27 Jan., 17 Feb. and 7 Mar.

207 *L'Etendard*, 22 Feb. 1889, 15 Jan. 1890; *L'Electeur*, 14 Nov. 1889; *Elections provinciales de 1892*, pp. 109, 117–18.

208 *La Presse*, 6 Mar. 1895.

209 *L'Electeur*, 19 Sept. 1894.

Liberal publicists had been trying hard to free the party from its old anticlerical image:

There was a time when the idea was firmly set in the minds of certain community leaders that the Liberal Party was hostile to the Church.

But Mr Mercier came to power, and he did more in four years to consolidate our Catholic institutions in the province than all his predecessors since Confederation.

It's been said that the clergy later forgot his services; but that is a mistake and a grave injustice to the clergy.

Before the coming of Mr Mercier, influenced by prejudices stirred up in the interest of the Bleus, there were not ten priests in the province who were sympathetic to the Liberal Party.

Today there are more than five hundred out of a thousand.[210]

Liberals need not fear, therefore, that the clergy would intervene in politics against them. If some clerics still occasionally did so, it was only because the Bleus had hoodwinked them into mistaking their true friends.[211] 'It's not the clergy who go running after the politicians; it's rather the latter who are continually chasing them. ... '[212] But good Liberals would not try, like the Bleus, to manipulate the clergy. They were 'submissive in every way to the teachings of our holy mother Church, devoted to the interests of religion more than to those of politics,'[213] and they knew that their duty was to follow clerical guidance while encouraging the electorate to do the same.[214]

In claiming to be the pro-Catholic party, Quebec Liberals were aided by their English-Canadian allies. Ever since the days when Edward Blake had attacked Macdonald's government for allowing the execution of Louis Riel, English-Canadian Liberals had been losing their old stench of Grit franco-phobia and taking on a sweeter aroma.[215] When McCarthy the Tory attacked

---

210 Ibid., 17 Apr. 1895. Also, 29 June 1896.

211 Ibid., 28 Jan. 1896.

212 La Patrie, 4 May 1896. That it was Conservative politicans who dragged a reluctant clergy into the remedial bill question and the 1896 elections is borne out by Professor Crunican in Priests and Politicians.

213 L'Electeur, 14 Feb. 1896. Also, 16 Apr. 1895.

214 L'Union des Cantons de l'Est, 4 June 1896. Not content with proclaiming their piety and obedience, Liberal editors opened their columns to Ultramontane articles by priests (eg., L'Electeur, 10 Apr. 1895), and L'Electeur even referred to Jules-Paul Tardivel as a guide to political events (17 Feb. 1896)! No wonder L'Union des Cantons de l'Est, could claim (21 Mar. 1895) that the old notion that Liberals were hostile to the clergy while Bleus were the champions of Catholicism was, in fact, the very opposite to the truth.

215 Even the Ultramontane L'Etendard (4 Feb. 1887) reprinted passages from Blake's speech on the censure motion to win Quebec support for the Liberals.

the French language in the North-West, Blake the Liberal declared himself 'the champion of the French language in Canada' and defended it.[216] It was the Ontario Liberal premier, Oliver Mowat, who had chaired the 1887 inter-provincial conference at Quebec and worked with Mercier to defend provincial autonomy. It was that same Liberal Mowat whose government maintained French and Catholic schools in Ontario while the Tories attacked him for it.[217]

All these circumstances were cleverly exploited by Liberal publicists. Their psychological astuteness is well illustrated by an 1894 report in *L'Electeur* about a provincial by-election in London, Ontario. The Conservative candidate, who had lost to his Liberal opponent, had been the leader of the infamous Protestant Protective Association. 'Catholics and Protestant Liberals had united,' commented the paper, 'to crush the bigots.' At the head of the article was a sketch of the red ensign, and over it were printed the words 'Catholic and Liberal'.[218] This was the image which a decade of Liberal propaganda finally succeeded in establishing.

When, in the midst of the 1896 election campaign, the Quebec episcopacy issued its collective pastoral letter on Manitoba schools and the duty of Catholic voters, it reflected the new constitutional and political attitudes. What they wanted, said the prelates – what all Catholics must want – was 'the triumph of rights which have been guaranteed by the Constitution.' To restore Catholic schools in Manitoba would be to show 'the respect due to the Constitution and to the British Crown.' In saying this, the prelates were expressing the new Quebec views about the constitution and minority rights, and in telling Catholic voters that they should vote only for candidates who would support remedial action in Parliament, they expressed the new view of the role of Ottawa in enforcing those rights.[219]

The pastoral letter also expressed the new political outlook by declining to give any explicit support to the Conservatives, who had already presented

---

216 *L'Electeur*, 17 Feb. 1890. Also 8 Nov. 1889. J.R. Miller points out that Blake had also helped the Liberals win Catholic sympathy by opposing the incorporation of the Orange order and by choosing Laurier to succeed him as party leader ('This Saving Remnant', p. 34). Even the Conservative *La Presse* had to praise Blake's good will and benevolence toward French Catholics (15 Feb. 1890).

217 *Laurier à la tribune*, p. 503; *L'Etendard*, 1 Apr. 1890; *La Patrie*, 28 Aug. 1889; *L'Electeur*, 1 Apr. 1890.

218 *L'Electeur*, 21 Nov. 1894.

219 The pastoral letter was published in most or all newspapers between the 18th and the 21st of May, 1896.

remedial legislation in Parliament. Bleus might claim that the letter 'approved the government's conduct',[220] but in reality they were disappointed by it. Liberals reported gleefully that after the reading of the letter from the pulpit, Bleus had come out of church complaining that it 'favours the Liberals – we're done for.'[221] Indeed, the letter's very neutrality did favour the Liberals, for the declining credibility of the Bleus and the increasingly Catholic aura which had come to surround the Liberals in recent years made it possible for the latter to gain a better hearing when they gave the undertaking required by the bishops. Well, then, might Liberals praise the letter for putting an end to the Bleus' 'odious exploitation of a holy authority'. French-Canadian Catholics would now have an even 'greater respect, livelier affection, and higher consideration for the hierarchy which commands us all, Conservatives and Liberals alike, in the spiritual domain.'[222]

In fact, the Rouges claimed they would get more than the Bleus for the Manitoba Catholics. Years of stalling and evasion had proved the duplicity of the Conservatives, who simply would not 'respect the constitution' by remedial action. The Liberals, on the other hand, 'would have done it five years ago.'[223] The Orangemen had realized this all along, and had attacked Laurier because 'his policy would have been favourable to the Catholic minority of Manitoba.'[224] Liberal papers proclaimed this in Laurier's own words:

What I want and what I ask is that the minority in Manitoba should obtain the privilege of teaching their children their duties toward God and society in the manner in which they have been instructed by their religious authorities. ...

The Liberal Party's policy has always had as its aim to protect the minorities. I want the Liberal Party to follow that policy under my leadership, and I believe that, in the name of all the members of the Liberal Party, I can make a

SOLEMN COMMITMENT

that the Liberal Party will undertake to settle the present problem on a basis which will

---

220 *Le Courrier de St-Hyacinthe*, 20 June 1896. Also, *Le Nouveau Monde*, 22 May; *La Presse*, 22 June; Bernard, *Manifeste libéral*, p. 36.

221 *La Patrie*, 18 May 1896.

222 *L'Electeur*, 18 May 1896. The Liberals did so well with the pastoral letter that their opponents later accused them of having shamelessly and dishonestly exploited it. Eg., Bernard, *Manifeste libéral*, p. 52; *La Minerve*, 25 June 1896.

223 *L'Electeur*, 28 Jan. 1896. Also, *L'Union des Cantons de l'Est*, 7 Feb. 1895. On the duplicity and unreliability of the Conservatives, see *L'Electeur*, 25 Mar. and 10 Apr. 1895; *L'Union des Cantons de l'Est*, 4 and 11 Apr. 1895.

224 *L'Union des Cantons de l'Est*, 23 Mar. 1893.

be found just, equitable, and satisfactory by the minority, on that liberal basis of equal rights and justice for all which is the spirit of our constitution.[225]

In other words, while the Tories' remedial bill only *pretended* to help the Manitoba Catholics, the Liberal Party was 'committed to the re-establishment of separate schools just as they existed before 1890.'[226] Thus the Liberals outbid the Conservatives in their claim to satisfy the demands of Quebec's Catholic voters in 1896 – to satisfy, that is, the demands which arose from the new conception of the constitution and of the nature of Confederation.

What made the Liberals particularly unbeatable, however, was that in satisfying new demands they were able to respect old values. Here Laurier's race and religion were precious assets. To vote for the party he led was to get rid of 'the Orange machine and put at the head of the country [a] compatriot and co-religionist'.[227] English Canadians understood what that meant. 'COMPATRIOTS!!' screamed a giant headline in *L'Electeur*. 'LEND AN EAR.' Here was what Tupper, the Tory leader, had said two days before in a speech at Port Arthur: 'Can you vote to overthrow the present government and put into power a French and Roman Catholic prime minister?'[228] In Quebec, of course, this sort of thing could only lend credibility to Liberal promises to do more than the Bleus for the Manitoba minority. That it did so, however, was a reflection of the continued belief that MPs were the representatives in Parliament of their nationality and religion. And as, in the traditional view, race and religion were connected with province, so that MPs were also seen as the representatives of their provinces, it was particularly important that Laurier was a Quebecker. 'We of the province of Quebec should be particularly proud of the statesman who is now the leader of our party; he is of our race and our little homeland.'[229] His coming to power would enable 'his province to gain the ascendancy in Confederation.'[230] But it was also a traditional view (still current, as we have seen) that Quebec was the protector of the minorities. Was it not clear, then, that a federal leader who was also the

---

225 This was printed in every issue of the *Union des Cantons de l'Est* from 25 July to 22 Aug. 1895. It was all in bold-face capital letters, with the words SOLEMN COMMITMENT standing out in extra-large type.

226 *L'Electeur*, 13 Mar. 1896. Also, 17 and 29 Sept. 1894; *La Patrie*, 16 Apr. 1896; *L'Union des Cantons de l'Est*, 21 May 1896; David, *Le Clergé canadien*, p. 68.

227 *L'Electeur*, 28 Jan. 1896.

228 Ibid., 15 May 1896. Also, 16 May; *La Patrie*, 8 May; *L'Union des Cantons de l'Est*, 21 May 1896.

229 *La Patrie*, 24 Apr. 1896.

230 *L'Electeur*, 24 Nov. 1894.

representative of French Quebec would be the man most likely to bring justice to the Manitoba Catholics? In February, Laurier had told the House of Commons that he would not take his stand as a Catholic and a French Canadian on the remedial issue. But in the Quebec campaign, that was exactly what the Liberals promised that Laurier would do.

This was borne out by the post-election commentaries. To the rueful Bleus it seemed Quebeckers had been taken advantage of, 'and that in voting for Mr Laurier they imagined that they were really giving their support to a French Canadian, who would defend the rights of our Manitoba brothers.'[231] Liberals, far from rueful, noted that Manitoba had voted Tory, and concluded that Manitobans, like Quebeckers, had understood which party was really for Catholic schools.[232]

The same ideas show up in the comments on the settlement which was negotiated in the fall of 1896. While the talks were going on, Bleus found it prudent to remind Laurier 'that you are a Catholic and that your MPs got themselves elected by promising, in compliance with the pastoral letter of the bishops, to vote for a remedial law'.[233] When the agreement was announced, Bleus found it particularly disappointing because it was the work of a French Quebecker. The Liberals had only been elected because Quebeckers were 'convinced that Laurier, a Catholic of French race, would do more and better for our oppressed brothers than an English Protestant like Sir Charles Tupper.'[234] Instead of keeping his promise, though, 'Mr Laurier has signed the abdication of his race and the subservience of his brothers in Catholicism'.[235] Interestingly, Liberal commentators agreed with the Bleus' assessment both of Laurier's election promise and of his duty. That was why, in *praise* of the settlement, they maintained that he had acted as 'a patriot, a devoted friend of all his brothers by race and by religion.'[236]

But in the election campaign Laurier offered more than the promise to act as leader of French Quebec and defender of the minorities. While, in 1872, Cartier had claimed that the New Brunswick Catholics could not be defended

---

231 *Le Courrier de St-Hyacinthe*, 27 June 1896. That the Liberals had won credibility for their promises by stressing Laurier's nationality was the contention of *La Minerve*, 25 June 1896; *Le Nouveau Monde*, 24 June; *La Presse*, 24 June; *La Revue Canadienne*, XXXII (1896), p. 444; Bernard, *Manifeste libéral*, pp. 56–8.

232 *L'Electeur*, 29 June 1896. Also, David, *Clergé canadien*, pp. 98–9.

233 *Le Courrier de St-Hyacinthe*, 12 Nov. 1896. Also, 17 and 21 Nov.

234 *Le Nouveau Monde*, 21 Nov. 1896.

235 *Le Courrier de St-Hyacinthe*, 26 Nov. 1896. Also, Bernard, *Manifeste*, pp. 215, 220.

236 *L'Electeur*, 21 Nov. 1896. Also, 20 and 23 Nov.; *L'Union des Cantons de l'Est*, 15 Oct., 26 Nov., and 3 Dec. 1896.

without some threat to Quebec's autonomy, Laurier undertook in 1896 to restore the schools of the Manitoba Catholics without endangering provincial autonomy.

Since Conservatives had looked increasingly to the central government over the past decade for action, responsibility, and identification, it was not surprising that they ended up with a remedial bill that seemed to *coerce* Manitoba into restoring Catholic school rights. The logic of the situation seemed to require it. Was it not federal action, after all, that Liberals had been demanding all this time? And what other choice was there once Manitoba had refused to comply with the order-in-council?

The more it goes, the more we're convinced that negotiating with fanatics of this sort ... is a waste of time. There only remains one thing to do: to act on the privy council decision and *force* them to do their duty.[237]

But was coercion really the only recourse? Was it really desirable, or was it only the natural tendency of a Conservative Party which had been accused for years of excessively centralizing tendencies? Had not Mercier already had to face 'a conspiracy of Sir John Macdonald against the independence of the provinces'?[238] Macdonald had always preferred legislative union to federalism, and his party remained a party of centralization.[239] All in all, therefore, it was easy to see the Conservatives in 1896 as offering a solution to the schools problem which, while not effectively restoring Catholic rights, nevertheless endangered provincial autonomy.

Was it not safer all round to turn to Laurier, who offered to get more for the minority by 'sunny ways', by negotiation? Laurier was a French Quebecker and therefore understood the value both of minority rights and of provincial autonomy. And he proposed to make Oliver Mowat a special commissioner to resolve the school problem to everyone's satisfaction – Mowat, who, as an English-Canadian Liberal, could deal with the Manitobans, who had fought for provincial rights as premier of Ontario and chairman of the interprovincial conference, and 'who for so long has fought against the Tory leader Meredith to preserve the separate schools of the Ontario Catholic minority.[240]

---

237 *Le Courrier de St-Hyacinthe*, 19 Oct. 1895 (emphasis added). Also, 21, 28, and 30 Jan., and 3 Mar. 1896.
238 *L'Electeur*, 12 Oct. 1889. Also, 5 and 9 Mar. 1892; *Elections provinciales de 1892*, pp. 153, 155.
239 *L'Electeur*, 2 Feb. 1895.
240 *L'Union des Cantons de l'Est*, 21 May 1896. Also 21 Mar. 1895. For an extra hedging of bets, Laurier added that if this method didn't work, he would resort to remedial legislation – and more effective legislation than what the Tories proposed. See the report of his St-Roch speech in *L'Electeur*, 8 May 1896.

This was an unbeatable programme. It responded to the ambivalence of Quebec attitudes, to the need for *both* provincial autonomy and provincial rights. Here we see how the notion of a bilingual or bicultural Canada came to coexist with the vision of an autonomous Quebec in alliance with other autonomous provinces. Although Laurier would inevitably disappoint some of the expectations his own campaign had encouraged (for it was impossible to be at once both a *federal* leader and the special representative of French Quebec), these ideas were carried into the new century. Henri Bourassa, who had followed Laurier in 1896 precisely because he believed in the implications of the campaign,[241] expounded them in opposition to Laurier, developing them into his bilingual theory. By the generation of Lionel Groulx, these ideas had become commonplace. They would remain so until the rise of modern separatism in the 1960s.

---

241 Bourassa, *Pour la justice*, p. 28.

X

CONCLUSIONS AND
CONJECTURES

We are accustomed to thinking of Confederation as a national unification transforming a scattered collection of colonies into a single people under a strong national government. From the foregoing chapters, however, it appears that French Canadians in the 1860s did not share this point of view.

By 1864 French Canadians had long been accustomed to thinking of themselves as a nation and of Lower Canada as their country. They were scarcely aware of the existence of French-Catholic groups elsewhere in British North America. French Canada and Lower Canada were, in their eyes, equivalent terms. Consequently, what they sought in Confederation was to strengthen the French-Canadian nation by strengthening Lower Canada. They wanted to be separated as much as possible from the other provinces, to have an autonomous French-Canadian country under the control of French Canadians. Conservative propaganda made Confederation attractive by stressing, and even exaggerating, the powers which the provinces would have, and by minimizing those of the federal government. It emphasized the separateness and sovereignty of the provinces. French Canadians in Quebec would 'constitute a state within a state' and enjoy 'the formal recognition of our national independence.'

That independence, however, could not be complete. 'We are still too young for absolute independence,' and some sort of collaboration with the rest of British North America was therefore necessary, both for military defence and for economic viability. To stop the alarming emigration of French Canadians from their native province, it was necessary to create jobs there. And since French Canadians could not do this all on their own, economic integration with the other provinces and encouragement of English business in Quebec were necessary.

But the degree of integration must be the minimum necessary to make Quebec viable. The greatest possible amount of provincial *sovereignty* was to be combined with a modicum of federal *association*. This meant that Confederation would be an 'alliance' or 'association' of autonomous provinces, with a central government dealing only with certain limited matters of common interest while the provinces took care of their respective nationalities. In this federal alliance Quebec would be the French-Canadian country, working together with the others on common projects, but always autonomous in the promotion and embodiment of the French-Canadian nationality.

In this scheme of things there was little place for bilingualism and biculturalism. The French-Canadian fathers of Confederation wanted to put education, for example, under the absolute control of the provinces. They declined to co-operate with the Archbishop of Halifax in getting restrictions placed on that control to protect Catholic schools in the Maritimes, and they only reluctantly agreed to constitutional guarantees for certain Protestant and Catholic school rights in Quebec and Ontario. Such provisions were not really desirable, since they limited French Canadians' control of their own province and might tend to erode that province's French-Catholic character. 'What we preferred was for there to be no concession of privileges to any religious minority in the new constitution.'

Unfortunately, the Quebec minority simply *had* to be given certain privileges: official status for its language, protection for its schools, guarantees for its political representation. The first government of Quebec could only be formed on condition that it produce legislation giving Protestants new educational privileges. When the bill was presented in 1869, it brought criticism from both parties for giving extravagant privileges to the minority at considerable cost to the Catholic majority. And when it passed, nevertheless, editorialists charged that it had been *forced* on the government by the overbearing minority.

But the minority forced more than just its schools on Quebec. In the decades after Confederation, complaints against the excessive prominence of the minority language, minority culture, and minority men were frequent and familiar in the French press. English Protestants occupied too many public places in Quebec. They refused to recognize the French language in dealing with French Canadians. And Protestants paraded through the streets in offensive demonstrations of their alien culture.

Thus, the decades after Confederation saw an increasing frustration in Quebec, as people realized that the highly autonomous French-Catholic province they had been promised in 1867 was, in fact, far more English and Protestant than they liked. And this frustration was intensified by the discovery of the French-Catholic groups living in other parts of Canada. Unfortunately, the circumstances in which that discovery was made were disagreeable ones.

The harassment of Métis in the North-West, the dismantling of Catholic separate school systems in New Brunswick, Prince Edward Island, and the prairie provinces, the disestablishment of the French language on the prairies, the attempt to eliminate French from Ontario schools – these were the events which brought the minorities to Quebec's attention. As the minorities appealed to Ottawa to defend them against their provincial authorities, their plight came before the French Quebeckers, who were represented at Ottawa. And it was natural that Quebec, which was *the* French-Catholic province, should sympathize with and support those minorities.

More than that, it was impossible to escape the bitter contrast between the way the minority was treated in Quebec and the way minorities were treated elsewhere in Canada. Whenever Catholic minorities were harassed or deprived of what had seemed to be rights, French-Quebeckers asked themselves: What if we were to do that to our minority? We could never get away with it. The result was to intensify resentment at the fact that Quebec could not be unilingual and unicultural like the other provinces, could not really be that French-Catholic country promised in 1867. Thus, one result of the discovery of the French-Catholic minorities was to intensify the Quebec nationalism which Confederation had appealed to originally. The outburst of separatism at the end of the nineteenth century was a manifestation of this phenomenon.

But the discovery of the minorities produced another effect as well. To fight for the Métis, to fight for the Acadians, to fight for French in the West, to fight for the Franco-Ontarians, was to develop among French Quebeckers a new interest in the French fact, a new commitment to the flourishing of French-Catholic communities in those other parts of Canada.

The most important area influencing these developments was the prairie West. Initially, Quebec's interest in the North-West was strictly commercial. The shipping of its grain by rail to the ports of Quebec for loading onto Europe-bound ships would stimulate the commerce of Quebec's cities, build up her ports, and provide jobs for French Canadians, who would no longer have to emigrate to the United States. All this benefit French Canadians would gain from the North-West without settling there themselves.

The Red River uprising made Quebeckers begin to look on the West in a new light. Initially unsympathetic or hostile to the Métis resistance, they began eventually to defend it as they became convinced that Ontarians were holding their race and religion responsible for it. It appeared, in fact, that Ontarians had isolated French Catholicism as the distinguishing characteristic of the uprising, and that many Ontarians were more interested in suppressing the Métis because they were French and Catholic than because they were rebels. This provoked a natural reaction from the French-Catholic province of Quebec: 'Ah, but on that point the province of Quebec has only one answer: to protect and aid our brothers of the West.'

The Manitoba Act appeased both Métis and Quebeckers. But although its guarantees for the French language and Catholic schools made it easier for French Canadians to live in the West, and although the missionaries were eager to see them settle there in order to reinforce their native Catholic population, the following decades saw no significant French-Canadian settlement on the prairies. Since Quebec was the French-Canadian homeland, emigration to the West meant exile, and if it came to that, New England was closer to home.

But if Quebeckers were not eager to go and live in the West, they did increasingly have another interest in the region. The continued harassment of the French Métis, the long delay in granting an amnesty, the arrest, trial, and conviction of Lépine, the expulsion of Riel from the House of Commons, the exclusion of the French and Catholic members of the Red River provisional government from the amnesty that finally was granted in 1875 – all these things bolstered the idea in Quebec that it was French Catholicism that was being persecuted in the West, and that Quebec, therefore, the French-Catholic province, had something important at stake there: the protection of that persecuted element.

This is the feeling we see in the Riel affair. Convinced that he was mad and not responsible for his actions, believing that there were extenuating circumstances in his favour, French Quebeckers reasoned that if he had been English, Scotch, or even Turkish, Riel would never have been hanged. It was not the criminal, therefore, that English Canada had hanged at Regina; it was the French Canadian. His execution was thus an attack upon French Canadianism, upon the French-Canadian nation. That nation, argued Mercier, must assert itself in its own defence. French Canadians of all political parties must unite to form a single National Party with the aim of fortifying the French-Canadian stronghold of Quebec.

Mercier's election, and his loud assertions of autonomy and of French Catholicism, frightened many English Canadians. They feared that French-Canadian insistence on special status, special privilege, would tear the confederation apart. Canada needed to become a nation – like the United States, united and strong. Only national unity (it's at this point that that phrase becomes current) and a single Canadianism could end the threat of French-Canadian nationality and separateness.

As English Canadians became increasingly agitated, French-Canadian leaders became frightened. Would nationalism and counter-nationalism not lead to a war between the races and the inevitable defeat of the weaker, less numerous, French-Canadian race? Far better for the two peoples to co-operate, to live together in peace and harmony, to share Canada between them on friendly and equitable terms.

French-Canadian calls for peace and harmony did not prevent Manitoba from scrapping the French language and Catholic separate schools in 1890. The resulting Manitoba schools question aroused a much stronger reaction in Quebec than the New Brunswick affair had done two decades before. In New Brunswick, the status of the French language had not been in question, nor had the French-origin population been well known to Quebeckers – at least until 1875. Consequently, while Quebeckers had protested on behalf of their new Brunswick co-religionists, they had accepted in the end Cartier's advice not to risk Quebec's autonomy by interference in New Brunswick.

The West was a different matter. For two decades Quebeckers had been finding their emotions increasingly involved in western affairs. They were very much aware now of the French-speaking community on the pariries. And they knew that prairie constitutions were defined not only by the BNA Act of 1867, but also by a series of special acts which spelled out French language and Catholic school rights. Moreover, they had been telling themselves for some time that Canada's stability and internal peace required French and English to live together with mutual tolerance and respect. When the Privy Council decided in 1895 that the federal government was constitutionally entitled to intervene in Manitoba to restore separate schools, French Canadians could have no doubt whatever that 'the constitution' guaranteed French-Catholic rights in the West.

From here it was a short step to the idea that minority rights were firmly guaranteed everywhere in Canada. To the continuing English-Canadian demand for a single, unhyphenated Canadianism, people like Bourassa responded with a dualist theory. Confederation, they said, was the result of an agreement between two races to live together on a basis of equality and co-operation. To ensure this equality they had established minority rights as the keystone of their system.

Not that French Quebeckers abandoned their old view of Quebec as the special French-Canadian country. It was still the only province which, as the majority, they could shape in their image, and its autonomy, therefore, must still be jealously guarded. But it was also in a partnership with other provinces. And a partnership can work only if each partner respects the integrity of the others. In the Confederation partnership that meant that each province must respect the nationality of the others, and that Quebec should be able to expect that its French-Canadian nationality would be respected in other parts of Canada. In this sense, bilingualism and special status for Quebec were not alternatives to each other; they went necessarily together.

A pivotal factor in the process described above was the readiness of French Quebeckers to accept that their province had a special responsibility for the French and Catholic minorities. It was the exercise of this responsibility that led to the emotional involvement and the identification with the French-Catholic element in the other provinces, and ultimately, therefore, to the bicultural view of Canada.

Why was such a responsibility accepted so readily? Why, when they considered *Quebec* to be the French-Canadian country, when they had been so concerned to secure its autonomy, to assure it the greatest possible degree of independence, did they feel so strongly about French-Catholic groups outside Quebec's borders? It may be suggested that the answer to this question is self-evident, that it was only natural for the province which defined itself as French and Catholic to identify itself with French Catholicism throughout Canada. But perhaps this naturalness is only apparent from a *Canadian* point of view – that is, only if we consider Canada a single nation, so that what affects French Canadians in one part necessarily affects them in general. However, French Quebeckers in 1870 did not have this *Canadian* point of view. It is precisely their autonomist attitude that creates the problem, for it is by no means inevitable that an active concern about Franco-Manitobans will go together with a storng adherence to the *Quebec* nation. Thus, the 1956 report of the Tremblay Commission, which argued for special autonomous status for Quebec as the country of a distinct French-Canadian nation, specifically renounced the right to interfere in other provinces on behalf of the minorities.[1] And Quebec separatists have argued increasingly since 1960 that the 'natural' thing would be for Quebec to be French and the other provinces to be English. In any case, the active interest of nineteenth-century Quebeckers in the status and rights of the Franco-Americans also indicates that support for the Canadian minorities was not just a result of their common Canadianism, their living in one country.

We live in an age of national self-determination and anti-colonialism. A Quebec separatist, appealing to these principles, would be inconsistent if he were to attempt to impose special rights for his compatriots on British Columbia or Nova Scotia. But the last third of the nineteenth century was a

---

1 Quebec, Royal Commission of Inquiry on Constitutional Problems, *Report* (Quebec 1956), II, 82.

different age; it was a time of imperialism, when countries normally interfered outside their own borders to defend their interests, their values, or their nationals.

French Quebeckers were neither ignorant of nor indifferent to the great events of their times. Their newspapers carried regular reports and comments on these imperialist interventions throughout the decades which concern us. What's more, they usually approved of them. The imperialist notion that a civilized – a Christian – power had both a right and a duty to protect those without power and enlighten those without civilization was a notion that Quebec's editors were quite ready to accept. Thus, the 1878 British takeover of Cyprus was praised in Quebec as 'an invaluable conquest for civilization'.[2] French forces were cheered on as they advanced in Indo-China and Madagascar;[3] 'Christian France' was urged to intervene in the Turkish empire to protect Armenian Christians;[4] and the Christian nations of Europe were asked to join in a crusade in Africa to put down slavery.[5] French-Canadian Catholics could rejoice at Brazza's peaceful conquests in the Congo, where the French flag sheltered Catholic missions just as it had done in the first days of Canada itself.[6] And in 1900, at the time of the Boxer Rebellion, *La Revue Canadienne* urged the western powers to do their duty in China 'with unbending energy. Those who have murdered Christians and perpetrated massacres must receive an exemplary chastisement.'[7]

Sometimes the imperial enterprises of great powers touched French Canadians particularly closely. In 1890 a number of them volunteered to join a proposed French military expedition to help put down slavery in Africa.[8] In the 1860s several had actually gone to Mexico to join French forces defending the Catholic empire of Maximilian.[9] This enterprise earned much praise in Quebec, where Maximilian was seen as saving Mexico from the 'anarchy and confusion' created by the previous, revolutionary régime,[10] and where the

---

2 *La Minerve*, 25 July 1878.
3 *Le Nouveau Monde*, 31 Mar. 1885; *L'Union des Cantons de l'Est*, 17 Oct.; *Le Pionnier de Sherbrooke*, 5 Nov. 1885; *Le Monde Illustré*, fall of 1884 through spring of 1885; *La Revue Canadienne*, XXIII (1887), pp. 214ff.; etc.
4 *La Revue Canadienne*, XXXII (1896), p. 188.
5 *Le Nouveau Monde*, 23 Oct. 1888.
6 *Le Courrier de St-Hyacinthe*, 3 Oct. 1889.
7 *La Revue Canadienne*, XXXVIII (1900), p. 227. Note also the sympathy for France in *L'Electeur*, 1 Sept. 1884.
8 *Le Nouveau Monde*, 24 Feb. 1890.
9 Among the Canadian volunteers were Honoré Beaugrand, the future mayor of Montreal, and N.H.E. Faucher de St-Maurice. See the latter's account, *De Québec à Mexico* (Montreal: Duvernay Frères et Dansereau 1874), dedicated to J.A. Chapleau.
10 *Le Journal des Trois-Rivières*, 31 Aug. 1866. Also, *La Minerve*, 7 Nov. 1866.

French army which fought for him was portrayed as the 'sublime personification of right supported by valour and courage.'[11]

In 1884 French Canadians were invited to participate in imperial adventure on a much grander scale, as nearly four hundred Canadians went off as boatmen to carry the British expedition up the Nile to the relief of Khartoum. This expedition was portrayed in the Quebec press as a righteous mission, and Gordon, the hero of the besieged town, as a saintly personification of persecuted and martyred Christianity.[12] The call for French-Canadian boatmen brought the appearance of this advice in *La Minerve*: 'Think about it, seek counsel, sign up, go, and as always, if necessary, let us die nobly. If we act in this way, God will assist us.'[13] The expedition was followed as closely as the communications of the time would allow, and special pride was taken in the role of the Canadian boatmen. 'Everyone is interested in this adventurous expedition of our French-Canadian boatmen on the Nile, and everything concerning it is read avidly.'[14]

The doctrines of nineteenth-century imperialism, then, made familiar the notion that it was proper to intervene outside one's own borders in the defence of right, and to those doctrines and their implications French Canadians responded positively. The idea of right, however, was a difficult one. The nineteenth century was a revolutionary period in which conflicting

---

11 Faucher de St-Maurice, *De Québec à Mexico*, p. 171. Also, *La Minerve*, 11 Sept. 1866, and 2 July 1867. Not *all* Quebec opinion favoured Napoleon III's Mexican enterprise (see *L'Union Nationale*, 31 July 1866, or *L'Ordre*, 16 July 1866), yet even among Liberals there was some support for it. Beaugrand was an example of this. So was the journalist Médéric Lanctôt, who only cooled to the enterprise after he became persuaded that American power would doom it to failure.

12 Eg., *L'Union des Cantons de l'Est*, 28 Mar. 1885; *Le Monde Illustré*, 7 Mar. 1885; *L'Etendard*, 21 Jan. 1889.

13 *La Minerve*, 6 Sept. 1884. Indeed, God did assist them, at least according to the *Union des Cantons de l'Est* (4 Apr. 1885), which reported that divine intervention had saved French Canadians from drowning in the Nile on two occasions.

14 *La Minerve*, 18 Oct. 1884. As a matter of fact, French Canadians were far from composing the entire contingent of boatmen, among whom were considerable numbers of Indians and English Candians. The Quebec press, however, presented the expedition as a *French-Canadian* enterprise. *L'Electeur*, for example, predicted the expedition would be a success because French Canadians had already proved, by their performance as Zouaves, that they were among the best soldiers in the world (30 Aug. 1884); and when it was reported that the Canadians had impressed the British troops by a particularly daring exploit, *La Patrie* commented by exclaiming, 'Bravo, Jean-Baptiste!' (20 Nov. 1884). See also, eg., *Le Courrier de St-Hyacinthe*, 21 Oct. 1884, 24 Jan. and 28 Feb. 1885; *L'Electeur*, 6, 9, 15 Sept., 3, 5 Nov., 5 Dec. 1884; *Le Journal des Trois-Rivières*, 15 Sept., 23 Oct., 10 Nov., 11 Dec. 1884; *Le Nouveau Monde*, 8 and 25 Sept., 22 Nov. 1884; *La Presse*, 6 Mar. 1885.

conceptions of political, social, and religious right vied for supremacy. In both Old World and New the battle raged between a conservative, religious ideology and a modern, liberal one. Republicanism challenged ancient monarchies; liberalism defied established prerogatives; Church and State fought fiercely for social and moral influence, and especially for control of education. In France, Belgium, Germany, Switzerland, and the United States the clergy was chased from its old place in the schoolroom by the forces of secularism and modernism.

It is interesting to note these battles over education, for some of the main conflicts discussed in the preceding chapters were about schools. In those conflicts it was not just a French-Canadian conception of education that was at stake but a clerical conception. The kind of schools wanted by the minority in New Brunswick or Manitoba was not French-Canadian *per se*. English-Canadian, American, French, German, and Swiss Catholics all wanted the same sort of schools.[15] Nevertheless, French Canadians saw these school questions from their own national perspective. They did not distinguish between 'the Catholic and [the] French cause in Manitoba'.[16] since it seemed to them that both 'the religion and *the nationality of the Catholics*' were in danger.[17]

Why this nationalization of a religious issue? Why this insistence that Catholic rights were automatically French-Canadian rights? After all, most Catholics outside Quebec were not French-Canadian. Nor did attacks on Catholic school systems necessarily involve any assault on the French language, as we saw in the case of New Brunswick.

The answer is probably to be found in the way in which French Canadians defined their own nationality, in the nature of the dominant ideology in French Canada during the second half of the nineteenth century. Much has been written on this subject in recent years, and the overwhelming tendency of this writing is to confirm that the ideology espoused by Quebec's élite in this period, and in terms of which it defined its society, was decidedly

---

15 It will be recalled that less than half of New Brunswick's Catholics were of French origin at the time when the controversial school law was passed. In Manitoba, the French-origin group became a minority among the Catholics during the decade of the school controversy. In any case, Gilbert-L. Comeault has shown in his paper on 'Les Franco-Manitobains face à la question des écoles' that it was the *English*-speaking Catholics of Manitoba who were hardest hit by the application of the 1890 school law and for whose sake the Archbishop of St Boniface kept up the pressure for remedial action.

16 *La Revue Canadienne*, XXXII (1896), p. 444.

17 *L'Union des Cantons de l'Est*, 28 Dec. 1889 (emphasis added). See also 19 Oct. 1889 and 16 Feb. 1893; *L'Electeur*, 16 Oct. and 13 Nov. 1889; *Le Nouveau Monde*, 8 Mar. 1895; *Le Courrier de St-Hyacinthe*, 24 Oct. 1889; *La Revue Canadienne*, LVII (1909), p. 133; Bernard, *Manifeste libéral*, p. 37.

conservative and clerical;[18] that this ideology was shared with conservative and religious elements in other countries;[19] and that its influence in Quebec was so pervasive as almost to exclude all others.[20]

Without re-analysing Quebec's clerical-professional élite, its 'dominant ideology', or the degree of that ideology's dominance, we can at least observe that when the French-Canadian journalists and other writers whom we have been reading looked at the world events of their time, they almost invariably sided with the conservative-religious elements in the ongoing conflicts. Thus, for example, the French intervention in Mexico was praiseworthy not just because it was French but because it represented Catholicism and order. Maximilian's régime pursued 'the struggle against the invasion of republican ideas', which, despite its eventual defeat in Mexico, 'will continue with no less ardour on this little territory which we occupy in America.'[21]

Republicanism, though, was on the attack in Europe as well as in America. In 1870-1 came the overthrow of Napoleon III and the establishment of the Third Republic. At Paris the revolution had for a time been pursued to outrageous lengths, with violence directed against the Catholic clergy. 'There,' commented a Quebec paper, 'we see a complete absence of any feeling of honour, patriotism, or humanity! There we see only rage, desperation, frenzy. ... '[22] The Third Republic was scarcely better. Within a few years it was expelling the Jesuits from France while getting ready to grant an amnesty to the 'communards'. Obviously 'the revolution intends to carry on energetically with its satanic work.'[23] Republicanism was pushing France 'into the abyss'.[24]

Perhaps the most dramatic challenge to the ideas prevailing in Quebec was

---

18 Eg., see the essays in Jean-Paul Bernard, ed., *Les Idéologies québécoises au 19ᵉ siècle* (Montreal: Editions du Boréal Express 1973); Fernand Dumont et al, *Idéologies au Canada français, 1850–1900* (Quebec: PUL 1971); Nadia Eid, *Le Clergé et le pouvoir politique au Québec* (Montreal: Hurtubise HMH 1978); Jacques Monet, 'French-Canadian Nationalism and the Challenge of Ultramontanism', in the *CHAR*, 1966.

19 Eg., Pierre Savard, *Jules-Paul Tardivel, la France et les Etats-Unis* (Quebec: PUL 1967); Philippe Sylvain, 'Quelques aspects de l'antagonisme libéral-ultramontain au Canada français', in *Recherches Sociographiques*, VIII, 3 (Sept.-Dec., 1967).

20 Jean de Bonville, 'La Liberté de presse à la fin du *XIXᵉ* siècle: le cas de Canada-Revue', in the *RHAF*, XXXI, 4 (Mar., 1978). Jean-Paul Bernard shows in *Les Rouges* how liberalism was forced into an increasingly marginal position in nineteenth-century Quebec. For a nineteenth-century complaint about this, see Arthur Buies, *Lettres sur le Canada* (1864), reprinted at Montreal by Réédition-Québec, 1968.

21 *La Minerve*, 11 Sept. 1866.

22 *La Gazette des Familles*, II (1870-1), pp. 349, 351 (15 May 1871).

23 *Le Journal des Trois-Rivières*, 5 July 1880.

24 *La Minerve*, 1 Sept. 1880.

the attack by Italian nationalism upon the temporal power of the papacy. Papal government over Rome and surrounding territories was an obstacle to the desire for a unified Italy under a modern, liberal régime. Already in 1848 the revolution had expelled the Pope from Rome, only to see him returned by aid of French arms. When the republican Garibaldi marched against Rome in 1867, French troops once more supported the papacy, and this time Catholics came from around the world to help the French Zouaves in the task. Quebeckers were not the least numerous among them. Over the next few years almost six hundred men, trained and equipped by public subscription and clerical leadership, participated in the great crusade. These 'champions of the rights of God'[25] were sent off by huge, cheering crowds, after special masses and special sermons in their honour. To Catholic editors they seemed to be 'soldiers of truth and justice',[26] inspired by Providence itself[27] to perform 'acts of sublime devotion'.[28] Even the withdrawal of the French troops in 1870 did not stop more French Canadians from leaving 'to die for their religion under the walls of Rome.'[29]

The Zouave affair is interesting not only because it shows French Quebeckers siding with clerical and conservative forces against tendencies considered progressive in the nineteenth century, but also because it shows them fighting outside their country for the cause they considered right. In doing so, they represented 'the devotion shown by [French] Canada to the cause of the Holy See'.[30] They had thus won glory for Quebec, enhanced its prestige in the world, and merited much both 'from Religion and from the Homeland'.[31] They had shown that the papacy was a French-Canadian national concern – something Quebeckers confirmed in the winter of 1870–1, when thousands signed petitions asking for a British intervention on behalf of the Pope,[32] and when, as a sign of national mourning, they suppressed St-Jean-Baptiste celebrations. 'Thus, patriotism and religion, which have made an eternal alliance with our people, continue to flourish among us as closely united as in the first days of our history.'[33]

This marriage of religion and patriotism led Quebeckers to follow with concern the victories and defeats of Catholicism throughout the world. A

---

25 Ibid., 23 Apr. 1870. From a cantata written to honour the Zouaves by A. Bellemare.
26 L'Union des Cantons de l'Est, 14 Apr. 1870.
27 La Revue Canadienne, VII (1870), pp. 559–60.
28 Ibid., p. 617.
29 Le Franc-Parleur, 8 Sept. 1870.
30 Le Journal des Trois-Rivières, 7 Apr. 1870.
31 Le Franc-Parleur, 8 Sept. 1870. Also, Bellemare's cantata in La Minerve, 23 Apr. 1870.
32 La Revue Canadienne, VIII (1871), p. 237. Also, Le Journal de Québec, 12 Apr. 1871.
33 La Revue Canadienne, VIII (1871), p. 480.

relaxation of anti-Catholic regulations in Prussia, or a census increase for Catholicism in Britain, might be greeted with joy.[34] The Zouave veterans' journal carried a regular column of 'Echoes from Rome', and announced in its second issue that it would also publish regular accounts of the 'Catholic Movement in America':

> The great struggle so courageously undertaken by the present Pope against the dangerous tendencies and doctrines of this century has its repercussions on our continent; therefore, we shall closely follow our compatriots and our neighbours in the vicissitudes of each day; we shall record the struggles of the worthy and venerable episcopacy of the United States. ... [35]

Such reporting was apt to be an unhappy affair, for since the Pope's struggle was against the tendency of the century, it more often involved sorrows and defeats than joyous victories. The summer of Canada's Great Coalition witnessed Russia's suppression of a Polish uprising ; a small Catholic nation was crushed by heretical oppressors. 'Poland,' lamented a Quebec newspaper, 'heroic Poland lies mutilated and bloody at the feet of her powerful tormentor. ...'[36] The triumph of Italian nationalism over the papacy was another torment. 'Who would not groan, who would not weep, at the thought that the best, the tenderest of fathers is a prisoner, exposed to the outrages of a godless and sacrilegious rabble?'[37] In 1884 the Poles were back in the news, as a delegation of Polish and Russian Catholics appeared at the Vatican to ask for papal intercession with the Czar on their behalf.[38] In 1886 it was Chinese Christians who were oppressed;[39] in 1896 the Armenians.[40]

Of all the oppressions of Catholicism, the worst was not by uncivilized pagans but by the triumphant new ideology in the West. Having destroyed most Catholic states by 1870, modernism turned its attention to replacing the Church in its traditional role as educator. Quebec newspapers followed the struggles in Europe and America.[41] In Germany and Switzerland, just as in New Brunswick, priests who opposed the new school laws were arrested or

---

34 *La Minerve*, 10 Oct. 1886; *Le Courrier du Canada*, 29 Jan. 1872; *L'Union des Cantons de l'Est*, 13 Dec. 1894.
35 *Bulletin de l'Union-Allet* (Montreal), I, 2 (Nov., 1873), p. 36.
36 *Le Courrier du Canada*, 15 Aug. 1864.
37 *La Gazette des Familles*, II (1870–1), p. 108 (15 Dec. 1870). Also, p. 158 (15 Jan. 1871).
38 *La Revue Canadienne*, XX (1884), p. 631.
39 *Le Monde Illustré*, issues of autumn, 1886.
40 *La Revue Canadienne*, XXXII (1896), pp. 186–8.
41 Eg., *Le Journal des Trois-Rivières*, 2 and 9 Oct. 1884; *Le Courrier de St-Hyacinthe*, 7 Apr. 1870; *Le Nouveau Monde*, issues of July, 1874, especially the series on 'Le Monde catholique'.

had their property confiscated to pay the public school tax. Quebec's bishops expressed their solidarity in a public letter to their brother prelates of Germany and Switzerland, assuring them of the support of their French-Canadian co-religionists.[42] As the 1870s advanced, the situation failed to improve. 'In Germany the religious persecution grows ever worse.'[43] Soon France began to imitate it, with the anti-Catholic school reforms of Jules Ferry. In 1880 public demonstrations were organized in Quebec to protest against France's expulsion of the Jesuits, and at Trois-Rivières 'the whole population of the town' – Liberals included – were reported to have assembled in front of the town hall to join their mayor in expressing support for the French Jesuits. They decided to send a cable 'signed by all the citizens of this town' to the Jesuit Superior in France.[44] By 1883 the situation seemed universally bleak. 'The Christian education of children, particularly in France, Italy, Germany, and Belgium, has become more difficult under the Masonic governments of those countries than it was even under the empire of Nero.'[45]

The defeats suffered by Catholicism in France were the most depressing of all, for had France not been 'the eldest daughter of the Church', who, only a few years ago, had sent troops to Rome to defend the Holy See? Of all the World's nations, surely France had always had a special mission to fight for Catholicism. Both Joseph de Maistre, the father of nineteenth-century ultramontanism, and Louis Veuillot, its best-known publicist, had said so.[46]

The vision of France as champion of Catholicism was an important reason for the excitement that gripped Quebec during the Franco-Prussian war. Several young men went overseas to fight for France, and those who remained

---

42 La Gazette des Familles, IV (1872–3), pp. 524, 548–50.
43 L'Opinion Publique, 28 Jan. 1875.
44 Le Journal des Trois-Rivières, 5 July 1880. See also Le Nouveau Monde, 9 June 1879; La Minerve, 1 Sept. 1880; La Revue Canadienne, XXVI (1890), pp. 281–7.
45 Le Journal des Trois-Rivières, 10 May 1883. Also 4 Feb. 1886, 25 Jan. and 27 May 1872.
46 Joseph de Maistre, Considérations sur la France, ch. 2; Louis Veuillot, 'Le Pouvoir temporel des Papes', in Œuvres complètes (40 vols.; Paris: Lethielleux 1924–40), vol. VII. Letters from Veuillot and extracts from his newspaper, L'Univers, appeared regularly in the Quebec press. Christine Piette-Samson, in her essay in Idéologies au Canada français, 1850–1900, p. 237, notes that at the time of Confederation all French-Quebec newspapers except Le Pays depended on L'Univers for European news and information. Bishop Laflèche considered Veuillot 'the foremost publicist of Europe' (in Quelques considérations, p. 139). De Maistre, more distant and difficult than Veuillot, nevertheless exercised a great influence on French-Canadian ultramontanes. In Idéologies, 1850–1900, p. 59, René Hardy points out his influence on Laflèche. A.-B. Routhier, the author of O Canada, once wrote to Le Nouveau Monde that he never went on a trip without a copy of de Maistre.

contributed to a 'national subscription' to send food and medical supplies. Crowds of people spent whole nights in front of newspapers offices, where the latest bulletins from the battlefield were posted as they arrived.[47] In the papers themselves, the war received far more attention than Manitoba, where Ontario militiamen were spreading violence and terror among the French Métis.[48]

Of course, this excitement must be largely attributed to a feeling of Frenchness. In contributing to the public subscription, Quebeckers were able 'to show ourselves French.'[49] The wounded French soldiers were 'our brothers',[50] and the defeat of France would be taken personally by Quebeckers because 'we are French!'[51] But the identification was not just racial. For France was defending the cause 'of right and of justice' in this war.[52] She was fighting as the embodiment of a principle:

God has made of this people (still the most Catholic in Europe despite all its faults) His instrument in the past; and it is reasonable to see in this war a struggle on which will depend the future of Europe – whether or not predominance will go to the Prussian principle: tyrannic, Protestant, rationalist, Hegelian.

As for us ... our sympathies are with France ... whose flag has always protected, all over the world, the cause of the weak, of justice, and of Truth.[53]

And yet, even as she went into this war, France abandoned the very principles whose defence was her sternest duty, by withdrawing her troops from Rome. This was the beginning of her destruction.[54] Was it any wonder, in view of this failure toward the Pope, that she lost her war with Prussia? Not to Catholic editors:

Rome abandoned, Napoleon a prisoner, Paris under siege: these are facts in which we can all read a salutary lesson. ...

However it may be, Napoleon III ought to have preserved Rome. As sovereign of

---

47 N.H.E. Faucher de St-Maurice, 'Le Canada et les Canadiens-Français pendant la guerre franco-prussienne', in *La Question du jour*; *Le Pays*, 13 Sept. 1870; *Le Pionnier de Sherbrooke*, 24 Feb. 1871.

48 During the Franco-Prussian war, the headline 'La Situation' in a French-Canadian newspaper referred to France, not the Canadian North-West.

49 *Le Franc-Parleur*, 25 Aug. 1870.

50 Ibid., 8 Sept. 1870.

51 *Le Courrier de St-Hyacinthe*, 27 Aug. 1870. Also, *Le Pionnier de Sherbrooke*, 22 July 1870; *L'Opinion Publique*, 11 Aug. 1870; Oscar Dunn, *Pourquoi nous sommes Français* (Montreal: La Minerve 1870), p. 6.

52 *Le Pays*, 21 July 1870.

53 *Le Nouveau Monde*, 18 July 1870. Also, *L'Union des Cantons de l'Est*, 21 July 1870.

54 *Le Franc-Parleur*, 25 Aug. 1870.

France, he could not, considering his honour and his interest, abandon the traditional policy of the French people.[55]

But this was only the beginning of France's troubles. Out of defeat came the republic, and out of the republic came persecution of the Church. Some might call it progress, but French Canadians could only lament at the 'mob of atheists, freethinkers, Jews, and other foreigners, who are now dancing upon the disfigured body of our unfortunate mother-country, insulting everything which is most dear to us.'[56] These were the elements which supported Ferry's school laws in the name of liberalism, secularism, and individualism:

Freemasonry has undertaken to dechristianize France by means of a godless education. With that devilish cleverness that makes it so dangerous, it has proceeded by degrees ... to the ruinous law it got passed under pretence of neutrality, expelling God from the schools, and thus from the hearts and minds of children – a law which Leo xiii has called a criminal enterprise.[57]

Nor was this the only triumph of the anti-Christian forces in France. The anti-Masonic 'revelations' of Léo Taxil[58] and the anti-Semitic 'exposés' of Edouard Drumont[59] seemed to reveal others. Were not the latter confirmed by the Dreyfus case, which clearly showed to France 'Jewry's subterranean efforts to stifle her'?[60]

But if Christian France was being undermined, there was, fortunately, a Quebec to keep her spirit alive. French Canada, under the leadership of its conservative and clerical élite, was (in the words of Louis Veuillot) 'that other

---

55 *Le Courrier de St-Hyacinthe*, 29 Sept. 1870.
56 *L'Etendard*, 3 Feb. 1883.
57 Jules-Paul Tardivel, quoted in Justin Fèvre, *Vie et travaux de J.-P. Tardivel, fondateur du journal 'La Vérité' à Québec* (Paris: Arthur Savaète 1906), p. 80.
58 On Taxil and his accounts of Masonic satanism, see Eugen Weber, *Satan Franc-Maçon* (René Julliard 1964). Taxil, who made a noisy conversion to Catholicism in 1885, began painting a horrifying picture of the forces at work against the Church in his 1887 *Confessions d'un ex-libre penseur*. This and other exposés by Taxil were published in serial form in Tardivel's *La Vérité*. Aspects of Tardivel's 1895 novel, *Pour la patrie*, were based on Taxil. For the Tardivel-Taxil connexion, see Pierre Savard, *Jules-Paul Tardivel, la France et les Etats-Unis*, pp. 275–302, in which the affair is followed to Taxil's final revelation in 1897 that everything since and including his conversion twelve years before had been one gigantic hoax.
59 For examples of the positive reception given Drumont's charges of a Jewish takeover of France, see *Le Courrier de St-Hyacinthe*, 27 Mar. 1890, and 2 Mar. 1895; *L'Etendard*, 11 Jan. 1890; *La Revue Canadienne*, xxiv (1888), p. 472.
60 *La Revue Canadienne*, xxx (1894), pp. 778–9. Also xxxiv (1898), p. 220, and xxxvi (1899), pp. 66, 154, 313–15; *Le Courrier de St-Hyacinthe*, 17 Jan. 1895.

France, young, sincere, believing, ardent in the cause of good'. Bidding farewell to the Zouaves on their return to Canada, Veuillot was lyrical:

Bon voyage, sons of France, who have renounced nothing and lost nothing of wisdom, spirit, or heart; return safely to your homes, where the old honour is still alive. ... Keep the flame of France, keep the flame of Rome and of Christ.[61]

Veuillot told the French Canadians what they wanted to hear. L.-F. Laflèche had already written that their national mission was to be learned 'from the mouths of the Most Christian Kings and the zeal of the élite souls of France, eldest daughter of the Catholic Church.' And that mission was to work for '*the extension of the kingdom of Jesus Christ*'.[62] Providence had made Quebec 'a new France ... grand-daughter of the Church, governed by the laws of her mother'.[63] The Zouave experience, by bringing Canadians together with Frenchmen in the fight for the Catholic cause, encouraged the tendency to associate the national missions of the two peoples:

If France has been great, it is because she has protected the papacy. ... Why may we not believe that [French] Canada will play the same role in America that France has played in Europe? What may we not expect from a country which, so young, has already produced so many missionaries, and which, like her mother-country, has sent soldiers to defend the successor of St Peter?[64]

That French Canadians identified their national mission with the extension of Catholicism was not surprising. Their own Church had begun as a mission, and the ultramontane revival of the nineteenth century had owed much to the work of French religious orders like the Oblates and the Jesuits.[65] The Church's missionary orientation certainly struck people at the time. It seemed an essential characteristic of their society 'to produce priests by the hundred and send them to carry the Good News to the rich cities of the United States as

---

61 In *Le Journal des Trois-Rivières*, 7 Apr. 1870. See also a pamphlet by the French consul at Quebec, Albert Lefaivre, published under the pseudonym J. Guérard, *La France canadienne* (Paris: Douniol 1887), especially pp. 5–7 .

62 Laflèche, *Quelques considérations*, p. 71.

63 Philippe Masson, *Le Canada-Français et la Providence* (Quebec: Brousseau 1875), pp. 52–3.

64 *La Revue Canadienne*, VII (1870), p. 860. See also XIII (1876), p. 477; Faucher de St-Maurice, *La Question du jour*, p. 110; Lanctot, *Avenir des Canadiens-Français*, p. 9.

65 Léon Pouliot, 'Un Siècle d'expansion religieuse', in the *RHAF*, XXI, 3a (1967), pp. 660–1. On the nineteenth-century perception of Quebec's missionary origins as model and inspiration, see Serge Gagnon, *Le Québec et ses historiens de 1840 à 1920* (Quebec: PUL 1978). Note, eg., pp. 20–1, 74–5.

to the frozen plains of Red River. ... '[66] In this work there were no boundaries to French Canada's activity:

Lower Canada is the instrument chosen by Providence to evangelize the American continent, to instruct the ignorant, help the poor, care for the sick, guide children on the right path of life, over the whole face of this immense continent. To Chile, Brazil, Peru, Oregon, Red River, Newfoundland, and even to the immense, frozen steppes of Russian America and Hudson Bay, [French] Canada sends bishops, priests, missionaries, and nuns. ... [67]

Embodying Catholic principles in its own society while carrying on this vast missionary work, Quebec had become 'the bulwark of Catholic principles, the beacon light of the new world.'[68]

Aware, then, of ideological conflicts raging in other countries, conscious that their own Church and ideology were vitally engaged in those conflicts, French Quebeckers felt that they too must 'gather their strength for the combats of the future'.[69] Quebec must be 'a dam against the flood of modern errors.'[70] It must act, moreover, outside as well as within its own borders, wherever it could, wherever it was needed by the cause it held dear.

If Quebec had a mission in the world at large, how much more particularly must it uphold the Catholic cause in other parts of Canada. 'As you were at Rome,' Bishop Laflèche told the returning Zouaves, 'so you will be in Canada ... the soldiers of truth and of justice.'[71] As France had defended Catholicism in Europe, 'we Lower Canadian Catholics are the defenders of our faith in the confederation.'[72]

And the enemies of the faith were the same. Was not the source of the New Brunswick school law to be found in the 'laws of the Paris Commune, from which it has been borrowed'?[73] Everywhere it was the same 'war against the

---

66 Oscar Dunn, *Pourquoi nous sommes français*, pp. 33–4.
67 *La Revue Canadienne*, VII (1870), p. 545. But French-Canadian missionary work was not confined to the Americas. The British and French colonial empires offered significant fields as well, and before the end of the nineteenth century French-Canadian missionaries were labouring in India, North Africa, the Sudan, and British East Africa. See, eg., Lionel Groulx, *Le Canada français missionnaire* (Montreal: Fides 1962), pp. 81–2. At the same time, it will be noted that missions in other parts of Canada could also be looked on as foreign missions. This was natural in so far as Quebec was considered the homeland. On missions in British Columbia and the North, see *La Revue Canadienne*, XIV (1877), p. 906, or *Le Courrier du Canada*, 2 Feb. 1872.
68 *La Minerve*, 28 June 1880. Also, *Le Courrier du Canada*, 9 Aug. 1871.
69 *Le Franc-Parleur*, 15 Sept. 1870.
70 Tardivel, quoted in Fèvre, p. 86.
71 In *L'Union des Cantons de l'Est*, 14 Apr. 1870.
72 Ibid., 6 June 1872.
73 *Le Journal des Trois-Rivières*, 13 June 1872.

Church'. Opposed by the same forces as in Europe, and 'like the Catholics of the United States, the Catholics of New Brunswick are reduced to defending themselves against the godless system of public schools. ... '[74] Yes, in New Brunswick one saw the triumph of 'the revolution ... the socialists, the instruments of the secret societies' who were also present in the Paris Commune and among the Red-Shirts of Italy.[75] Manitoba too, in passing the 1890 school law, was applying the principles of Jules Ferry,[76] and it was the international Freemasons and Jews whose occult influence would keep Ottawa from remedial action.[77] As a result, Manitoba Catholics were suffering from a persecution comparable to what Poland had been suffering at the hand of Russia.[78] Two decades before, Mackenzie, in his refusal to grant an amnesty to Riel and Lépine, had been compared to Bismarck, waging an insidious war against the Church of Christ.[79]

It was against these forces that Quebec had to fight:

There has been reserved for her a nobler and loftier mission than to compete for a share in the patronage distributed by the central government. ...

Our adversaries would perhaps not have dared to turn their dominating and discriminatory attacks against us directly, but they have directed them against our co-religionists and co-nationals of the other provinces who are weaker than we.[80]

These co-religionists and co-nationals Quebec would defend, just as France had defended the Catholic and French cause in distant parts of the world. France had fought for 'justice, equity, and principles ... [and] the future peace of Europe.'[81] In the same way, Quebec, when she went to the aid of the minorities, fought for 'the rights of religion',[82] 'justice',[83] 'right',[84] 'honour',[85]

---

74 Ibid., 25 Jan. 1872. Also, *Le Courrier de St-Hyacinthe*, 7 Apr. 1870.

75 *Le Journal des Trois-Rivières*, 23 July 1874. Also, *Le Courrier de St-Hyacinthe*, 15 June 1869.

76 *Le Journal des Trois-Rivières*, 13 Dec. 1892.

77 *L'Electeur*, 10 Apr. 1895 and 17 Feb. 1896. For more on the efforts of international Free-masonry to wreck Catholic school systems, even in Quebec, see *Le Journal des Trois-Rivières*, 10 May 1883, and *Le Courrier de St-Hyacinthe*, 20 Jan. 1891.

78 *La Presse*, 6 Mar. 1895.

79 *Le Courrier du Canada*, 26 Feb. 1875. See also *Le Journal de Québec*, 10 July 1871, accusing Canadian Protestants of Bismarckian tyranny.

80 *Le Nouveau Monde*, 1 June 1874.

81 *L'Union des Cantons de l'Est*, 21 July 1870.

82 *Le Courrier du Canada*, 16 July 1873, on New Brunswick schools.

83 *Le Pionnier de Sherbrooke*, 21 Apr. 1871, or *Le Journal de Québec*, 16 May 1873, on New Brunswick schools; *L'Opinion Publique*, 9 Oct. 1873, on the arrest of Lépine.

84 *Le Nouveau Monde*, 15 Apr. 1874, on the amnesty question.

85 *La Presse*, 17 Nov. 1885, on the hanging of Riel.

'humanity',[86] 'Truth',[87] and the 'union, concord, and peace' of Canada.[88] These were principles French Canadians had defended in Mexico and at Rome.

Helping the minorities was not only a matter of fighting. It was an exercise of Christian charity, like helping the religious missions. In 1868, when Red River was suffering from flood, fire, and grasshoppers, *L'Ordre* used almost the same language to encourage Montrealers to help as it had used to ask for contributions to a Mesopotamian mission.[89] *L'Union des Cantons de l'Est* asked its readers to help Bishop Taché as they had recently helped two visiting priests from Algeria.[90] This habit of contributing to the missionary effort would carry over into the pursuit of a wider mission. We have seen Bishop Taché appealing to the tradition of support for western missions to persuade Quebeckers to send him settlers.[91] In 1890, when the French language was under attack in the West, *La Minerve* proposed an apostolic model for an organization to defend it: 'We already have the Propagation of the Faith. Its results are marvellous. Let us apply it also to the national cause.'[92]

But to carry out her mission Quebec had to act as an imperial country. P.J.O. Chauveau, the first prime minister of this Catholic metropolis, told representatives of the Canadian and u.s. minorities in 1874 that 'our role toward you is the same that France, our old mother-country, played toward us.'[93] Albert Lacombe agreed: 'French Canadians in the United States and Manitoba must regard the province of Quebec in the same way as she once regarded France, and we must expect the same support from her that she expected from Europe.'[94] Honoré Mercier took up the same theme when he told the Quebec legislature that this province was 'the mother-country' of the Franco-Americans. *La Presse* used another imperial analogy when it compared Quebec's concern for the Métis to the 'interest which the English and Scotch show for their compatriots and co-religionists in the Irish province of Ulster.'

Also reminiscent of nineteenth-century imperialism was a certain military language people sometimes used. The penetration of French-Canadian

---

86 *La Patrie*, 18 May 1885, on Riel.
87 *Le Journal des Trois-Rivières*, 25 Jan. 1872, on New Brunswick schools.
88 *La Presse*, 11 Nov. 1885, on Riel.
89 *L'Ordre*, 16 July 1866, and 9 Sept. 1868.
90 *L'Union des Cantons de l'Est*, 9 Sept. 1868.
91 Above, p. 135. This sort of appeal became the subject of a notable dispute between Albert Lacombe and Jules-Paul Tardivel. Tardivel objected to the mixing up of missionary work with land settlement. The former deserved the fullest support from Quebec; the latter was a completely separate matter. See *La Vérité*, 3 July 1886.
92 *La Minerve*, 19 Feb. 1890.
93 Reported in *L'Opinion Publique*, 2 July 1874.
94 Ibid.

population into eastern Ontario, for example, was described by the expression 'spreading like an oil stain', made famous by the French general Gallieni in Indo-China and Madagascar.[95] Colonizers spoke of sending out detachments of settlers as if they were units of soldiers on military campaigns.[96] Parliamentarians fighting for New Brunswick's Catholic schools were 'valiant soldiers fighting in a sacred cause.'[97] And some people seemed to take literally Bishop Laflèche's advice to the Zouaves that *they* should be soldiers of truth in Canada as in Rome. Thus, the North-West Mounted Police was hailed on its creation as a force for order, justice, and the protection of the weak.[98] Several former Zouaves joined the force, and the Zouave bulletin expected their experience at Rome would inspire them to be 'the faithful and loyal supporters of authority.'[99] Such a role seemed to attract young French Canadians more than that of settlers, for the response to the recruiting campaign of the ex-Zouave E.A. Brisebois was greater than that attained by the St Boniface colonizers.[100] Nor was this the only manifestation of the desire to keep alive the Zouave tradition. In 1874 the Union-Allet attempted to obtain the creation of a special Zouave militia regiment, complete with Zouave uniforms and banners.[101]

It may, perhaps, seem odd that although French Quebeckers responded to the sense of mission that ran through their religion and through the imperialism of the nineteenth century – although their missionaries went to the far corners of the world and their adventurous young men travelled to Mexico, Rome, and the Sudan – they did not seem to respond to the call for prairie settlement.

One simple answer to this is that we are dealing with very different kinds of movement. Settlement offered neither the glamour of military adventure nor the spiritual exaltation of a religious vocation. What's more, while the Zouave came home to Quebec when the wars were over, and while the politician and the journalist could fight for the minorities without going farther away than

95 *La Revue Canadienne*, xxx (1894), p. 337.
96 *L'Opinion Publique*, 9 July 1874.
97 *La Gazette des Familles*, iii (1871–2), p. 400.
98 *Le Franc-Parleur*, 7 Oct. 1873.
99 *Bulletin de l'Union-Allet*, i, 2 (Nov., 1873), p. 31.
100 Men of French origin constituted 15 per cent of the 'orginals' in the NWMP (list made available by RCMP Historian S.W. Horrall), while according to the censuses of 1871 and 1881, people of French origin accounted for only six per cent of Manitoba's population increase in that decade.
101 *Bulletin de l'Union-Allet*, Dec., 1874, Apr. and May, 1875. See Desmond Morton, *Ministers and Generals* (Toronto: University of Toronto Press 1970), pp. 49–50. Even without special uniforms, the Quebec militia units attracted former Zouaves. Several participated in the Manitoba expedition of 1870 and in the North-West campaign of 1885.

the parliament buildings at Ottawa, the Manitoba settler had to leave the homeland forever.

Beyond this, we have seen that the dominant ideology in French Quebec was conservative and religious. The principles which Quebeckers defended in other provinces or other countries were conservative principles: order, stability, religion. These, however, were not the most prevalent values in the settlement of Manitoba. English-Canadian expansionists believed that settlers would be attracted by 'rich inducements to go in and possess the land'.[102] They promised 'any man whose capital consists on his arrival of little but brawny arms and a brave heart' the chance to become 'the proud possessor of a valuable farm, which has cost him little but the sweat of his brow.'[103] Not only could 'an energetic man' participate in and benefit from the 'rapid development of the country',[104] become an 'independent' farmer,[105] and even 'MAKE A FORTUNE in two or three years',[106] but what was more, this participation by individual men seeking to better their own condition in 'the race of progress' was 'enlightened and noble'[107] and would contribute to 'human progress, freedom and civilization in every province of the Dominion.'[108]

This sort of race for 'a fortune in two or three years' seemed rather less noble to the editors and writers whose views we have been consulting than it did to William McDougall. There was more to life than this seeming obsession with material goods:

The French Canadian ... knows that man does not live by bread alone, that if he is poor on earth, he is rich in heaven, and if death comes to him, his wife, or his children, with all its sadness, the doctor of souls is there to open wide the gates of the heavenly Jerusalem.[109]

Not that French Canadians needed to be deprived of material well-being. But it must be sought in a reasonable, a moderate way. There was no need to 'race' to economic development:

---

102 Alexander Morris, *Nova Britannia* (Toronto: Hunter, Rose 1884), p. 29.
103 Thomas Spence, *The Prairie Lands of Canada* (Montreal: The Gazette 1880), p. 10.
104 *Manitoba, the Canadian North-West* (n.p., c. 1883), pp. 12, 20.
105 *Province of Manitoba: Information for Intending Emigrants* (Ottawa: Grison, Frechette 1874), p. 48.
106 *The Letters of Rusticus: Investigations in Manitoba and the North-West* (Montreal: Dougall and Sons 1880), p. 13.
107 *The Globe* (Toronto), 3 Feb. 1863.
108 William McDougall, *The Red River Rebellion*, p. 7.
109 Antoine Labelle, *Projet de la société de colonisation du diocèse de Montréal pour coloniser la vallée de l'Ottawa et le nord de ce diocèse* (Montreal: Imprimerie Canadienne 1879), p. 7.

What would be wrong with Canada taking its time to develop at its own natural rate, as long as it is governed well enough that the people who inhabit it, be they few or many, enjoy the material, moral, and religious well-being which are appropriate to them.[110]

The idea of a degree of well-being which is appropriate or fitting to a people ('qui lui convient') is a curious one. It reflects the conservative and religious outlook of its author. Had not Bishop Laflèche written that every person, every family, every society had a place and a purpose in the divine scheme of the universe, and that each had received from Providence the character and the facilities necessary to fulfil the purpose? Was it not precisely to teach children how to occupy their place in this scheme that Catholic schools were necessary?[111] Thus, 'French Canadians – it cannot be too often repeated – only need, in general, that moderation of wealth and possessions which befits their peaceful, honest, and virtuous character.'[112]

The idea of a divine scheme discouraged both the pursuit of wealth for its own sake and also the pursuit of social change. The English settler without capital who became an independent farm-owner was changing his social position. But the Laflèche system – the ultramontane ideology – did not encourage such a thing. It was a hierarchical system, according to which persistence and fidelity in labour were to be counted among the chief virtues of the ordinary farmer. Thus, one writer saw a moral lesson in the docility of the farmer's ox:

Poor old animal! how much cause for reflection there is in your patience and your constancy in work. What a lesson you teach us in showing how to quietly plough the furrow from which will grow our well-being. ... [113]

Given this social attitude, it is not surprising that our French-Canadian writers did not expect their compatriots to participate in the kind of spontaneous individual movement to the prairies that English writers seemed to expect and encourage.

The French, an essentially hierarchical and Catholic people, do not possess that individual initiative which is the characteristic of Protestant nations. ... They expect action to come from above, being accustomed to find in their leaders more knowledge, wisdom, and enlightenment than elsewhere.[114]

---

110 [T.-B. Pelletier], *Considérations sur l'agriculture canadienne, au point de vue religieux, national et du bien-être matériel* (Quebec: Côté 1860), p. 145.

111 Eg., A.-A. Taché, *Pastoral Letter of His Grace the Archbishop of St Boniface, on the New School Laws of Manitoba* (St Boniface 1890), p. 4; *Idéologies au Canada français, 1850–1900*, pp. 35–6 and 39 (quoting from Catholic teachers' manuals); B.A.T. de Montigny, 'De l'éducation', in *La Revue Canadienne*, XXVI (1890), p. 386.

112 *Considérations sur l'agriculture*, p. 21.

113 *La Revue Canadienne*, XXIII (1887), p. 231.

114 Ibid., III (1866), p. 622.

Joseph Royal, one of the leaders of the St Boniface community, noted the difference between the French-Canadian approach and that used by Ontario in settling the prairies:

For us the priest, the cross, the church, the assurance of aid for the life to come, and a colonization movement produced at great cost in heroic examples, sacrifice, and pleading. For them, it's enough just to see the chance of making money. A company is set up, a few payments are put down, a risky prospect for their settlers to survive, and there you are – a settlement is established.[115]

Royal's mention of the cross, the priest, and the church referred to some of the protective measures French-Canadian colonizers thought it necessary to take for their settlers. You needed to settle a priest and build a chapel in a new area before you could expect settlers, according to one colonizer.[116] Another called for roads and railroads, schools and model farms, laws controlling interest rates, 'powerful aid from government and the clergy ... and every kind of help for the first settlers.'[117] The organizers of the movement aimed both to aid and to protect the settlers, and to ensure that the form of settlement would be consistent with their own values. Would-be settlers seeking a fast fortune were discouraged.[118] Ideal settlers were sober, without debts, and having certificates of honesty and good conduct.[119] Families were wanted, not single men.[120] And capital was needed to begin with.[121]

The effort to select only those who, in the view of the organizers, would make proper settlers, appears in marked contrast to the English-Canadian invitation to 'any man whose capital consists on his arrival of little but brawny

---

115 Ibid., XVII (1881), p. 46.
116 Projet de la société de colonisation, p. 6.
117 Considérations sur l'agriculture, p. 49. A recent comparison of settlement strategies in the Ontario and Quebec sectors of the Abitibi region shows that Ontario tended to build access roads and utilities, leaving settlers and private companies to do the rest, while Quebec tended more to provide direct aid to the settlers and to the Church for support of settlers. See Benoît-Beaudry Gourd, 'La Colonisation des Clay Belts du Nord-Ouest québécois et du Nord-Est ontarien', in the RHAF, XXVII, 2 (Sept., 1973).
118 Le Nord-Ouest canadien: brochure compilée par un colonisatuer de neuf ans d'expérience (n.p., n.d.), p. 1; Le Canada agricole: l'immigration française (Edmonton: Le Courrier de l'Ouest 1910), pp. 3, 26. Written during the most spectacularly successful decade of prairie settlement, this pamphlet aimed specifically to discourage those not likely to be desirable settlers.
119 Albert Lacombe, circular letter to the clergy of the diocese of Montreal (Montreal, 5 Apr. 1884), in Archives Deschâtelets, St Boniface papers, mfm no. 750.
120 See, eg., Joseph Royal to G.-E. Cartier (St Boniface, 1 June 1872), in PAC, Cartier papers, correspondence (MG27, I, D4, vol. 5).
121 Lacombe, circular letter; Le Grand occident canadien (Ottawa 1881), p. 15.

arms and a brave heart'. Lacombe reported to Taché that he had turned away
many would-be settlers precisely because their capital did consist of little but
brawny arms and brave hearts. 'I'm overwhelmed with people who want to go
to Manitoba,' he wrote in 1876. 'Poor people, I tell them, what do you expect
to do among us, you have hardly enough money to pay for your
transportation.'[122] Claiming that 'if I wanted, I could get a large movement of
emigrants to Manitoba,' Lacombe admitted that 'I stop a number of families
who are ready to leave but whom I don't consider likely to succeed. ... '[123]

This paternalistic attitude undoubtedly helps to explain something we
noticed earlier – that colonizers were spoken of as a sort of officers leading out
directed and controlled detachments of settlers. Ontario was said to be
'fortifying her colony in Manitoba' in the pursuit of her 'particular
interests'.[124] Ontario was engaged in a 'crusade ... to direct a numerous
emigration to Manitoba'.[125] This notion that somehow the movement of
Ontarians to the West was controlled and directed by an Ontario leadership
was a mistaken idea. But it reflected the attitudes of those who expressed it.[126]

The conservative, hierarchical, Catholic ideology of Quebec's élite, therefore, is a thread which we can follow through the turnings and ambiguities of
our subject. It was that ideology which attached editors, writers, sermon-
izers, and politicians to a form of education different from what was
increasingly favoured by a majority of English Canadians, and thus gave rise
to the separate school issue. It was that ideology which they saw embattled
around the world and requiring their action in its defence. It was that ideology
which led to the sense of mission, of responsibility for the Catholic cause, and
which, therefore, made them responsive to the paternalistic strain in colonial
imperialism. This was what made it Quebec's responsibility to act as
'defender of the oppressed' in New Brunswick,[127] to 'uphold the demands of

---

122 Lacombe to Taché (Montreal, 30 May 1876), in Archives Deschâtelets, St Boniface papers,
   mfm no. 486.
123 Lacombe to Taché (Worcester, Mass., 14 Apr. 1876), in Archives Deschâtelets, St Boniface
   papers, mfm no. 481. See also letters from Montreal, 7 Feb. 1877, and 6 June and 22 Apr.
   1876 (mfms no. 505, 486, and 484).
124 L'Union des Cantons de l'Est, 5 Nov. 1874.
125 Le Nouveau Monde, 8 July 1871.
126 A.R.M. Lower, in his study of settlement and the forest frontier, describes the Quebec
   colonization movement as 'militant for the faith and the race. ... The priests are the
   officers and the habitants are the private soldiers, and together they go forward toward
   victory looking for inspiration to the achievements of their own past and for reward to
   the life beyond' (quoted in Gourd, p. 237).
127 La Minerve, 1 June 1872.

the Acadians',[128] and, in the West, 'to protect and help our brothers out there.'[129]

At the same time, the very distinctiveness of this ideology reinforced the tendency to look on Quebec as the French-Canadian country. The difference between these social values and those prevalent in English Canada made autonomy necessary, for only in a province which they controlled could French Canadians hope to apply these values through their legislation and their institutions. Moreover, the conservative and hierarchical content of the ideology was not conducive to the kind of individual and isolated enterprise that would have been involved in prairie settlement, but rather encouraged French Canadians to remain in Quebec or at least to move only to contiguous areas like New England or eastern Ontario, where they could, in a sense, remain part of a single society and geographically compact group, find parishes already organized, schools established, and jobs and housing waiting for them.[130]

The theory expounded by Bishop Laflèche, that every person and every community has an appointed place in the divine plan, leads to a great emphasis on the idea of the place in which one belongs, that is, one's proper home. Laflèche himself wrote that the proper home of the French-Canadian nation was the St Lawrence valley, or Quebec. Yet the idea of the universal plan implies that people have appointed places within Quebec and that Quebec itself has a proper place in a wider context. It is interesting that nineteenth-century anti-emigration literature often lamented not just the departure from Canada, or Quebec, but even more, the loss of 'the paternal farmstead',[131] the native village, the 'place of one's birth'.[132] Emigrants were far not only from their province but also from a much more personal homeland:

Far from the slopes where their fathers sleep!
Far from the dear sites consecrated
By the golden days of childhood. ...
Far from the steeple that watched o'er their birth,

---

128 *Le Courrier de St-Hyacinthe*, 30 Jan. 1872.
129 *Le Journal des Trois-Rivières*, 18 Apr. 1870.
130 It is interesting that some writers discussed the Franco-Americans as if the old rural parish had been transplanted to the u.s. mill town, with the mill owner in the role of the seigneur! Eg., Beaugrand, *Jeanne*, pp. 172, 218; Hamon, *Les Canadiens-Français*, pp. 12, 21, 25–8, 32–5, 40–7; Rumilly, *Franco-Américains*, p. 42.
131 Patrice Lacombe, *La Terre paternelle* (Montreal: Beauchemin et Valois 1871).
132 Beaugrand, *Jeanne*, p. 189; *La St-Jean-Baptiste à Québec en 1865* (Quebec: Duquet et Cie 1865), p. 16.

Whose bells in pious tones
Weep for the absent ones
Whom the priest will bless no more.[133]

But beyond the borders of Quebec, the sense of belonging did not disappear at once. Bourassa called Quebec the particular heritage of French Canadians, but at the same time he proclaimed himself a Canadian, and, beyond that too, he reminded his compatriots that they belonged to the British Empire, to which they also had duties.[134] The French-speaking world, the Catholic world, for which French Canadians had been willing to fight and die – these too were wider homelands for their people.

In a world of nation-states, however, the possibilities for a political homeland were limited to two: Quebec and Canada. No doubt originally, and in a profound sense, Quebec was the more satisfying of the two, as offering French Canadians a definite, familiar territory on which they had lived for centuries, in which they were the majority, and in which they could pass their own kind of laws, set up their own kinds of institutions, create a society in keeping with their own values and aspirations.

Yet they could not have Quebec entirely as they wanted it. On its own it was not viable, so it had to be associated in the Canadian partnership. That association alone forced a certain identification with Canada. But more, it brought French Quebeckers into contact with other French-Catholic groups, involved them in their causes, their destinies, and ultimately led to a desire and an expectation that beyond the still-special home of Quebec, all Canada should yet be a country for French Canadians.

Is it now too late to meet that hope?

---

133 L.J.C. Fiset, *Jude et Grazia, ou les malheurs de l'émigration* (Quebec: Brousseau et Frères 1861), p. 17.
134 Bourassa, *Le Patriotisme canadien-français*, pp. 3, 4.

« »

BIBLIOGRAPHICAL
NOTES

T HE most important source for this study was the periodical press. As circulation figures were not available for the
early period and not entirely reliable in any case, lon-
gevity was also used as a guide to the influence of papers. Those which survived ten
years or more were used. Two exceptions to this rule were *Le Défricheur* (L'Avenir)
and *L'Union Nationale* (Montreal), which are generally considerd to have been
important as organs of anti-Confederation opinion.

For the early years, the papers used here represent the greater part of the
French-Quebec press. For the later years the sampling is proportionately smaller but
does include the papers with the largest circulations and the leading party organs.
Many of these can now be consulted on microfilm in libraries far from the cities where
they were published. Other than the two mentioned above, papers used were:

Bulletin de l'Union-Allet (Montreal)
Le Canadien (Quebec)
Le Courrier de St-Hyacinthe
Le Courrier du Canada (Quebec)
L'Electeur (Quebec)
L'Etendard (Montreal)
L'Evénement (Quebec)
Le Franc-Parleur (Montreal)
La Gazette de Sorel
La Gazette des Familles (published first as *La Gazette des Familles Canadiennes*, then
 as *La Gazette des Familles Canadiennes et Acadiennes*; place of publication varies)
Le Journal d'Agriculture (Montreal)
Le Journal de Québec
Le Journal des Trois-Rivières
Le Métis (St Boniface)
La Minerve (Montreal)

Le Monde Illustré (Montreal)
Le Moniteur Acadien (Shediac)
Le National (Montreal)
Le Nouveau Monde (also published for a time as *Le Monde*; Montreal)
L'Opinion Publique (Montreal)
L'Ordre (Montreal)
La Patrie (Montreal)
Le Pays (Montreal)
Le Pionnier de Sherbrooke
La Presse (Montreal)
La Revue Canadienne (Montreal)
L'Union des Cantons de l'Est (Arthabaskaville)
La Vérité (Quebec)

Pamphlets and brochures were often a sort of extension of the periodical press, or concentration of its contents. There seems no useful purpose to be served in repeating here all the information contained in the footnotes, but the following are some of the most useful of the pamphlets, and some of the most widely accessible in university and public libraries.

ON CONFEDERATION

La Confédération couronnement de dix années de mauvaise administration. Montreal: Le Pays 1867
Contre-Poison: la confédération c'est le salut du Bas-Canada. Montreal: Senécal 1867
Nouvelle constitution du Canada. Ottawa: Le Canada 1867
Réponses aux censeurs de la confédération. St Hyacinthe: Le Courrier 1867
Taché, J.-C. *Des Provinces de l'Amérique du Nord et d'une union fédérale*. Quebec: Brousseau 1858

ON RIEL AND THE MÉTIS

L'Histoire d'un crime. n.p., n.d.
Louis Riel, martyr du Nord-Ouest. Montreal: La Presse 1885
La Mort de Riel et la voix du sang. n.p. n.d.
Ontario et Manitoba: la vérité. n.p. c.1872
Sulte, Benjamin *L'Expédition militaire de Manitoba, 1870*. Montreal: Senécal 1871
Taché, A.-A. *L'Amnistie*. Montreal: Le Nouveau Monde 1874
– *Encore l'amnistie*. St Boniface: Le Métis 1875
– *La Situation au Nord-Ouest*. Quebec: Filteau 1885
Le Véritable Riel. Montreal: Imprimerie Générale 1887

LANGUAGE AND SCHOOLS IN THE WEST

Bourassa, Henri *Pour la justice.* Montreal: 1912

Bernard, P. [P.T.D.C. Gonthier] *Un Manifeste libéral.* Quebec: Brousseau 1896

Faucher de St-Maurice, N.H.E. *La Question du jour: resterons-nous français* Quebec: Belleau 1890

Taché, A.-A. *Ecoles séparées: partie des négotiations à Ottawa en 1870.* St Boniface 1890

- *Mémoire de Monseigneur Taché sur la question des écoles en réponse au rapport du comité de l'honorable conseil privé du Canada.* Montreal: Beauchemin et Fils 1894
- *Une Page de l'histoire des écoles de Manitoba.* Montreal: Beauchemin et Fils 1894
- *Pastoral Letter of His Grace the Archbishop of St Boniface, on the New School Laws of Manitoba.* St Boniface 1890

AGRICULTURE AND SETTLEMENT

Beaudry, D.H. *Le Conseiller du peuple.* Montreal: Senécal 1861

Bernier, T.A. *Le Manitoba, champ d'immigraton.* Ottawa 1887

Labelle, Antoine *Considérations générales sur l'agriculture, la colonisation, le repatriement et l'immigration.* Quebec 1888

Le Nord-Ouest canadien: brochure compilée par un colonisateur de neuf ans d'expérience. n.p., n.d.

[Pelletier, T.B.] *Considérations sur l'agriculture canadienne, au point de vue religieux, national et du bien-être matériel.* Quebec: Côté 1860

Société de colonisation de Manitoba *A nos compatriotes des Etats-Unis et du Canada, émigrez à Manitoba.* n.p., n.d.

Tassé, Elie *Le Nord-Ouest.* Ottawa: Imprimerie du Canada 1880

OTHER PAMPHLETS

Beaubien, Louis *Les Chemins de fer: nos communications avec l'Ouest.* Quebec 1875

Blanchet, J. *Discours de l'honorable J. Blanchet, secrétaire de la province de Québec, sur l'autonomie des provinces.* Quebec: A Côté et Cie 1884

Bourassa, Henri *Le Patriotisme canadien-français: ce qu'il est, ce qu'il doit être.* Montreal: Revue Canadienne 1902

Correspondances parlementaires: session fédérale de 1875. Lévis: L'Echo 1875

Le Coup d'état, ou le renvoi du cabinet de Boucherville Quebec: Le Canadien 1878

Dunn, Oscar *L'Union des partis politiques dans la province de Québec.* Montreal: Desbarats 1874

Lanctot, Denys *Avenir des Canadiens-français.* Montreal 1902

Masson, Philippe *Le Canada-Français et la Providence.* Quebec: Brousseau 1875

Manuscript sources were not very important for this study, although it will be seen from the text and footnotes that the papers of most prominent figures were consulted where possible. Only one collection proved very valuable: the St Boniface archiepiscopal papers. These have been microfilmed, and it is possible to obtain permission to see the films at the Oblate seminary in Ottawa, the Scolasticat St-Joseph, where the archivists are remarkably kind and helpful. Of special importance are the letters sent to Archbishop Taché by Albert Lacombe and other priests who toured Quebec and New England, trying to organize a movement of settlers to Manitoba.

The official records of parliamentary debates were not used as a source for this study. Parliamentary speeches were exploited only if they were reprinted in some more popularly accessible form, such as pamphlets, newspaper columns, or collections of speeches like Ulric Barthe's *Wilfrid Laurier à la tribune* (Quebec: Turcotte et Menard 1890), or Joseph Tassé's *Discours de Sir Georges Cartier* (Montreal: Senécal et Fils 1893). The one exception to the above rule was the *Parliamentary Debates on the Subject of the Confederation of the British North American Provinces*.

Two royal commissions were of obvious use: Quebec's Royal Commission of Inquiry on Constitutional Problems (The Tremblay Commission), and the federal Royal Commission on Bilingualism and Biculturalism. Appendixed to the latter as its Study No. 4 is an important study by Ramsay Cook, *Provincial Autonomy, Minority Rights and the Compact Theory, 1867–1921* (Ottawa: Queen's Printer 1969).

Readers wishing to consult other secondary sources will find that Confederation and the intentions of its fathers concerning French-Canadian status and rights have been the subject of considerable debate. Some of the following may prove of interest:

Arès, Richard *Dossier sur le pacte fédératif de 1867.* Montreal: Bellarmin 1967
Bonenfant, J.-C. 'Les Canadiens français et la naissance de la confédération', in the *CHAR*, 1952
– 'L'Esprit de 1867', in the *RHAF*, XVII, 1 (June, 1963)
Creighton, D.G. 'Confederation: the Use and Abuse of History', in the *Journal of Canadian Studies (JCS)*, I, 1 (May, 1966)
– 'John A. Macdonald, Confederation, and the Canadian West', in the Historical and Scientific Society of Manitoba, *Transactions*, series III, no. 23 (1966–7)
Hall, D.J. 'The Spirit of Confederation: Ralph Heintzman, Prof. Creighton, and the Bicultural Compact Theory', in the *JCS*, IX, 4 (Nov., 1974)
Heintzman, Ralph 'The Spirit of Confederation: Prof. Creighton, Biculturalism, and the Use of History', in the *CHR*, LII, 3 (Sept., 1971)
Morton, W.L. *The Critical Years: The Union of British North America, 1857–1873* (Toronto: McClelland and Stewart 1964)
– 'Confederation, 1870–1896: The End of the Macdonaldian Constitution and the Return to Dualty' in the *JCS*, I, 1 (May, 1966)
Waite, P.B. *The Life and Times of Confederation.* Toronto: University of Toronto Press 1962

On Riel and the Métis, two books by G.F.G. Stanley remain essential: *The Birth of Western Canada* (Toronto: University of Toronto Press 1960), and *Louis Riel* (Toronto: Ryerson 1963). W.L. Morton's *Manitoba: a History* (Toronto: University of Toronto Press 1957) and his *Manitoba: the Birth of a Province* (Altona: Friesen 1965) are also to be consulted on the first uprising. For later problems in the West, see Paul Crunican's splendid work, *Priests and Politicians: Manitoba Schools and the Election of 1896* (Toronto and Buffalo: University of Toronto Press 1974), and Manoly R. Lupul, *The Roman Catholic Church and the North-West School Question,* published at the same time by the same publisher.

J.R. Miller's new book, *Equal Rights: The Jesuits' Estates Act Controversy* (Montreal: McGill-Queen's University Press 1979), will be useful and interesting. Those who read French will certainly profit from Andrée Désilets, *Hector-Louis Langevin, un père de la confédération canadienne* (Quebec: PUL 1969) and Marcel Hamelin, *Les Premières années du parlementarisme québécois* (Quebec: PUL 1974). Robert Rumilly, that remarkable prolific historian whose passionate and unfootnoted style may upset some readers a little, provides a wealth of information on a wide range of topics. Of relevance here are the first six volumes of his *Histoire de la province de Québec,* his *Honoré Mercier et son temps* (2 vols.; Montreal: Fides 1975), *Histoire des Acadiens* (2 vols.; Montreal: Fides 1955), and *Histoire des Franco-Américains* (Montreal 1958).

Finally, it should be noted that since the present text was completed, Gilbert-L. Comeault's paper has been published in revised form as 'La Question des écoles du Manitoba – un nouvel éclairage', in the *RHAF*, XXXIII, 1 (June, 1979).

INDEX

This book

was designed by

HAROLD KURSCHENSKA

and printed at

UNIVERSITY OF

TORONTO

PRESS

1982